Harold Wilson and Europe

Harold Wilson and Europe

Pursuing Britain's Membership
of the European Community

Melissa Pine

LONDON · NEW YORK

Revised paperback edition published in 2012 by I.B.Tauris & Co Ltd
6 Salem Road, London W2 4BU
175 Fifth Avenue, New York NY 10010
www.ibtauris.com

Distributed in the United States and Canada
Exclusively by Palgrave Macmillan
175 Fifth Avenue, New York NY 10010

ISBN: 978 1 78076 037 7

A full CIP record for this book is available from the British Library
A full CIP record for this book is available from the Library of Congress

Library of Congress catalog card: available

Printed and bound by CPI Group (UK) Ltd, Croydon, CR0 4YY
Camera-ready copy edited and supplied by the author

CONTENTS

LIST OF ABBREVIATIONS

ANZUS	Australia, New Zealand, United States
CAP	Common Agricultural Policy
CDU	*Christlich Demokratische Union Deutschlands* (Christian Democratic Union Party of the FRG)
CSU	*Christlich Sociale Union* (Christian Social Union Party of the FRG)
CERN	*Conseil Européen pour la Recherche Nucléaire* (European Organisation for Nuclear Research)
CET	Common External Tariff
DEA	Department of External Affairs
EC	European Communities
ECSC	European Coal and Steel Community
EEC	European Economic Community
EFTA	European Free Trade Association
ELDO	European Launcher Development Organisation
ESRO	European Space Research Organisation
EURATOM	European Atomic Energy Community
EURM	Ministerial Committee on the Approach to Europe
EURO	Official Committee on the Approach to Europe
FCO	Foreign and Commonwealth Office
FO	Foreign Office
FRG	Federal Republic of Germany
GATT	General Agreement on Trade and Tariffs
GDR	German Democratic Republic
GITA	'Go it alone'
HMG	Her Majesty's Government
JIC	Joint Intelligence Committee

MOD	Ministry of Defence
NAFTA	North American Free Trade Association
NA	National Archive
NATO	North Atlantic Treaty Organisation
OECD	Organisation for Economic Co-operation and Development
OPD	Defence and Overseas Policy Committee
PUS	Permanent Under Secretary
SOSFA	Secretary of State for Foreign Affairs
SPD	*Sozialdemokratische Partei Deutschlands* (Social Democratic Party of the FRG)
UKMis	United Kingdom Mission
UKRep	United Kingdom Representative
WEU	Western European Union

ACKNOWLEDGEMENTS

This book would not have been possible without the support of a large number of people and institutions. First, my thanks go to my doctoral supervisor, Dr Anne Deighton. Anne read drafts of chapters, of the thesis, the corrected thesis and now the book, and offered invaluable observations and guidance. My DPhil examiners, Dr Jonathan Wright and Dr Piers Ludlow, made significant comments on my text, and Piers has made numerous important and helpful suggestions in the preparation of this book, for which I am very grateful. My colleagues at the University of Plymouth, especially Professor Kevin Jefferys, have counselled me and assisted my efforts towards publication, as well as providing a supportive workplace since September 2004. At different times, I have discussed the manuscript with Andrea Benvenuti, Helen Parr, Lasse Boehm and Vicky Shields, and I thank them all for their comments. I owe a great debt of gratitude to the staff at the National Archive, Kew, London; at the Bodleian Library in Oxford, particularly Colin Harris in the Modern Papers Room; and at the Archive Centre at Churchill College, Cambridge. My thanks must also go to Elizabeth Munns and Kelly Hallett, my advisors at I.B.Tauris, and especially to Dr Kate Heard, copy-editor extraordinaire. Christ Church Boat Club, Oxford University Women's Lightweight Rowing Club and, more recently, the PSOF triathlon club have all given me outlets beyond work and kept me sane throughout the preparation of this manuscript.

For financial help I thank St John's College and Keble College, Oxford, for awarding me scholarships. Dr Anne Deighton employed me as a research assistant. Keble College, the Department of Continuing Education at the University of Oxford, Queen Mary and Westfield College (University of London), the Stanford Programme in Oxford, OPUS, the University of Tomsk and the University of Virginia offered me teaching opportunities during the course of my DPhil.

Finally, I would like to thank my family. Their moral and financial support has been invaluable, and I could not have done it without them. This manuscript is dedicated to my mother, Tina McEwen.

INTRODUCTION

In May 1967, Harold Wilson's Labour Government applied to join the European Communities.[1] In November, the opening of negotiations was vetoed by the French president, General Charles de Gaulle. Undeterred, Wilson pressed on with his effort to join the Communities, only to lose office in June 1970 – just twelve days before the opening of negotiations for British membership. As a result, Wilson's successor as prime minister, the Conservative leader Edward Heath, has been credited with taking the United Kingdom into Europe.

This book addresses three historical questions. First, why was the British application maintained after General de Gaulle's veto in November 1967? Second, how did a government whose cabinet was divided over the question of Europe sustain the momentum for membership at home and abroad? Finally, did Wilson's tenacity contribute positively to the ability of Heath to open and successfully conclude negotiations in 1970?

The book argues that the application was maintained as part of a deliberate strategy that was shaped and led by Wilson. The commitment to Europe was upheld not only because the British saw no alternative. Key players like Wilson and his two foreign secretaries in this period, George Brown and Michael Stewart, had made a positive commitment to its success and were determined to take Britain into Europe. It was maintained by unremitting diplomatic pressure, imaginative work with continental allies, and flexible responses when the situation inside the Communities changed. This work, finally, was vital to the eventual success of the British application. Heath's government used the official team, the negotiating briefs and the timetable prepared under the Wilson government. In the interim period much progress in the Communities had been held up, specifically and openly in response to the French veto. Wilson's actions and those of his government between 1967 and 1970 were therefore fundamentally important to Britain's eventual entry into the European Communities on 1 January 1973.

Literature

There is a large body of literature on British foreign policy in the 1960s, on European policy more generally, and on Wilson himself. Literature on Wilson's broad foreign policy focuses on disparate subjects such as the retreat from East of Suez.[2] With the exception of Andrea Benvenuti, who links British European policy with difficulties in Anglo-Australian relations, this literature minimises the significance of Wilson's efforts in Europe.[3] Frankel, for example, writes of Wilson's 'abortive application'; Bell argues that it was of no consequence; George comments that British membership had to wait for de Gaulle to resign; Butler and Pinto-Duschinsky claim that in June 1970, there 'was still no prospect of British entry into Europe.'[4]

The literature focusing on European policy specifically is, of course, more detailed. One of the earliest books was Uwe Kitzinger's *The Second Try* in 1968.[5] Most recent are Oliver Daddow's edited collection, *Harold Wilson and European Integration*, and the chapter on Europe in John Young's volume on the international policy of the Labour Governments of 1964-70, both published in 2003, and Helen Parr's analysis of Wilson's turn to Europe, published in 2006.[6] Most writers focus on the period up to and including the veto: as documents have become available under the thirty-year rule, the making and implementation of European policy – the process of Wilson's decision to apply – have come under increasing scrutiny.[7] Others take a broader overview to follow Wilson's European policy from about 1960 to 1975. These writers draw attention to Wilson's apparent about-turns on Europe, from supporting Gaitskell's opposition to the first, Conservative application in 1961-3, to making his own bid in 1967, to opposing the terms negotiated by Heath in 1972, and ultimately to renegotiating and leaving the final decision to the people in 1975. Daddow, for example, writes of Wilson's 'vacillating stance.'[8]

Kitzinger and Young acknowledge the work done between 1967 and 1970. Kitzinger records that Pompidou had made a bet in January 1968 that the veto would soon be forgotten, and that the Common Market would get going again.

> But Britain did not just go away. The other five did not give up trying to get her in. The Common Market's progress was severely held up right through 1968 and 1969, to the point where *Der Spiegel* in Germany just before The Hague summit devoted the core of its issue to 'the break up of the Common Market.' Progress in European integration had reached stalemate: Pompidou lost his bet, and no doubt paid up.[9]

Even then, however, Kitzinger is elliptical on British policy in the period 1968-1970. Young is more expansive, briefly tracing some of the key developments after the 1967 veto and concluding that 'Wilson's policy on European integration can be seen as quite successful.'[10] The more general lack of attention to the veto period, however, has given rise to the myth that there were three British applications to join the EC: Gowland and Turner write that Heath lost little time in submitting his application.[11] In fact, as Young acknowledges, there were only ever two.[12] O'Neill, the top British official negotiator, wrote that there was 'no discontinuity between [Wilson's application] and its success, or between the policy of the successive British administrations which made it, and which converted it through negotiations into the Accession Treaty signed in Brussels on 22 January, 1972.'[13]

Finally, the literature on Wilson himself falls into two groups: biographies and memoirs. Wilson's plethora of biographers pays little attention to his European policy. The authorised biographer, Philip Ziegler, commented that 'nothing much happened' in British European policy between November 1967 and June 1970.[14] Paul Foot, writing in 1968, acknowledged that Wilson left the application 'on the table' but prophesied, wrongly, that the veto would allow Wilson to swing back to opposition to entry.[15] Ben Pimlott skipped from de Gaulle's veto to the general election of June 1970.[16] Austen Morgan gave a damning verdict on the French veto: another 'Wilsonian initiative had bitten the dust', although he also noted, without giving any detail, that by 1970 it looked as though Labour would take Britain into the EC.[17]

Ministerial and other diaries present divergent pictures of Wilson's views. James Callaghan, home secretary, saw Wilson as a pragmatist, willing to see how negotiations would go and seeking something to counter the 'drifting, rudderless nature' of policy in other areas.[18] Cecil King, the chairman of the Mirror Group, thought that Wilson 'was in no way interested in the Common Market except as a ploy to help him in his Parliamentary manoeuvres.'[19] Foreign Office minister Alun Chalfont believed Wilson was 'more sceptical', and Michael Stewart believed him 'more cautious' than Brown (although that would not have been difficult).[20] Chancellor Roy Jenkins described him as 'genuinely much less committed on the issue than I am'.[21] Wilson's personal secretary Marcia Williams felt that he 'wanted to get us into Europe if the terms were right', and to 'find out what the Europeans were offering.'[22] George Brown was taken aback by the 'surprisingly firm line' in favour of entry that Wilson took on the tour in late 1966-67, and first secretary of state Barbara Castle was 'convinced [that] he is anxious to get in.'[23] The 'father of Europe', Jean Monnet, believed that Wilson had 'made his mind up' in favour of entry.[24] Richard Crossman, secretary of state for social services, described him as 'fanatically anxious to get in', and transport minister Richard Marsh 'was never in any doubt from the beginning that Harold Wilson was determined to get this country into the European Economic Community'.[25] Ascertaining Wilson's true position is therefore something of a puzzle.

Sources and methodology

The book is largely based on primary state and private papers. In the National Archive in London, prime ministerial, cabinet and Foreign Office archives newly released under the thirty-year rule, and hitherto unconsidered in this debate, have been consulted. Additionally, the book draws on the private papers of Lord Wilson of Rievaulx, Lord George-Brown, Lord Stewart of Fulham and Sir Patrick Reilly (British ambassador to Paris 1965-68). The Wilson papers were not wholly open, while access to other collections, such as that of Lord Soames (British ambassador to Paris from 1968), was denied. As the book is concerned with British perceptions of the actions of others rather than the actions themselves, research has been restricted to documents in British collections. Altogether approximately three and a half thousand documents have been consulted. These primary sources have been supplemented by secondary literature, including that mentioned above, and interviews.

The book presents a dense historical narrative, with research questions derived from the existing literature on Wilson and European integration. It explains and analyses why, how and with what consequences the British application to the EC was maintained in the post-veto period. It tracks the management of the British application, in the cabinet and internationally, from the French veto in November 1967 to the end of the Wilson administration in 1970. It demonstrates the ways in which the British government managed and used its international relationships, the extent to which it built alliances on the continent, the imaginative range of solutions found to the veto situation and the mistakes and successes in the diplomacy of the Wilson administration. The importance of personality is highlighted, as is the role of contingency in the timing of, for example, the May 1968 riots in France and the coming into power in the Federal Republic of Germany of Willy Brandt's Social Democrats. The research questions are problematic given the multilateral setting of British foreign policy making, and the book is primarily a study of prime ministerial power and diplomacy.

It is not, however, a general account of Anglo-European relations, and does not address the Labour Party more generally, the role of elite pressure groups, or public opinion. As will be seen, the enormous size of the government's majority in the March 1967 parliamentary decision to apply for membership of the EC was taken by Wilson as an absolute mandate to continue to pursue membership. The existence within both the parliamentary and the broader Labour Party of a vocal group opposed to British entry could therefore be ignored. In part, this strategy was possible because de Gaulle's veto meant that European policy did not require any parliamentary votes: there was no opportunity for anti-Europeans effectively to challenge or to block government policy.[26]

There certainly existed pressure groups that campaigned both for and against British entry – Kitzinger even suggested that had the anti-market campaigns not existed, then the government would have had to invent them in order to protect the vitality of British democracy.[27] Wilson engaged with some of the pro-European campaign groups, ultimately agreeing to become a patron of the British Council of the European Movement, and joining Jean Monnet's 'Action Committee for a United States of Europe.[28] There is, however, almost no mention of the anti-European campaign groups in the prime ministerial and Foreign Office archives, indicating their lack of importance to the shaping of European policy in this period.

Likewise, although during the period after the veto a popular majority against entering the EC emerged, it too could be safely ignored, even during the 1970 election campaign. First, public opinion had been notoriously fickle on the European question over the previous decade, with a majority in favour of entry as recently as March 1967. Second, even when the majority of the population stood opposed to entry, there were many issues of greater political saliency or domestic importance: the Common Market came very low down the list of priorities. It was not, therefore, an election issue, and Wilson could ignore the will of the majority of the British population with relative impunity.[29]

Overview

The next chapter gives a short outline of British domestic policy and international circumstances, and of developments in the EC in the late 1960s, in order to provide a context. It also gives a brief overview of Wilson's European policy leading up to the application and veto in 1967. Chapter two looks at the first month after the veto, during which Wilson and Brown procured authority from the Cabinet to maintain the application and began to instigate alternative arrangements with members of the Six. Chapter three follows a sharp change in European diplomacy in the first two months of 1968, from Brown leading pressure for co-operation with the 'friendly Five' (that is, the Six minus France), to Britain putting the onus for a new initiative on the Six. Chapter four analyses abortive British and continental efforts during March-September 1968 to translate the resulting proposals into something concrete.

Chapter five describes a significant change in Anglo-European relations between October 1968 and January 1969, as real progress was made towards co-operation outside the EC. The months from February to April 1969, covered in chapter six, were an eventful period for the British and their allies. Further progress towards Anglo-European co-operation was complication by the so-called 'Soames Affair' and, soon afterwards, by de Gaulle's resignation as president of France. Chapter seven traces the effect of the consequent French elections and the later German election on the British application. Concluding with scrutiny of a major summit in The Hague in December 1969, this chapter sees the raising of the French veto on negotiations. The last chapter, covering the final six months of the Labour government to June 1970, investigates the British effort to come to terms with this new situation and with the prospect of entry into the Communities.

1

Approaching Europe 1964 – 67

This chapter illustrates the development of Wilson's commitment to a British application during 1964-67, in the context of the international and domestic environment. It sets the stage for the book's argument that, after November 1967, Wilson was so committed to the 'approach to Europe' that the veto did not lead to a change in policy.[1]

While it is a truism to cite Dean Acheson's famous comment of 1962 that Great Britain had lost an empire and not yet found a role, the more nuanced approach taken in the Foreign Office (FO) is revealing. An official wrote that if 'Britain has managed to acquire a new role, it has done so very hesitantly and appears not to have much idea what to do with it.'[2] The first three years of Wilson's government can be understood as the final acknowledgement of the loss of the empire and of world power status, after a long battle to hold on to the world role. As Greenwood notes, in 1964 Labour was determined to conserve the overlapping objectives of the parity of sterling on international markets and a British presence throughout the world.[3] Kaiser and Staerk's description of the foreign policy possibilities open to Britain as 'contracting options' is apt, as circumstances contrived to close down the alternatives available for a medium-sized island off the north-west coast of Europe.[4] It took time and brutal economic truth to convince Wilson that his options were narrowing. As he acknowledged that Britain could no longer punch above its weight, he found in the 'approach to Europe' a plausible and increasingly attractive alternative.

The chapter introduces several themes. Cold War bipolarity, difficult relations with the United States, pressure on the sterling area, troubles in the Commonwealth, lack of satisfaction with the European Free Trade Association, and the contrast between British stagnation and growth and prosperity in the EC all combined to bring increasing pressure on British policymakers. These themes played into and were in turn influenced by domestic issues: the weak economy, turbulent industrial relations and efforts to modernise. While these factors and the government's response to them were not always explicitly linked with making a renewed application to the EC, taken together they provided momentum towards Europe. At the same time, it did not matter that there was no cabinet consensus on this issue, because the balance of power within the cabinet shifted so that those who wanted to pursue membership of the EC held strategically important positions. It is evident that the application must be seen in the wider context of British foreign and, indeed, domestic policy and the chapter gives a brief account of the first British application to the EC in 1961-3, the domestic economic context in 1964-70, the impact of domestic constraints on foreign policy, and finally, the making of the second application itself.

The first application

Of course, pressure for a turn to Europe had been present for some time, and had been acted upon by Harold Macmillan's Conservative government. Yet, as Ellison argues, the first application was not a radical turning point in British policy: it was a change of tactics aimed at securing traditional goals. Membership would have protected several British interests: in placating the Americans (who urged British entry), it would have made safe the Anglo-American nuclear relationship, while at the same time avoiding British isolation from a French-led EEC and providing a regional basis from which Britain could regain its former position in the world.[5] Sked and Cook also argue that Macmillan had no intention of making Britain a European power but instead wanted to find a 'theatre' in which Britain could act the leading role and thus increase her reputation on the international stage.[6] Ludlow thus describes the first application as an 'essentially defensive move.'[7] The truth of these assertions is clear from the conditional nature of the first British application. The government wished to maintain its preferential trading relationship with the Commonwealth, for example, to arrange protection for the special interests of the EFTA states, and to have a say in the negotiation of the nascent common agricultural policy.[8] There remained an unwillingness to see the United Kingdom as 'just another European country.'[9] Hugo Young describes the atmosphere:

> The altogether larger question concerns the nature of the approach: a conditional and tentative venture, creeping in a state of high suspicion towards this moment of historic destiny, declining to make a commitment until the Europeans had shown what ground they

were prepared to surrender, and reserving even then the option of a British veto....The British were not prepared to do more than negotiate and hesitate. They were not, actually, applying.[10]

At the time the Labour Party was split on the issue. The Party's senior figures included those, like George Brown, Roy Jenkins and Geoffrey de Freitas, who had been representatives at the Council of Europe. Others, like Wilson, Denis Healey and, eventually, Hugh Gaitskell, opposed entry either absolutely, or on Macmillan's terms. The National Executive Committee set 'five conditions' for entry: protection for Commonwealth and EFTA interests, the right to an independent foreign policy and to plan the British economy, and safeguards for British agriculture.[11] However, membership was not seen as necessary for economic recovery. As Kitzinger notes, 'from the seat of power the world soon looked different.'[12]

The British domestic context

Wilson won power in 1964 with a majority of just four, increased to ninety-six in the election of 1966. Labour's 1964 and 1966 election manifestos and speeches promised great things. Wilson spoke all over the country for state-sponsored science, an overhaul of education and general modernisation, and the Labour leadership castigated the Tories for 'thirteen wasted years'.[13] Some aspects of the optimism that greeted the new government were fulfilled. The 'Swinging Sixties' saw many liberal changes in Britain, with legislation decriminalising homosexuality and abortion, easing divorce, encouraging the equality and rights of women, and ending the death penalty.[14] But the Labour governments of 1964-1970 are often remembered for the things that went wrong: industrial relations proposals, unpopular diplomatic support for the United States in Vietnam, or even the second French veto.[15] As Daddow notes, 'Harold Wilson is not a fondly remembered Prime Minister'.[16] This dichotomy is reflected elsewhere. Kenneth Morgan identifies two themes for the 1960s: socialism and libertarianism, and argues that they came together in the Wilson cabinet. His conclusion is harsh: while libertarianism changed everything; socialism left 'a tangle of half- or unfulfilled expectations.'[17]

The possibility of fulfilling those expectations was, however, limited: the Tories left behind a massive balance of payments deficit of £800 million. Dealing with this economic legacy occupied Labour almost to the last minute of the 1966 government.[18] The maintenance of sterling as an international reserve currency, Wilson's initial determination not to devalue and consequent financial dependence on the US hampered Britain's freedom of manoeuvre. Sterling crises in 1966 and 1967 eventually forced the government's hand, leading to devaluation by 14.3% on 18 November 1967 and the replacement as chancellor of the exchequer of Callaghan by Jenkins. Jenkins oversaw the overturning of policies that Labour held dear, such as the re-introduction of prescription charges and the postponement of plans to raise the school-leaving age to fifteen; and introduced austere economic measures, including the impromptu bank holiday that was to lead to Brown's resignation as foreign secretary in March 1968. Despite further loans and contingency plans for another devaluation, Jenkins' 'two years of hard slog' were bearing fruit towards the end of 1969, with a balance of payments surplus recorded from April to September 1969 for the first time in Wilson's second government.[19] By January 1970 Britain was able to pay off debts ahead of schedule, and looked set to approach the general election called for June with a surplus of nearly half a billion pounds.[20] The surprise May deficit announced two days before the election may have contributed to the five per cent swing resulting in a Conservative victory on 18 June.[21]

Tied in with Wilson's economic difficulties were turbulent industrial relations and a failed attempt to put them on a stringent new legal basis. He faced no major strikes at first, and announced that any incomes policy would be voluntary, with a 'beer and sandwiches' format for negotiations in Downing Street.[22] Soon after the 1966 election, however, an indefinite strike by the National Union of Seamen set the scene for the following years: there were major strikes by dockers and blast furnacemen among others, with more than six million days lost in the first six months of 1970.[23] Wilson's stance gradually hardened, with the introduction of a prices and incomes bill in July 1966 and the white paper *In Place of Strife*, by Barbara Castle, now secretary of state for employment and productivity, in January 1969. Their isolation and defeat over the proposed legislation, however, meant that the unions only made a 'solemn and binding undertaking' to self-monitor. This reversal was not only catastrophic for the government's prestige: internal labour relations were 'the key to improved productivity, a stronger trade balance and a check to domestic inflation'. Without their reform, the positive effect of decisions like devaluation and defence retrenchment could only be limited.[24] Similarly, Wilson's own pet project of scientific and technological modernisation could not be realised within the tiny domestic market. The 'white hot technological revolution' needed large markets if the Europeans were to avoid becoming 'economic helots' of the US.[25]

The impact of domestic constraints on foreign policy

The state of the domestic economy did not seem to allow for a world role for Britain, although Wilson was initially determined to maintain the parity of sterling and world power status. The message given out by the Labour leadership was mixed. Pickering draws attention to 'Wilson's romantic conception of the world role....[his] speeches on the overseas role were filled with both emotion and romantic imagery.'[26] This ambivalence was reflected in the policy: the government was 'determined to reduce what they saw as runaway defence expenditures while at the same time preserving Britain's status as a world power.' Changes to defence policy were a manifesto commitment and followed on from significant modernisation and retrenchment under the previous Conservative government. As the cuts were implemented the gap between commitments and capabilities grew.[27]

The first Wilson government continued the Conservative assault on the defence budget. Healey described it as a 'runaway train' and introduced American criteria of 'cost-effectiveness'. He quickly persuaded cabinet to cut three major aircraft programmes: the P1154 fighter, the HS 681 jet transport and, most controversially, the advanced TSR-2 strike aircraft, replacing each with American versions for about half the total cost. In February 1966 he axed the Navy's new CVA 01 aircraft carriers, and announced a new policy rationale: 'Britain will not undertake major operations of war except in co-operation with allies' – meaning the USA. Yet at this time the thrust of policy was still traditional. International defence commitments were maintained but the capability of the armed services to honour them was emasculated.[28]

The trend of cuts continued throughout the 1966-70 government, with an order for American F-111A aircraft being cancelled in 1968. From the summer of 1967, however, there was a more significant and far-reaching attempt to match commitments to capabilities. Wilson claimed that he and Healey were considering terminating British deployments east of Suez as early as the autumn of 1966, following the sterling crisis of the summer and consequent need to make more savings.[29] Pickering asserts that the final decision was taken in April 1967 in the Defence and Overseas Policy Committee, to halve British forces in the Far East by 1970-1 and to pull out altogether sometime in the 1970s. Devaluation provided the final boost, and the policy was forced through Cabinet in January 1968.[30]

Anglo-American relations

It is impossible to discuss this decision, however, without examining the links between Britain's world role and its relations with the United States, which in turn link back to the domestic economic situation. Anglo-

American relations in the later 1960s were a mix of interdependence and reassertions of British independence. There was no easy relationship between Wilson and presidents Lyndon Johnson and Richard Nixon as between Churchill and Roosevelt or Macmillan and Kennedy.[31] Indeed, as Brown confessed, 'I think the fact of the matter was that Mr Johnson didn't really like the Prime Minister much'.[32] The Suez and Cuban crises had demonstrated British impotence in the face of American interests, yet for Wilson the connection was, initially at least, 'axiomatic'.[33] He returned from visiting Washington in December 1964 jubilant that the Americans wanted and needed close relations with Britain.[34] As will be seen, the Americans underwrote both of Wilson's initial aims – maintaining the parity of sterling and the world role – but for their own reasons. In doing so they delayed the transformation in British foreign policy that was to begin in 1967-8.

The most important factor in the relationship was Vietnam. South East Asia was the principal hot arena of the Cold War, and a British presence in the region was symbolically important to the Americans.[35] Wilson continued the informal arrangement of maintaining a world role in return for American nuclear, diplomatic and financial support.[36] In 1965 Wilson and Callaghan made a secret deal with the Johnson administration: they would avoid devaluation (to help to defend the dollar) and maintain a presence East of Suez in return for American support for sterling.[37]

However, as US involvement in Vietnam escalated, Johnson increased the pressure on Wilson to send a military contribution.[38] Wilson, faced with significant domestic opposition, stood his ground, and what was left of the 'special relationship' began to break down.[39] Johnson crushed Wilson's effort, in February 1967, to negotiate a peace deal for Vietnam, while Wilson rejected a US proposal to create a joint sterling-dollar area.[40] When Wilson revealed the decision to withdraw from East of Suez Johnson was furious, writing that 'the US would no longer consider Britain a valuable ally in any strategic theatre, including Europe.'[41] Wilson's reply revealed the non-negotiable nature of the British decisions: Britain was 'sick and tired of being thought willing to eke out a comfortable existence on borrowed money' and 'must no longer overstrain our real resources and capabilities in the military field abroad.'[42] Some Americans acknowledged Wilson's point. Secretary of the Treasury Joseph Fowler accepted after the 1966 British currency crisis that the US could no longer block both devaluation and retrenchment. The administration as a whole recognised that the intense pressure applied to their closest ally was 'increasingly inappropriate.'[43] Wilson saw the possibility of regaining greater equality with the US through membership – and perhaps leadership – of the EC.

The Commonwealth

Domestic decisions also had repercussions for the Commonwealth. Wilson was known for Commonwealth sympathies, while troubles within the organisation kept it firmly on the agenda. There were problems linked with decolonisation in Rhodesia, Nigeria, Cyprus, Anguilla and Indonesia as well as in areas of more informal British influence such as the Middle East. Trouble in the Indian Ocean area in the first years of Wilson's government made strategic withdrawal from the region impossible: the so-called 'Confrontation' between Indonesia – a country with the third largest Communist party in the world and an avowed intention to build a nuclear bomb – and Britain's ally, Malaya. The defence treaty with Malaya was honoured with sixty-eight thousand troops and a third of the surface fleet.[44] Across the world, Anguilla's intention to secede from the Associated State (St Kitts and Nevis) in 1969 resulted in a British frigate, troops and special political representatives being sent to the Caribbean.[45] In Africa, civil war in Nigeria and the Unilateral Declaration of Independence in Rhodesia occupied tremendous amounts of government time. Crossman recorded that Wilson saw Rhodesia as 'his Cuba', in which he could make his mark as a world statesman.[46] The Commonwealth did not break up despite these challenges, but the slow process continued of the reorientation of Commonwealth countries and Britain towards their natural, regional allies. Australia sent troops to support the US in Vietnam under the ANZUS pact. Changing trade patterns, with only 24.4% of British exports going to the Commonwealth in 1970 compared to 47.7% in 1950, and 25.9% of imports coming from the Commonwealth in 1970 compared with 41.9% in 1950, made the organisation progressively less important in economic terms.[47] Britain sent 60% of its investment to the sterling area in 1960 but only 38% in 1970. Even before the decision to withdraw from East of Suez, the defence cuts meant that Britain was no longer able to guarantee the security of the outlying members.[48] Altogether, the Commonwealth was not a cohesive body, and the costs it engendered for Britain – including that of its defence – were beginning to outweigh the benefits it brought.

The changing EC

At the same time as Britain was stepping back from its relations with the United States and the Commonwealth, the EC began to look more attractive. This is not the place for a detailed analysis of EC developments in the 1960s, but it is important to note that, in a meaningful sense, the EC was a moving target for Britain. In the period since de Gaulle's first veto, the member states had been implementing the policies, such as the common agricultural policy and the common external tariff, set out in the

Treaties of Paris and Rome, and were working through the so-called 'transitional period' of the Communities.[49]

Despite the fears of many, the EC had not raced towards the sort of supranational federation that might have caused the British to shy away from re-applying. On the contrary, the 'empty chair crisis' and the 'Luxembourg Compromise' that resolved it ensured that the principle of national interest was entrenched. Faced in 1965 with proposals including those for more majority voting and a stronger Commission, president de Gaulle withdrew the French representatives from Community institutions. They only returned in 1966 when de Gaulle secured from the other five member states a 'gentlemen's agreement' that, where 'vital national interests' were concerned, the national veto would be retained.[50] This explicit recognition of the role of the nation state in European integration perhaps made it easier for a British government to decide to re-apply: the supranational elements of European integration had never been welcomed in the UK.[51] Meanwhile, EC growth was outflanking that in Britain. 1960-5 saw growth in real GNP per head at 3.9% in the Six, compared with 2.6% in Britain. Growth in real wages and industrial production were also significantly higher in the Community than in Britain. EFTA, disappointing from the outset, could not provide Britain with the size of market it needed to match European growth or compete globally in the technological sector. The Labour government had revealed its views on EFTA almost immediately on coming in to power, with the imposition of an import surcharge without prior consultation or warning.[52] EFTA could not match what the EC had to offer.

The second British application

It is not possible to understand 1967-70 without some knowledge of 1964-67 and the making of the second British application to join the EC. This section draws heavily from the most recent research based upon newly released archival resources. The economy was suffering through exclusion from a successful common market on its doorstep. The Commonwealth was costing much while offering few benefits. The relationship with the United States brought benefits, such as nuclear sharing, but at a price, and brought the British less influence than expected in international affairs. Meanwhile, the Six grew more tightly integrated, gaining political legitimacy and influence. As noted, the links between these domestic and international developments were not explicit: 'in the prime minister's mind any moves the government made towards Europe did not equate with a simultaneous desire to abandon Britain's commitments in the wider world.'[53] Frankel adds that the turn to Europe was not 'clearly connected with the Commonwealth in political argument.'[54] Yet the changes in policy were, if nothing else, coterminous, and it is difficult to imagine that they were not connected on some level.

Wilson commented regularly on the subject of Europe before he became leader of the Labour Party. When discussions on the free trade area were underway in the late 1950s, he rhetorically asked, 'Can we afford to stay out?' The answer was 'I am sure the answer is that we cannot' but he followed it later with '[t]here is no suggestion that Britain should join the Common Market.'[55] These comments suggest that Wilson was not doctrinaire, but weighed up the costs and benefits and made his decisions accordingly. This pattern would continue over the following years. In the House of Commons debate on EFTA in 1959 he noted the distinction between the 'original dreamers and idealists' who had thought up the Community and the 'highly realistic ideas' that they had produced to implement the dreams. While he still resisted entry into the Community, he acknowledged that there was 'a strong desire for a really effective and intimate basis of association between Great Britain, and Scandinavian countries on the other hand, and the community of Common Market countries on the other.' He was also worried that Western Europe would attract investment and that Britain would become a scientific backwater.[56] The technological potential of European integration interested Wilson for years as a rationale for membership and as a tool to assist entry.

Once the Tories entered negotiations in 1961-2, however, Wilson took a virulently anti-European position, most famously declaring that Britain was 'not entitled to sell our friends and kinsmen down the river for a problematical and marginal advantage in selling washing machines in Dusseldorf.'[57] When he became party leader after Gaitskell's death in 1963, his opposition to Europe grew, and he said that '[n]ever again must a British minister be put in a position of sitting outside in a cold ante-chamber while six European nations decide the fate of his country.'[58] He stressed both the 'American alternative' and 'links with the Commonwealth.' Yet throughout this period (when Wilson appeared most opposed to British entry), he took care to stress that it was the Tory *terms* with which he disagreed. The tortuous state of the Brussels negotiations gave Wilson the opportunity to unify his party without worrying about damaging the government's effort on the continent.[59] Without such unity, Wilson could have no hope of winning the forthcoming general election. This prioritising of one rational interest over another, party unity at one moment, Britain's international interests at another, was to continue throughout Wilson's leadership of the Labour party. It gave the impression that he held no strong position on the issue of British membership of the European Communities.

The Labour Party manifesto of 1964 said little about the EC. It stated that 'although we shall continue to seek to achieve closer links with our European neighbours, the Labour Party is convinced that the first responsibility of a British Government is still to the Commonwealth.'[60] When Wilson took office, his government had 'no intention whatsoever of renewing the previous application.'[61] As prime minister, however, new opportunities and resources became available to Wilson. Parr asserts that he thought little about the process and ramifications of making an application at this time.[62] Cynthia Frey also argues that his decision to apply was not inevitable, nor was he pushed into it by circumstances over which he had no control.[63] At a public meeting in Westminster he said that entry was

> at the present time not a real issue. If it were to become one, we should be prepared to consider negotiations for entry if, and only if, we can secure the conditions vital to British interests, vital to Commonwealth interests and vital to the pursuit of an independent foreign policy which we have laid down and to which we have all agreed.[64]

He felt that there was no question of being invited to, or of asking for, discussions with the Six on the subject.[65] Instead, meetings with continental leaders in 1964-6 focused on 'bridge-building' between the EEC and EFTA. It was only towards the end of this period, under pressure from Whitehall (especially the FO), that Wilson accepted the need to raise more comprehensively the question of membership.[66] The balance began to shift more quickly in 1966: majority opinion in cabinet slowly swung in favour of making a new application, with the conversion of Michael Stewart, the promotion of Roy Jenkins and Anthony Crosland, and a lessening of the former antagonism of Richard Crossman and Denis Healey.[67] The 1966 manifesto did not suggest a significant shift in policy, noting only that 'Labour believes that Britain, in consultation with her EFTA partners, should be ready to enter the European Economic Community, provided essential British and Commonwealth interests are safeguarded.'[68] More important, however, was the fact that Wilson had made up his own mind.

Wilson's decision soon became clear to one of the officials working most clearly with him. In an interview that resulted in Michael Palliser becoming Wilson's private secretary, Palliser expressed concern that his own strongly pro-European views would cause difficulties in their working relationship. Palliser was surprised by the response: "Oh', [Wilson] said, 'that doesn't matter. You'll see. We won't have any problems over

Europe.' So we agreed that I would join him and I went over there a week later. And sure enough we didn't have any problems over Europe.'[69] Bringing Palliser into No. 10 also had the effect of reinforcing pro-European opinion around the prime minister. Not only was Palliser enormously and passionately knowledgeable about the Community and its member states, but he also spoke perfect French, was married to the daughter of one of the 'founding fathers' of the EC, Paul-Henri Spaak, and had a brother-in-law in the Commission.[70] Shortly afterwards, Wilson revealed to Palliser that some of his comments had in fact had a tactical motivation. Palliser commented,

'You know, you seem to be more interested in the European Community than I expected.' And he said, 'Oh, I've been interested for quite a long time. You've got to realise that the Labour Party is pretty hostile, and I can't sort of go out on a limb, without having the Party behind me. So it's difficult.' I said, 'Well, you made a speech just before the election which everybody took to be a very anti-European speech.' And then – typical Wilson – he said, 'Oh, well I only made that speech to anticipate a far more anti-European one which I knew Barbara Castle was going to make.'[71]

Wilson is well known for such tactical manoeuvring, and this characteristic has been taken to mean that he did not care about anything except tactics. In fact, in the case of European policy at least, he was consistently working towards the particular goal of securing Britain's entry into the European Communities.

One of the episodes that contributed to Wilson's change of heart was the Communities' own crisis of 1965-66, mentioned above. He did not see sovereignty as self-evidently desirable, saying in August 1961 that an argument about it would be

out of harmony with this modern age. The question is not whether sovereignty remains absolute or not, but in what way one is prepared to sacrifice sovereignty, to whom and for what purpose....The question is whether any proposed surrender of sovereignty will advance or retard our progress to the kind of world we all want to see.[72]

Nevertheless, he told de Gaulle in January 1965 that Britain, like France, preferred a *Europe des patries* to a supranational Europe.[73] Moreover, the notion of attracting Britain may have played some small part in de Gaulle's calculations in 1965-6. In his memoirs for 1964-6, the then British ambassador in Paris, Sir Patrick Reilly, noted that de Gaulle 'thought that what he had been doing should make our entry easier, and surely with some reason.'[74] Parr asserts that in November 1965 de Gaulle went so far as to invite Britain to join the EEC, in order to prevent the Labour Government from teaming up with the Five in support of supranationalism. The invitation forced the British finally to consider what sort of Europe they might be interested in joining.[75]

In the end, however, it was a British problem rather than a French action that made the difference to Wilson and the British government. Parr argues convincingly that it was the sterling crisis of July 1966 that finally tipped the balance from guarded interest to determination. Economics made it imperative that the EEC issue be addressed, so that Wilson could no longer, as Foot put it, shrink from a final decision. The crash underlined both the failure of Wilson's domestic policies and the danger of dependence on the American economy to bolster sterling – for as he saw it, sterling was bearing the brunt of an attack directed primarily against the dollar. A new initiative abroad was thus crucial.[76] In Parr's analysis, however, it was not yet a decisive break with the past. A truly radical transformation would involve the path advocated by the new foreign secretary, George Brown: devaluation and retrenchment in overseas commitments. Wilson was not ready to face this course, and turned towards the EC partially in the hope that doing so would allow him to avoid Brown's more drastic route.[77] Thus the application in its final form was a sort of third way between the UK remaining an imperial power and becoming a regional power.

Forced into contemplation of a policy he had not hitherto considered seriously, Wilson announced after a Chequers cabinet meeting that he and Brown would tour the capitals of Europe. Peter Shore asserted that Wilson made this decision 'in spite of the unanimous advice of all the government advisers that membership was against the economic interest of the UK', and thought that Wilson only undertook it in order to show Brown that membership was impossible.[78] Palliser recollects that even Brown was alarmed at the thought of Wilson accompanying him, telling him over coffee that the idea was 'dotty, and if anyone's going to do it I must do it.' Palliser calmed him, pointing out that

'If he goes with you round these capitals he is absolutely committed, publicly, to this enterprise. Surely that's what you need – want?' 'Ah!' said George, 'I hadn't thought of that.' So they did go round the capitals together, and it was a fairly comic performance at times, but it was important in the sense that I said, identifying Wilson with the policy of wanting to go in.[79]

Brown himself recorded that '[g]radually our line got firmer and firmer, and by the time we had finished we had virtually decided to make our application.'[80] Palliser confirms that the prime minister was convinced. 'Wilson – this was the slightly warped thinking of the politician – he was quite convinced a) that he was right, which he was, and b) that he could persuade the General, which he couldn't.'[81] The tour not only convinced Wilson that membership of the Communities was desirable, however, it also made clear that any application would have to be unconditional. As Parr noted, '[e]veryone had had to accept unwelcome consequences for the benefits of membership and so too would Britain.'[82] Before attempting to negotiate, however, Wilson and Brown had to convince Cabinet and Parliament, and this was the task that occupied them in the months during and after the tour.

Castle and Crossman, among others, described the series of cabinet meetings leading to the decision to seek membership. Most interesting was Wilson's ability to finesse his colleagues into supporting his own objectives, reassuring them that no final decision was being taken, boring them with long, repetitive sessions, and threatening that, without following the European road, Britain would end up as America's lackey, forced even to join the conflict in Vietnam. Benn's acknowledgement that they were 'a defeated cabinet' illuminates the extent to which economic crisis and the lack of resources for pursuing international policy had boxed the government into a corner.[83] A number of different assessments of the cabinet decision to make the application have been made. Wilson's own, sent to Brown after the final Cabinet meeting in April 1967, was that at best only two and at worst, four to five ministers would vote against making a new application.[84] Massive parliamentary support followed, with 488 MPs in favour and only 62 against. Future divisions were suggested, however, in the 36 Labour MPs who voted against and 50 who abstained, despite a three-line whip. Nevertheless, this victory would serve as the main legitimising factor during the months and years in which Wilson pursued British entry. Six parliamentary private secretaries who had defied the whip were dismissed, but otherwise Wilson ignored the voice of dissent within his party – another tactic to which he would frequently return. Similarly, in formulating his policy

the Prime Minister had virtually ignored Labour's NEC and the Party Conference. Only in the fall of 1967, with Government and Parliament already committed, did he seek the endorsement of these bodies. At that time he succeeded in obtaining virtually unconditional support from the NEC; and…the Annual Conference itself endorsed the Government's Common Market application by a margin of more than 2 to 1.[85]

The victory over cabinet and parliament were short-lived, however, for just days after Wilson announced Britain's intention to apply for full membership of the European Communities, de Gaulle delivered his 'velvet' veto.

Before looking at the French response itself, its immediacy begs the question of Wilson's expectations of the General in making the application, and lays doubt upon his intentions and sincerity. Some commentators have focused on assertions by Healey and Crossman that they only allowed the application to go forward in the knowledge that de Gaulle would save them. Healey erupted in one of the April cabinet meetings, exclaiming that some ministers 'were always opposed to making these approaches at all' and that he had only supported the decision on the tour because 'we were assured that we would not be committed in any way'.[86] Crossman told Marsh that he had felt able to vote in favour of the application because 'the General will save us from our own folly.'[87] Presumably on the basis of these comments, some authors have assumed that the Wilson application was simply a public relations exercise, made in order to show the pro-Europeans that entry was not possible and to unite the party behind a new position, or to distract attention from the economic situation. Cecil King believed that Wilson was telling different things to different people – George Brown that he supported an entry bid, Jay and Peart that 'there was many a slip betwixt cup and lip'.[88] More subtly, perhaps, there were many who 'knew' for themselves that de Gaulle would veto, and either could not believe that Wilson did not know, or thought he was deluding himself. As King noted, '[y]ou cannot break through Wilson's façade of buoyant optimism….One must just wait for events to reveal to the world that the emperor has no clothes.'[89]

Palliser, however, believed that 'Wilson was determined to get us in, and it was part of a very carefully thought-out strategy, and the evidence was that when de Gaulle made his veto, Wilson said, 'Well, our application will remain on the table. We want to get in'.[90] Crossman agreed, noting in January 1967 that Wilson was 'clearly very confident. He feels he can woo [de Gaulle] without giving away any vital position.'[91] Wilson himself told Hugh Cudlipp, editor of the *Daily Mirror*, that de Gaulle had told him in Paris that he accepted Wilson's sincerity, and that he was 'handling' cabinet well. Cudlipp concluded that Wilson's confidence was 'dangerously immense.'[92] In his own memoir, Wilson was ambiguous, noting that de Gaulle had given his 'benediction' to the British application in their January meeting, but then asking 'what did it mean?' In reporting on the May veto he commented only that Britain would not take no for an answer.[93] Yet if Wilson still retained hope that he could convince the French president after the May press conference, he had lost it after meeting de Gaulle in June 1967. Despite the latter's acknowledgement that he might not be able to keep Britain out of the Community in the long term, Wilson recognised that, in the short term at least, he would continue to do so.[94] This impression was reinforced by de Gaulle's further press conference in November.

Contingency planning

Before de Gaulle's November press conference there had been a debate within the Foreign Office about whether the British should press for an clear answer from France. Sir Con O'Neill, deputy under secretary in the FO, worried that publicly admitting that there was no hope of entry until after de Gaulle left power needed careful consideration.[95] Wilson insisted that they should be ready for a French 'non', wondered if they should make another application immediately, and declared that the government should 'keep the ball before every meeting.'[96] Part of the problem was conflicting information about French intentions. Reilly, in Paris, warned in late September that a veto was imminent.[97] Yet Brown was still holding out hope in the same month that negotiations would open, since French foreign minister Maurice Couve de Murville had told him in New York that talks could begin by the end of the year.[98] The Bonn embassy confirmed that 'they really had no reliable indication of which way the French cat might jump.'[99]

Wilson's determination to be ready for a 'non' meant that contingency planning for a veto began in Whitehall long before November. In July an Italian diplomat warned that de Gaulle was 'showing increasing signs of madness' and advised that, should he issue a veto, 'we should all of us consider seriously refusing to acknowledge that it existed.'[100] O'Neill felt that a French veto would 'be *par excellence* the moment for 'not taking no for an answer'.' He acknowledged then, however, the importance of having the friendly Five on side:

> the Five must <u>not</u> acquiesce in the kind of position they adopted in January 1963: namely a reluctant acquiescence in the fact that the French attitude effectively terminated, or interrupted, the possibility of further negotiations with us. Thus, if the French say no, the Five must continue loudly and determinedly, in season and out, going on saying yes. For instance, the discussions on our application (and the Commission's report on it) should, by the action of the Five, be continued indefinitely until eventually a different French position is

arrived at. The matter should not be removed from the Council's agenda. On the contrary, it should be automatically placed on the agenda of each meeting of the Council of Ministers, and discussed at each meeting.[101]

O'Neill's path was ultimately followed. An FO draft paper emphasised that the British application should be 'debated and approved' in all the national parliaments, the Consultative and Western European Union (WEU) Assemblies, and 'in as many bodies and organisations as we can drum up.' While it was recognised that these tactics would not be enough to force de Gaulle's hand, it was equally acknowledged that the point was not to alienate France completely, since 'our major objective is to become part of a European Community which includes France.' The possibility of working with the Five in areas outside the Rome Treaties was raised, as was the notion of the Five holding up progress within the Communities.[102] Officials suggested both a 'solemn declaration' by Britain and the Five, and a high-level meeting. The final draft of the paper highlighted the irony of the situation: the government would need to act quickly after the expected veto, but must not give any hint of the action being considered in the meantime.[103]

The secrecy that would become a feature of European policy was already notable: Wilson, Brown and Callaghan agreed that contingency planning would be discussed interdepartmentally, but with officials attending in their personal capacity. The papers were therefore not circulated to the different departments. The group of officials from the Treasury, Board of Trade, Department of Economic Affairs and Foreign Office, after consulting the Commonwealth Office and the Ministry of Agriculture, agreed that there was 'no alternative to maintaining the objective of joining the Community and...this would require the strongest possible reaffirmation of purpose by the Government buttressed by supporting statements in some form by the Governments of the Five.'[104] Months before the veto, therefore, both British policy in case of rejection, and its management, were already set.

The 'Opinion', devaluation and the November veto

The publication of the European Commission's 'Opinion' on enlargement in September strengthened British policy. It was ruthless in dealing with the British economic situation, but concluded that the accession of the four applicant countries (the UK and Ireland, Denmark and Norway) 'could both strengthen the Community and afford it some opportunity for further progress, provided the new members accept the provisions of the Treaties and the decisions taken subsequently. This they have said they are disposed to do.' Negotiations should be opened at once.[105] While the Five welcomed the Commission's contribution and agreed that negotiations should be opened, the French focused on the comments about Britain's economy. At a Council of Ministers meeting on 23-24 October, Couve argued that the four applicants were 'extra-continental' and that their accession would cause fundamental changes in the Communities. The Six should define the conditions of membership, including a stable British balance of payments and a strong pound. Britain must also be prepared to accept the common external tariff and agricultural policy. The Council, Couve concluded, must study all these questions and destroy the 'myths' about negotiations: meanwhile, Community life must continue. He finished by saying that this was 'the only way of preparing British entry, against which – I repeat – we have no objection in principle.' While the Five felt that the problems raised by France were surmountable, they accepted the French wish for preliminary discussions among the Six. Belgium and the Netherlands demanded that there must be no delay beyond the end of the year.[106] While the Six were conducting this internal debate, however, the British finally accepted that the parity of sterling would have to be modified.

Many hoped that devaluation would help British European policy by indicating that the government was prepared to address the country's persistent economic weakness in preparation for taking on the economic burdens of membership. The Treasury brief stated that devaluation 'will not lessen the Government's determination to join the European Economic Community.' Rather it would 'put beyond doubt this country's ability to accept the obligations of membership.'[107] Members of the Six were reassuring. The Belgian prime minister, among others, wrote to Wilson, welcoming the economic measures taken by the British government: '[e]lles renforcent le désir du Gouvernement belge de voir rapidement les négociations entamées entre le Royaume Uni et les Six pays membres, dans le perspective d'une adhésion prochaine. Je ne puis donc que vous réaffirmer la détermination de mon gouvernement de vous soutenir dans vos efforts que nous approuvons entièrement.'[108] Wilson himself felt that the devaluation 'clearly…ought to help'.[109]

Straight away, however, the cabinet secretary was concerned that 'the operation does not seem to have made any difference, so far, to the French attitude.…Perhaps it was too much to hope that it would – the French have their own reasons for not letting us get off the hook too easily.'[110] Wilson himself had doubted 'whether it will in any way affect the General's long-term strategy.'[111] Both were correct. At a meeting of EEC finance ministers on 19 November, the Six expressed their unanimous appreciation of the courageous decision of the British government, but also expressed their own Community solidarity in deciding not to devalue themselves. French finance minister Michel Debré noted that the devaluation would 'not fundamentally change the French view on the British candidature for membership of the Common Market', despite having stressed in the summer that devaluation was a condition of membership.[112] The foreign ministers of the Five requested an oral report from the Commission on the consequences of devaluation for enlargement, pressing for a written report after formal talks with the UK. However, Couve opposed this step on the grounds that the press would interpret formal talks as *de facto* negotiations. The Belgian and Dutch ministers formally recorded their disappointment at the French attitude, but that did not stop it from being confirmed in de Gaulle's press conference, held just nine days after the devaluation announcement.[113]

So why did the British plan to press on? As Kitzinger noted, Wilson could hardly have coined the phrase 'not taking no for an answer' if the answer had looked like being yes.[114] Deighton suggests that so much had been invested in the policy that backing off would have been politically unacceptable: 'having got so far, the Labour government clearly could not yet take France's third *Non* as a final no.'[115] Lieber takes a slightly different approach, arguing that once the decision was made, 'Wilson was absolutely determined in his course'.[116] Neither concern for political appearances, nor plain stubbornness, however, take account of the long-term importance of the second British application.

De Gaulle's reasons for opposing British entry to the Communities – economic weakness, the 'special relationship', links with the Commonwealth – were the very issues with which governments were trying to come to terms in the later 1960s. This chapter has shown their importance to the subsequent story:

> Just as Macmillan had done...Wilson exhausted other options before turning toward the EEC. In 1964, Labour had come to power with its own variant of the three circles conception of Winston Churchill. But the Commonwealth, Eastern Europe and the Atlantic relationship proved to offer few possibilities. The realities of governing presented a different perspective than the realities of winning power....It did not take Wilson long to judge that the most realistic position for Britain to adopt was that of a European rather than a world power.[117]

As Frankel concludes, 'domestic and external developments converged...to the point of persuading the leadership of the reluctant Labour Party also to decide in favour of Britain's entry.'[118] Wilson's foreign policy was both reactive – to straightened economic circumstances in particular – and pro-active, with Wilson's government taking its own decisions and resisting US pressure to shadow American policy. Yet the reorientation towards Europe took the whole period of 1964-1970. The recognition of 'contracting options' and the creation of new policies to replace the old took considerable time and painful effort. This book argues that once Wilson decided on Europe, he used all tools at his disposal to get Britain in.

2

November – December 1967: reacting to the veto

In the months following de Gaulle's press conference, Wilson and Brown procured authority from cabinet both to maintain the application and to seek arrangements with the 'friendly Five' for the duration of the French veto. Their joint management of cabinet at this time was essential to its acquiescence in the 'approach to Europe' later on. At the same time, however, Brown's untactful treatment of the Federal Republic of Germany (FRG) in his rush to arrange a 'high level meeting' of Britain and the Five underlined the problems of division among the Five, with Germany on one side and the more helpful Italy and Benelux on the other. Brown alienated Brandt and, by the end of the year, caused a serious breach in the solidarity of the Five.

The Six: 'A certain wish for revenge was born'[1]

Any remaining British speculation on the General's position was quashed on 27 November 1967. In 'words of undisguised hostility', de Gaulle focused on two main issues concerning the British application: the extent to which it would change the Community, and the weakness of the British economy as made evident by devaluation. Britain could not join the EC, the General said, 'without disrupting or destroying what already exists.' He questioned the speed of the British application, and accused the government of 'embarking on all imaginable promises and pressures to get it adopted'. International and domestic problems led Britain to look to the EC for a safeguard which would 'allow her to play a leading role again.' But in order to do so, 'fundamental changes...radical modification and transformation' were needed. De Gaulle argued, wrongly, that the

Commission's report showed the UK economy to be incompatible with those of the Six. He listed Britain's chronic balance of payments deficit and distinctive production, sources of supply, credit practices, working conditions, food supplies, capital movements and the role of sterling. Furthermore, if Britain joined 'it would obviously mean the breaking up of a Community which has been built and which functions according to rules which would not bear such a monumental exception.' Britain was not a part of Europe 'as we have begun to build it.' There was no point in negotiating. It would be possible to include Britain in something new, thereby sacrificing the Community, but 'France is certainly not asking for that.' He wanted to see Britain accomplish 'the immense effort' needed to make the transformation, and France would be happy to help with any association or agreement that would increase commercial exchanges between the Six and EFTA. But the most important change would have to come from within the UK: 'the will and action of the great British people, which would make them into one of the pillars of a European Europe.'[2] There was absolutely no room for manoeuvre in this 'very clear rejection of any negotiations for our entry.'[3]

While Reilly in Paris described de Gaulle's performance as 'so exaggerated and divorced from reality that it did not seem to carry much conviction to his audience', the General undoubtedly brought about a new reality, to which Britain and the EC member states had to adjust.[4] Wilson immediately set in train the contingency plans worked out in Whitehall, and reaffirmed his determination to succeed with the application. Wilson and Brown met the day after the veto, agreeing to press for a reply from the Community as a whole at the next Council of Ministers in December. They agreed that a confirmation of the veto would not mean a change in course 'in the sense of withdrawing our application or looking for NAFTA-type solutions', and Wilson said that he was 'completely opposed to the pursuit of alternatives.'[5] He dealt with de Gaulle's statement in a point-by-point rebuttal speech at a luncheon of the Parliamentary Press Gallery, drawing on the Commission's 'Opinion', pointing to economic difficulties in France itself, insisting that Britain was prepared to make both the commitment and the changes necessary for entry, and trumpeting the technological contribution that Britain could make to the Communities. In his memoir he commented that he enjoyed dictating these points, 'though I did not affect to believe that they would have any effect on the General.'[6] He gave a statement in the House of Commons that the government had 'slammed down our application on the table. There it is, and there it remains.'[7] By the time cabinet met on 30 November, messages of support had already begun to pour in from the Five. Before turning to the more detailed and complex relations with the

EC, however, the chapter addresses the UK's wider relations and their impact on the maintenance of the British application.

The superpowers, EFTA and the Commonwealth

Throughout this period, the United States administration continued strongly to support the British line on the EC. In dismissing NAFTA, an official paper on the consequences of the veto noted that the Americans were more interested in protecting their own economy than in joining such an association, and preferred British membership of the Community.[8] Yet they were not able to be particularly helpful. Overt American pressure would be taken as justifying de Gaulle's assertion that the British were a 'Trojan horse' who would enable the Americans to gain dominance over the EC. For this reason, care was taken over the announcement of Wilson's trip to the USA, planned for early 1968, which Palliser worried could be 'interpreted as a hastily organised meeting designed to search for alternatives to the present European policy'.[9]

Nonetheless, American advice was sought.[10] Their ambassador in London said that the British had been absolutely right and would continue to be right to insist on negotiating with the Community as a whole, and that the government should not be deflected from this course. NAFTA was emphatically not a possibility at present, and therefore the British should do everything possible to bear down on the French with one proposition: namely that all the French difficulties could be discussed as part of a negotiation.[11] The US undertook to ask their Brussels mission to reflect this position in their contacts with the Commission.[12] When secretary of state Dean Rusk visited London in December, he offered to do something 'to help', supporting British policy to force a decision at the forthcoming Council of Ministers meeting.[13] Although Rusk resisted the 'founding father' of European integration, Jean Monnet's advice to speak out against French policy, the Americans continued publicly to support British accession. Rusk stated in early December that the European states 'must merge their strength so that they can act and grow together' and that 'if that merger is to be complete and secure, Britain must be a part of it.' He confirmed that the US 'still stand[s] in support of Britain's entry into Europe.'[14] In reality, there was little at this time that the USA could do practically to support the British policy of accession.

It had always been unlikely that the three other applicants for EC membership, Ireland, Denmark and Norway, would continue their applications in the event of a French veto on negotiations with Britain. The British therefore worked on the assumption that EFTA would continue in being in the interim period.[15] In some cases this attitude was welcomed: the Portuguese government, for example, which had not applied for membership, hoped that the French veto would postpone the effective disappearance of EFTA, which they were sure would follow EC enlargement.[16]

The British focus was firmly on what could be achieved in concert with the friendly five, to the exclusion, if necessary, of the other three applicants. Fortunately, they were initially as opposed to association as the British.[17] The Norwegians asked in December for the British to include them in any initiative for contacts with the Five, when the British ambassador in Oslo warned that they might be attracted to association if the Germans appeared to be looking favourably on that option.[18] The Danish took a pessimistic view, willing to go along with any British initiative but noting that 'if there was any alternative to the enlarged Common Market which was once again denied us, we should all have thought of it before.'[19] Sweden was torn between its neutrality and its fear of losing three of its most important customers to the EEC. For economic reasons Austria had applied for its own association agreement with the EC, making it clear that it was prepared to leave EFTA in the process, and prime minister Kreisky was immediately critical of the political nature of Britain's application and arguments for enlargement.[20]

Therefore both EFTA and the bilateral relations between the UK and other EFTA states languished after the veto, with all waiting to see the outcome of the December Council of Ministers. At the same time, the British hoped to use the unity of EFTA to strengthen their bid: the chances of success would increase 'if all EFTA countries maintain the pressure of their own bids for participation, in one way or another, in an extended EC. This is one way in which EFTA should maintain its unity and demonstrate its strength.' In contrast, trying to build a stronger EFTA would only 'dissipate our energies and create the impression that we were losing interest or confidence in our bid.'[21] This stance, of trying not to do anything in foreign policy that could undermine the membership bid, became a pattern for Britain over the next two years.

Brown had spelled out the British position on the Commonwealth when he presented the British case for membership in WEU on 4 July.[22] The African, Caribbean and dependent territories were to have Associated Overseas Territory (AOT) status; Asian countries should see a revival of the provisional 1963 agreements; the Commonwealth Sugar Agreement should be preserved until its expiry in 1974 and thereafter there should be discussions with the Six to safeguard the long term interests of countries whose economies were overwhelmingly dependent on sugar; New Zealand butter should likewise be protected. Transitional arrangements would be needed for the whole field of Commonwealth trade.[23] Britain's plans for the Commonwealth could hardly have been more different than in 1961-3, when the Macmillan government had, initially at least, hoped to retain special terms for Commonwealth access to EEC markets.[24] Disunity in the Commonwealth in general, and difficulties over arms exports to South Africa and over Rhodesian independence made it an increasingly unattractive institution, so that its claims on British loyalty were less than at the time of the first application.[25] The Commonwealth countries accepted this British position, and were more concerned to learn the British fall-back position than to pursue their own interests.[26] Brown promised the deputy prime minister of New Zealand that while there might be differences of opinion about the extent of New Zealand interests, he would never make a bargain at New Zealand's expense. John Marshall, evidently convinced of the finality of the French veto, explained that his government considered it premature to take the discussion of their interests any further at this stage.[27] Similarly, when Wilson met John McEwen, prime minister of Australia (albeit for just twenty-three days), the subject was barely mentioned. The Australians asked only if Wilson thought the French attitude was simply that of de Gaulle, presumably wondering if the stance would change when de Gaulle left office.[28] Clearly, the Commonwealth countries were waiting for greater certainty about Britain's relations with Europe before making any concrete plans of their own.

Back to Europe: 'Dealing with Britain' again[29]

Britain's friends in the Community were anxious for certainty. Dutch foreign minister 'Joe' Luns announced that press conferences did not constitute a method of negotiating: proper Community procedure must be followed. The 18 December Council meeting would be the 'hour of truth'.[30] Italian foreign minister Amintore Fanfani asserted that de Gaulle's comments were 'not valid' and did not change Italy's belief that British membership was 'desirable, useful and necessary for a constructive evolution of our continent.'[31] With Chancellor Kiesinger absent in Asia, the German line appeared reassuringly strong. Foreign minister Willy Brandt announced that negotiations should begin as soon as possible, and that since the French had raised no objection in principle, it was premature to pass a final judgement.[32] Harmel, the Belgian foreign minister, was inclined to maintain a very strong position in the face of France, and the Belgian ambassador told Brown that he wanted Britain to do all possible to move closer to the Communities so that there would be gradual integration with the EC, regardless of the outcome of the application. Brown replied that Britain would pursue all possible European initiatives – the prime minister's November proposals for technological co-operation would be a case in point. But it was membership alone that the UK wanted. Readiness to pursue co-operative policies in Europe was conditional on not being sidetracked into 'association' or any other relationship with the Community that fell short of full membership. Brown hoped, therefore, that the Benelux foreign ministers would agree a tough line in response to de Gaulle's press conference.[33] Their resulting line was more than satisfactory, stating that de Gaulle's comments 'in no way constituted a form of negotiation and that his press conference had as such no validity.' Luns indicated that the Five would meet together before the December meeting and that they would take a tough line with France.[34] The Six would have to make a collective decision in Council, towards the end of December.

Cabinet

Cabinet was faced with this situation on 30 November. Brown presented various options, from leaving the Five to take a decision on the future with no British input, to the possibility of association with the Community. He favoured the most assertive course: urging the Five to fix a date for the opening of negotiations in January, thereby forcing the issue with the French, and suggested that due to other issues it was 'possible that de Gaulle can be forced to give way.' On the other hand, if the French confirmed their veto, the British Government would at least know where it stood. He therefore sought authority to follow this course with the Five over the next weeks.[35] Brown added that he feared for the credibility and standing of the Government should there not be early negotiations: support for the policy would be lost both at home and abroad. In discussion several qualifications were raised. Denis Healey pointed out that there were risks in pressing for early negotiations and suggested that the idea of a NAFTA deserved further study. Made anonymously in the style of post-war cabinet minutes, where only the main speakers are identified, concerns were raised regarding the future of EFTA, relations with the Commonwealth, the potential humiliation of continuing with the application and the opportunity to focus on British economic interests. Clearly therefore, there were differences not just of emphasis but of policy within the cabinet. Nevertheless, all agreed with Brown that they must seek an 'early termination' of uncertainty, and Wilson therefore summed up by saying that cabinet agreed with Brown's proposed course, while noting that British interests were paramount and that officials would carry out a study of the consequences of exclusion.[36]

This discussion was important for two main reasons. First, as seen above, Wilson and Brown had already agreed on the line to try to take after de Gaulle's press conference: cabinet was persuaded to confirm their hope to press the Five for an early decision. This prior agreement implies that Wilson's acceptance in cabinet of the focus on the domestic economy and of an official study was intended at least in part as a sop to the less than enthusiastic members of cabinet. Why though did those members of the Government endorse the decision? Barbara Castle noted that Brown's line was accepted for 'conflicting reasons', but acknowledged that 'we all wanted to know where we were so that we could plan our next steps accordingly.'[37] Peter Shore asserted that the decision 'not to take no for an answer' was a face-saving public relations exercise.[38] He had already informed Wilson of his own views, writing that,

> while I appreciate your wish not to react petulantly to de Gaulle and to await the December meeting of the Council of Ministers, I do feel strongly that, with soft answers, we are in danger of losing a unique opportunity of rallying opinion, of asserting our self reliance, and of identifying ourselves with the national cause.
>
> People in Britain, as you have so often observed, are tired of being pushed around. The General's veto compounds the feeling of national humiliation which followed last week's devaluation....
>
> Surely this is the moment, in a measured and serious way, to be 'Gaullist' in the British sense and to rally the nation...in the task of making ourselves both strong and independent.[39]

Yet Shore did not make a stand in cabinet.

Hints of the explanation for the cabinet's acquiescence may be found during the 1967 decision to apply for membership. Castle wrote after the key 30 April cabinet meeting that, 'as always, H[arold] would do what he intended to do and one could only judge one's own course at the last minute when face to face with the implications of the decision he had made.'[40] Benn's portrayal of a 'defeated cabinet' and Crossman's cynical expectation of a saving French veto, both noted above, suggest the atmosphere in cabinet. The increase in the volume of opposition to the application after de Gaulle's resignation and the lifting of the veto at the summit at The Hague in December 1969 makes Crossman's comment seems particularly relevant. Until then, those who opposed entry felt that they could allow the policy to drift. Cabinet meetings over the next five to six months followed the same model of activism by Brown and Wilson combined with acquiescence by 'Euro-sceptics'.

Second, the decision to press for consultation with the Five, reinforced in a subsequent meeting, was used as sufficient authority for all the diplomacy of the coming months. It was not examined in cabinet as different proposals emerged from the Continent, although the foreign secretary made several reports and there was occasional discussion, as will be seen below. The initial apathy of Euro-sceptics was therefore crucial in allowing Wilson and his foreign secretaries to press on with the 'approach to Europe'.

Diplomacy

Cabinet certainly made little difference to Wilson and Brown's planning with the Five. The Italians were strong in their defence of the British application and their condemnation of the French. They told the Germans at the beginning of December that Five-solidarity was more important than ever, and that they must continue to insist on the opening of negotiations.[41] Luns advised Crosland that diplomatic pressure should be concentrated on Bonn.[42] Brandt himself told the Belgian ambassador to Germany that his aim at the Council meeting was

> to find a middle way between the French position which was to avoid negotiations, and [the British] position which was to insist on immediate negotiations. For Germany, the essential thing was to keep the talks going. The British should be asked to moderate their pressure and consider some form of association.[43]

The British gave the same response to all. Brown came down hard on suggestions of association as being the 'wrong road', and wrote to Brandt that it 'has been hard work hitting these ideas on the head. As you will know, all we are interested in is full membership.'[44] Brown was only partially reassured when the Belgians acknowledged that there was no point putting such suggestions forward if they were unacceptable, and Brandt told him in person that he accepted this line and promised to 'bring things to a head' at the Council meeting: he and Wilson nevertheless felt the need to 'nail...Willy Brandt down even more firmly'.[45] Wilson focused on the political arguments for British membership, telling the leader of the Austrian Socialist Party, Dr Kreisky, that while the economic arguments for joining were finely balanced, 'the political arguments for creating a much stronger and more united Europe, able to play its rightful role in world affairs, were very powerful indeed.'[46] He stressed that this political role was important not just for Britain, but for Europe:

> [t]he political consequences for Europe as a whole of the adhesion of the United Kingdom were equally important for Europe's influence on world affairs generally....If Europe were not even able to solve its own problems, it could not expect the rest of the world to pay much heed to its advice on world problems.[47]

Clearly anything less than full membership would be unwelcome to Wilson.

Like Brandt, Commission president Jean Rey was concerned to avoid either controversy or deadlock. Nevertheless, he stood by the Commission's 'Opinion', and argued that association, as provided for in the Treaty, was not suitable for Britain: '[f]ull membership was the only solution.' At the same time, however, he warned against trying to divide the Six.[48] Overall, the atmosphere in both Britain and Continental Europe between de Gaulle's press conference and the 18-19 December Council meeting was one of 'wait and see.'

There was little contact between Britain and France: evidence of the French position came from the media, reports of speeches by ministers, and information from the Five.[49] In a rare low-level meeting, the diplomatic counsellor at the Elysée attacked the very basis of the British application, arguing that the government should have concentrated on bilateral relations with France. It was 'more essential for the future of Europe', he said, 'that Franco-British relations should be close than either Franco-German or Anglo-German relations should be close.'[50] In a precursor of the 'Soames affair', the FO dismissed this apparent effort to improve bilateral relations as a delaying tactic intended to draw attention away from the application, while noting that (secret) talks might be a possibility in the future.[51] De Gaulle's biographer Lacouture therefore aptly described the relationship as 'an underhand guerrilla war of unappeased jealousies and cleverly cooked-up plots'.[52] The French felt that they were in an unassailable position. De Gaulle thought that the failure of Wilson's European initiative would cause the British public to turn against him. He did not expect a crisis in the Community as a result of his veto, acknowledging only that there would be a period of difficulty.[53]

Urgent diplomacy between the British and the Five continued throughout the run-up to the Council of Ministers meeting. As well as fending off proposals for association and other interim measures, Brown began to work hard for a 'high-level meeting'. On 1 December he suggested to the Italian ambassador that such a meeting could be useful, and could be held in the fringes of the forthcoming NATO meeting in Brussels.[54] A meeting of the Five was already planned that day, so arrangements would be simple. Brown told the Luxembourg foreign minister that he would arrive for the meeting a day before it started: Grégoire took the bait and suggested that the Five could meet him after their own meeting.[55] Brown broached this idea to Luns, arguing that if the French veto were confirmed, the more treaties and arrangements that could be made between Britain and the Five the better. Luns agreed, suggesting that they use the Franco-German Friendship Treaty of 1963 as a model. As with Grégoire, Brown managed to present this idea as Luns' own, even as the FO continued to prepare its own plans.[56] The Germans were more sceptical. Brandt conceded that *if* the French confirmed their veto on 18-19 December, they would discuss the next stage together, but no dates were mentioned.[57] In fact, he was still working on Kiesinger for permission even to attend the meeting of the Five on 12 December, let alone planning for one of the Five and Britain.[58]

Ultimately, with the focus at the NATO meeting on the new 'Harmel Doctrine' of defence, deterrence and détente, there was no Five – Britain meeting, although there were several bilateral and multilateral meetings on the fringes of the main event. Couve told Brandt that the French were not in favour of negotiations – neither full negotiations nor negotiations in any other form. The British economic position would have to be re-established first.[59] The French position met opposition from the Five, however: at a breakfast meeting, Germany, Italy and the Benelux countries decided that the further development of the Communities, such as agricultural price levels and aid to francophone countries, would be bound up with British entry.[60] Brandt himself, reporting on the meeting to the Bundestag, said that ending the division between the EEC and EFTA would be in the interests of Europe, international progress, closing the technological gap between Europe and the superpowers, and the furtherance of peace. He sent a sharp message to France:

> We are not inclined towards citing power relationships, engaging in demonstrations, and least of all making threats. But our own interest and Europe's interest too…compel us to speak clearly. We feel obliged at this moment to recommend urgently to our French neighbour not to make things too difficult for France itself and for others.[61]

Despite this clear line, however, Lord Alun Chalfont, minister of state in the FO, was worried that the attitudes of the Five 'oscillate violently between resolution and compromise, between solidarity and disintegration.'[62] No one knew quite what to expect on 18-19 December.

The German factor
Despite the solidarity at the NATO meeting, the Germans continued to cause concern. The British were aware of divisions within the German government regarding the extent to which pressure should be put on the French, particularly between the more cautious Kiesinger and the more enthusiastic Brandt.[63] Several members of the German administration

continued to offer support. Brandt made a 'firm and clear and excellent' speech in the Bundestag on 15 December, arguing that a decision should be made to open negotiations, and explicitly isolating France in his description of the situation.[64] Brown immediately wrote to thank him.[65] Strauss, the minister of finance, advised that the British would have to show the traditional quality of 'bull-dog tenacity' in order to overcome French opposition.[66] The German parliament put strong pressure on the government to support enlargement of the Community whole-heartedly.[67] However, other signals, less welcome to the British, continued to emerge from the German government. Although Brandt was determined to achieve a common position of the Five with which to confront France at the Council meeting, some ministers like state secretary Lahr clung to the idea of some halfway house stage before full membership could be achieved.[68] Most important, Kiesinger's position was clear from the start: he would support the British position with 'all possible emphasis…but without this leading to a final break' with France.[69] As ambassador Frank Roberts noted, the 'key to German policy remains in Kiesinger's hands. It is good that he is now under such strong political and other pressures, but his attitude, despite his undoubted anger with de Gaulle over his press conference, does not seem to have changed….'[70] This division within the German government was a problem with which the British would have to deal until the victory of Brandt's SPD in the autumn of 1969.

Nevertheless, the British continued to work with the Dutch on proposals that they hoped would include all five friendly member states. At a meeting in mid-December, officials from the two foreign ministries discussed the possibility of co-operation in defence, technology, economics and political union.[71] A Dutch paper noted that action would be most effective if all the Five took part, but acknowledged that bilateral action might be all that was possible.[72] Chalfont and Brown agreed to pursue this line, accepting that they would have to get authorisation from at least some of their ministerial colleagues to do so.[73] The Official Committee on the Approach to Europe (EURO) immediately produced a paper on the UK contribution to a high-level meeting with the Five.[74]

The December Council of Ministers
At the Council of Ministers meeting, the British were pleasantly surprised at the strength and cohesiveness of the Five in facing France. The Council communiqué stated that,

> [f]ive member states are in agreement with [the Commission 'Opinion' on the need to open negotiations]. They think, moreover, that it is necessary to begin immediately negotiations with a view to

the adhesion of Britain, Ireland, Denmark and Norway in order that these negotiations can be parallel to the recovery of the British economy.

One member state is of the opinion that the process of recovery of the British economy ought to be brought to its conclusion so that the request of Great Britain can be reconsidered.[75]

The French veto had been confirmed. The FO issued a statement on the same day:

It is a matter of grave concern that the Government of France has been unable to accept the unanimous view of its partners that negotiations for Britain's accession to the European Communities should start at once. This can only delay the inevitable progress towards a united Europe including Britain, which is in the interest of Europe as a whole.

There is no question of withdrawing Britain's application. H.M. Government believe that, given the support of the Five Governments and the overwhelming majority of opinion throughout Western Europe, European unity is bound to be achieved. H.M. Government will be consulting about the implications of the present situation with other European Governments who share Britain's views on the future of Europe.[76]

The Five shared Britain's disappointment. Harmel made a statement, saying that 'Europe had not lived up to itself'.[77] Luns, supported by the leaders of the governing and opposition parties, said that it 'was of particular importance that the UK and other candidates did not turn their backs on Europe and the Five must be ready to give factual proof of their readiness for integration.'[78] The Italians were equally supportive: Fanfani agreed on the necessity to work out a plan of action, while nothing 'should be done which would make the ultimate goal more remote. The Italian Government had much appreciated the British decision not to withdraw their application for membership of the Communities.'[79] Prime minister Pierre Werner stressed Luxembourg's continuing support for Britain, and added that Benelux governments had made 'great efforts to keep up some momentum.'[80] Sir William Nield, deputy under-secretary in the Cabinet Office, stressed that the Five 'have stood up very well to the French and declared themselves in favour of early negotiations.' Again, however, the awkward position of Germany, caught between its 'special relationship' with France and its desire for British entry into the Communities, became clear. Harmel pointed out to the British that while 'Herr Brandt had been

quite excellent in the meetings…his position was rather more difficult
than that of his four colleagues.'[81]

As the Five demonstrated their support for Britain, Brown, in
preparation for cabinet, wrote to selected ministers about his intentions
for a high level meeting. He set out three aims for the veto period: to
maintain the objective of full membership as a credible policy; to prevent
unwelcome developments within the EC; and to preserve, insofar as it did
not interfere with the first two aims, freedom of action in the economic
field pending membership.[82] The first two of these aims were to remain a
top priority throughout the veto period. Having succeeded in pressing the
Five to extract a clear veto from France, Brown wanted to move on to
extra-Rome Treaty consultation and collaboration with them. He told
cabinet that they were anxious to develop mutually advantageous
activities, and that Luns had assured him that the Netherlands were
prepared to block internal Community developments unfavourable to
Britain. Brown therefore sought approval from his colleagues and
authority to consult confidentially with the Five in order to make the most
of their resentment of French intransigence, initially by means of a high-
level meeting. As before, the response from ministers was qualified. UK
freedom of action and relations with the US should not be endangered,
while it was important not to give the impression that anything short of
full membership would be acceptable; otherwise the determination of the
Five to fight the British cause might be undermined. Brown undertook to
'take account' of the views expressed, and Wilson's summing up
established that the response to the Council meeting should be such as
would strengthen the determination and position of the Five, including
the possibility of a high level meeting between the Five and the four
applicants to consider the consequences of the French veto.[83]

Once again, therefore, Brown and Wilson were seeking authority from
cabinet for a process they had already begun. On an issue of such
importance, and given the divisions among ministers, Wilson's and
Brown's actions were significant. Benn had even approached Wilson in
response to Brown's preparatory minute, writing that he had 'considerable
misgivings' about the proposal for a high level meeting, and stating that
the 'issues of policy raised are of such importance that I presume you will
want to let Cabinet discuss it.'[84] Yet Benn did not raise these 'considerable
misgivings' at the meeting – at least not persuasively enough to prevent
Brown from receiving the necessary authority.

Meanwhile, Brown subtly addressed the misgivings brought up in the
previous meeting. The desire of some members of cabinet to focus on
British economic self-interest was clearly stated on 30 November, and was
accepted by Wilson in his summing up. Yet at this meeting on 20

December, Brown accepted freedom of action in the economic field only as far as it did not interfere with what he saw as the two primary objectives: the maintenance of the full application and the prevention of Community development in undesirable ways.[85] Given that cabinet gave him authority, his semantic nuance clearly worked. He made a statement in the House of Commons the same day, paying tribute to the Five and the Commission, reaffirming that the government 'still regard ourselves as committed to our main purpose in Europe', and announcing that they 'now propose to enter into consultations with those Five members...who supported the Commission's view that negotiations should be started at an early stage.' As for France, 'we shall not indulge in any peevish or petty reaction...[but] it would be idle to pretend that what has happened is not a grave blow to our relationship.'[86]

Unfortunately, Brown's pursuit of these plans for consultations with the Five pushed Germany towards France and broke the solidarity of the Five. Relations with France remained cold. Chalfont met members of the French embassy on 18 December and reported the ambassador's position as being one of 'almost total intransigence and bitterness.' Chalfont was tempted by the embassy's offer of a 'clandestine' meeting of British and French experts to discuss monetary affairs, but accepted O'Neill's point that 'the French point about bilateral talks is a completely phoney one.'[87] O'Neill felt that any conversation with the French would be a *dialogue des sourds*.'[88]

Brown's aggressive diplomacy for a 'high-level meeting' between the Five and Britain alienated Britain's strongest supporter in Germany, Brandt. In a telegram to Rome, Brown argued that continuing common action between Britain (and the other applicants) and the Five would be 'essential' and that Britain 'must move quickly if we are to make the most of current irritation with France' and to achieve something before Kiesinger and de Gaulle met in January. He stressed that it was not 'realistic to think in terms of common action including France', suggesting for the rest projects like joint weapons development and industrial collaboration. His ambition was revealed at the end of the telegram, where he said that the 'aim might be to establish a form of political union between the Five, Britain and the other applicants'.[89] He asked whether Italy would be prepared to call the initial meeting, and if any conditions would be attached. Brown's aim was to avoid placing Britain in an environment in which the French could use their veto, and he was willing to use the threat that, were nothing done, pro-entry sentiment in Britain would surely falter. Moreover, he calculated that if Britain, Italy and Benelux showed themselves willing to proceed without the Germans, 'this…would induce the Germans to attend.'[90] This assumption was incorrect.

Initially only Italy and the Netherlands were consulted on the 'high-level meeting', although the ground was tested in Belgium as well and the idea of increased contacts between the Five and Britain was circulating after the Council meeting.[91] The Italians were initially somewhat cautious: the proposal was 'more audacious' than the 'next steps' they had been considering.[92] However, on Christmas day Fanfani invited Brown to a meeting to discuss the idea.[93] Sir Evelyn Shuckburgh, the British ambassador in Rome, warned that Brown would need to 'shake [Fanfani] up quite considerably', convince him of the need for a striking joint political action, and come prepared with precise, well-prepared ideas.[94] The Dutch also stressed the need for a well-planned meeting, anticipating that the reactions of the Five would vary 'in inverse ratio to the serious content and implications of the action proposed.' Luns agreed to urge the Italians to call a meeting, and his government got to work immediately on a list of subjects for discussion.[95] A few days later Luns emerged in 'fighting mood', ready to consider talks without Germany if necessary and, if it came to the crunch, talks between Britain and the Netherlands alone. 'In any case he was ready to press the other members of the Five to go as far as possible, and was still maintaining his refusal to set a date for the next Council of Ministers.'[96] Less than a month after the veto, the Netherlands had emerged as the strongest and most consistent supporter of British entry, a position it would retain for the rest of the veto period. The British ambassador in The Hague immediately warned that HMG should be careful not to take the Dutch for granted, and as will be seen in the following chapters, Wilson and his ministers were careful to nurture the relationship.[97]

When the idea of consultations between the Five and applicants was floated with other members of the Community, James Marjoribanks, the British representative to the Communities, felt that even the Commission might be persuaded to support increased contacts between the Five and the applicant states. He warned that the Commission would naturally be suspicious of contacts that might undermine the Community itself but concluded that it would therefore be important for the Government to carry the Commission along, making clear that they were moving to European unity along the only roads at present open to them.[98] Grégoire in Luxembourg 'thoroughly approved' of the idea of a Five-four meeting.[99] Harmel was slightly more guarded, resolute that any such initiative must come from the Five, not Britain, that it must be very carefully prepared, and that the matter should be presented in such a way as to cause the fewest problems for the Germans.[100] When the Belgians were formally consulted they took a similar line to the Dutch, prepared to encourage the Italians but adamant on the need for preparation. They also felt that an initial meeting of the Five alone would be appropriate, since they had agreed on 19 December to consult in the New Year on their future relations with the UK.[101] Having received this encouragement, Brown informed the governments of Germany and Benelux that he had accepted an invitation from Fanfani to discuss the decisions taken at the Council meeting and the British application. In keeping with the newly intimate relations with the Netherlands, Luns was informed first.[102]

The actor obviously missing from these consultations was Germany, and there were early warning signs that the Federal Government was not happy. Shortly after the Council meeting Roberts cautioned that the Germans wanted time for thought and consultation within and outside the Six, to maintain Franco-German relations on as even a keel as possible and therefore to avoid any early demonstrative acts which might aggravate matters. Roberts did not think the Germans would attend any early meeting, and questioned the ability of the Four to hold together in the absence of German support. Since the next de Gaulle-Kiesinger meeting had been postponed until mid-February, there was now time to think and prepare carefully.[103] Roberts warned, too, of the dangers of appearing to go to the Italians and Dutch behind Brandt's back. GF Duckwitz, a state secretary in the ministry of foreign affairs, felt that two or three months would be necessary for the dust to settle and tempers to calm.[104] Kiesinger made clear that he was prepared to consider consultation among the Five, but was still considering some kind of association between Britain and the Community.[105] Lahr reported that the Five had agreed on 19 December to think things over with a view to meeting in January. If the British were willing to consider some kind of 'arrangement', the Five could discuss that with France. With no authority yet to tell Lahr of the 'high-level meeting' idea, Roberts noted that there had been separate Dutch and Italian suggestions for a meeting of Britain and the Five, and that HMG was trying to discover what they had in mind. Lahr poured cold water on the idea, seeing no advantage in it and indeed suggesting that it could do more harm than good. Roberts warned that the Germans must be taken into British confidence as soon as possible, and permission was given on 22 December for Roberts to approach Brandt after Christmas – just days before the planned meeting between Brown and Fanfani.[106]

If Brown was not already alerted to the Federal Republic's rejection of the idea, Brandt made the German position icily clear. He told Roberts on 28 December that 'he must frankly admit that he had not been thinking in terms of such rapid or demonstrative developments'. He would of course consider any ideas that emerged from the Brown-Fanfani meeting, but felt the efforts of the Five should be focused on France, who, being responsible for the current state of affairs, should have to come up with some solution. An overly demonstrative act of solidarity among the Five and Britain, without sufficiently solid content, would surely, Brandt said, weaken the reasonable elements in France and even give de Gaulle an excuse to say that the Community had broken up. Instead, perhaps contacts could be developed at ambassadorial level between Britain and the Five in WEU. Brandt was upset that the British had approached Rome and The Hague before Bonn, and was obviously shocked and discomforted at the progress of events. However, Roberts felt that he was open to the ideas: it would be important to keep him closely in the picture from now on.[107]

The meeting with Fanfani therefore went ahead in a potentially difficult atmosphere. By the time Brown arrived in Rome, Harmel had suggested a modified approach to the high-level meeting, proposing that it take place immediately before a WEU meeting in Brussels at the end of January rather than on an earlier date. He recognised that the British government's policy was 'a very European one', but felt that it was essential that the Five must stay together as they moved forward. 'If any one of them were to drop out this would merely reinforce de Gaulle's position.' Fanfani was therefore prepared to support Harmel's proposal instead of making one of his own, believing that it would be easier for the Germans to attend a meeting in such a framework.   Brown, although disappointed, agreed under three conditions: the fact of the meeting must be public; it must be thoroughly prepared; and it must be the start of a continuous process. He stressed that the meeting must be before the next Kiesinger-de Gaulle meeting.[108] Harmel was quickly informed of the agreement between the two ministers, and the planning got underway.[109]

Although Brown was careful to send Brandt a personal message about his Italian trip, the Germans were unimpressed.[110] Roberts reported that 'Brandt was obviously put out by the fact that we had consulted Fanfani and others before him about future moves...and this took a little smoothing over.' It was clear to Roberts that 'Germany would prefer action with France inside the Community to action between us and the Five outside it', and that Brandt was interested in some arrangement between the Six and the applicants, not as an alternative to membership but as a step towards it. Roberts felt that Brandt genuinely wanted to help Britain, but shared the 'deep-seated German reluctance' to get on a collision course with France. If Britain took a strong line against such an arrangement, even 'our best friends' in Germany might feel that this was an unreasonable position and be less inclined to join the other Four in seeking co-operation outside the Community. Roberts concluded that the best – indeed the necessary – course of action was to 'smoke out the French', in addition to pursuing increased contacts with the Five. If Gallic hints about 'arrangements' could be shown to be false, the Germans might come on board.[111]

So despite support from the Four, 1967 ended with the solidarity of the Five in support of the British application, so recently shown in the Council meeting, significantly undermined. The full extent of Brandt's anger would not be revealed until January, when it would become clear that Brown's bull-headed diplomacy in pursuit of a high-level meeting, without taking account of the sentiments of his most important ally in the EC, had caused significant harm.

Conclusions

Kitzinger's assertion that 'the political initiative that began with the announcement of 10 November 1966 came to a halt with the Council's communiqué of 17 December 1967, and thereby forms a finished chapter in Britain's post-war relations with Western Europe', is clearly incorrect.[112] At the very least, the veto opened a new chapter in Britain's relations with Europe. More important, European policy after the veto and its confirmation in the Council of Ministers was presented as a continuation of the original application, a continued insistence that Britain's place was at the heart of Europe.

Yet it was Brown, the supposed 'Europhile', who undermined the British 'approach to Europe' at the end of 1967. By annoying Brandt he upset the most stalwart and sure German supporter of British entry into the Communities. Brandt had wanted time to ease the Federal Government towards closer contacts between the Five and Britain, ensuring at the same time that France was not made to feel isolated. Instead, Brown's actions prevented Brandt from being able to help the UK, forcing him instead to focus on mending fences with France. It would be almost a year before Brandt was able to persuade his government to prioritise co-operation with the British instead of relations with France. Although not unexpected – indeed, in an echo of Chancellor Konrad Adenauer's move to de Gaulle's side in 1962-3 – the French veto created a dual political schism within the Community. Germany's core loyalty to France meant that the initial solidarity of the Five in support of Britain was soon replaced by a division between the Franco-German alliance on one hand, and the other four member states on the other.[113] In January and February the British were therefore taken in new directions in their European policy, as members of the Six began to make proposals for managing the period of the French veto.

3

January – February 1968: new ideas

George Brown's indelicate handling of the proposal for a meeting between Britain and the Five coloured the first weeks of 1968, but the most striking characteristic of this period was the intense effort directed towards finding an 'interim solution' to the problem of the British application. The spring saw apparently contradictory policy decisions from the British. Financial constraints dictated the final decision to withdraw from 'East of Suez' and a consequent focus on Western Europe, while the same constraints compelled Britain's departure from a number of European technological and particularly space projects. Throughout, Wilson sought to keep attention focused on 'the citadel': the application itself, and not on any alternative arrangements. Cabinet was bypassed where necessary, while extra-European support was drafted where possible.

Wilson's own view was revealed in a private letter to Lord Wayland Kennet, a Labour peer and minister. Wilson wrote that

> Anyone who has talked to de Gaulle as I have three or four times in the past two years knew perfectly well that he was ill-disposed towards our membership of the Community. But this knowledge did not – and does not – make me consider it wrong for us to have decided to go for membership – to apply for it and to maintain our application in the face of last December's veto. Things have changed a lot since 1963, as the reaction in this country and in Europe to our application has shown. Of course, the tactical handling still needs care and skill...but I believe the strategy to be right....'[1]

Wilson had not been knocked off his preferred course by the confirmation of the French veto in December. The extent to which the tactical handling of this course had upset Germany, however, was about to be revealed.

Soothing Germany: An 'intricate series of confusions and misunderstandings'[2]

As preparations for a high-level meeting between Britain and the Five continued, reports began to arrive from Bonn about the extent of Brandt's unhappiness.[3] While the German ambassador in Rome reported merely that Brandt had been 'a bit put out' by the speed with which the British had come up with new proposals over Christmas, and state secretary Harkort delicately noted that Brandt had hoped for 'a little more time' in which to work out a possible approach to the French, Lahr was instructed to make clear that his foreign minister was 'upset' ('*veraergert*') by the British approach to the Italians.[4] Much time was to be invested in soothing Brandt, but difficult relations were compounded by German reluctance to be parted from their closest ally, France. An element of frustration with the German government appeared amongst British ministers and officials. As one FO official commented, 'I am struck by the number of occasions on which the Germans from Brandt downwards have tended to argue that there was no crisis, that they should go on talking to the French, and that meetings between the Five and the Four [applicants] were unwise because provocative.'[5] The frustration increased as the member states made new proposals for managing the veto period.

The British therefore invested significant efforts in trying to keep the Germans on side. Intelligence reports in January indicated that the French were trying to make the Germans believe that 'they will move towards the USSR if the Germans get too far out of line with French policy', hinting to 'official German representatives in Paris that France [would] "enter into associations with the USSR" in proportion to the extent to which German policy deviates from French interests.' Wilson suggested, perhaps tongue in cheek (and certainly hastily rebutted by the FO), that '[m]aybe we should drop the same hint to the Germans!'[6] Trying both to address these fears and smooth ruffled feathers, Chalfont told Brandt that he 'very much hoped [he] would not think of abandoning the very leading role he had played' and 'would not surrender the role he had played of champion and friend to Britain'.[7] Brown returned early from a visit to Tokyo in order to visit and 'butter up Brandt.'[8] Much diplomatic time was wasted and two ministerial visits necessitated by Brown's inept handling of the immediate post-veto situation.

The FO therefore concluded that the Germans should be given a limited period of time to work on the French.[9] Wilson agreed, saying that he would 'prefer to see the Germans draw a blank in Paris – then let all of us, including them, review the situation.'[10] He was increasingly worried that 'further pressure on the Germans will be highly counter-productive'. On the other hand, a less rushed approach would allow the post-devaluation economic measures to produce fruits, so that Britain would be in a stronger position in its application.[11] For, O'Neill concluded, 'in the end, German participation in action with us is bound to be depend on her readiness to draw the line somewhere with France.'[12] When the French provisional agenda for the scheduled Kiesinger-de Gaulle meeting in February did not mention the question of the British application, Lahr assured the British that should the French prove negative in that meeting, the Germans would be much less inhibited about consultations between Britain and the Five.[13] This was to be an oft-repeated German promise.

The Benelux proposals: 'Much Diplomatic Activity'[14]

While the British were repairing relations with the Germans, other countries were working on plans to bring the UK and the EC closer together. The first detailed plan for an 'interim arrangement', in January 1968, emerged from the Benelux states, and announced a new level of consultation between them that would be open to other members of the Community and the applicant states.[15] The British were kept informed and consulted throughout – Wilson agreed that they had possibly been too concerned with procedure, and that it was time to turn to substance. He asked if any concrete proposals were being prepared in Britain, for example on technological co-operation.[16] Harmel told the British ambassador in Brussels that the three countries had agreed that their objective must remain full British membership, and that their tactics would have to be devised to keep this aim in the foreground.[17]

The 'Benelux proposals' planned for increased co-operation both within and outside the Community structure. They suggested that the Commission should continue its studies of enlargement and that a means should be found for permanent consultations between the member states and the applicants, perhaps by extending the 1954 ECSC-Britain agreement. The Benelux countries themselves were prepared to undertake joint action in fields outside the Treaty with any one of the Ten (that is, the six members and the four applicants). They would make a commitment to political consultation amongst themselves, but others were invited to join.[18] Brandt would be asked both to attend the WEU meeting at the end of the month, and to organise a meeting of the Five before it. Then the Benelux ambassadors would formally launch the proposals.[19] In announcing these proposals, Harmel stated that he believed the UK would join the EC, thereby creating 'a vast Community equal to that of the other great powers the United States and the USSR'. The aim was to decrease differences between the members and applicants, and to encourage political co-operation, since 'progress would be illusory if progress was not made at the same time along the road to political unification.'[20]

Early responses to the Benelux proposals were mixed. The Commission jealously guarded any activity that should remain within the Community, but nevertheless described the plan as 'excellent.[21] The Italians privately welcomed the new proposals, although they had hesitations and were uncertain about the German attitude. Fanfani warned that little could be done until after the de Gaulle-Kiesinger meeting in February.[22] Brandt publicly welcomed the proposals, although the Germans were repulsed after Brown made a speech in the House of Commons in which he spoke of 'becoming a leader of a major group of European nations'. Lahr warned Roberts of the dangers of such talk, either after membership or indeed in the context of the Benelux proposals.[23] The French were negative from the start: Couve dismissed the suggestions for political co-operation since, he said, the necessary will did not exist in Europe.[24] An official told John Robinson, head of European Integration Department in the FO, that French policy was to get the British to lose interest in the application. They regarded the development of a 'Community of nine' [presumably the Five and the four applicants] as a serious danger to their interests. 'They were therefore proposing to play Kiesinger along with talk of alternative "arrangements", although they would not allow such schemes to achieve fruition.'[25]

The British ambassadors in The Hague and Luxembourg urged the FO to respond to the new proposals.[26] The problem was complicated by a disagreement within the FO over whether to accept the proposals, and whether cabinet authority was needed to do so. The cabinet secretary's advice that the proposals could be accepted without committing Britain to anything more than discussion, and that such discussion might restrain Kiesinger in his February talks with de Gaulle, was persuasive.[27] When cabinet met on 25 January, Brown successfully recommended that the proposals be welcomed and accepted, and after some discussion Wilson agreed: ministers could raise any questions they might have at a comprehensive review of foreign policy scheduled for the following month.[28] Meanwhile, the FO was still working on its agenda for a 'high-level meeting' with the Five, while a group under Wilson's scientific adviser, Sir Solly Zuckerman, was preparing proposals for a European institute of technology.[29] Both of these plans were, however, already being overtaken by events.

Since the Benelux proposals involved co-operation outside the Treaty of Rome rather than a stage towards membership of the Community, and there was no possibility of a French veto, the British were relatively free to accept or reject them. Governments in the Six and the other applicant countries were therefore told of Britain's acceptance (Brown, obviously learning from experience, told Brandt himself over the phone).[30] But despite British encouragement and the early welcome to the proposals from some members of the Six, the Benelux proposals never really got off the ground.[31] The British and others continued to refer to them over the coming months, and to hope that they would be elaborated and implemented, but they were overshadowed by new German proposals until the end of September when they were reinvented by Harmel.

The Franco-German declaration

During early 1968, de Gaulle made 'vague' comments about a possible arrangement with the British, and Reilly mentioned 'nebulous rumours' from the *Quai d'Orsay*.[32] Couve and the former president of the Commission, Marjolin, suggested that the Six should concentrate on helping Britain to overcome her economic difficulties, 'without arguing about the formal date for entry into the Common Market.'[33] De Gaulle complained during German Federal President Lübke's visit in February that there was too much 'excitement' to talk about Europe.[34] As the Benelux states revealed their proposals, however, the French became increasingly concerned that this delaying tactic was not working.[35] With the Germans determined to pin down the clearly-defensive French, the evasive manoeuvres could not go on indefinitely, but the British were worried that the French could continue 'to use vaguely encouraging phrases towards the Germans, and a good deal depends upon how clearly the Germans see that there is nothing beyond the phrases.'[36]

While the French were attempting thus to muddy the waters, Brandt continued to elaborate German ideas. In a radio interview in early February, he spoke of the Commission as the 'hinge' between Community and applicants, of creating something like the 1954 ECSC-UK agreement, and of enlarging EURATOM. He promised to ask the French what they meant by an 'arrangement'.[37] The British tried to strengthen the German position in two main ways. First they stressed their own 'European nature', shown by such events as the shift to decimalisation and the metric system.[38] Second, they passed on negative comments by French ministers and thus revealed the way in which they were using the Germans: Duckwitz was 'deeply shocked' to discover the true French intentions, and said that the French attitude 'reminded him of Soviet diplomacy in the worst days of Stalin.'[39]

The British tactics seemed to have proved successful when, after Kiesinger visited Rome, the Italians issued an *aide mémoire* confirming plans for a meeting of the foreign ministers of the Six, or, if France declined to attend, the Five, immediately after Kiesinger's talks with de Gaulle in February.[40] Given the earlier hesitations, this agreement marked a significant step forward, but Brown was disappointed that it did not include a commitment to a meeting including the applicants. In true Brown style, he made his disappointment 'unmistakeably clear' to Guidotti, the Italian ambassador in London.[41]

The Franco-German meeting
When Kiesinger went to Paris he took with him the largest delegation ever to go to Paris since the signing of the Franco-German Treaty in 1963, but it did not help him to stand up to the General.[42] Shortly before the Germans arrived, Couve more forcefully denounced the activities of Britain and the Five, arguing that Britain's position of 'all or nothing' was problematic.[43] In the meetings with the Germans, the French emphasised the need for the Six to maintain solidarity, insisted that the discussion of the British question would have to take place first within the Six, not with the candidates, and stated their preference that any proposal for an 'arrangement' should come from Bonn, not Paris. A first discussion could take place in the margins of the Council of Ministers meeting on 29 February, and the British application should be on the agenda of all future Council meetings.[44] Later Kiesinger and de Gaulle concurred that it would be a great advantage if Britain could join, but went on to agree that they wanted the Community to develop, and did not want difficulties caused by enlargement to prevent it from progressing.[45] At the end of the visit, the French and Germans issued a joint declaration, stating that

> [t]he two Governments affirm their determination to continue the work undertaken by them and their partners since the creation of the European Economic Community. They intend to make all efforts to complete and develop the Common Market: they reaffirm in particular their desire to achieve the fusion of the three existing Communities.
>
> In this spirit, they wish the Communities to be enlarged to include other European countries, particularly those who have already applied for membership, once those countries are in a position, either to enter effectively into these Communities, or as the case may be, to link themselves with them in another form. This applies particularly to Britain and means that the evolution begun by this country should continue.

It went on to suggest interim 'arrangements', which would be 'designed to facilitate the above-mentioned evolution and would in any case contribute to the development of relations between the European countries.'[46] The French counterblow to the Benelux proposals had been struck.

The German interpretation of and response to the Declaration was enthusiastic: it was the first real French concession, 'won by a hard fight'.[47] Lahr 'personally was convinced that a real change for the better had taken place' and that 'the European train could now move out of the station' – although its speed was not known, and nor was whether it would reach the goal of enlargement. France would not admit that it was possible, and 'even though their position had changed nearly one hundred per cent they would continue to assert that it was still the same.'[48] When Lahr and Duckwitz visited London, Lahr said that the arrangements would not be a substitute for membership but an 'interim arrangement', and that the French had specific ideas for their content, including British participation in a European patent convention and the development of European company law. Moreover, the Germans had not renounced the Benelux proposals.[49] Brandt confessed to Brown that he might find the public results of the meeting 'rather thin', but stressed that it offered 'important openings' and that talks with the applicants would begin soon.[50] However, Kiesinger told the Paris correspondent of *Die Welt* that his visit to Paris had put an end to the idea of revolt by the Five, and that he was glad.[51] Revolt by the Five was exactly what the British wanted.

In contrast, the French put the strictest possible interpretation on their Declaration, and Brunet said that it 'represented no great change in the French attitude'.[52] A leaked French guidance telegram revealed the French bottom line: in declaring their resolve to complete and develop the Common Market, while awaiting possible enlargement, and in proposing an 'arrangement', the French and German governments were implicitly rejecting the Benelux proposals. No precise proposal was to be expected until the British government abandoned their 'all or nothing' posture and took up a position on the Declaration. The 'arrangements' contemplated would be commercial in nature and would not cover technological co-operation, which was the business of the Community. Industrial tariffs would be reduced but not abolished, while agricultural arrangements would have to be adapted to the CAP framework. Finally, there was to be no distinction between the applicants and other members of EFTA: the arrangements could be extended to any of the latter.[53] The British source in the *Quai d'Orsay*, Hervé Alphand, revealed that de Gaulle had given just one order and that 'good care' had been taken to leak it to his guests: 'if the Germans formed a common front with the Four against France, this would mean "the automatic and immediate end of the Common Market".'

The Declaration was intended as a 'face-saving device' for the Germans, but as far as British entry into the Community was concerned, Alphand had said, 'the General had not budged a hair's breadth.' De Gaulle regarded the outcome of the talks 'with great satisfaction', and the mood in the *Elysée* was 'euphoric'.[54] Later, the British authorised their ambassadors in the Five to pass on this information to their host governments, so that the French and Germans would not be allowed to get away with glossing over 'their very different interpretations of the declaration.'[55]

The discrepancies between the two interpretations were clear, and the Kiesinger visit and Declaration were assailed by the continental press.[56] The Commission described it as 'economic nonsense'.[57] Duckwitz himself drew attention to the 'extreme harshness' of de Gaulle's language about the Americans: the General had again identified British Atlanticism as a barrier to her entry.[58] In Britain, Palliser at first saw the Declaration as 'really not too bad', although he conceded that a 'great deal therefore is now going to depend on the British Generals, and their partners in the Five, keeping cool heads and responding skilfully to exploit this slight tactical advantage.'[59] Soon, however, the FO pointed out the lack of concrete proposals and the Paris embassy advised that 'the Germans have done the French a considerable service. They have broken the isolation which the French were finding increasingly uncomfortable.'[60] The British were saved from having to comment publicly on the Declaration by taking a stance that they would only consider proposals for interim arrangements that had the support of the Six as a whole.[61] Privately, they told the Five that they had not yet made up their minds about the Declaration, while the Benelux proposals 'should not be allowed to fall under the table', and asked for views and advice.[62]

The Four were as disheartened as the British. Luns, Harmel, Grégoire and Fanfani all deplored the discrepancy between the French and German interpretations.[63] But in order to appear 'European', the British were forced to pay lip service to the Franco-German initiative, which served few British interests. Partly in response to consequent British pressure, the Italians produced a memorandum, proposing that when the Council came to discuss the applications for membership, the Franco-German Declaration and Benelux proposals 'be taken into account' and went on to make five points. First, the Six should return to 'normal life' in the Communities and get on with the process of fusion (of the three Communities into one). Second, they should abstain from measures that might widen the gap between Community and applicants. Third, they should adopt measures to reduce the existing gap. Fourth, there should be 'harmonisation between the measures already taken and the external development of the European communities.' Finally, the Six should develop a policy for European unity, and formulate a declaration of intent that could eventually be signed by the present and any future applicants. Once the Six had studied these ideas, a meeting should be called of the ten foreign ministers and the Commission, 'to agree on procedures for achieving a closer co-operation between their governments in view of a political and economic unification of Europe.'[64] This memorandum not only put the British application and the various ideas for interim arrangements firmly in centre stage, but also devised new and imaginative ways of ensuring that they stayed there, to be discussed continually in bi- and multilateral meetings over the coming months. Thus began a period of considerable debate over the best way to manage the interim period.

Cabinet

Debate was not confined to the continent, although Wilson kept cabinet away from European policy for as long as possible.[65] When Brown reported on the above events to cabinet in mid January, Wilson had addressed the concerns of the less enthusiastic ministers with the promise of a 'comprehensive review' of external policy. He stated that while the government should seek to maintain the interests of European friends in the British application, and should continue to consider what positive proposals might be put forward by the UK, they should beware of promoting discussions in Europe of a kind that might be divisive and thus counter-productive.[66] Wilson thus skilfully used cabinet to restrain Brown, but at the same time he ensured that his European policy was, at least nominally, supported by his colleagues.

For the general review of foreign policy, held on 27 February, Brown presented a paper, the first part of which suggested that decisions already taken, especially the decision to withdraw from East of Suez by the end of 1971, had helped to shape the options open to Britain, guiding the Government towards a European-based policy. 'Going it alone' or becoming part of a new European 'third force' autonomous of the US, did not provide an opportunity to influence future world events or protect worldwide interests. Thus the 'logic of events' provided 'no satisfactory alternative' to seeking to play an influential part, as soon as possible, in a cohesive Western European grouping, acting generally in harmony with the United States. If this were true, the UK must meanwhile prevent the development of the EEC in ways that would make it more difficult for Britain to join later. Cabinet eventually backed Brown, despite suggestions from some ministers that institutions other than the EC should be considered.[67] In summing up, Wilson noted that the Cabinet generally supported Brown's paper as the basis for Britain's future policy towards

Europe, although the priority must be British economic strength and non-military means of building up British influence in the world, such as economic aid, trade and cultural activities, should also be considered.[68]

Wilson's management of division

Castle's diaries for these months illustrate more clearly than cabinet minutes how Wilson dealt with disagreement. She described what she saw as Brown's motives: he 'had put in a couple of papers which, under the disguise of a philosophical analysis of our new role in the world, were merely designed to lead us to the conclusion that we were right to go on trying to get into the Common Market by every means.' She records that she thought the papers presented were 'pretty meaningless' and was disgusted when other members praised or at least welcomed them. In reaction she recalled that she 'burst out with one of my usual diatribes. I told them that we all ought to be uttering paeans of praise and thankfulness for the fact that our application to join had been turned down.' The economy could be strengthened without the application: devaluation and the resulting investment could be had without entry; technological research would be best done through the Organisation for Economic Co-operation and Development. In sum, Castle believed her intervention was 'pretty devastating' and was surprised when it was received in 'deathly silence.' When Anthony Greenwood, minister of housing, told her afterwards that he agreed with her, she was furious that he had not supported her in the meeting. After her lone opposition, Wilson, who she thought was 'clearly bored', said, 'Well, we've had a pretty uneventful, not to say dull, debate, but I think we are all broadly in agreement with the Foreign Secretary's papers.'[69]

Clearly, there was substantial opposition within cabinet to the continuation of the European policy, yet those who felt it did not articulate this opposition successfully. Why? First, as suggested in the previous chapter, few in the winter and spring of 1967-1968 believed that entry was possible. The policy could therefore be pursued without risk of success. Second, it was clear that both prime minister and foreign secretary supported the policy, so that it might not be politically expedient to oppose it categorically. Opponents knew, furthermore, that there would be future opportunities to protest since there would have to be cabinet, parliamentary and party consideration of the eventual terms of entry. It is also possible that the majority were simply bored of the whole subject, which had been exhaustively examined over the past year and a half.[70]

In contrast to their apathy on general European policy, ministers insisted on cuts in spending on European technological projects. The Five had welcomed devaluation and the withdrawal from East of Suez as evidence of British determination to heal the economy in preparation for membership.[71] But the economic strains that necessitated those decisions also required the British government to be very careful about where and how much money would be spent on grand European projects. In 1968 a large number of bilateral and multilateral technological and scientific projects were underway or being considered in Europe, and Britain had a stake in several: the European Launcher Development Programme (ELDO), the European Space Research Organisation (ESRO), the European Organisation for Nuclear Research (CERN), Concorde and the Gas Centrifuge project are just a few of the better known examples.[72] However, when financial constraints demanded the sacrifice of symbolic Labour initiatives like free prescriptions and raising the school leaving age, there was little support for maintaining prestigious but non-cost effective space and technology projects for the sake of European policy.[73] The decisions to minimise government expenditure on technological projects were taken in January and February, and ministers even considered pulling out of Concorde.[74] During the comprehensive review, the minister of technology presented a paper emphasising the need to push forward with technological co-operation within the structure of the Benelux proposals, but added that collaboration should only be undertaken where 'it is judged in our economic interest to do so' and stressed the role to be played by private industry.[75] Cabinet agreed with Benn's recommendations, on the understanding that they would not entail participation in unnecessary projects involving large expenditure.[76] As will be seen in the next chapter, these decisions, particularly those to withdraw from the joint space efforts, had important ramifications for Wilson's efforts to portray the UK as a 'European' country.

The superpowers, EFTA and the Commonwealth

During this period of debate, other countries continued to pay attention to the developments in Britain's European policy – some more closely than others. The ramifications of EEC membership for Britain's relations with the United States began to become clear from early 1968. It was seen in the introductory chapter that issues such as devaluation, the decision to withdraw British troops from East of Suez, and the continued American presence in Vietnam placed significant strains on the relationship. Documents for 1968 onwards show that Wilson's government made an important choice in this period: the application for membership of the EC took priority over close relations with the United States. At the same time, however, the British relied on the Americans to provide discreet support for British entry into the Communities.

There was a clear awareness in Whitehall of the diminishing influence that the UK had with the western superpower, partly as a result of the financial and strategic decisions taken at this time. Not all were sanguine about the prospect: writing about the decision for withdrawal from the Far East and the simultaneous cancellation of the contract for the F-111, the British ambassador in Washington warned that if Britain proceeded, 'we shall have crossed a watershed in our ability to influence world affairs and above all in Anglo-American relations, which have been our foundation and our lifeline for the last fifty years.'[77] Despite Dean's worries, there was also a sense within Britain that closer integration in Europe might be the way to regain influence. A Foreign Office paper of January 1968 – that Wilson had a hand in drafting – echoed British concerns of the early 1960s, stating that 'the temper of the people and Administration of the United States is that while we shall get a sympathetic hearing we shall henceforth not exercise much influence *unless we can speak on at least some occasions with the voice of Western Europe*' [author's italics]. That is, Britain's continuing influence with the United States was seen as dependent on British integration into Europe. The paper went on to say that the government should try to ensure that Europe and the US were working towards similar aims, but acknowledged that

> we need not be shy about putting forward means of attaining them which may differ from those currently being pursued by the United States. We should not differ for the sake of differing but if we think our own views or the European views are preferable on the merits of the case there will be advantage in not hiding our light under a bushel.[78]

Senior officials, and ultimately Wilson himself, thought that there was no more 'special relationship', and that the best way to exert influence on the US – and indeed the Soviet Union – was as the leader of a unified Europe. Cabinet accepted this view in the same month in the comprehensive review, agreeing that,

> [i]f we can join them while we still have a substantial lead in various aspects of modern life and industry we should be able to play a major part in shaping the future of Europe and of European relations with the United States. But we have to acknowledge that time is not on our side. Our position in the world league is steadily slipping. The EEC is enormously much more powerful than we are and even the individual countries of the Six eg Germany and France, are in some respects stronger than we are. In some aspects of the

race Japan has already passed us. We must therefore bend every effort to join the European Communities at the earliest possible moment.[79]

This willingness to let the 'special relationship' go and determination to focus on Europe as a vehicle for British influence marked a significant step in British foreign policy, albeit one that had been developing for years. The aim was a '[v]oice in the world alongside [the] superpowers', where they 'could try and bring some European experience into world problems such as Vietnam' while being able to influence both the United States and Soviet Union 'in a way that no individual European country could hope to do today'. For their part, the Americans also hoped that Britain would urge the Community to follow lines acceptable to the US.[80] Indeed, when Wilson visited Johnson in February 1968 conversations focused on Vietnam and did not mention European policy.[81] The new British position demonstrated an awareness of the new realities of the UK's geo-strategic position, and a resolve to overcome them in order to retain an important role.

Despite the conscious step away from the United States and concomitant wish to have influence with its administration, Wilson sought support for his European policy from the US. Doing so was a delicate matter, however, given French accusations that the British would be a 'Trojan horse' for American influence over the Communities. Therefore when the State Department suggested making an open speech of support for enlargement in early 1968, Brown replied that while the Government was grateful for being consulted in this matter, 'we are inclined to feel that the reasons which have led to American Government to maintain public silence on this question [that is, the danger of provoking France]...continue to apply.'[82] No tool other than bilateral conversation could be used: when it was suggested that the US might be induced to offer differential financial concessions to Community countries, penalising France, the Foreign Office quickly concluded that 'there is too great a risk of our intervention becoming known for us to make any suggestion of the sort to the Americans.'[83] Subject to these caveats, the British Government did ask that in private, bilateral conversations with the governments of the Six, the US Administration support the British application and exert its influence in that direction.[84] While he rejected the offer of a public statement in February 1968, Brown informed the State Department that 'we would welcome it if the United States Government could continue as appropriate to make clear to Community Governments, especially the German Federal Government, their continuing support for our membership of the Communities.'[85]

Dean set out the nuances of the relationship clearly in a letter to the Foreign Office. Asking to what extent the British should take the Americans into their confidence, he noted that they were 'keenly interested' in the European policy. Since they were bound to express views to the Five, it was important that they should have a clear idea of what the British were trying to achieve, but at the same time, 'we do not want to give them too many opportunities to offer us gratuitous advice or to interfere when our policies may seem to them to be contrary to what they conceive to be their or our interests.' Dean stressed the need to show the Americans that British European policy was imaginative, constructive and viable, so that it might act as some consolation for the less welcome decisions taken in foreign policy and defence. He concluded that he was not suggesting that the government be deterred from following policies, for example in arms collaboration, which might conflict with some American interests, only that such policies should be presented to the US in the most favourable light.[86] The ambassador's advice was closely followed over the following two years.

The US responded positively to this pressure, at least in direct conversation with the British. In January 1968, when the first interim plans were beginning to emerge from the Community, a State Department official informed the British Embassy in Washington that 'in the view of the US Government the basic policy at present being pursued by HMG was exactly right. We should stand out for full membership and refuse to be satisfied with anything short of that.'[87] He later sent instructions to the US ambassador in Bonn to make plain to the German government that the US saw no point in solutions short of membership and were not interested in them.[88] When the Germans persuaded under secretary of state Nicholas Katzenbach to urge the British to take 'half the loaf' (that is, something less than full membership), Wilson took him to task. Katzenbach was impressed by Wilson's firm rebuttal of German ideas and thought it 'extremely salutary' that the prime minister should have used such robust language with him.[89] The US Embassy in London later confirmed that the German ideas were 'totally unacceptable' to the US, and when the Franco-German proposals were officially launched in February, asked to be kept closely informed.[90]

In contrast, the attitude of the Soviet Union towards the enlargement of the EC was whole-heartedly negative. Publicly, the Soviet leadership focused on calling for the greater uniting of Europe by means of a pan-European security conference instead of the selective and exclusive integration of Western Europe.[91] Indeed, the joint communiqué at the end of Wilson's visit to Moscow in January 1968 acknowledged that a conference could be valuable, providing that it was properly prepared.[92] In private, the British considered that the Soviets were playing the same old game of trying to divide Western Europe from the US and to dominate the continent themselves. Sir Denis Greenhill, deputy under secretary in the FO, argued that the 'real prize for the Russians is the break-up of NATO and the final check to the movement for European unity. They evidently still rate high their chances of success'.[93] Interestingly, when asked in February 1968 by the Austrian federal chancellor, Chalfont denied that the Soviet Union had expressed any reservations on the subject of EC enlargement during Wilson's January visit, perhaps seeking to reassure Klaus that Austria's application for association with the EC would not anger the Eastern superpower.[94] The British tried to turn the Soviets' supposed fears back against them, arguing that

> if no more that one per cent of the Soviet anxieties about German intentions was true and well-founded, anything which the British Government could do to unite Western Europe in terms both of defence and of economic and political co-operation would provide the best safeguard against those anxieties becoming a reality....In short, the greater our influence in Western Europe, the more we could do to ensure that Western Germany continued to hold its present peaceful attitude.[95]

Wilson even joked to Kosygin that if the Soviet Union was so concerned about Germany, perhaps it should offer to pay for the maintenance of British troops there.[96] With the aim of increasing peaceful relations, the British signed an agreement in January for Anglo-Soviet co-operation in applied science and technology, including links between British and Soviet firms and the DEA and *Gosplan*.[97] Wilson thus took care to soothe Soviet fears about the consolidation of Western Europe. While the USSR had no real means of influencing British European policy at this time, it will be seen that Franco-Soviet relations, Soviet actions like the invasion of Czechoslovakia, and the place of the USSR in West German *ostpolitik,* were all important in the unfolding and eventual success of Wilson's European policy.

Less important were the views about and participation of EFTA states in any interim arrangements.[98] A few officials were concerned that the government might provoke a hostile reaction from EFTA countries if it pressed ahead with plans for consultation with the Five without informing them, but there was some room for manoeuvre in that the Danes and Norwegians had shown little inclination to participate, at least in the first round of talks, and seemed to be content to be informed by the British of progress.[99]

The relative incoherence of the organisation was demonstrated by the different responses to the new proposals emerging from the Six, and a further difficulty was caused by plans within EFTA for greater Nordic co-operation. In a policy response agreed by Brown, Crosland and Wilson, the British sought to place themselves in the role of intermediary, reporting on the progress of proposals for Five-four collaboration and seeking to head off emerging plans for Nordic union through pre-emptive ministerial meetings.[100] Although plans for closer co-operation within EFTA were later to provide a complication for British European policy, EFTA members had little to offer Britain, and therefore little influence over her European policy.

Relations with the Commonwealth had an even smaller impact on British European policy than relations with EFTA members. Wilson rejected the possibility of meeting the prime minister of Jamaica during his spring visit to Canada and the US, not wanting to set a precedent of meeting Commonwealth leaders (except Canada) during other visits.[101] The old days of spreading British culture and institutions across the world had given way: a draft paper on future foreign policy stated that 'we should encourage an enlarged EEC to accept a limited responsibility for the development of Africa. But we ourselves should accept no more responsibilities than our partners in the EEC are willing to share.'[102] The usual Commonwealth problems continued: decolonisation, immigration, Gibraltar, Rhodesian independence and Nigerian civil war, the Falkland Islands.[103] Defence commitments continued despite the withdrawal from East of Suez announced in January, and a new defence agreement was signed with Mauritius.[104] Commonwealth Office officials were relieved that the FO did not press for a dramatic British initiative in defence, which would have 'had no chance of success in Europe but which would have offended our most important Commonwealth partners.'[105]

From the opposite side, there was little urgency on the part of Commonwealth countries to press for their Community-related interests as long as the French veto remained in place. Leslie Pearson, prime minister of Canada, saw little prospect of early change – and anyway expressed his own anger with de Gaulle, who 'had certainly been trying to break up Canada.'[106] At the same time, however, some Commonwealth countries were considering the possibility of association with the EC, particularly since the Yaoundé Convention was due for renewal in 1969. None of these countries – of the superpowers, EFTA and the Commonwealth – was the focus of British foreign policy in early 1968. The decisions taken by the Wilson government about Britain's role in the world, dictated by the financial situation, contributed to the concentration on Europe. That concentration then decreed a policy of continued extrication from far-flung commitments.

Conclusions

The first months of 1968 therefore saw a significant shift in the way in which the British pursued their European objectives. The changing characterisation of relations with the USA and lack of concern for the interests of EFTA and Commonwealth states were indicative of the importance placed on European policy. The goal, membership, remained constant, but whereas in late 1967 Brown had attempted to take the lead and direct co-operation between the UK and the Five, in early 1968 the lead was left to the Community. The position taken by Wilson and Brown, that they would consider any proposals coming from the Six and linked with full membership, handed the initiative back to the Six. Brown's initial efforts had been too risky, offending Brandt and driving Germany back towards France. Showing interest in new proposals from the Six, however, demonstrated the government's continuing commitment to European integration and to bringing Britain into closer co-operation with the member states. Therefore, despite the bad feeling created over the space decisions, British efforts towards and participation in discussions for 'interim arrangements', as well as decisions to focus strategic interests on the continent, helped to create good 'European credentials' for Wilson and his government. There was a secondary effect too, one that would become increasingly apparent over the coming months. During a period when the Six should have been focused on the transition to the common external tariff and new integration in the areas of technology, company law, a European patent, economic union and the fusion of the three communities, they were instead faced, repeatedly and insistently, with the British demand for membership.

4

March – September 1968: a war of attrition

By March 1968, the seeds of all the proposals for 'interim arrangements' during the period of British exclusion from the EC were on the table. The Five, with British encouragement, immediately set to work to develop the various ideas. However, the main characteristic of the next few months was frustration, particularly the frustration of the British with the Germans as the latter sought to produce a plan acceptable to the French. Two important changes occurred: the first was the replacement of George Brown by Michael Stewart as British foreign secretary in March. The second was the lengthy process of Germany's acknowledgement of French intransigence, and consequent shift towards more fruitful co-operation with Britain and the Four.

The Benelux proposals were not forgotten in the spring of 1968 but attention was focused on Brandt's forthcoming paper elaborating the Franco-German Declaration.[1] The Belgians and the Commission insisted, to Brown's satisfaction, that any interim arrangement must be linked with membership.[2] The Italians produced a new *aide memoire* urging Brandt to create serious plans in March and to convene a meeting of the Ten as soon as possible in order to give a real demonstration of intent. They stressed the need for the Six to agree on proposals and a 'statement of intentions' to put to Britain.[3] Yet the difficulties facing Brandt were revealed in the contradictory signals coming from France and Germany. It was clear almost from the moment that the Franco-German Declaration was released that the two governments had fundamentally different views on how it should be implemented – if at all.[4] Reilly made clear that the French had fully intended to place the Federal Republic in this position, writing that they were satisfied that the Germans had 'taken the French bait, to have put an end to any five to one line-up and to have put Britain in the position of refusing what is available or accepting much less than she really wants.' They did not doubt Couve's ability to 'kick the ball into touch' should the Germans 'go in the wrong direction.' However, the British posture of waiting for a proposal from all Six was discomfiting the French, and on no account should the British give any sign of welcome to Brandt's new plan before the French.[5] In Brussels, Marjoribanks added that as long as there was 'an internal squabble' in the Communities, it was likely to hold them up 'in fields where progress would be unwelcome to us.' Meanwhile the Five were coming to realise that a tight 'line-up' was the best way of exerting pressure on the French.[6] Roberts warned from Bonn that the Germans would resent any British pressure, and officials agreed, therefore, to wait for Brandt's paper before making any new move.[7]

Brandt's proposals and the March 1968 Council of Ministers
The Germans sent their proposals to the British, confidentially, the day before the Council meeting.[8] The eight point paper stated that the Six

> have the common wish to complete the construction of the Community and to enlarge it by the inclusion of other European countries particularly the countries which have sought membership.
>
> The dynamic further extension of the Community is in the interests not only of the six member countries but also of those states who wish to join them. The objective of enabling Europe, by combination of its political and economic strengths, to occupy and in future to maintain its proper place can only be achieved if the Community includes all European countries which accept the same political and economic objectives as the founder states.

Despite this ambitious prologue, the contents of the paper were modest. The commercial proposals involved reducing trade barriers to create a uniform preference zone. Reductions of tariffs within EFTA were to be maintained, and the final aim of enlargement to be clearly stated. There was no automatic transition to entry, but the plan would 'serve the thought of enlargement of the Community.' The technological proposals suggested that the Community act on its Marechal report of September 1967: the Six should begin co-operation in technological matters and then involve other states. European co-operation in all areas where Europe was 'behindhand' or where expenses were great, such as atomic energy, should be intensified, both inside and outside the Treaty of Rome. The candidates should have opportunity to participate in discussions on a European patent and on European company law before entry. The Six should make plans and then hold negotiations with the states concerned. Finally, Brandt stated that all the current proposals had been used in the preparation of the paper, but that the aspects that involved co-operation outside the Treaties should be left to the foreign ministers.[9]

The night before the Council meeting, Duckwitz and Brandt expressed appreciation for the UK's 'very correct attitude'. However, Duckwitz said that prospects were very bad: the French had expressed 'strong displeasure over the German eight point programme', and said that the Germans had misinterpreted the Franco-German Declaration. Brandt was livid, commenting that the French 'had clearly supposed their German partners to be more stupid and gullible than they were.' He felt 'calm and confident', however, and Duckwitz said that if the French persisted in such behaviour, 'the Germans would leave them alone to take the sole responsibility for future disappointments.'[10]

The pessimism was well-judged. Brandt's paper was the only item on the Council agenda, and it received little support. It was insufficiently ambitious for the Four but too tightly linked to enlargement for the French to accept, and the Six could barely agree to ask the Commission to report on all the proposals before them.[11] The atmosphere at this March meeting was 'almost as strained as on…19 December'. Harmel described the French as 'cold and uncompromising', with Couve 'increasingly irritated that the Five had not accepted the French veto of 19 December.'[12] Lahr said that while Couve had been outwardly more polite to the Germans than the others, he had not shown the slightest support for their proposals.[13] In Couve's post-Council press conference, there 'were no little jokes, and the cockiness had gone out of his manner.'[14] Yet despite Couve's isolation, the solidarity of the Five was not perfect. Brandt was disappointed at the reactions to his paper and there was no agreement among the Five on the best way forward.[15]

In this situation, Wilson decided that the government should not express a view on any proposal until it had the support of all member states, although Brown wanted to pursue the Benelux proposals. Brown's impatience was evident: the British government was prepared to wait until the next Council meeting on 5 April 'but they could not be expected to wait while an indefinite series of meetings took place'. He suggested that a planned meeting on technology in Rome in July be extended to cover discussion of the Benelux proposals.[16] Supporting the proposals helped to reinforce Britain's 'European credentials', while continually focusing on entry brought attention back to the government's main aim. As one FO official noted, 'so long as the Six spend their Council time quarrelling about British membership, we are at least achieving the twin objectives of keeping the issue of our membership alive, and preventing the development of the Community meanwhile.' Pat Hancock, assistant under-secretary in the FO, suggested that the British should think of taking some initiative themselves, to convince the Five that Britain was 'not a mere alternative to France – but a better bet as a European partner than France.' Otherwise they would continue to judge that the British issue was not a sufficiently important one over which to force a showdown with France. O'Neill suggested that economic recovery might improve British prospects in Europe more than any initiative. Chalfont underlined the need to decide: 'we shall have to consider, after April 5th, the choice between a positive initiative and a policy of masterly inactivity. We cannot go on for long treading the unsatisfactory path between them.'[17] There would shortly be a ministerial battle over this choice.[18]

A new foreign secretary

Before that battle began, however, Brown resigned as foreign secretary. Brown went on 15 March after the ongoing financial crisis led to a decision to call an extra bank holiday being taken in his absence.[19] Michael Stewart, foreign secretary in 1964-66, replaced him. There were worries both in the UK and on the continent, that the replacement of such a well known pro-European with a less passionate person would be interpreted as indicating a change in British policy.[20] However, the change was beneficial to the 'approach to Europe': it ended what Reilly described as 'a lamentable and even a shameful period' in the history of the FO.[21] Stewart got on well with and shared ideas about policy and strategy with Wilson – indeed, Wilson made him his 'No. 1 Deputy in grave emergency.'[22] His less abrasive style allowed for easier relations with foreign ministers abroad, and, according to Castle, his boring and verbose reports allowed him to sneak difficult information past cabinet.[23] Stewart immediately wrote to his European colleagues, emphasising his commitment to the British application.[24] More important, perhaps as a result of his belief in de Gaulle's 'complete intransigence', he kick-started the plans for a new British initiative mentioned above.[25] For the first time in the veto period, Britain had a foreign secretary who was not only an activist, but was also sensitive to the needs and anxieties of friends on the continent.

Unfortunately, Stewart's proposal for an initiative in defence or political union faced obstacles on the domestic front almost immediately. Healey was obstructive, Stewart recorded, of 'anything that smacks of approach to Europe' [sic].[26] O'Neill, who had initially endorsed the early FO preparation, recorded that he was 'suffering from second thoughts.'[27] Moreover, when embassies in the Six were asked for their views, responses were mixed.[28] Stewart's perseverance led to a bitter fight with his colleagues.

As Stewart began his preparations, the Commission, with the three French commissioners abstaining, published its new 'Opinion'. The Opinion of October 1967 had recommended opening negotiations; the new one now said that any 'commercial arrangement' must aim at a customs union in pursuit of the desire of full membership, suggesting that it could be part of the transition period before full membership. Meanwhile, the strengthening of the British economy, the strengthening of the internal Community structure and progress towards economic union should continue, and the normal functioning of the Community should be resumed. The British felt that French arguments about the British economy were given credence, while no guidance was given about the form of interim arrangement to be adopted. The Opinion failed to meet the Commission's own requirement of 'facilitating the subsequent membership of the applicants.'[29] It was hardly surprising, therefore, that the April Council meeting ended in the same deadlock that had been seen in March, and the Five were unable to prevent Couve from deferring the discussion to the next meeting in May.[30] The same deadlock was seen when Stewart met the Six in WEU at the end of the month, although the Germans appeared to respond to his strong re-statement of the British position.[31] Clearly the British were right continually to re-emphasise the importance they placed on maintaining their application.[32]

Space decisions

However, the British had first to survive the negative effects of the decisions taken earlier in the year on participation in European space projects. Stewart suggested, further to his support for a general British initiative, that officials should work 'urgently' to set out proposals for a European space policy that he would be able to represent as a reasonable alternative to the activities from which the UK planned to withdraw. He suggested participation in an experimental television relay satellite and a meteorological satellite, on the condition that American launchers were used to place them in space.[33]

Stewart's proposals came before the Ministerial Committee on the Approach to Europe (EURM) on 4 April. Formed in May 1967, it was composed of Stewart, Castle, Jenkins, Thomson (Commonwealth Secretary), Callaghan, Ross (Scottish Secretary), Crosland, Peart (Minister of Agriculture) and Chalfont.[34] Stewart was defeated, as Palliser noted, in a 'major disagreement...with the Foreign Office in a minority of one against the other departments.' Palliser warned Wilson that not all Whitehall departments were as convinced as he was of the desirability of pursuing technological co-operation, and that technology, a 'major trump card' in the approach to Europe, was not being played skilfully.[35] Even Zuckerman, not known for pro-European beliefs, wrote to Wilson of his

> grave concern at the danger that we should find ourselves having in effect opted out, for perfectly valid reasons, from most of the main European projects in this field, without having made any constructive proposals for alternative technological projects which could fruitfully be developed on a European scale. The result was to undermine our credibility in Europe and to increase scepticism about our real intentions towards European co-operation.[36]

Stewart repeated Zuckerman's warning in a minute to Wilson, and suggested that a new committee be set up, chaired by Chalfont, to maintain momentum and 'take some of the edge off our decision on space projects'.[37] Wilson consented to the setting up of the new committee, and Stewart informed cabinet that he was considering the possibility of a British initiative.[38]

Stewart still had to inform his European colleagues of the decisions taken by cabinet in February. Although he tried to place the decisions in the best possible light and said that the government continued 'to attach the greatest importance to the development of European technological co-operation', the credibility of British European policy was severely undermined.[39] Wilson and Stewart therefore pressed on. Wilson wanted Benn to be included in any ministerial discussions, since he was 'taking a most active interest' in technological co-operation. Stewart agreed that Benn should join EURM, which would discuss any papers referred from Chalfont's new sub-committee.[40] Conversation returned, however, to the problem consistently faced by the UK. Stewart acknowledged that 'the credibility of our European approach and thereby the general credibility of our foreign policy' had suffered because of Britain's unfulfilled promises for technological co-operation. At the same time, he and Wilson recognised that the government needed to focus attention on what made economic sense and not on highly costly and impractical projects. In other words, the economic reality that had led to the decisions on space projects still existed.[41]

The FO therefore recommended that the British initiative should be framed as the logical follow-up to the Benelux proposals, and should cover: consultation with the Community; joint actions in science and technology; co-operation in aid; defence co-operation; political consultation; and Britain's attitude to the future development of the Community. A caveat was included that the above should be limited to actions which it would in any case be in British interests to take, and should not impose any additional burden on British resources.[42] Despite Stewart's, Chalfont's, and eventually Wilson's praise for the paper, FO officials were worried from the start.[43] In EURO, officials (who were not aware that Wilson had seen and approved the draft paper) suggested that it might be better to wait until the autumn and that perhaps to try to get Italy or one of the Benelux countries to take the initiative instead.[44]

In EURM Stewart met continued opposition, facing near consensus that it was premature to decide on an early initiative. In contrast to Wilson and Stewart, who felt that a British initiative would help to prevent unwelcome progress within the Community, Crosland argued that because of the current difficulties facing the Six and the uncertainty created by recent events in France (see below), any such Community progress was unlikely. Stewart had to agree to reconsider his proposals; although he stressed that 'no member of the Committee considered that there should be any weakening in our determination to pursue [the] long-term objective of securing membership of the EEC.'[45] Palliser described this meeting as 'a very open clash...between the Foreign Secretary, on the one hand, and virtually all his other colleagues in EUR(M), on the other'. He concluded that 'it is clear that the approach on which you [Wilson] and the Foreign Secretary agree has no hope of carrying with it the other colleagues in EUR(M); and even less the Cabinet as a whole.' Even though he still felt that their position had been correct, Palliser advised Wilson not to force the issue of an initiative – especially since the unrest in France made May 1968 a natural breathing space anyway.[46] The FO decided in favour of 'delaying action' with no ministerial discussion: Wilson should 'hold himself in reserve at this stage.'[47] Stewart's summing up at the EURM meeting was important and his line was used again: Robinson noted in June that as 'long as this policy line remains to us, we have cover for a good deal of activity which should help to hold up Community progress' – one of the key aims identified by Brown before the veto.[48] In other words, the ministerial authority given in December and February was still being used.

The brake that it provided to Wilson's preferred policy ensured that EURM did not meet again, despite being asked for guidance by EURO, despite being reconstituted in October 1969, and despite the fact that EURO continued to meet and to produce papers.[49] Cabinet itself barely discussed European policy for the rest of the year, instead receiving brief reports from Stewart on various developments.[50] Instead, Wilson and Stewart worked through Chalfont's sub-committee on European

Technological Co-operation (EUR(M)(T)), agreeing that there was no need to inform cabinet of the members, who were second-string rather than cabinet ministers.[51] However, if the intention was to bypass EURM and cabinet in order to proceed with the Wilson-Stewart initiatives, it failed, for one reason. Benn was invited to join the first meeting in May 1968, and made clear that he would uphold the previous cabinet decisions on technological co-operation. He also rejected the idea of seeking technological projects merely to boost European policy.[52] As a result, the remaining three meetings went on to discuss purely technical considerations of pre-existing technological initiatives: the European Technological Institute, the European counter-proposal for an International Institute of Science and Technology, and civil nuclear co-operation.[53] Foiled again, Wilson and Stewart would go on to set up yet another committee in the autumn.

The impact of the May events in France

The urgency underlying Stewart's pursuit of a British initiative diminished, however, as France slid into crisis. The strikes and disruptions of May and subsequent election seemed to have the potential to undermine de Gaulle's authority and thus his grip on foreign policy.[54] Reilly wrote from Paris that the crisis could have repercussions for EC policy in general and the British application in particular, but warned that it was 'hardly possible to judge' the outcome until the new government was in place. There had been comments from some Gaullist deputies that French opposition to British entry was looking rather foolish. However, knowing de Gaulle's powers of regeneration, Reilly was sceptical that the crisis would help the British cause at all, advising that it 'would be unwise to expect any immediate change of policy in our favour.' He added, however, that 'I would…hope that this crisis will bring nearer the day when French opposition to negotiations will be withdrawn.'[55] Reilly was right to be cautious, and indeed Davignon, Harmel's *chef de cabinet*, reported that the Germans had urged that nothing should be done to embarrass the French in their present difficulties.[56]

As the French prepared for elections, there were hints that Couve was working to persuade de Gaulle that British entry was inevitable, although they were 'energetically spreading the canard that [Britain was] losing interest in the whole affair.'[57] Although the Germans continued to work on their proposal, there was in Brussels little confidence that the May Council would produce any concrete result.[58] Stewart visited Bonn at the end of May to try to strengthen the German position. Brandt said that he would propose a trade arrangement, technological co-operation, consultation and an agreement to resume progress on internal Community matters, and that 'Germany would continue to make every effort to try to convince the French.' He accepted that proposals must come from all Six and have a clear tie to membership, but asked if Britain would welcome proposals for tariff reductions. Clearly French insinuations about British lack of interest had been hitting home. Stewart replied that Britain would certainly not wish to shut the door on a trading arrangement, and asked about co-operation in technology, political consultation and defence. Brandt said the most important thing was to close the economic gap. He did not think there was much substance in the other proposals, although he would like to see more life put into WEU. In general, he went on, the German government wanted to avoid situations where only some Community countries would meet with other countries. Tantalising as ever, Brandt hinted that, should the French attitude remain entirely negative, the German position on this point could change.[59] Just after the Stewart-Brandt meeting, however, the French managed once again to convince the Germans that they were making concessions, for example accepting that the preamble to any agreement should say that it should serve to facilitate and prepare the 'generally desired' entry of Britain into the Communities. The German ambassador in London told Stewart that 'agreement existed' that the end of the period during which tariffs had to be reduced should coincide with the entry of the applicants, without actually giving a date for that event.[60] The tortuous semantics suggest that the French knew how to give the Germans just enough to indicate that their position was changing, without saying anything definite.

'...it is all rather dull and unexciting.'[61]

Lahr presented the amended German proposals at the Council meeting on 30-31 May, proposing that tariffs should be cut by 30% in three annual steps beginning on 1 January 1969. For technology, the Marechal Group should be reactivated and start discussions on the possibility of involving other countries in technological co-operation. Lahr confessed that his proposals were German ideas, not an agreed Franco-German position, and Boegner, representing France, simply said that he had no instructions. Given the French internal situation, it is hardly surprising that this meeting made so little progress: indeed it was even interrupted after ten minutes for delegates to listen to de Gaulle's radio speech announcing the dissolution of the National Assembly.[62]

By June, therefore, European policy seemed to be at an impasse. Progress with all the interim proposals seemed to have stopped, while domestic constraints had ensured that there would be no British initiative. Officials were wary of advising Stewart 'to go into bat again', but also acknowledged that, as Chalfont put it, a 'clear Ministerial directive on

EEC policy' was needed. Chalfont suggested a series of talks '*à deux*' between Stewart and Wilson, Jenkins, Crosland and Thomson 'to see if we can rally the good Europeans back to the cause', and the FO concluded that the most useful first step would be to try and reach some common view with the Treasury.[63] Meanwhile the FO asked ambassadors across the Community for their thoughts on whether or not the events in France would have any effect on the readiness of Community governments to consider British membership as a more desirable and more immediate objective.[64] Although the responses all recommended avoiding being seen to be trying to profit from French weakness, and waiting until the autumn before any re-launch of efforts, they indicated a subtle change in the atmosphere, condensing around a new awareness of French fragility and comparative German strength.[65]

The original proposals for interim arrangements remained. Throughout, the British maintained the same line: Wilson told Rey at the end of June that the government's attitude was 'entirely unchanged' and the application was 'firmly in.'[66] By July there was real impatience. The Commission released a statement saying that 'efforts to enlarge the Community and to unify the European continent must be resumed'.[67] In a press conference, Kiesinger said that he hoped the question of the admission of Britain and the other applicants could be eased, and promised to work in that direction when he met de Gaulle in September. He advocated a summit meeting, without Britain, to seek progress.[68]

At a WEU meeting in July, Brandt tried to give new impetus to his 'trade arrangement' proposals, which he said would speed progress towards enlargement. He asked that everything should be re-examined 'in a positive light' in Council in September, and said that 'his government were open to any suggestion likely to hasten a solution. They did not intend to insist on their own proposals.' The Four all supported the idea of a fresh start in September, but Alphand repeated that while France supported the principle of enlargement, the time had not yet come. The Six must reach agreement on a commercial arrangement before it could be discussed with the applicants: the tension between EC business and enlargement therefore continued. Reminding his colleagues of the newness of his government – after the May crisis Couve replaced Georges Pompidou as prime minister, while Michel Debré became foreign minister – Alphand said that the French position would become clearer over the coming months, and that he was glad to hear of the UK's economic progress.[69]

Although the French had thwarted progress for the time being, others gave new assurances to Stewart. During WEU, Stewart spoke to Harmel and Brandt together. Harmel said that nothing could be done before the holidays, but that the first Council meeting in September would be entirely devoted to the question of enlargement. Brandt agreed, although he pointed out that the Kiesinger-de Gaulle meeting at the end of September would probably take the focus off the Council meeting to some extent. Harmel showed his impatience, noting that the Benelux proposals could be taken up at any time and that there should be discussion of what could be done without France. Brandt conceded that if Italy and Benelux supported such an idea, he did not see how the Federal Government could stand aside, 'even in the absence of France.' He would prefer though, not to have to make the choice. Asked about his 'commercial arrangement' Brandt confessed that, although he did not exclude progress along those lines, he was not 'in love with the German ideas' and that if something better were produced, he would go along. Harmel gave the first hints of an imaginative new proposal. He wondered if WEU could be used in the interim before enlargement: the Brussels Treaty allowed for the attendance of other states on the Economic Day. Perhaps a measure of consultation or even 'pre-negotiation' could be facilitated without needing to create new machinery? Harmel called this notion a *'passerelle'* between the present situation and the opening of negotiations, but all agreed that it would depend on a notable shift in the French attitude.[70] Privately, Stewart and Harmel agreed that the latter would develop his idea, and it took on increasing importance in the autumn.[71] In other bilateral meetings, Brandt sought support for Kiesinger's idea for a summit meeting.[72] There was thus a subtle shift in the balance of power at this WEU meeting. The Five were increasingly aware that the French might be induced to make concessions in the near future. Stewart did not think that there would be a 'mere return to old positions' in the autumn.[73]

The British were as satisfied as possible with this state of affairs. Hancock recommended that the aim should be to ensure that British membership was 'inextricably enmeshed' in every aspect of Community business: both the Commission and Harmel should therefore be encouraged to take initiatives. Britain should continue to 'stick pins into the French from time to time': a stagnant Community would increase pressure on France to change her policy on British membership, while in the meantime, British economic recovery could proceed. Pressure for entry must be maintained, and 'above all', the Five must be encouraged. If the government gave the impression of faltering, 'we shall lose the improved position which HMG has achieved in European terms over the last eighteen months.'[74]

British resolution was necessary, since the new French government came out fighting. Once the new government was installed, it was clear that the French line had not changed at all. Couve told *Paris Match*

magazine that that he could 'only see advantage in enlargement of the
Common Market, particularly to include Great Britain' and that 'the whole
of British policy [was] directed towards solving' the economic and
financial problems that were keeping her out, but in a press conference he
said that Britain was not in a condition to fulfil the obligations of
membership. He also repeated the French argument that British entry
would transform the 'very nature of the Community.'[75] Although Debré at
times appeared to present a softer French line, an FO official wondered if
'in some ways we weren't better off with Couve. At least he made the 5
angrier!'[76]

As the new government settled in, the Paris embassy advised that de
Gaulle's need to focus on domestic policy would reduce his resources for
implementing his European policy, and suggested that by October it
would be feasible for HMG and the Five to bring renewed pressure on
France to agree to the opening of negotiations. Much depended on the
relative British and French economic situations.[77] A first bilateral contact
with the new junior minister at the *Quai* was ambiguous: Jean de Lipowski
indicated slight movement towards the possibility of including in the
German proposals a date for the consideration of membership, but also
said that French economic difficulties made them more reluctant to face
British competition inside the Community. They were unlikely in any case
to allow negotiations to open in 1969, when the agricultural finance
regulations were to be renegotiated.[78] When the Council met on 30 July, it
spent only fifteen minutes on enlargement: the Five were resolute that
there must be substantive discussion on this subject in the autumn, and
Debré conceded this point, but it was clear that the French position had
not changed.[79] The impatience of the Five was growing: Luns told a
journalist with 'the French were being quite impossible about British entry
but they would find out that they were not the only people who could
make life impossible for others.' He intended to return to the Benelux
proposals in the autumn.[80] In this context the British continued to
consider the possibility of a new initiative directed at the Five.

Domestic considerations

The FO was determined not to give ministers any opportunity to
undermine the policy.[81] The only cabinet level European policy debate in
the summer of 1968 was over Monnet's invitation for the Labour Party to
join his Action Committee for a United States of Europe. Monnet was a
source of support and information to the British government, visiting
London regularly for top-level ministerial visits.[82] The Government saw
his invitation as important because it was 'the result of conversation
between all the existing members of the Committee...senior people in all

the political parties in the Six except the Gaullists and the Communists.'[83] Monnet's tact and patience in allowing Wilson to work out the best way to have the invitation formally dealt with (by cabinet, parliamentary party or party) was important in its final acceptance: he provided Wilson with a draft invitation in July 1968 while leaving the official invitation until after the summer vacation, as requested.[84] At the same time, he hinted at the positive results membership could have for Britain, revealing that a 'number of European ministers and particularly Herr Brandt had emphasised the need for direct and informal relationships to supplement the more formal diplomatic contacts which were all that existed at present.'[85] Both in this case and when invited to become a patron of the British Council of the European Movement, Wilson was initially suspicious, worried that he would be tricked into supporting a federal super-state.[86] Ministers too requested more information before considering the informal invitation, which Peart, then Lord Privy Seal, saw as a 'Common Market plot' to get a little extra pressure for entry.[87] But in both cases the invitations were eventually accepted, adding new credibility to Wilson's European policy.

Among pro-European ministers there were hopes that increasing German fortitude combined with French weakness would provide opportunities.[88] Chalfont felt that there 'were signs that [the Germans] were becoming disillusioned with the abortive negotiations on the arrangement.'[89] However, there was still uncertainty about the best way forward. Some officials rejected Harmel's ideas as a 'non-starter', while German ideas of a summit meeting were dismissed as 'unrealistic' at this stage.[90]

Christopher Soames, the ambassador-designate to Paris, approached these questions from a different angle. Soames was Churchill's son-in-law, and was appointed in an effort to improve bilateral relations with France – to impress the General.[91] He had suggested in April that the government could try to reduce ill feeling in France.[92] In July he again suggested that Britain turn to trying to win France over rather than 'batter[ing] our way in in the face of French opposition' and advocated that the government play the 'nuclear card'. The FO was unimpressed, noting that the 'sooner Mr Soames realises the limits and dangers of thinking in terms of nuclear keys and bilateral deals with France the better.' Robinson saw 'no ground for supposing that the basis of a deal exists between France today and Britain.' The French wanted 'a French bomb'.[93] Soames did not back down. He thought the FO 'had become mesmerised by the idea of EEC membership...[and] were insufficiently flexible as regards ideas of outflanking the French by making advances on other fronts.'[94] When he presented his credentials to de Gaulle he made clear that he saw it as his mission to improve Anglo-French relations.[95] When Soames took over the embassy from Reilly in September, therefore, he was given very strict instructions to the effect that British policy did not allow his embassy 'an active role in the immediate future.'[96]

For the time being, though, Palliser proposed a more dynamic approach than simply waiting for new initiatives to emerge from the Six. He suggested a meeting with Kiesinger in order to 'keep up a certain continuity and momentum in our relations with Europe.' It might be wise to visit other capitals again, since 'the plant of continental confidence in Britain's choice of the European option is still very tender and needs a lot of watering. If I may put it that way, no one can water it more effectively than you!' Wilson concurred.[97] He and Stewart agreed shortly afterwards on this course of events, as well as that nothing should be done to discourage Harmel from pursuing his ideas for co-operation using WEU.[98]

British representatives across the continent also argued for a more activist policy.[99] John Ford in the Rome embassy entreated Stewart for more British participation in joint technological projects, arguing that 'we have got to show our friends in Europe that our will is stronger than France's and use all the cards we can play relatively cheaply to maximum advantage in an attempt to outflank France politically and seize the initiative in Western Europe.' Instead, he said, 'we seem to be relapsing into our bad old ways of the post-war decade when we so often killed European initiative and discouraged our European friends.'[100] Perhaps as a result, the British were loath to give a negative response to a new Italian initiative in mid August for confidential Anglo-Italian-German talks, not yet cleared with Germany, to consider all of the proposals, with the aim of making recommendations to the September Council of Ministers.[101] The FO believed that such talks would do more harm than good, but were saved from having to say no by the inability of the Germans and the Italians to agree combined with the extremely negative attitude of the French to Italian ideas for future work between the Community and candidate states, such as inviting finance ministers to the economic day of WEU council meetings.[102]

The invasion of Czechoslovakia

More than any new initiative, however, the Soviet invasion of Czechoslovakia on 21 August gave added impetus to British European policy. First, it undermined the legitimacy of French foreign policy with its emphasis on rapprochement with the USSR.[103] Second, it reinforced German feelings of vulnerability about their own security and consequently their determination to achieve the unification of Europe.[104]

Wilson stepped into the opportunity created by these two divergent responses, saying in a House of Commons statement that

> all of us in Europe must be ready to move more positively in the direction of European unity. We must show not only that we are united in our defensive purpose but even more our conviction that only on the basis of a real political and economic unity in Europe can our continent heal its divisions and regain, through that ever-widening unity, its rightful influence for peace.[105]

Wilson thus portrayed himself and the UK as a more effective guarantor of German security than the French. The new British ambassador in Bonn, Sir Roger Jackling, emphasised the importance of maintaining this position. It had been conclusively demonstrated that France could not 'deliver the goods' on issues vital to the FRG, and the UK should encourage Kiesinger's consequent focus on strengthening European unity, in NATO as well as the EEC.[106]

In this new situation of potentially greater German determination, Debré argued that the Six should agree on outstanding matters before enlargement was considered. The only way to progress was for the Six to take all decisions on outstanding policies first.[107] When Stewart questioned de Courcel on this new stance, the French ambassador took his point that there would always be outstanding matters in the Community that could be used to delay negotiations, but argued that the Community could not be expected to stand still for the four or five years that negotiations would take. Although de Courcel maintained that the French government desired enlargement in principle – indeed, it had 'always said that Europe would be better balanced with the UK in' – and acknowledged that the Czech crisis underlined the need to strengthen Europe, he concluded that the economic difficulties of enlargement were 'formidable.'[108]

As the summer ended, therefore, the atmosphere was still pessimistic. A meeting between Brandt and Debré on 9 September failed to make any progress, and on the same day, de Gaulle stated that the 'desire to avoid the risk of Atlantic absorption is one of the reasons which has so far caused us to postpone, to our great regret, the entry of Great Britain into the present community.' Palliser commented that de Gaulle had made it very clear to Wilson in January 1967 that Atlantic ties were 'the real reason for his opposition to British membership of the EEC. But, to my recollection, this is the first time he has stated it in public quite so specifically.'[109] De Gaulle made similar points to Reilly in the latter's farewell interview on 10 September. He said that his criterion for the UK being qualified to enter the Common Market was that 'we should follow a

policy that was really European', in the monetary, military and political
fields. British entry would 'bring the Americans'. If France and Britain
could agree, all would be well, since they 'were the only two countries that
counted. But, alas, we did not agree.' De Gaulle said that Britain was quite
capable of doing what was needed: Eden had 'come nearest to doing so';
once or twice Macmillan had seemed to be 'on the brink'; Wilson 'had
seemed to catch a glimpse of what was needed. When it came to the point
of action, however, we never took it.' Replying to a question from Reilly,
de Gaulle agreed that while the economic reasons for the veto were
important, the 'essential point was that we should take the right political
decisions.'[110] Evidently de Gaulle's position had not moved at all since
November 1967: Reilly 'left Paris with Franco-British relations in a much
worse state than I found them.'[111]

Despite the general's obstinacy, Brandt still insisted that agreement
could be reached on a trade arrangement.[112] The Germans gave the
British, in confidence, a draft of the paper that they would put before the
Council on 27 September: it called for the participation of the applicants
in Community work on technology and regular consultation between the
governments of member states and non-member states at government
level, as well as giving new proposals for the commercial arrangement.[113]
Others, however, returned to looking outside the Community structure
for an interim solution. Informal talks between British and Italian officials
ended with an agreement to press the French to say what they meant by a
trade arrangement, and if they again proved negative, to concentrate on
co-operation outside the Rome Treaties.[114] Spaak told his son-in-law
Palliser that the UK must keep the application 'firmly and evidently on the
table' but that in parallel, HMG should try to take 'fresh initiatives in the
political and defence fields', perhaps along the lines of the 'Fouchet plans'
for political co-operation of the early 1960s. Moreover, Spaak went on, the
British were not doing enough to exploit the possibility of joint research
and development in weapons, aircraft and other defence tools, as well as
civil nuclear co-operation.[115] Britain's friends on the continent were still
torn over the best way to proceed.

The superpowers, EFTA and the Commonwealth

Throughout this deliberation, the USA continued to support the British
application at the highest level. However, a certain ambiguity began to
emerge as various groups began to realise that their interests were
threatened by the prospect of an enlarged but still protectionist EC.
During 1968, this ambiguity was not yet clearly expressed, although the
force with which the Johnson administration denounced the German
'trade arrangement' proposals made clear the American dislike for

economic integration without political content.[116] Otherwise, the Americans continued to respond to British requests for private support without public endorsement of their European policy, to offer advice, and to dissuade those, like MP Peter Bessel, who continued to believe NAFTA was a viable alternative to entry into the EEC.[117] Meanwhile, the main impact of the Soviet Union on European policy during these months came from the invasion of Czechoslovakia, as was seen above.

In EFTA, all welcomed Brandt's 'Eight Point Plan' but shared British scepticism that the French could ever be brought to accept it.[118] However, frustration with the speed of progress facilitated other projects, and in April the Nordic prime ministers announced a study of closer co-operation, with the aim of a 'closely integrated Nordic Union'.[119] The British response was relaxed. Wilson did not believe that much headway was being made: the Nordic countries were merely seeking to fill the void left by the veto.[120] Even when it became clear that the Nordic countries were considering building a secretariat and a ministerial council there was little concern in Britain: such institution-building could neither harm British interests nor offer anything desirable.[121] The foreign minister of Sweden, Lange, made this fact clear in EFTA Council when he asserted that Nordic co-operation was not an alternative to closer integration with the EEC, and foreign minister Nyboe Andersen of Denmark added that Nordic Union was in fact open to all EFTA countries.[122] Under the guiding hand of the pro-EFTA President of the Board of Trade, Crosland, some extra co-operation was agreed. It focused on improving trade, new interpretations of the EFTA Convention, especially regarding competition, and extending consultation in a number of fields.[123] Throughout, the British continued to keep their EFTA colleagues informed about progress – or lack of progress – with interim EC arrangements.[124] The British focus on the Six was, however, revealed in one letter from the British ambassador in Copenhagen: '[o]ne doesn't see the telegrams, one is all agog, and one wants to be able to talk intelligently to one's clients.'[125]

As in January-February, the Commonwealth had little impact on European policy, although it was troubling that some countries, particularly Malta and the East African members, might make association agreements with the EEC before the UK achieved membership.[126] Commonwealth leaders did not expect progress: for example, president Sir S. Ramgoolan of Mauritius was convinced that British efforts to gain membership were fruitless.[127] The Commonwealth Office was concerned that no interim arrangement with agricultural content should be agreed without consultation, but lack of agreement among the Six meant that this question never had to be addressed.[128] Nevertheless, the British were prepared to risk Commonwealth preferences and consequent retaliation from Commonwealth countries if necessary to achieve an agreement with the Six.[129]

The hope of progress

In the autumn Wilson and Stewart met to discuss tactics. Wilson said the application must continue: 'there must be no suggestion that we were not still standing at the main gate awaiting entry....This was the centre-piece of our European policy.' However, other initiatives should aim at both increasing de Gaulle's isolation and, somehow, ensuring that 'the potential resistance to British entry of the post-de Gaulle regime should have been weakened as far as possible beforehand.' Little progress could be made with technology, so perhaps they should 'try to launch the Fouchet plan again in some form.' The Five would welcome it and (because the 1962-63 deliberations had been largely shaped by France) it would be difficult for France to refuse. Wilson was 'impressed by the need for some fresh political impetus to be given to our European approach so as to outflank the embattled positions, such as the Benelux plan which, while valuable, had not so far led to much progress.' He felt that, given the post-Czechoslovakia situation, Kiesinger realised that the Franco-German relationship was not enough, and that he should visit him soon 'as a means of strengthening the Chancellor's tendency to take a broader look at the European scene.' The two concluded that EURM or a sub-committee should examine areas for a fresh initiative, perhaps in the monetary field as well as the political.[130] Robinson sharply pointed out that the FO had tried to follow exactly this path earlier in the year, only to be blocked by ministers in EURM and cabinet. He concluded that 'the answer to the Prime Minister's suggestions must depend almost entirely on the political judgement of what the Secretary of State's colleagues will agree to in the way of a revival and intensification of our European efforts.' If ministers gave authority for a new initiative, HMG would have to show the Five that they were willing to take a lead in the direction of political union and defence and technological co-ordination.[131]

However, even as Wilson and Stewart were considering their next move, Harmel wrote to Stewart from Rome, where he was having talks with the new foreign minister, Medici. He wrote that the Belgian government believed that they 'must truly carry out a European renewal in all directions where that approach appears possible, rather than search for a single solution, even partial, to the obstacles which have arisen on the road to Great Britain's membership of the Community.' On 27 September they wished to find out the 'exact nature' of the 'suspensive condition' impeding enlargement. In the meantime, article VIII of the Brussels

Treaty (of WEU) prescribed 'an extremely general and complete form of co-operation' – members could build new links in all those areas that were not specifically subject to the Treaties of Rome. An initiative could therefore be taken at the WEU council in Rome on 21-22 October. He proposed strengthening political and military co-operation, and beginning technological and monetary co-operation. Harmel went on to regret the British decisions on space collaboration, saying that it would be difficult to give content to technological co-operation if the crises in ELDO and ESRO were not surmounted.[132] Harmel and Medici agreed that they should seek from Brandt an absolute minimum proposal for a trade arrangement, on which the Five would aim to reach agreement before putting it to the French on 27 September. Harmel considered this effort necessary in order to make his subsequent WEU initiative more acceptable.[133]

The British were initially unsure of how to respond to this new proposal. Bernard Ledwidge wrote from Paris to say that there was no likelihood of the French agreeing to discussions including the UK that could so easily lead on to a kind of negotiation on enlargement terms.[134] Palliser wondered if WEU was the 'right vehicle' for co-operation, but concluded that 'perhaps it is all we have!'[135] Stewart feared that the Five were placing themselves in a dangerous position by attempting to agree a proposal amongst themselves before putting it to France, and tried to dissuade them. Instead the French should be forced to make their own proposals, since they had agreed to a commercial arrangement.[136] Although Luns shared Stewart's reservations he revealed that the Germans had said they needed only one more 'no' from the French before changing their attitude. Luns was worried that the British would not agree to proceeding with the Four in the event that they failed to detach Germany from the French.[137] Stewart wanted to do all possible to secure German participation in multilateral action on the lines of the Benelux proposals, which included allowing them one last effort to get French agreement to a commercial arrangement, but reassured Luns that if necessary, he was willing to envisage action on a narrower basis if the Germans could not be brought along.[138]

As the Five seemed to be creeping towards the possibility of co-operation with Britain, the French line hardened. Debré attacked the political aspects even of the Treaty of Rome: the economic parts alone were ambitious, and enlargement 'would at present be a leap into the unknown in which all that has been achieved would risk being destroyed.' He could envisage technological co-operation with extra-Community states in specific fields, but only if it would help to reinforce European independence, and he did not think that British membership would help in this respect. Debré's comments thus contradicted even the modest Franco-German Declaration.[139]

When they met on 18 September, therefore, Stewart and Harmel now agreed that after the Council on 27 September they would pursue multilateral co-operation outside the Treaty of Rome, and, if France obstructed work in WEU, outside that institution too. As Harmel said, '[p]rogress had to be made and we had to know where we were going': he was 'pleased and encouraged'.[140] The Germans continued to consult the British on their proposal for a 'trade arrangement', while the Dutch kept the British informed of their efforts to exert pressure on the Germans to take a stronger line.[141] The Italians prepared a draft 'decision' for the consideration of the Five, so that they could present a common front to the French on 27 September, and this 'decision' was discussed both bilaterally with Britain and multilaterally among the Four.[142] On the evening before the Council meeting, the Four agreed that they would accept the German paper, without enthusiasm, as the absolute minimum that their governments could contemplate. They agreed that it should be regarded as an indivisible entity (that is, that the French could not accept some parts and reject others) and that it could, on these conditions, be the basis for discussion with the UK provided that it was accepted by all Six.[143]

As the Council meeting began there were indications from leading Germans that they might finally be prepared to join in co-operation without France.[144] In particular, Kiesinger said that if no positive or constructive result emerged from his meeting with de Gaulle after the Council of Ministers meeting, the Federal Government would be prepared to take the initiative in calling a summit meeting, initially to discuss defence co-operation but later to cover other issues as well.[145] Wilson sent a long message to Kiesinger, stressing the 'fundamental identity of views between our two governments' and the need further to unite Europe in the post-Czechoslovakia environment, attacking French accusations that the UK was too 'Atlantic' to be a member of the Community, and pressing for extra-Treaty co-operation should Brandt's proposals fail.[146] Kiesinger welcomed the message, saying that broadening the Community to include Britain had been his constant aim for the past two years. 'All indications from Paris were that the French attitude was still opposed but until he had actually discussed matters face to face with the General he was not going to give up hope.' While he was prepared to 'press strongly for progress, he was reluctant to contemplate pushing things to the points of a break with France.' Nevertheless, some forward step must be made: Kiesinger mentioned 'a European core in NATO' and technology.[147]

The September Council of Ministers

The Council of Ministers meeting of 27 September revealed a real strengthening of the German position. Brandt formally presented his updated 'trade arrangement' proposal. He said that it should facilitate enlargement, and was conceived in the framework of GATT.[148] The initial participants should be the Community and the four applicants, although others could be considered later. The content involved three annual tariff reductions of ten per cent. On a broader level, three issues should be tackled in parallel: the enlargement, strengthening and fusion of the Communities. The negotiations over agricultural finance could be linked with enlargement. In response, Harmel presented the agreed position of the Four. Debré, however, was 'quiet, unemotional, but utterly negative'. He could not accept a link between the internal development of the Community and enlargement, although France would be willing to discuss an 'arrangement' with no link with enlargement and which was open to all European countries. If the Five continued to press for enlargement to the detriment of the development of the Community, he would be forced to argue that it should be removed from the Community agenda. The Five agreed that they could not offer the French further compromise: as Luns said, what was un-reconcilable could not be reconciled.[149] This meeting was the first occasion when the Five stood firmly together against the French since 18-19 December 1967. The French were forced to state explicitly that they would not allow the 'arrangement' to be linked to accession, and the Five refused to accept this position.[150] The Germans maintained that the Brandt proposals were still on the table, but it was clear that it would be impossible to reach agreement on a 'commercial arrangement'.[151] The Belgians told the British that they would now proceed to 'the working out of a plan for political and defence co-operation to include Britain.'[152] The British efforts to persuade the Five to co-operate with them seemed to have paid off.

Before much progress could be made, however, the new German position had to survive one of Kiesinger's regular meetings with de Gaulle. Initially it looked as though it had fallen at the first fence: Kiesinger assured de Gaulle that a European policy without France would be 'destructive for Europe', and the two leaders agreed that their governments would seek to activate policy in Europe by means of their 'special co-operation'. While the French opposed an automatic link between an 'arrangement' and enlargement, 'both sides agreed that eventual entry might be facilitated by an 'arrangement'.' There could also be co-operation on energy policy, space research and defence equipment. On German television, Kiesinger said that some progress had been made and there was scope for useful interim action. He emphatically stated his opposition to the view that Europe must be strengthened with Britain and Scandinavia even if France would not co-operate: 'Europe could only be built with France.' It emerged that de Gaulle had told Kiesinger that France had done without the Common Market before and could do so again – a threat that, as Palliser noted, 'always brings Kiesinger to heel.' It seemed that Kiesinger had reneged on the agreement reached among the Five only the day before.

However, press coverage of this meeting was very negative towards Germany, and Brandt told Jackling that the chancellor was disturbed and upset: his remarks had been taken out of context. While he had said that Europe could not be built without France, neither could it be built without England [sic]. And while the FRG would take no initiative against France, 'this by no means [excluded] taking action with others in appropriate matters even though France did not take part.' He had spoken firmly to de Gaulle about the need for progress in Europe. Moreover, Brandt did not believe de Gaulle's threat to withdraw from the EEC: it was too important to the French economy. Jackling concluded, however, that Kiesinger was 'no more ready than he [had] ever been to put any real pressure on the French'. Soames said that the impression in France was that de Gaulle had 'won yet another round over Kiesinger whom he has successfully frightened...into abandoning any attempt to speak up for Britain'. Wilson agreed, commenting that 'I think we are being taken for a ride [and] I'm getting fed up with this A[rse] L[icking] attitude of ours' and suggesting that it was time to 'start putting the fear of God into Kiesinger' and 'playing German politics.'[153]

Conclusions

For once, however, Wilson was wrong. The FRG, as will be seen, stood by its September commitment to co-operate with Britain even if France did not join in. The seven months covered in this chapter thus saw the Germans desperately attempting to delineate a proposal that both France and Britain could support, followed by a sudden step towards the possibility of extra-Treaty collaboration. The FO followed up Wilson and Stewart's request for consideration of a British initiative, with Robinson elaborating proposals for political, defence, technology and monetary integration, and asking for authority to start sounding out senior ministers.[154] Stewart later agreed to talk to Healey and Jenkins.[155] There were hints that the Five would gain leverage over France as the time for renegotiating CAP drew closer – indeed, at one point the French even accused the Germans of wanting British accession in order to have an excuse to change the agricultural finance arrangements![156] For the time being, however, attention was focused on Harmel, and all awaited his proposals for co-operation using WEU.

5

October 1968 – January 1969: progress – without France?

As the first post-veto year drew towards a close, the Five displayed hints of a new solidarity. The failure of Brandt's September proposals pushed Germany towards extra-Rome Treaty co-operation with the Four and Britain, while the French were increasingly isolated. Trends emerged that would take on greater significance from February 1969: collaboration on foreign policy between Britain and the Five; and fleeting hints from the French about the possibility of closer Anglo-French relations. This chapter again demonstrates the importance of Wilson and Stewart in guiding and implementing European policy: as Crossman commented, they could not 'take their hands off the effort to get into Europe.'[1]

In October Wilson finally accepted Monnet's invitation for the Labour Party to join his Action Committee for a United States of Europe, much to the latter's pleasure.[2] The announcement was made on 25 October, and made a good impression across the Community.[3] More important, the Action Committee immediately set to work on reports intended to show that the obstacles in the way of British entry could be overcome.[4] The *rapporteurs* were to keep in close touch with the British during the drafting period: Monnet regarded the process 'as a kind of "pre-negotiation" to reach an agreed view as well as demonstrating conclusively the possibility of British membership.' Wilson preferred the words 'blue print', but agreed that the reports would help to demonstrate to 'realistic and intelligent people in Europe' that the problems of British membership could be solved.[5]

Relance européene

Monnet was not the only European working for British admission. Harmel proposed that the foreign ministers of Britain and the Four hold preliminary discussions on his new proposals when they were in New York for a United Nations meeting in mid-October. Palliser was worried that acting without the Germans would push them back towards the French and 'let them off the hook on which they are half-impaled.' Jackling, in Bonn, and the German ambassador in London, were equally worried. However, Harmel was taking a calculated risk that fear of being left out would coax the Germans away from France. Robinson too thought the Germans would find it difficult to stand aside from a 'determined effort' in political co-operation in an existing institution.[6] Despite these divided counsels, Stewart encouraged the Belgian initiative, welcoming the suggestion for a meeting in New York, but advising that the Germans should be handled carefully. The Belgians did not think the Germans would resent preliminary talks among the Four, and Brandt was not planning to be in New York anyway. Harmel would tell him that Belgium would make proposals at the end of the month, and if he expressed an interest in preliminary discussions, all to the good. To help the Germans to participate, the French would be informed about the proposals, and any proposals would be open to them.[7]

Harmel unveiled his plan to journalists on 3 October. He spoke of '*une insatisfaction, une impatience, un désenchantement*' with the construction of Europe, the first basis of which had been the Brussels Treaty that led to the WEU and the second, the EC. Attacking '*solidarités préférentielles*' within the Communities, Harmel wanted to move past the stage of declarations. He did not intend to replace the Community, or replace France with Britain: on the contrary, the internal development of the EC must continue. Nevertheless, internal development was not a substitute for '*une vision politique commune de l'avenir de l'Europe, qui s'exprime au sein des Communautés ou ailleurs. Même si l'ouverture de l'Europe se faisait ailleurs qu'au sein des Communautés, nous sommes persuadés, qu'au bout de chemin, les Communautés retrouveront leur place naturelle au centre de l'Europe de demain.*' Technological and monetary co-operation came under the Community purview but also could be pursued under Article VIII of the Brussels Treaty; defence collaboration could be developed through WEU, within NATO; the co-ordination of foreign policy was also available. He would prefer to go forward with seven, but '*[a]ucune train ne circulerait jamais s'il fallait attendre que tous les voyageurs soient tous prêts au depart*', and Europe was at '*l'heure de choix*'.[8] Harmel's speech was a powerful advocation of the need to continue European integration and to include Britain and other interested European states.

Harmel's speech also succeeded in pricking Germany into action. His point about cliques within the Community stung: the federal spokesman said that close-Franco German co-operation was meant merely to serve the furthering of work in the Communities, and that the federal government would examine any new proposals from its partners with the greatest interest.[9] Brandt also sent a circular telegram to all posts stressing that the German government 'remained prepared to react positively if other partners wished to take an initiative to co-operate with candidate members in fields falling outside the operations of the Treaties of Rome and Paris.'[10] Nevertheless, Palliser was still anxious that pursuit of Harmel's initiative would, in isolating the French, 'inevitably' isolate the Germans too.[11] He therefore passed to the FO Wilson's earlier comments deploring British sycophantism vis-à-vis Germany and suggesting that they should start 'playing German politics'.[12] The FO, however, resisted Wilson's extreme suggestions that the UK could 'put the fear of God into Kiesinger' by threatening to recognise East Germany or to withdraw British troops from the FRG. Instead, continuing to propose and even participate in European co-operation was a more effective and immediate way of imposing pressure on Germany.[13] Had Brandt not been so positive in New York, this embryonic split over tactics might have become more problematic.

Sidestepping cabinet

In the meantime, Stewart required ministerial consideration of the new proposals. He did not want to go to the ministerial committee on the approach to Europe (EURM), officially because the Harmel proposals were for co-operation outside the Communities while EURM's remit was the application for membership. In reality, Stewart's memories of the reception accorded in May to his ideas for a British initiative made him wary of returning to EURM. His preference was for an *ad hoc* group of ministers, and Palliser agreed that if possible, Wilson should chair it. Wilson and Stewart agreed that an *ad hoc* committee should meet on 16 October – that is, after Stewart returned from the preliminary talks in New York but before the Rome WEU Council at which Harmel would formally present his proposals. Wilson left Stewart to decide the membership of what became 'MISC 224' – one of 236 *ad hoc* committees created by Wilson. They would then decide on whether to report to cabinet.[14] Stewart spoke privately to Jenkins and Healey on 4 October. Stewart rehearsed the developments since May and noted a 'widespread feeling that Europe must move closer together'. He suggested that Britain would have to react to events and initiatives from others while doing what was possible to shape those initiatives. It would have to be cheap, but a move towards political union with real defence content would constitute no additional burden on the balance of payments. 'Such a move could revive the momentum towards European unity, and could provide us with an opportunity to recover some measure of leadership in Europe; and secure a position from which we could inhibit the development of the Community as long as we are prevented from joining it.' Stewart noted that the defence aspect would have to be within the Atlantic Alliance, but that the initiative would have to be 'something of a dramatic approach' in order to secure German support. A 'clear and firm' directive from ministers would therefore be required when he returned from New York. Jenkins and Healey's 'broad agreement' with this line ensured that Stewart had at least some ministerial support for his plans when he left for New York.[15]

Progress with the Five

The French took a hard line on the Harmel proposals. They were demonstrably unsettled at the prospect of a new proposal in Rome, arguing that it would mean the end of any prospect of political co-operation *à Six* – a development welcomed by Palliser. They threatened that if the rest of the Five adopted the Dutch line of refusing to allow progress in the Community except on condition of progress towards enlargement, they 'could not guarantee what the consequences would be in 1969.'[16] As the New York meeting drew closer, they tried to bring attention back to proposals for a 'trade arrangement'.[17] The ability of the French to obstruct discussion of the new proposals had, however, been diminished by the Five's frustration with such tactics over the previous months.

Frustration with the French perhaps explained Brandt's unexpected appearance in New York, and Stewart reported that he no longer regarded further clarity on a trade arrangement as a necessary condition for considering other approaches. In the first French delaying tactic directed towards the new proposals, Debré told Harmel in a separate meeting that France would not object to a procedural decision being taken at the Rome WEU. France would allow the establishment of a study group, to report back in January, but would oppose decisions of substance being taken in October. Officials immediately began work on 'the general political objectives which we should have in mind'. They decided that there should be a new agreement to co-operate in the fields of defence and foreign policy, the former in NATO, the latter in 'a similar institutional structure' if France obstructed the use of WEU. While no one had any illusions about French intentions, Debré's apparent readiness to contemplate procedural decisions made it easier for Germany to participate. Stewart was pleased at the progress, and convinced that this was the right approach. In the atmosphere of insecurity after the invasion of Czechoslovakia, and with elections in the US making their future policy uncertain, foreign policy co-operation was the most promising field for action. If the UK did nothing, Stewart felt, Italy and Benelux might lose heart, and the Community resume its development under French leadership now, and German leadership in the future. Medici, Luns, Harmel and, provided that France was not deliberately excluded, Brandt, all agreed that progress would have to be made without France if necessary.[18] The first small step in the veto period towards real, multilateral co-operation with Britain had been taken.

Domestic deliberations

Despite this progress, Stewart was in no doubt that 'considerable pressure' would be needed to make it as difficult as possible for Brandt to withdraw.[19] He therefore sought ministerial agreement to work for closer co-operation in Europe, especially in foreign policy and defence; to seek agreement in the Rome WEU Council to the establishment of a small group to report, if necessary without unanimity, in January; and to proceed without France from October if agreement could not be reached.[20] Although the proposal had come from Belgium, not Britain, Stewart therefore wanted the authority, denied him in May, to take a new direction in European policy. The brief for the first meeting of the new MISC 224 committee stressed the urgency of the situation. It stated that '[i]mpatience with de Gaulle's European policies seems...to be growing in Germany and as the split within the Six widens the German Government must become increasingly uncomfortable at the prospect of being aligned with France on the big issues against Britain, Benelux and Italy.' Stewart's ideas should therefore be pursued, without Germany if necessary.[21] Palliser doubted that the UK would be able to go forward without Germany, since he saw the Federal Republic as the key to British entry. However, he also thought that HMG could exert more influence over Germany than the FO believed. He suggested a new British initiative along the lines of the Fouchet plan; closer links with leading Christian Democrat politicians other than Kiesinger; and using Jean Monnet as a liaison with 'the top Germans'.[22] Palliser's return to the Fouchet plan was the continuation of a split between the FO and No. 10 over the best way to pursue closer European integration.

In the FO, Robinson wanted to put off any ministerial decisions about proceeding with or without German participation for as long as possible – sensible advice since, as will be seen, the Germans eventually came on board. Regarding Fouchet, he pointed out that the original proposals had been a cause of division between France and the Five in the early 1960s, and that the more recent proposals for political co-operation should therefore be cast in as non-controversial a way as possible.[23] When MISC 224 met for the first time on 16 October, therefore, Stewart invited his colleagues (Wilson, Crossman, Peart, Benn, Jenkins, Healey, Crosland, Chalfont and Lever) to agree that Britain should support the Harmel proposals and that they should proceed without France if necessary. While Healey took care to defend the concentration of European defence collaboration in NATO, all recognised the need to 'make every effort' to increase collaboration as well as maintaining the application, the need to keep the pressure on the Germans, the need to maintain technological co-operation, and the need to be seen to be active, 'otherwise the momentum of our approach would be lost.' Still, neither relations with EFTA nor the balance of payments should be jeopardised.[24] Wilson and Stewart had finally succeeded in getting ministerial authority to pursue an initiative for further integration in Europe, including the 'high politics' area of foreign policy. Robinson had predicted that the ability to build on the Benelux proposals would be inhibited by majority opinion in Cabinet, but despite the 'very strong' efforts of one or more ministers to argue that the time had come to end the 'fruitless initiatives' towards entry, and with Healey again identifying NATO as the correct forum for defence collaboration, OPD and then cabinet broadly endorsed the decision already reached in MISC 224.[25] As Castle later commented, while the use of MISC committees was necessary and justified, and Wilson was careful to bring their conclusions to cabinet for ratification, 'by the time things have gone as far as that it is very difficult for the rest of Cabinet to change them. All one can do is to decide whether the existence of the near *fait accompli* makes the continuation of one's membership of Cabinet impossible.'[26] Clearly European policy as pursued through MISC 224 did not.

Rallying Germany

The British therefore exerted pressure on the Germans, using hints about closer collaboration on defence procurement and attacks on the inequality of the Franco-German relationship.[27] Chalfont made a long and eloquent speech to the WEU assembly, re-stating HMG's whole-hearted determination to seek full membership of the Communities and insisting that they could 'not afford to put Europe into cold storage because of the refusal by one member of the Community to permit it to be enlarged.' He concluded that they 'must now recognise clearly who are the real Europeans.'[28] However, a sign of weakness in the German position came in a *Bundestag* speech by Kiesinger, in which he repeated that 'Europe would...not be extended by ousting France from her chair in order to

accommodate Britain.'[29]   Despite 'unusually strong and united press
criticism', expected *Bundestag* attacks on the chancellor's speech did not
materialise.[30] Apparently there had been a 'development in German
thinking' since the New York meeting. Duckwitz said that Germany still
fully supported the Harmel initiative, including the procedure worked out
in New York.

> But they wanted [Britain] to know that they thought it essential to
> work with the French in this operation. Should it prove impossible
> to obtain the agreement of all member Governments within the
> framework of WEU, then the German Government did not expect
> that anything could be achieved outside WEU. They, therefore,
> thought we should avoid setting up any new institution and they
> attached importance to the proposed study group being established
> within the framework of WEU, perhaps using the help of the WEU
> secretariat.

The Germans had effectively given the French a veto. Stewart found it
hard to believe that the German position could have changed on so
fundamental a point in a matter of days, and he took a hard line. Asking
Jackling to speak to the German government 'in emphatic terms', he said
that he was determined to move forward on the lines agreed in New York,
with the door kept open for French participation. Palliser commented
'quite right too.'[31] In a personal message to Brandt, Stewart said he was
'very much concerned' and hoped that the German foreign minister would
be able to set his mind at rest.[32] While there were increasing signs of
dissent within Germany, Stewart clearly took these indications of German
backsliding seriously and immediately moved to counter them at a high
level.[33]

French manoeuvres
Concurrently, the first indications of a possible change in policy emerged
from the French. In an article described as 'very interesting' by Palliser, a
Gaullist commentator regularly used by the *Elysée* and the *Quai* wrote of
the need for Anglo-French reconciliation, suggesting that Wilson should
'give up trying to get into the Common Market against the will of France,
and…seek the means of entering with her blessing.' The article explicitly
acknowledged that while France had succeeded in keeping Britain out of
the EC, Britain had equally well succeeded in paralysing the Common
Market: the resulting situation was harmful for everyone.[34] It is impossible
to say whether or not this article was a 'trial balloon' for the proposals that
would spark the 'Soames affair' four months later, but it was certainly an

indication that the French administration might be considering an effort to improve bilateral relations with the UK.

The situation was complicated when the British embassy in Paris indicated that a radical reassessment of French foreign policy might be underway, and Chalfont, having heard from de Lipowski that the French might accept certain parts of the Harmel proposals, did not think that the possibility could be discounted.[35] Stewart concluded that the French were nervous at being left out, and that he should therefore stick firmly to the substantive objectives, especially that of developing the mandate to WEU agreed with the Five in New York.[36] The French did not respond well to British pressure for immediate action, however, and Soames warned that they might, after all, resist even the setting up of a study group in WEU.[37] Moreover, the French later claimed that Debré had only agreed in New York to the inclusion of the Harmel proposals on the WEU agenda on the condition that there was no discussion and that no study group was set up.[38] The apparent warmth of Soames' first meeting with Couve as prime minister did not extend to a reversal of this position, and the French soon returned to destructive tactics.[39]

The Germans were therefore walking a tightrope between the British (backed particularly strongly by the Dutch, who wanted to take an even harder line) and the French.[40] Duckwitz responded to Stewart's message to Brandt with some very tight conditions for participation in the Harmel proposals, including that the decision to set up a WEU working group must be unanimous, and that if the seven WEU countries could not agree on a mandate to that group in October, discussion should be postponed until the next ministerial council. Germany would not favour the elaboration of a new treaty or new institutions.[41] The German permanent representative to the EC confused the situation further by commenting that his government was convinced that the trade arrangement proposals were the best approach.[42] Jahn then indicated to Chalfont that they might be prepared to consider the Harmel proposals on a less-than-seven-country basis, but not at the Rome WEU.[43] It seemed that the federal government would never take a consistent position, and British officials were uncertain of the best tactics to pursue: a serious clash at WEU might push the Germans back into the arms of the French.[44]

The Rome WEU Council

In fact, the 'serious clash' in Rome pushed the Germans out of the arms of the French and towards the others. Fearing the French reaction, Harmel hesitated the day before the meeting, but after an hour's talk with Stewart, he agreed to go ahead.[45] He launched his proposals for extra-treaty co-operation with the clear, long-term aim of bringing all forms of co-operation under one institution. For the time being, ministers should establish a special group to consider the possibilities and report in January: all countries except France had already agreed (in New York) the group's mandate. Stewart reported that the Italians, Dutch, Germans and Luxembourgers joined him in welcoming Harmel's initiative, agreeing to the mandate. De Lipowski alone rejected it, together with a German compromise solution of a study by the WEU's permanent council. All delegations agreed to prepare in a 'suitable' manner for the January meeting, although obviously, there was no agreement between France and the rest about what 'suitable' meant.[46]

Breakthrough: the first meeting of Britain and the Five

With the French having comprehensively isolated themselves, Medici convened a meeting of the Five and Britain. Stewart explained that the Harmel proposals had been drafted to maximise the chances of French acceptance. Since the French had rejected not only Harmel's proposal but also the German compromise, and refused to discuss European co-operation at all, 'the six governments should now agree to appoint representatives to a special group of the six.' It would not be a WEU group, but its report could be considered at WEU council in January, where the French would not be able to prevent discussion of political issues. While Luns and Medici supported Stewart, the Luxembourg, German and Belgian representatives felt unable to take a decision that night. Medici, in the chair, consequently postponed the decision to the margins of the next NATO meeting in November in Brussels, and charged Stewart with contacting the other five in preparation.[47] Another small step towards co-operation had been taken, and the British were to prepare the next.

The second day of WEU also saw strong support for the British position, with the Dutch and Italians commenting on the improved British economy, the Germans hoping to see practical results coming from the Brandt and Harmel proposals, the Dutch renewing their self-exclusion from (and *de facto* veto on) Community work on technology for the duration of the French veto, and Chalfont repeating that the application remained the cornerstone of British European policy. Even de Lipowski, for France, said that his country was prepared to accept the possibility of co-operation with Britain in the patent field. However, his inability to agree to an Italian proposal for economic and finance ministers to attend a WEU economic day in the future meant that the second day too ended with France isolated.[48]

Moreover, the French were 'throughout completely negative in substance and offensive in tone', so that 'resentment at the French attitude ran deep in all other delegations.' The psychological barrier to co-operation without France was therefore at least partway down: the meeting of the Five and Britain at the end of the first day was the first such meeting since 1963, and all six agreed to meet again.[49] French newspapers – which Soames identified as 'clearly briefed' – characterised the Rome council as 'most unpleasant', where France was 'confronted without warning with a cut and dried scheme', and accused Britain and the Netherlands of working on Harmel to step up his ideas.[50] Cabinet merely took note of the small but significant development in Rome, apparently without discussion.[51]

Stewart's diplomacy: disarming France and strengthening Germany
Stewart immediately set to work to fulfil his mandate of preparing the November meeting. He wrote to Brandt saying that they must go on: the 'purpose in all of this must be to preserve what we can of the prospects for European integration'.[52] A second message suggested that Britain and the Five meet on 14 November, before the NATO proceedings began.[53] He sent instructions to other missions, stating that the French were determined that all work in the field of European co-operation should be instituted on the basis of the Six, where they had a veto and the threat of withdrawal. The government could not, however, accept French efforts to veto progress outside the Rome treaties, and would consult further with their friends.[54] Stewart was determined to succeed.

The French changed tactics to show supposed warmth towards the 'trade arrangement' (which they had already rejected in five versions) as seen on the second day of WEU, and hopeful words about future British accession at a Chamber of Commerce lunch.[55] When Soames met Debré at the end of the month, the latter insisted that France was serious about the trade arrangement – although they had not yet worked out serious proposals. In another indication that the French government was considering a wholesale revision of its policy towards the UK, Debré also suggested that Britain and France should have more bilateral technological and political (that is, foreign policy) co-operation. He asked for time to reflect.[56]

The resulting suspicion of France, on the continent and in Britain, was clear. The Dutch PR said that France was seeking 'excuses to postpone the question of British membership' and the Italians – the first to accept Stewart's invitation to the November meeting – warned that they were trying to divide the Five.[57] These tactics nearly worked: some of the Five were worried about progressing without France, with Luxembourg and Belgium seeking ongoing bilateral contacts with Britain as a form of reassurance.[58] The Italians warned that it would be better not to have the

November meeting than to end up divided on the way to proceed.[59] Harmel, disappointed that his initiative had not been properly accepted on 22 October, wanted to investigate Debré's and Brandt's positions at the next EC council meeting before committing himself to Stewart's meeting. He did not want the latter to be a mere gesture, but for something useful to be achieved.[60] Stewart took care to reassure and encourage Harmel, sending a message through the Belgian ambassador in London that his road was right.[61]

The real concern, however, remained the Germans. Perhaps as a consequence of Stewart's messages to Brandt, the Germans informed the British that they wanted a full discussion of the Harmel proposals at the January WEU council.[62] Brandt's reply to Stewart's messages contained positive and negative aspects: he wanted the next WEU council to reach definite conclusions on intensifying foreign policy co-operation, and was 'always prepared to discuss and examine proposals for specific projects of co-operation between interested governments.' However, he still preferred bilateral preparation for the WEU council, wanted to avoid giving the impression that a 'special group' of six countries had been formed within WEU, did not think a working group of the six could serve any purpose, and wanted Stewart to invite Debré to his proposed November meeting.[63] Clearly Brandt was still trying to walk his tightrope.

As these discussions about WEU continued, the EC Council of Ministers met on 4-5 November. The French produced actual outline proposals for a trading arrangement – the first time they had done so since the Franco-German Declaration in February. They included mutual tariff reductions on certain products together with non-EC states' purchase of member-state agricultural produce, and would not be linked with the question of UK membership of the Communities. In response, the Five formally stood by Brandt's proposals of 27 September, which Debré again rejected. The Council asked the PRs to consider the French proposals along with all the others so far put forward (except the Harmel proposals, which lay entirely outside the Community) and to report back early in the New Year. As Robinson commented, the French ideas were even less attractive to the British than the earlier German version, and agreement was unlikely, particularly because of the French refusal to countenance a link with membership.[64] The British responded with the standard line, that they would consider any proposals coming from all member states that led to membership.[65] It is difficult to see the French proposals as anything other than an effort to divert attention from the work proceeding in WEU.

The French rebuff and Brandt's balancing act helped to push the reconstituted Foreign and Commonwealth Office (FCO) towards taking a strong line with the Germans.[66] An Office meeting agreed that Stewart would urge Brandt (and Harmel) to attend the 14 November meeting, and would remind him of his New York commitments. Stewart and his officials also agreed that Britain would attend the meeting even if only Italy and the Netherlands attended, and try to bring the others back on board afterwards. On the trade arrangement, it was essential to maintain the condition of a link with full membership. In terms of presentation, it was important to avoid the issue appearing as a struggle for the leadership of Europe: it must appear as a struggle between Europe and France, not Britain and France.[67] Stewart's reply to Brandt's message reflected these views, saying particularly that it was the French attitude that had made necessary meetings of Britain and the Five in the first place.[68] In response, Brandt said that there had been some movement in the French position, and that progress on a seven-country basis might be possible.[69] However, when he met Stewart at a European Movement meeting, he agreed to attend the 14 November meeting provided that Debré was also invited. It was important to Germany for tactical reasons that the French at least be asked. Harmel took the same line.[70]

At the same time as Stewart was trying to win over Brandt, his officials were working closely with the Italians to prepare for the 14 November meeting. They agreed that the Italians would be asked to prepare a paper for the WEU council in Luxembourg in the New Year. In order to help the Germans to participate, they would proceed on the basis of using WEU and the paper would be made available to all seven WEU members.[71] In the light of Brandt's and Harmel's position, and with the reluctant acquiescence of the Dutch, Stewart invited Debré to attend the meeting on 14 November.[72] The French foreign minister told Soames two days later that he did not think he would be able to accept, but the fact of his invitation was enough for Harmel to agree to attend.[73]

Cabinet

Before the meeting in Brussels, however, Stewart had to face cabinet. In a discussion at the end of October, the OPD had decided that cabinet needed to discuss NATO and European policy side by side, not to seek new decisions but to ensure that there was harmony: eventually the Harmel proposals for political and defence collaboration would, 'for sound practical reasons', be pursued separately.[74] A paper was prepared for cabinet, discussing this parallel progress. On Europe, it concluded that the government had

> kept the issue of European integration and our participation in it alive. French obstruction is increasingly recognised by the other

members of the EEC. It is our hope that continued exposure of the French attitude will encourage other members of the EEC to pursue a more robust and independent line.[75]

On 12 November Stewart described this parallel approach to cabinet, noting that the five foreign ministers had agreed to attend his meeting and that the defence ministers of the five, Denmark and Norway had similarly accepted an invitation from Healey to discuss collaboration on European defence. Stewart stressed that his discussions in Brussels, if successful, would involve neither new expenditure nor new commitments for the UK. Ministers agreed that the main objective in European policy must be to detach the Germans from their too-ready compliance with French wishes. It was also pointed out that the French proposals for a trade arrangement would hold attraction for some members of EFTA, and that tactics for the forthcoming EFTA council must therefore be carefully prepared, but no general protest was raised.[76] It should be noted that cabinet was during these months preoccupied with, and divided over, the 'Fearless' proposals for a settlement in Rhodesia and with the first discussions of Castle's white paper on industrial relations that would eventually become the disastrous 'In Place of Strife'.[77] There were thus more important things than European policy on which to take a stand.

New commitment from Germany?

As Wilson and Stewart received the go-ahead from cabinet, a welcome sign of German stout-heartedness came in the form of a letter from Kiesinger. Replying to Wilson's September message of support after the invasion of Czechoslovakia and in preparation for a planned Wilson visit to Bonn, Kiesinger agreed with the need to strengthen NATO. Although he again said that 'Europe can neither be built up without France nor can it dispense with the co-operation of Great Britain', he also argued that the European nations 'ought to take advantage of any opportunities presenting themselves and also to develop new and unconventional forms of co-operation which accord with the realities of our present situation.'[78] It was a cautious welcome to the Harmel proposals.

Despite Kiesinger's words, however, Duckwitz explained that the Germans were genuinely afraid that if they went too far, 'de Gaulle was an irrational enough character suddenly to pull out of the Common Market as a means of expressing his dissatisfaction.'[79] It remained to be seen whether the Germans would consider that pursuing the Harmel proposals would be pushing the general 'too far.' Stewart's determined diplomacy succeeded in rallying his colleagues and the planned meeting went ahead on 14 November: Brandt, Medici, Luns, Harmel, Grégoire and Stewart all attended. Debré had formally declined on 13 November, saying that he had not had enough notice.[80] They agreed that rather than setting up a formal working group, the Italians would prepare a paper to be the basis for discussion and decision at the next WEU meeting. Medici agreed to invite France, 'though no one expected them to come.'[81] Brandt's position was slightly more qualified than the others: he said that in the absence of other ways forward, progress was being made on three narrow fronts: the trade arrangement in the EC, defence in NATO, and other progress in WEU. Stewart concluded that all agreed they should proceed, with discussions on foreign policy in WEU to be parallel to those on defence in NATO. He added that it might be necessary to create some new mechanism for co-operation if progress within WEU proved impossible (because of French obstruction). They would make clear to France that the door remained open but also that a French refusal would not stop them: progress must be made at the Luxembourg WEU meeting in February.[82] Another small step had therefore been taken towards extra-treaty co-operation between Britain and the Five.

Work on 'interim arrangements' now continued in two separate ways. In WEU, the Italians called a meeting of representatives of Britain and the Five to consult on the paper that they had agreed to produce. Countries that did not want to come would be contacted bilaterally, and all member governments (that is, including France) would be kept informed.[83] Robinson was the British representative.[84] In the EC context the Belgians circulated to the Six, the applicants, Sweden and the Commission, a working document with the stated purpose of bringing together the various interim proposals. It said that neither internal nor external development of the Community should be pursued at the expense of the other. It went on to affirm that the moment for opening negotiations should be known, or at least agreement should be reached on the nature of the event that would provoke the opening, so that a 'suspensive, concerted and known' condition, or trigger, would exist. Finally, the paper stated that Belgium was prepared to participate in a trade arrangement, but attached strict conditions for that acceptance: an arrangement must contribute effectively to enlargement and to European unity; it should conform as closely as possible with GATT; and it should distinguish between the states with a 'vocation' for membership, and other states. Moreover, applicants should be consulted on some aspects of the internal development of the EC, such as company law, and priority should be given to these aspects within the Community. This practice would help to avoid an increase in the divergence and even lead to convergence in the policies of the Six and Four.[85] Both the Italian and the Belgian work, therefore, took close account of British interests.

The Italian paper

Discussion of the first draft of the Italian paper confirmed this impression, despite French efforts to brand the meeting 'illegal'. It took the form of a declaration, concentrating on foreign policy and defence but providing for discussion of the possibilities of co-operation in other fields.[86] The British concluded that the broad agreement reached in Rome 'owed a great deal to the absence of the French' and that further success would 'depend on the French not coming'.[87] The British were not the only ones to fear that the French would find a way to veto further work in WEU: one junior Belgian even suggested that the whole operation be transferred to NATO in order to protect it from the French.[88]

Attention was momentarily diverted by a financial crisis in Europe. Economic integration had received a boost in July, when all industrial tariffs among the Six were abolished and the common external tariff came into force, eighteen months ahead of schedule.[89] However, in the autumn, expectations of an upward revaluation of the Deutschmark and a devaluation of the French franc led to enormous flows of capital into the FRG and reserve losses by France and Britain. Crossman records that, in what the chancellor described as a 'ludicrous piece of misjudgement', Wilson, Jenkins and Stewart told the German ambassador that, if there were another financial disaster Britain would no longer be able to maintain her troops in Germany.[90] Unsurprisingly, given the incredible nature of this threat and despite more orthodox pressure from France and Britain in a meeting in Bonn on 20-22 November, the Germans refused to revalue. A rescue package was put together for France, and Jenkins announced more stringent domestic economic controls.[91] The Dutch described the financial talks at which the Germans made their stand as 'the complete failure of Europe', but others saw the financial difficulties as underlining the need for monetary integration in Europe, and Jenkins later gained back some of his good reputation by calling for closer collaboration in this field.[92]

This acrimony spilled into discussion of the trade arrangement at a divided and confused Council of Ministers meeting in December, where Harmel presented the Belgian paper noted above. The Six were split over whether and how agriculture should be included in a proposal, as well as the possibility of a link with enlargement and conformity with GATT.[93] Real decision was therefore postponed again. In this chaotic atmosphere, work continued on the Italian paper. There was little optimism about the possibility of progress, and the Italians feared that the Germans, who had announced that they would circulate a paper of their own, were about to 'torpedo' their work.[94] Birrenbach, a CDU parliamentarian who was close to Kiesinger, bluntly stated that there could be no move on enlargement while de Gaulle was in power, warning that 'the Government of the Federal Republic had virtually no influence in Paris, and that anyone who believed that the key to French attitudes to our application lay in Bonn was very much mistaken.'[95] Birrenbach's comments were not encouraging: while favourable to British accession in the long term, they did not indicate that the Federal Republic was prepared to take a strong stance against France in the immediate future – quite the opposite.

The Italians collected comments on their paper on 12 December, in Paris, and Davignon said that Harmel would attend the Luxembourg WEU no matter what the French did.[96] The German 'paper' turned out not to be a separate initiative but general observations and comment on the Italian paper, substantially watering down the Italian approach.[97] Back on the tightrope, state secretary Frank confirmed that they had decided not to submit a rival paper because they did not want to give the impression that their position was basically different from that of the Italians. They would reconsider this position if, however, the Italian paper died at the Luxembourg WEU. Frank told the Italians that he had informed the French of Germany's support for the Italian paper, particularly the principle of obligatory consultation, and that the French had responded with two threats. First, they might refuse to attend the WEU meeting in Luxembourg, and second, de Gaulle might be tempted to wreak vengeance on the EEC.[98] Meanwhile, in new hints of a French change in tactics, de Gaulle let it be known that he was looking forward to a good talk with Soames in the New Year, and Tricot, the secretary-general at the *Elysée*, said that 'events were moving in such a way as to bring our two countries more closely together'.[99]

In these circumstances, there was little optimism about the prospects for co-operation.[100] The French position became increasingly hysterical: Beaumarchais, the director of political affairs in the *Quai*, complained that the WEU meeting in Rome had been a severe shock to France, and that de Lipowski had been so ill-treated by his colleagues that he would take some time to get over it. Consequently they would need more time to reflect on the Italian paper: he would be ready to give the Italians a considered opinion in the second half of January. The Italians concluded that it was essential to put the French in a position where they must either accept political consultation in WEU at the request of their partners, or veto it in the certain knowledge that such consultation would take place elsewhere, without them. The British agreed. The more intransigent the French showed themselves to be, the more determined other members of the Five became to secure collaboration amongst themselves.[101]

The second draft of the Italian paper thus stated the need for further integration in Europe, and explained that it was necessary to proceed outside the Treaty of Rome and other institutions. It went on to suggest that the Council should discuss '*l'intensification de la coopération prévue par le Traité de Bruxelles modifié.*' It then set out a detailed version of Harmel's original design, including: foreign policy consultation '*à Sept*'; discussion of the political aspects of defence with a view to forming a European caucus within NATO as well as practical co-operation, for example, on the production of armaments; regular stock-taking by the WEU Council, so that new integration could be forged where it became necessary, such as in monetary and technological policy; and finally, '*la composition du Conseil tiendra compte des questions à traiter.*'[102] It therefore envisaged British participation in significant areas of European integration.

Domestic debate

One such area was, of course, technology, and Stewart's anxiety that the UK's position on European technological co-operation would be exposed as 'essentially hollow and negative' was clear.[103] Efforts to regain a good reputation continued, with, for example, an agreement in November for the continuation of the OECD 'Dragon' project for a high temperature reactor.[104] The importance of a good British reputation in this area was again demonstrated when Medici suggested that Britain take an initiative in setting up a European technological centre for Europe.[105] However, Wilson's original ideas for a European technological institute were 'trumped' by a similar proposal involving the OECD.[106] Wilson was loath to give up on his idea, and ministers in the EURM sub-committee on European technological co-operation were uncertain that Britain could afford to participate in the proposed 'European Institute of Science and Technology'. In December the government therefore contributed £10,000 to the new Institute but reserved its decision on whether or not to join.[107] At the second (and last) MISC 224 meeting, in November, Stewart finally got his wish that the UK should show willing in other European projects in order to underline the Government's commitment to Europe. The committee, composed this time mainly of second-rank ministers, agreed that the UK should express willingness to enter into a joint project for the development of an information transfer satellite, using funds liberated by the proposed withdrawal from the ELDO project.[108] The money would thus not be 'saved', but re-directed into other European technological projects.

Agreement on technology did not prevent the domestic arguments about broader European policy within the 'pro-European' camp, first seen in October, from re-emerging. Wilson, encouraged by Palliser, again pressed for consideration of a British initiative on the lines of the Fouchet Plan.[109] Stewart's private secretary acknowledged that, in its promotion of harmonisation of foreign policy and defence, the Fouchet Plan did resemble the Harmel proposals. However, Barrington felt that it was 'much more cut and dried' than Harmel's ideas and would have less chance of securing general approval. Again, the Five had disagreed strongly with the French version of the Fouchet proposals in the early 1960s, and their alternative proposals, with their 'strong flavour of supranationality', would cause difficulties for Britain. Barrington concluded that pursuing the plan 'would tend to separate us from our friends in Europe.' Palliser and Wilson did not give up, with Palliser suggesting that Wilson could raise the idea in February when he visited Kiesinger, 'FCO *volens* or *nolens*.'[110]

Wilson personally wrote to Stewart, adamant that he must be in a position in early 1969 to develop new ideas to Kiesinger. These should not be called a new Fouchet plan, but should be differently devised and dressed up. Wilson wanted to find something to discuss with the Germans 'which would both keep up the momentum and at least be difficult for the French to turn down out of hand.'[111] Wilson was not opposing the Harmel proposals, but trying to think ahead and come up with ways to further his European policy should Harmel's initiative fail. Stewart sought advice within the FCO and then wrote to Wilson, 'confident that there is no real difference of opinion between us on all this.' He agreed that, should the Harmel proposals fail, the UK should be ready with new ideas, and suggested a proposal to the Six and any other interested European countries for a treaty providing for co-operation in foreign policy and defence. The FCO would work on a draft.[112]

A nuclear deal?

At the same time, Soames began to exert pressure from Paris for a re-opening of dialogue with France. He told Palliser that there had been 'some fundamental changes in the past year or more, both within France itself and in the balance of France's relations with other countries' and wanted to base European policy on working with the larger countries, rather than relying on the smaller ones. Soames wanted authority to probe de Gaulle when they met in early February, and Palliser commented that at 'the back of [Soames'] mind there is the hope that he may at some point be authorised to hint to de Gaulle at the possibility of a nuclear defence relationship between Britain and France.' Even if this subject were out of bounds, Soames felt that there were other issues that should be discussed and that the UK could show itself to be more helpfully disposed to France than hitherto. Palliser noted that Soames felt he had been sent to Paris with the aim of making real progress in European policy before the next election, and that he had in mind a meeting between de Gaulle and Wilson in the autumn of 1969. Palliser supported Soames' views, and Wilson too noted that he had 'a lot of sympathy with Soames' views'… 'apart from nuclear defence, which is out.'[113] Two French officials had hinted at the notion of a nuclear deal over the previous months, but these seven words, written in Wilson's green ink, show that Wilson did not at this time consider a nuclear deal with France to be a price worth paying for improved Anglo-French relations and, by extension, the opening of negotiations for entry into the Communities.[114] Whether or not the British discussed these issues with the US government is unknown.[115]

The FCO therefore set out the case for a British initiative in the eventuality of a French veto in WEU. Since, as will be seen in the next chapter, Britain and the Five did succeed in implementing foreign policy collaboration, this paper does not need to be discussed in too much detail. However, it is interesting to note that the FCO was thinking in terms of a 'treaty of union of states', preceded by a trial period to harmonise foreign and defence policies. In order to attract the others, the British proposal would have to make clear that the aim was for a 'federal, or at least confederal, Europe', with a clear position on institutions, direct elections to the European parliament, and some federal policies.[116] Wilson liked the FCO proposals, although he wanted them to be sufficiently 'unfederal' so as to attract France too.[117] As this planning continued, Wilson and Stewart agreed that no ministerial discussion was needed before Stewart went to the Luxembourg WEU.[118]

The superpowers, EFTA and the Commonwealth

Adding to this domestic debate, other events had the potential to disrupt British European policy. As elections approached in the US, Britain requested the usual public silence and private support for European policy from the Americans. Johnson's last 'State of the Union' speech said that the US must continue to support efforts towards regional co-operation, and that among those efforts, 'that of Western Europe has a special place in our concern. The only course that will permit Europe to play the great world role its resources permit, is to go forward to unity. America remains ready to work with a united Europe – as a partner, on the basis of equality.'[119] President-elect Nixon's position was not immediately apparent, although it was clear that he shared Wilson's disdain for ideas such as NAFTA.[120] The longstanding friendship between Palliser and Henry Kissinger allowed for exchanges between Wilson and Nixon before the latter's inauguration, and revealed that there would be no difference of approach between the old and new American administrations'.[121]

As usual, there was little direct contact with the Soviet Union on the subject of Britain's European policy. However, the ramifications of the

Soviet invasion of Czechoslovakia continued to echo, and an FCO paper entitled 'The Longer-Term Prospects for East-West relations after the Czech Crisis' concluded that, in order to 'prevent the Soviet Union picking off Western countries one by one the West must co-ordinate its policies as closely as possible.'[122] Conversely, the Soviets interpreted Britain's hostile attitude to the invasion of Czechoslovakia as an attempt to curry German favour. Ambassador Duncan Wilson's annual review for 1968 stated that 'West Germany is, in the Soviet book, gaining in political importance within Western Europe, and HMG is furthering this development. We are adopting a strong anti-Soviet line to please the Germans, and in the hope of securing their support against the French for entry in the Common Market.'[123] Of course, as was seen in the previous chapter, Wilson *did* use the invasion of Czechoslovakia to try and stiffen German support for British entry. British perceptions of the international situation and the Soviet Union's intentions in it thus reinforced existing European policy.

In EFTA, Crosland's efforts to defend Board of Trade territory led to a slightly bizarre correspondence with Stewart – bizarre because they agreed that the main focus of European policy should be the application and consequent 'skirmishes', but differed over how it should be presented to EFTA.[124] Swedish pressure for discussion of a trade arrangement without a clear link to entry met a sharp rejoinder from Wilson, who reminded prime minister Erlander that 'HMG's objectives in Europe are fundamentally political.'[125] All EFTA countries continued to follow events closely, and as progress proved slow, some continued to discuss the possibility of Nordic Union. The British were still convinced that the idea would 'not get off the ground.'[126] The fact remained that EFTA had nothing to offer the UK that was more attractive than membership of the EC.

The same was true of the Commonwealth, where attention was focused on the conference of Commonwealth prime ministers in January 1969 in London. Prior to that meeting, the Jamaican high commissioner wondered if the WEU proposals would affect his country's interests, but his was a lone voice.[127] In Stewart's conference speech on 'World Situation and Trends', he tried to present British European policy as being in Commonwealth interests. He said that

> a united Western Europe would be much stronger to check dangers and ensure stability; this would be of benefit to the world as a whole and to the developing world in particular. A prosperous and united Europe would also be able to help developing countries much more

than a divided Europe and it would be the British Government's intention to see that Europe was outward looking.[128]

Commonwealth leaders acknowledged Britain's right 'as a sovereign nation' to enter the EC, and all 'that they asked of Britain was...that they should be mindful of the effects of their actions on high-cost producers who for centuries had been dependent on protective shelter in the British market.' They generally welcomed the British assurance that they would consult members of the Commonwealth Sugar Agreement if they entered the EC before 1974, and hoped that the British would help to make the Community more outward looking. The communiqué 'reiterated the importance of continuing close consultation by the British Government with Commonwealth Governments in regard to developments of interest to them concerning the British application for entry into the EEC.'[129] The contrast with 1962, when the British guaranteed to protect certain Commonwealth interests, could not be clearer: only consultation was on offer in 1969. Stewart elaborated the government's position in a speech to a small Labour Party group towards the end of January. He said that those who thought EEC membership was incompatible with the continuing commitments to the Commonwealth failed to understand the nature of the latter. It was not a political union, military alliance or economic union.

> The Government's decision to join the EEC does not mean that we are turning away from the Commonwealth or from the world outside Europe. Our links with other members of the Commonwealth will help us to bring a new breadth of vision to Europe and ensure that European unity will not be a narrow, inward-looking concept.

Stewart concluded that Europe would then be able to work more effectively for détente and for solutions to the problems of the developing world, all of which were important to the Commonwealth.[130] The abolition of the Commonwealth Office on 18 October demonstrated more than anything else the institution's place in British policy.[131] Like EFTA, the Commonwealth was not to be an obstacle to British admission to the Communities.

Conclusions
Work on the Italian paper continued throughout and after the Commonwealth meeting, with Robinson and Stewart doggedly defending British interests.[132] Furthermore, while it might seem that attention was distracted, during these months, from the 'citadel' itself, the British

application was not forgotten. As has been seen, the British continually referred to it as the main aim of their European policy. The Queen's speech at the opening of parliament stated that HMG would 'maintain their application for membership of the European Communities and will promote other measures of co-operation in keeping with this.'[133] In his Guildhall speech on 11 November, as the Harmel proposals were beginning to draw the Germans away from France, Wilson was confident enough in his European policy that he did not need to 'dwell on this theme tonight.'

> No words of mine could add to our determination, not only as a government or Parliament, but as a trading country and a people, to stand firm in support of that application. To be neither disheartened by obstruction, nor distracted by plausible *soi-disant* alternatives or attractive and tempting blind allies. Our purpose is clear, known and respected.[134]

As a result of this clear British purpose, the Five continued to champion British membership. Although Stewart complained to his diary on new year's day that '[n]one of the difficult problems [in which he included Europe] seem any nearer solution', real steps had been taken towards meaningful co-operation between Britain and five of the Community states. Stewart's own determination and diplomacy, during a period of considerable confusion, had been essential to that progress.[135] While the domestic debate gives interesting indications of Wilson's and others' views on the future path of European integration, it was almost immediately cut off in February when president de Gaulle made certain proposals of his own to the British ambassador in Paris, Christopher Soames.

6

February – April 1969: the 'Soames affair' and its aftermath

Playing poker with the General, though fascinating, is not always a
profitable enterprise.[1]

In February 1969 collaboration between Britain and the Five was
interrupted, first by what became known as the 'Soames affair'; and
second, by de Gaulle's resignation. On one hand, Wilson finally succeeded
in isolating France, bringing Germany around to consistent support of the
UK, and participating in real, albeit extra-treaty, European co-operation
on foreign policy in WEU. On the other hand, de Gaulle's resignation
immediately eclipsed the significance of these developments, moving the
focus to the possibility of the removal of the French veto. The three
months from February also saw WEU meetings, Wilson's visit to Bonn,
Nixon's European tour, a Franco-German summit and an Italian state
visit to Britain. Wilson's navigation of this diplomatic minefield was
skilful, and this chapter argues that Wilson's European policy, in the
context of de Gaulle's continuation in office until April, showed real signs
of success.

In February, Wilson and Stewart were considering their next steps in
Europe. They agreed on the need to go on 'investing the citadel', co-
operating with Monnet's Action Committee to prepare the reports noted
above. Meanwhile, they decided to welcome the forthcoming Italian
paper on foreign policy co-operation in WEU, and agreed that a joint
Anglo-German Declaration, to be issued at the end of Wilson's visit to

Bonn, would be useful. There was no need for ministerial discussion before Wilson went to Bonn.[2]

The General's proposals

The British suspected towards the end of 1968 that the French were planning a change of policy, and hoped that the *entente* between the two countries was becoming increasingly *cordiale*. In this context, Soames met de Gaulle on 4 February. The French president began by 'playing the old record about our pro-American stance'. However, he

> then showed that his purpose was to suggest that the British and French governments might have far-reaching bilateral talks covering economic, monetary, political and defence matters to see whether we now saw things sufficiently in common to co-operate "in a way which our two countries have never done before".[3]

Initially de Gaulle presented 'word for word' the same opinions on Anglo-European and Anglo-American relations that he had expressed in his 1962 talks with Macmillan, in 1965 and 1966 with Wilson, and in 1968 with Soames' predecessor, Reilly. When Soames tried to show that the British position had evolved, de Gaulle responded that 'the fact remained that whereas France had succeeded in achieving a totally independent position this was not so in the case of either Germany or Italy or of the Netherlands, and certainly not of the United Kingdom.' The 'whole essence' of a 'European entity' must be 'an independent position in world terms', and he was not convinced that Britain could accept this situation. Replying to a question from Soames, de Gaulle said that independence did not require Britain to leave NATO, but once it was built, there would be no need for NATO as such 'with its American dominance and command structure.'[4]

De Gaulle continued that he had played no part in the creation of the Common Market, and had no particular faith in it. The changes resulting from enlargement 'would not therefore necessarily be any bad thing.' While the British seemed to have their hearts set on joining the Community, he would like to see it change 'into a looser form of free trade association with arrangements by each country to exchange agricultural produce.' He would gladly talk to HMG about this idea, but was also 'anxious to have political discussions with us.' He thought there should be

> a large European economic association, but with a smaller inner council of a European political association consisting of France and

Britain, Germany and Italy. But it was necessary first to find out whether France and Britain saw things sufficiently in common, because this was the key to any such political association.

He wanted to build a 'specifically Franco-British bond', based on 'a genuine desire to build something in Europe together.' Talks should be 'a positive attempt to mend our relationships with a view to arriving at a point where we could co-operate in a European sense.' He would therefore like to see a gesture by the British government suggesting that such talks would take place, which he would then welcome. Pressed by Soames, de Gaulle did not rule out the possibility that he himself might issue an invitation to bilateral talks, but he must first know whether or not it would interest the British. He hoped that 'his proposition would be secret until we decide to have talks. If we did decide to do so, the fact would then of course be public.' He hoped to meet Wilson soon to discuss the future of Europe.[5] All the factors that would contribute to the resulting controversy are present in this account: the replacement of the EC by a looser association and disappearance of NATO, the creation of a political 'inner council' and the request for secrecy.

The British reaction
From the ambassador to Wilson himself, the British were unsure how to react. When de Gaulle began, Soames thought that there was nothing new in his 'classic lecture on our pro-American position.' As the conversation went on, however, he 'had the impression that he was taking a line different from the one in the records of his talks with British leaders between 1961 and 1968. It was closer to the abortive proposals he made to Mr Churchill in Paris in November 1944 for a far-reaching Anglo-French entente.' Given this powerful assessment, and despite his back-pedalling later, Soames must therefore bear some responsibility for the furore that was about to erupt. De Gaulle's approach, Soames theorised, could be purely tactical, aimed partly at undermining German resolve to fight for British admission to the EC. On the other hand, the general might have been sincere: he had had the ideas in mind at the end of the war. His awareness of the growing strength of Germany might be inclining him to 'look to the West.'

Soames' uncertainty of the General's intentions led him to request authority only to probe the French government for elaboration, though he also intended to make the point that the government's application to the EC stood. They would only consider a new proposal if all six member states agreed to replace the Treaty of Rome with a new form of economic association including all of them. HMG would not put themselves in the position of appearing to want to break up the Community while the Five still saw it as the basis for building Europe. Moreover, it should be made clear that the initiative for new talks came from France. Soames concluded that de Gaulle had made the proposals with an open mind: de Lipowski had told him that they should be taken seriously.[6] Soames' desire to seek more information before making recommendations is understandable, but there is no recognition in his initial telegrams of the need for haste dictated by Wilson's forthcoming visit to Kiesinger, less than a week later.

Palliser felt that de Gaulle had said 'nothing new on Britain and EEC' but that the very act of making the proposals was something new. Like Soames, he thought that de Gaulle made the proposals with an open mind, and with both tactical and substantive objectives in mind. He advised Wilson not to turn de Gaulle down flat. Instead the government should carefully consider if it might be useful to move cautiously down the road that the general was indicating, and whether other European governments should be informed. In any case, Soames should be given authority to probe Debré further. Wilson, in contrast, was immediately suspicious of the General's motives, asking,

> [i]s this connected to Debré's invite to Chancellor [to visit Paris]? Or trying to put us off taking too hard (ie anti-French) line in Bonn? Or getting ready to say to Pres[ident] Nixon he offered this and we rejected/dithered? Certainly we [should] follow up – and given encouragement it is getting time for me to see him again.[7]

Stewart, in Luxembourg for the WEU meeting described below, twice ordered Soames to wait before meeting Debré so that he could talk to Wilson. When Soames replied that Debré had already asked to see him two days later, the pressure was on the British government to decide what to do.[8] Stewart first stressed that the matter must not leak.[9] He then set out two questions for Wilson. 'First, what sort of relationship can we have with a man whose concept of Europe and Europe's relations with the United States is so different from our own? Secondly, what can de Gaulle's motive be in making this offer to us: and why at this particular moment?' Stewart's distrust of de Gaulle was clear: he told Wilson to remember that de Gaulle had always been 'implacably opposed' to British interests and objectives in Europe and elsewhere. Stewart was sceptical of a change of heart: the general had given no sign of readiness to change his position on the basic issues. He might be trying to deter a new British initiative. The problem was that de Gaulle could use either a rejection or an acceptance of his offer of talks to harm British interests. If the offer were refused, he could say that he offered to try to settle differences with

Britain but was turned down, proving that Britain was not yet ready for Europe. If on the other hand the offer were accepted, he would be able to represent to the Five British readiness to do a deal with the French and to build something new in place of the Communities. Following de Gaulle would mean foregoing the advantages of the multilateral approach, which would be particularly costly since the differences with France were not over bilateral issues but derived from fundamentally different approaches to problems that affected other countries as well. Stewart concluded that it would be dangerous to make any positive response to de Gaulle: his terms were not a basis for discussion, or even for probing his intentions further. Indeed, the UK should go on the record as rejecting them. Stewart added that de Gaulle was 'on the way out' and it was not a good time to start something new with him, while the reasons why other Frenchmen might want better relations with the UK would only get stronger. Wilson should therefore tell Kiesinger of the approach, suggesting that they try to deal with de Gaulle together. Asking Kiesinger for his advice on how to handle 'this dangerous and out-dated French approach to world problems' would avoid the risk of de Gaulle presenting the British refusal to the Five in his own terms. No instructions should be sent to Soames until Wilson returned from Bonn.[10] A long FCO paper came to the same conclusions and added to the urgency by suggesting that the French might leak the proposals themselves.[11] Wilson 'greatly welcomed this advice and he particularly welcome[d] the conclusion...that [he] should speak to Kiesinger about this in the terms which the Foreign Secretary proposes.' Wilson's own initial reactions coincided closely with Stewart's, he said, 'particularly the possibility that de Gaulle may be hoping to condition Kiesinger and even Nixon. What we must clearly avoid is falling into a trap.'[12]

The situation became even more confused after a conversation between Chalfont and de Lipowski. Professing to be an Anglophile, de Lipowski said he thought de Gaulle was working towards the idea of a trade arrangement 'as a form of pre-entry', but that such an offer would be conditional on readiness by the British government to enter into serious high-level bilateral talks with France, mainly on the political structure of Europe and defence. France and Britain, the only countries with nuclear weapons, were the two powers in Europe that mattered. France had divorced its nuclear capacity entirely from that of the US.

> The time had come for us to do the same and to discuss seriously the possibility of nuclear weapons co-operation with France. This would not involve the transfer of hardware, but an exchange of technical knowledge together with agreement on targeting and

nuclear contingency planning. Why not...an Anglo-French Nuclear Planning Group? Nassau had been a disaster for Anglo-French relations and for Europe. There was now a chance to retrieve the position.

De Lipowski concluded that de Gaulle was going through a fundamental reappraisal of his foreign policy. A reluctant Chalfont confined himself to hoping that any new policies would allow relations to be improved and developed.[13] Although de Lipowski stressed that he was speaking privately, this conversation was the highest-level, officially-recorded, bilateral discussion during the second application of the possibility of nuclear collaboration. As far as can be told from the official record, Wilson did not consider it: the risks of making such an approach were too great. At the same time, the pro-active ambassador in Rome, Shuckburgh, wrote to warn that there must be no question of dealing with Paris behind the backs of the Italians. He requested authority to tell the new Italian foreign minister, Pietro Nenni, of de Gaulle's approach before any action was taken with Debré, thereby increasing pressure on the government to make a decision on how to handle the situation.[14]

The Luxembourg WEU Council

Meanwhile, the foreign ministers met in Luxembourg for the WEU Council to discuss the Italian paper on political co-operation. Gaston Thorn, Luxembourg's new foreign minister, reported that France had effectively told the Five on 1 February that 'the children had now gone far enough'.[15] De Lipowski, while hinting that France might agree to the need for improved political consultations within WEU, had instructions not to participate in a discussion or vote on the Italian paper, and the Germans were unwilling to go further than the French.[16]

No one expected a dramatic result in Luxembourg, and the success there was therefore a surprise.[17] The meeting lasted over six hours, partly because of French attempts to 'bog matters down in procedural discussion', but the Five held together in support of foreign policy co-operation.[18] Nenni introduced his paper, saying that WEU could make a real contribution to European integration. There followed a long and acrimonious discussion, in which Stewart proposed a first meeting to discuss the Middle East, and where the isolation of the French became increasingly apparent.[19] Finally, Thorn summed up as follows.

Seven Delegations expressed their resolve to improve consultations in the matter of foreign policy within WEU. They were unanimously of the opinion that a procedure should be devised enabling a meeting of Member States to be convened more rapidly in an emergency. They decided unanimously that in certain cases the Council could meet in more restricted session to ensure secrecy for their discussions. In addition, the Benelux Governments decided, in the Council, that before taking any decision on a list of foreign policy questions they will consult with their WEU partners…to further the adoption of positions agreed and harmonised to the fullest possible extent. The United Kingdom, Italian and German delegations agreed with this proposal. The French Delegation took note and reserved its position on all matters of substance and procedure arising from the Benelux proposal. The French Delegation will make its views known not later than the next Ministerial meeting.[20]

The French at first implied that there had been no acute conflict.[21] In contrast, Stewart told cabinet that the meeting had both emphasised French isolation and 'established that our not being members of [EEC] did not exclude us from consultation with those EEC powers who wished to consult with us, and that the EEC was not the only forum for consultation.'[22] This six-one division in WEU would soon become more apparent.

After the meeting, Stewart and Nenni discussed tactics. Stewart thought they ought to begin consultation immediately. Nenni expected Brandt to take an increasingly firm position, partly for electoral reasons (federal German elections were scheduled for the autumn). Meanwhile, although he was not prepared to upset the Common Market, Italy would not support any decision that served French interests, including those on agriculture, as long as France continued the veto. When President Saragat visited London in April there should be a joint announcement of all that the British and Italians were doing to show that they 'saw eye to eye on the future of Europe.' Stewart agreed.[23]

Divided counsel

In this context, of having received de Gaulle's proposals but uncertain of their meaning, and of a small but real step towards political co-operation with the Five being taken in WEU, Stewart tried to advise Wilson. He wrote that 'unless we can show progress in 1969/70 a great historical chance may have been lost', a point that Wilson appreciated. In order, Stewart went on, both to maintain the Atlantic Alliance and western cohesion created since 1948, and to 'make substantial steps forward', the UK would have to perform a difficult balancing act. He thought France would 'fight all the way against any move to bring Britain into European consultations.' It was more important to get relations with the FRG on to 'a basis of genuine confidence'. Germany also might be brought to agree that the best way to avoid substantial American troop withdrawals and US pressure for larger European contributions to NATO was through closer European co-operation on defence. In turn, Wilson should discuss with Nixon the ways in which the US could help. These might include 'conventional diplomatic support, generous attitudes with regard to our bilateral agreements on nuclear and other questions which at present tend to inhibit our co-operation with Europe, and the possibility of a similar linkage with any measures that are taken for reform of the international financial system.'[24] Clearly, Stewart increasingly perceived an interconnectedness among these different areas of foreign policy: the focus, however, remained firmly on Europe.

In this uncertain atmosphere, Soames met with Debré. He had taken the precaution of having the French agree his record of his original talk with de Gaulle, and Debré confirmed that 'there was nothing in it with which we disagree.' Debré said de Gaulle thought it would be a good idea to have bilateral talks on how the British and French saw the future economic structure of Europe. Debré himself felt that 'it was not possible for the Treaty of Rome to function realistically if we [the British] and our friends were to join'. There should also be bilateral talks on the question of future political development, 'in the strictest secrecy until we knew whether or not we could see the seeds of agreement.' Soames asked if it was a genuine attempt to resolve differences, and Debré replied that it was in French interests to reach an accord with Britain. Soames concluded that the idea for bilateral talks to improve Anglo-French relations had originally been Debré's, and that he himself should return to London for consultations before Wilson went to Bonn.[25]

Reading Soames' report, Palliser began to share the worries expressed by Wilson and Stewart. Nevertheless, he still felt that the government should consider the French offer. Stewart's hard line overlooked the fact that 'European unity is meaningless unless all three of the big powers ie Britain and France and Germany form part of it', and Palliser could not see how they could possibly reject talks.[26] In contrast, Shuckburgh in Rome argued that de Gaulle's move was confirmation that British European policy was working: the general was sufficiently worried about the effects of British persistence to have launched a major initiative to try and relieve the pressure. Again, if the Italians thought that the British condoned any element of de Gaulle's foreign policy, 'it would be the end of Italian confidence in HMG.' Shuckburgh urged Stewart not to budge from the positions taken up. Wilson commented that this advice was '[q]uite good.'[27]

In the context of this contradictory counsel Wilson and Stewart again met to discuss tactics. They agreed that 'in the spirit of consultation' just agreed at WEU, it would be desirable to inform Kiesinger and the governments of the Five of the French approach and to tell the French that this action was being taken. They would tell Kiesinger that they would not return a flat negative to the French, but that any talks would be in consultation with the Germans and others, and that they would not accept de Gaulle's approach to NATO and alteration to the EEC. When Soames was informed that Wilson intended to tell Kiesinger all, he was 'very upset.' He felt that his role as ambassador was being undermined, and said that telling the Germans would 'kill the French approach dead at the outset'. The government had taken from his original telegram 'a too clear-cut and too dramatic picture of his talk with de Gaulle, which had differed from that with Debré. The latter had talked of Britain joining the EC, seeing political discussions as taking place in parallel, and had shown discomfort at some of the general's views. The FCO nevertheless recommended that Wilson should tell Kiesinger of de Gaulle's approach on 12 February, the first day of his visit to Bonn. He should say that he found it 'interesting and far-reaching' but that he must consult his partners, as agreed in WEU. He should stress that he still wanted to join the EC, and that if de Gaulle preferred some other approach, it was up to him to convince us (Palliser added 'and the Five'). The UK did not agree with de Gaulle's views on NATO, the US or the concept of a four-power European political directorate. The rest of the Five and the US should be informed the same day, and France should be told of Wilson's actions either that evening or the following morning.[28] The FCO position was clear.

In protest, Soames telegrammed to Stewart, urging him to reconsider what he described as 'a betrayal of General de Gaulle's confidence.' He suggested that Wilson reveal only that de Gaulle had made his usual comments on the US and on the radical changes to the Common Market if Britain joined, and had suggested bilateral talks. Wilson should say that he proposed to probe further through diplomatic channels, and would keep the Germans informed. Soames wanted to tell Debré that Wilson was interested in talks and that he would inform Kiesinger and the rest of the Five on the lines outlined above. That way they would avoid the risk of France being able to exploit the proposals or accuse the UK of double-crossing them by betraying the General's confidence.[29] Palliser warned that Soames was being treated too harshly and might resign. Wilson should consider very carefully whether he really wished to speak as fully to Kiesinger and the rest of the Five and, if he did, whether his own relationship with de Gaulle could stand the strain.[30] As the debate went on, Wilson left for Bonn.

Stewart did not agree with Soames' and Palliser's position at all. If Wilson gave Kiesinger only a partial account, he or his staff would surely elicit the rest from the British advisers or the French. He recommended that Wilson give a fairly full account, and did not want Debré to have advance warning.[31] The speaking note prepared for Wilson's talks with Kiesinger reflected almost word for word Soames' original telegrams of 4-5 February.[32] Wilson hesitated, telling Soames that he would 'test the atmosphere in Bonn' and consult again with Stewart before deciding what to do.[33] He told Stewart that his object in Bonn would be to turn the four-two combination in Europe into a five-one combination, and that he would open by reminding Kiesinger that HMG was one hundred per cent determined to get into the EEC. Stewart, however, reiterated that the 'more I have thought about this issue…the more convinced I have become that you should not leave Bonn without telling Kiesinger the whole story.' The risks that the French would leak and that the Five would see any British consideration of de Gaulle's ideas as a breach of confidence were too great. Soames should tell Debré that Wilson accepted the idea of bilateral talks only on the basis of current British policy, and tell him that he was informing Kiesinger of the general's proposals.[34]

Stewart clearly expected Wilson to follow his advice, and telegrams were sent to Community posts instructing ambassadors to prepare to tell their host governments about the 'Soames affair'.[35] He was correct: Wilson telegrammed on 12 February to say that 'I intend to put Kiesinger fully in the picture about what de Gaulle has said to Soames…on the condition that the implications of the communication are pressed to their logical conclusion.' In other words, if Kiesinger did not react 'in the right way', Wilson wanted both the original proposals (showing de Gaulle's disloyalty to the EC) and Kiesinger's 'unsatisfactory reaction' (showing his continued subservience to de Gaulle) to be made public.[36] It is important to note that Wilson took this decision himself, choosing between different strategies suggested by Soames, Palliser and Stewart. His account in *The Labour Government*, in which he blamed the FCO for effectively forcing him to tell Kiesinger about de Gaulle's proposals, is therefore deeply misleading – as Ziegler, his official biographer, acknowledges.[37]

Wilson's meeting with Kiesinger

Wilson therefore reviewed the Soames-de Gaulle talk with Kiesinger 'as per the telegrams', and outlined the British response. Kiesinger was surprised. While de Gaulle had often said that British entry would change the Communities, he had never given as his objective that they should disappear. Kiesinger concluded that he 'would welcome talks between Britain and France, provided that there was first agreement between Britain and the Five on the maintenance and strengthening of NATO, on the development of the EEC and on its enlargement to include Britain.' He agreed with Wilson that the British and Germans should exchange information and co-ordinate their views, and undertook to keep Wilson informed of his own talks with de Gaulle. Germany would not accept a free trade area and four-power directorate: it would be very dangerous if the EC were to be undermined. Instead, 'we should all show patience and determination to see Britain as a member of the EEC.' Wilson took the opportunity gently to reprimand Kiesinger for siding with France over the trade arrangement proposals, arguing that there 'was no point in taking a side road which led nowhere.'[38] Wilson therefore used the apparent evidence of de Gaulle's treachery to push the Germans towards greater support of the principal British aim, admission into the EC, and of co-operation outside the Treaties. 'Her Majesty's Government', Wilson said, 'intended to advance their candidature with all the means in their power.'[39]

Kiesinger's response indicated that Wilson had chosen the correct course: Sir Denis Greenhill, the senior FCO official to accompany Wilson to Bonn, described the German chancellor as 'obviously shaken'.[40] The other four member states were informed of the whole affair on the same day that Wilson spoke to Kiesinger, and the Commission the following day. Ambassadors were instructed to say that Soames would seek an interview with Debré that evening to say that HMG regarded the proposals as significant and far-reaching, but that it was too much to expect Wilson not to say anything to his partners when he was in Bonn, in the post-Luxembourg situation. HMG rejected de Gaulle's ideas about NATO and the EC, but were willing to have bilateral discussions, provided that their partners were kept in the picture.[41] The Italians were actually informed *before* Soames saw Debré.[42] In general, the Four felt that the British had responded correctly to de Gaulle's proposals, appreciated being informed and wondered at de Gaulle's motives.[43]

In a move almost designed to infuriate the French further, and in the knowledge that Nixon was soon to visit Paris, the British also informed the Americans of the 'Soames affair'. Although they were sworn to secrecy, efforts at discretion were destroyed when the Italians, who asked specifically who had been told, were informed that the Americans knew.[44] Moreover, the FCO had begun to prepare for the possibility of a French leak on 12 February, when comments by the Swedish ambassador in London indicated to them that the French were already up to something, perhaps by stirring up trouble for Britain in EFTA.[45] Later EFTA ministers *were* annoyed not to have been informed about the 'Soames affair' at the same time as WEU members, and showed great interest in the matter (as they did in the increased co-operation in WEU).[46]

Meanwhile, Wilson was still in Bonn. Brandt warned him that de Gaulle would be 'deeply resentful' that the British had revealed the content of the talk, but recognised the force of Wilson's argument that he would be left in a difficult position if Kiesinger heard of the proposal and realised that Wilson had kept it from him. They speculated about de Gaulle's motives, concluding that it was extremely important to continue the closest consultation. Palliser, who was keeping the record, noted 'a strong current of hostility on Herr Brandt's part towards France and the General, such as had also been perceptible in Dr Kiesinger's comments. This was patent and obviously sincere.' While Brandt did not see anything particularly new in de Gaulle's proposals, he expressed himself 'strongly' about German difficulties in dealing with him.[47] Strauss, the finance minister, indicated that while Kiesinger would not be the instrument of expressing the German position to de Gaulle in 'lethal terms', Germany would eventually bring it home to the Frenchman.[48] Some Germans, at least, had been pushed past breaking point.

The Anglo-German declaration issued that evening affirmed the two countries' 'determination to go forward in partnership.' It went on to say that

[t]he security and prosperity of Europe demands unity: and only in unity can Europe exert her rightful and beneficial influence in the world. For both our countries a united Europe is inconceivable without Britain.

The British Government maintain their application to join the European Communities. Both Governments pledge themselves to further this aim. They both agree to work out together with other European Governments, the means by which a new impetus can be given to the political unity of Europe.

Concluding with a reference to the 'continuation and strengthening of the Atlantic Alliance', the declaration was a powerful reaffirmation of Anglo-German entente.[49] Wilson hoped to be able to use it to ensure a German commitment that they would keep Britain informed of any developments in the EC which could affect British interests as potential members: 'this should enable us to have something of a say in the deliberations on these matters that take place within the EEC.'[50] Wilson did 'not like guff for guff's sake', Palliser noted, so that the declaration 'represent[ed] a useful step forward.'[51] Wilson's handling of the 'Soames affair' therefore succeeded in drawing the Five closer together in support of the British position. Relations with France, in contrast, descended to icy depths. Instructions were sent to Paris on the evening of 12 February.[52] However, by the time Soames received them it was too late to see Debré, and instead he told Alphand, who 'reacted badly', fearing that the news would 'deeply anger' both de Gaulle and Debré.[53] When Debré met Jenkins to discuss international monetary matters, he was distressed that Wilson had seen fit to discuss the affair with Kiesinger, but said that he would give the matter more thought, and talk to Soames again in a few days.[54] Although the British were still trying to handle the matter discreetly, indications that it would soon leak catalysed the FCO to send a detailed account to EFTA, Commonwealth and other missions.[55]

Consultation in WEU
In the midst of these diplomatic manoeuvres and before the extent of the French reaction became clear, the WEU meeting that had been proposed by Stewart in Luxembourg went ahead. On 14 February the PRs met in London to discuss the Middle East.[56] The French did not attend and tabled a protest, arguing that *'cette réunion, qui c'est tenue en violation des règles statutaires, ne peut être consideré comme une réunion du Conseil de notre organisation'*. Shortly afterwards they announced a boycott of WEU activities.[57] The French boycott created great German anxiety, with Kiesinger moving away from the strong stance in favour of co-operation with Britain that had been taken by Brandt in Luxembourg.[58]

Cabinet and the leaking of the 'Soames affair'
When Stewart and Wilson first learned of de Gaulle's proposals, they had agreed that there was no need for consultation among ministers before Wilson's trip to Bonn. A paper was finally sent to OPD (apart from Wilson and Stewart, it was composed of Crossman, Healey, Thomson, Jenkins, Callaghan, Peart and Lord Shackleton) on 12 February, the day Wilson talked to Kiesinger. Even then the committee did not discuss the matter.[59] During the trauma over WEU, however, evidence of leaks about the 'Soames affair' surfaced in Paris, and the French began to present their own interpretation of de Gaulle's remarks.[60]

Stewart therefore gave a detailed description of the 'Soames affair' to cabinet on 20 February. He described the consultation that had been occurring without France in WEU, depicting the somewhat 'confused' German attitude to such actions. The discussion as recorded in the official minutes was mostly favourable to British actions regarding de Gaulle's proposals, the decision to inform the Germans and the continuing collaboration with the Five; Wilson then recounted his visit to Bonn.[61]

Castle's comments on this meeting suggest that Wilson had returned to a former tactic for ensuring compliance: boredom. She noted that 'we were all interested in the Soames conversations with de Gaulle but Michael's report dragged on and on with Harold interjecting gossip about his visit to Bonn. Really, under Harold, these discussions are more like conversations than Cabinet meetings.'[62] Crossman concurred: 'I must admit that I hardly listened to this item. As Michael Stewart had not suggested that the de Gaulle subject was particularly important and had preceded it with four other items, with his boringly dull voice drilling through your head, on and on for half an hour, I didn't really notice.'[63] Clearly, cabinet did not immediately grasp the importance of the 'Soames affair.'

As it leaked into the media, however, ministers could no longer 'hardly listen.' Telegrams poured in with requests for information, comments on the British and French versions of events, and replies to the FCO's enquiry as to where would be the best place to undertake a 'corrective leak' should the French leak 'in a slanted manner.'[64] On 21 February it seemed to be clear that the French had leaked: an article in *Figaro* reported a conversation between Soames and de Gaulle, accusing Britain of giving a 'sensational version misrepresenting Mr Soames' audience' to the Five.[65] An official French government statement that evening confirmed that Soames and de Gaulle had met, but denied that the president had expressed different opinions from those that had been 'publicly and steadfastly laid down by him in recent years.' It repeated that enlargement would change the nature of the European Communities, and that Europe could only take shape on the political level when it was independent.[66] The British at first responded unofficially, arranging a leak through the Italian newspaper *Messagero*, and stressing that their record of the talk had been agreed with de Gaulle's office.[67] In view of 'further leaks from Paris', however, the FCO decided to give the press in London an unattributable account, and the head of News Department held a briefing.[68] In truth it is impossible to discover who had leaked first: as the telegrams demonstrate, so many people knew about it and it was being discussed in so many different fora that the first leak could have come from one or more of at least twenty countries. Castle commented aptly in her diary: 'I can't make out what's happening.'[69]

On 22 February, the *Quai* issued an addition to their official statement, to the effect that de Gaulle had not proposed a political directorate: 'the idea of a directorate of four imposing its will on the small countries of Europe is so manifestly contrary to everything which the French Government have always expressed on the necessary independence of each people that it does not even warrant a denial.'[70] (One wonders, therefore, why a denial was issued). Debré repeated the French version on the radio, concluding, as always, that 'the present economic and financial condition of Britain did not permit her pure and simple membership of the [EC] as it exists at the moment to be envisaged.'[71] Soames finally met Debré that evening – ten days after Wilson had originally informed Kiesinger in Bonn. The French foreign minister expressed his great personal sadness at the situation. Both men knew, he said, that Soames had come to Paris to mend fences. Up until their own conversation on 8 February, he understood all that had happened – even that Wilson might have found it 'right and necessary' to tell Kiesinger something of the conversation. But he did not understand the *'diffusion, déformation et sensationalisme'* that had followed. Soames said Wilson had thought it right and necessary to tell not only Kiesinger, but also their other friends, since so much of what de Gaulle had said touched on their interests. Moreover, he had checked his record of the talk with the *Elysée* – on the same day that he had told Alphand that the British government accepted the offer of talks, subject to certain conditions. Debré's reply made clear the glacial nature of Anglo French relations. 'How could we possibly talk?' he said. 'The book had been opened in good faith on 4 February and it had been closed on 22 February.'[72]

Anglo-French relations
The Anglo-French relationship descended into farce. On 24 February, Alphand appeared to acknowledge that Soames' record of the talk had been agreed by the *Elysée* – or at least that officials had not said that there was anything wrong with it. On the very same day, however, the *Quai* issued a formal protest to Soames, which insisted that his account *'n'a reçu, à aucun moment, sous aucune forme, l'approbation ni du sécretariat général de la présidence de la République, ni du Ministère des Affaires Étrangères.'* Alphand said that the protest was required because of errors in the British press, which had said that Tricot had initialled Soames' record (he had not), that the confirmation of the record had come direct from the *Elysée* (it had come via Debré), and that Soames had tried to see Debré on the evening of 12 February (instead he had sought Alphand). Putting the record straight on these matters might, Soames felt, help to calm the atmosphere. Soames added, however, that 'in [his] judgement the French government [were] not telling the truth and they know it.'[73]

In this context, Stewart informed Debré that the British government had had no intention of exaggerating or misrepresenting de Gaulle's views, and indeed, had not. He was willing to show the government's instructions to ambassadors to Debré if necessary. He went on to accept de Gaulle's initial invitation to bilateral talks, saying that he knew that 'we start with serious differences between us but I do not see why we should not come, together with our partners, to a common view on the structure, purpose, and future of Europe.'[74] He resisted domestic attempts to get him to associate himself with the more critical remarks about de Gaulle, and repeatedly expressed British willingness to talk to the French.[75] This conciliatory attitude may have had some effect: when Chalfont met ambassador de Courcel the latter gave the impression that there had been a 'genuine and serious misunderstanding' rather than anything malicious. De Courcel said that Wilson's actions in communicating the substance of the talks to others without giving the French prior warning and the British leaks to the press were the cause of French anger. When Chalfont pointed out that the first leaks had appeared in the French paper *Figaro*, de Courcel said he could only assume that they had come from WEU, 'a notably incontinent organisation'. It would be difficult to retrieve the situation, but de Courcel hoped that they would stay closely in touch and that the whole affair would soon be resolved.[76]

Soames continued to try and minimise the damage to Anglo-French relations, again advising Stewart not to take a sensationalist line.[77] The French appeared to take a similar path, playing the 'whole affair down rather than up' with the Five, perhaps in the knowledge that they had not shown themselves to be very 'European' and needed to regain face. Interestingly, the Germans provided the UK with an account of Debré's first meeting with the ambassadors of the Five in Paris, despite an appeal from the French foreign minister for Franco-German solidarity, suggesting that they put increased priority on relations with Britain in the aftermath of the general's proposals.[78] On the other hand, notes exchanged between the British and French governments indicated that it would take some time to rebuild relations.[79]

Cabinet

In this situation, Stewart reported to cabinet again, stressing that both governments were anxious to 'take the heat out of the situation.' He emphasised that the action taken by the UK was justified by events, and that comment in other countries appeared to bear this out. This outcome made it all the more important to 'enhance the importance' of WEU and to 'make it into the forum of European consultation which it had originally been intended to be.' As long as Britain was not a member, he went on, the EC must not be the sole focus for European co-operation. The ensuing discussion revealed acceptance that Stewart, Wilson and officials had taken the correct action. Ministers believed that the episode would blow over, and that the harm done to Franco-British relations was not too great since de Gaulle respected those who stood up to him.[80] Castle's diary for 23 and 25 February reveal, however, how strongly both she and Crossman felt about the affair, with both deploring 'the fact that we had been so bored with last Thursday's Cabinet we hadn't really been listening to Michael.' Castle noted that her 'only relief was that another initiative to get ourselves in by sucking up to the Five had failed', and wished that Wilson would 'stop being so busy about issues like entry into Europe (which would be economically disastrous for us anyway)....Leave them alone a bit.'[81] Yet Castle did not appear to raise these points in cabinet on 27 February.

The continuing ramifications of the 'Soames affair' played out for the rest of the spring, and were mainly positive for Britain. As people continued to debate the rights and wrongs of the affair, British aims in Europe were plastered across European newspapers, almost all of which supported the UK, and which gave the government an opportunity to display its European character with statements like the following from Chalfont.

> The effort that we are making to enter the European Economic Community is one of the most great and important that this country has ever followed in the sphere of her foreign policy. It is an acknowledgement of the future role of importance and significance of Europe. The determination to pursue this line in spite of every difficulty and obstacle, patiently and tenaciously, does not seem to me to be at all humiliating; actually it is an important and courageous task which will be crowned with success and which will bring great benefit to a Europe really united.[82]

The 'Soames affair' therefore had the effect of raising the profile of the British application in the Community states.

After the 'Soames affair'

Although de Gaulle's proposals cast a shadow over European relations, 'normal' business went on as well, suggesting that the 'Soames affair' was something of a storm in a teacup. At the same time as pursuing damage-limitation with France, the British tried to strengthen Kiesinger's position on WEU and managed Wilson's first meeting with president Nixon. The usual Franco-German meetings, WEU councils and an Italian state visit to Britain all shaped British-European relations in the remainder of the spring.

WEU

Following FCO advice, Wilson sent a personal message to Kiesinger, noting that they had agreed in Bonn that the decision taken at

Luxembourg was a 'welcome step forward and should be encouraged.' It was unfortunate, he wrote, that controversy had now arisen over procedure, and 'essential that we should now agree together on the next step.' While Wilson hoped that the French would return to WEU, the other members must not allow themselves to be diverted. He thought it essential that the meeting planned for 26 February should go ahead – procedure could always be discussed there. Wilson concluded with a plea.

> What is at stake now is not the interpretation of a single article in the Brussels Treaty but the continuation of the efforts, on which we have worked together for so many months, to develop political consultation in the WEU as a step towards the development of European unity. I hope you will see this matter in terms of Anglo/German relations as well as in the context of wider European policy....This is the time to build on what has so far been achieved.[83]

Wilson's letter had the desired effect. Kiesinger explained that he had been concerned by the level of French suspicions about WEU, but claimed that a proposal to postpone the next meeting was no more than a suggestion. He agreed that there was no need to postpone the February meeting, unless doing so would persuade the French to attend the regular meeting of 5 March.[84] On 25 February, the Germans announced that they would, after all, attend the meeting the following day.[85] It covered only the procedural points brought about by the French absence, but the WEU Assembly later passed a resolution welcoming political consultations.[86] In March the Benelux countries decided to stand by their interpretation of the legal situation – that is, that the French could not veto meetings to discuss foreign policy, and the Council met on 12 March to consider the Nigerian civil war.[87]

While an analysis of de Gaulle's motives in the 'Soames affair' would require a comprehensive study of French archival material, it seems likely that the early indications of progress, in the face of French opposition, towards political consultation between Britain and the Five in WEU, played a part.[88] As Palliser and Brandt commented, most of the ideas raised by de Gaulle to Soames were not new. The timing of the conversation, however, is interesting, coming as it did just before the crucial Luxembourg WEU Council meeting. When his proposals failed to derail progress in WEU, de Gaulle turned to his familiar tactics of (attempted) veto and then boycott. These efforts did not, however, prevent small steps being taken, including Britain, to create a concerted foreign policy. Wilson's role in bringing Kiesinger to accept these steps in the face of French opposition cannot be overlooked.

Nixon's visit

While working on Kiesinger, Wilson prepared also to meet the new American president.[89] British aims and strategy vis-à-vis the US were unchanged: in order 'to maximise our influence with the Americans we need to convince them by our actions that the cohesive, strong, stable Western Europe which they think best suits their interests can only be built with Britain as the focal point. To do this we have to show that the West Europeans want us and that we have their confidence.' The Anglo-German Declaration would demonstrate the intention to form a strong and cohesive Western Europe, giving 'the Americans the sense of something solid in Europe on which to base their own policy.'[90] Wilson therefore set out to convince Nixon that the government was committed to European integration in the political as well as in the economic field and to secure his endorsement that a United Europe including Britain was the best sort of Europe for the US, so that American policies vis-à-vis France and Germany could be shaped to assist in this objective.[91]

Nixon made clear that whatever the position of other elements in the US administration, he himself was entirely in favour of British accession into the Communities. Moreover, he was aware of the difficulties posed by any question of American assistance in securing this goal – particularly important when his next stop was Paris. Stewart asked him to provide the usual discreet bilateral support, while Wilson pointed out that although both the US and Britain would have to pay a premium for Britain's entry, they would gain in the long term.[92]

In a press conference on 4 March, Nixon noted US support for the 'concept and ideal of European unity' but said it was a matter for Europeans: 'we should not become involved in differences among Europeans unless our vital interests are involved.' He also said that de Gaulle was right to want a European Europe, although he sited this comment firmly in the context of the Atlantic Alliance. The US would remain dominant simply because of its immense nuclear power and economic wealth. 'But on the other hand, the world will be a much safer place and, from our standpoint, a much healthier place economically, militarily and politically, if there were a strong European community to be a balance...between the United States and the Soviet Union, rather than to have this polarisation of forces in one part of the world.'[93] Kissinger later revealed that Nixon had left de Gaulle in no doubt that the US wanted to see Britain as a full member of the EC, although they recognised that this was a problem to be solved by Europeans.[94] Privately he continued to refer to a 'special relationship' existing between Britain and the US, but he asked that no one refer to it.[95]

The relationship was complicated, however, by indications that the French were trying to improve their bilateral relations with the US.[96] The closer Franco-American relationship that emerged after Nixon's election, revealed in more consistent and formal discussions about nuclear weapons including the repudiation of Johnson's condemnation of the French *force de frappe,* and in the purchase by the United States of a dozen French Mirage aircraft, suggests that the Americans were in fact nurturing several 'special relationships' with their European allies.[97] When Nixon visited France, he praised de Gaulle's 'wisdom and experience', calling him 'a giant among men' and admiring his 'epic leadership rarely equalled in history.' He described France as 'America's oldest ally and America's oldest friend,' and at a dinner for Pompidou in March, added that the friendship was 'so deep and so long that any minor irritation or bad manners or differences are not going to impair it.'[98] Warmer Franco-American relations had to be taken into account in the planning of British European policy.

The Franco-German summit
Despite the gentle progress made in WEU without France, everyone was waiting to see how America's new friend would treat Kiesinger in the mid-March summit, and how the chancellor would respond. Brandt felt that there was 'no sign of any change or any give in any aspect of French policy', and the Dutch were concerned that French actions would place irresistible pressure on the Germans.[99] They seemed to be correct. The French and German leaders agreed 'to pursue the common goal of an independent Europe.'[100] De Gaulle presented himself as a good European, saying that France found the Community to be beneficial and that it should be continued and developed. He said that there was no question of renouncing the alliance with the United States or the 'steadfast' economic links that France had with the western superpower, but that it was 'necessary that Europe should desire to organise itself in its own way in the economic, political and security fields.' It was not possible to admit all the states that wanted to join. 'Perhaps one day it will be necessary to do something in common with all European states. This is an open prospect and France is ready to talk about it with Germany.' For the present, however, there was the EC, which France wished to continue and develop.[101] Kiesinger agreed. He said that basically, 'between France and Germany there is the problem of Great Britain. But that must not be a reason for harming the development of the Community.'[102] Whether or not de Gaulle had threatened to withdraw from or destroy the EC, he

once again appeared to have convinced Kiesinger that their focus should be on the development of the existing Community, not on enlargement.

However, for the first time since the veto, Kiesinger stood firm on the commitments he had made to Britain and his other European partners. He told the British that he had left de Gaulle in no doubt that British entry remained a central objective of his policy, and that he had defended the work in WEU, describing the Luxembourg meeting as a step forward. He promised British representatives in Bonn that he would take no step towards 'the future Europe' without 'the closest consultation' with Britain.[103] Moreover, the FRG continued to participate in WEU foreign policy consultation without France. De Gaulle had told Brandt that political consultation in WEU was 'a matter that is of no interest to France'.[104] The Italians suggested that this comment gave Kiesinger a free hand to proceed as he wished in WEU, so that the danger of a German reverse was in fact reduced.[105]

Brandt also said that he saw no need to change German policy, which was first to develop the Community from within, and second to widen it. In a speech in the *Bundestag*, he said that Europe needed both France and Britain, explicitly saying that Germany had not gone back on its previous endorsement of enlargement. Nor would the FRG obstruct political discussions in WEU (that is, they would not be moved by the French boycott).[106] In fulfilment of his commitment to consult with and keep the British informed, Brandt also wrote a private letter to '*Lieber Michael*', giving his personal impressions of the talks in Paris, requesting that they stay in 'close contact' and encouraging Stewart to continue to pursue better Anglo-French relations.[107] Stewart's appreciation of Brandt's words was clear: he replied, not only thanking the German foreign minister, but also asking if he had any suggestions for talks tentatively planned with Debré.[108] Brandt suggested the Middle East and East-West relations, and Stewart was careful to keep him informed of the content of the talks, described below.[109]

Rebuilding relations with France

The British took some time to consider how best to approach relations with France after the disastrous start to the year. Soames suggested that 'bashing' the French would be counter-productive, and that it would be better to seek a new dialogue.[110] There were indications too, that even de Gaulle did not want to leave relations in such a parlous state. The French secretary of state for information told a British diplomat, Crispin Tickell, that 'the general did not want to make a bad situation worse and wished to leave open all the possibilities for the future.'[111] After much discussion including a recalled Soames, Wilson's preliminary reaction to agree with his ambassador was followed.[112] As Soames put it,

> [t]hough we will never get as far as we would like along the European road while the General is in power, I think that we should see how far we can get while holding fast to our principles in the hope that we will be able to travel farther and faster when he is gone. The alternative of waiting till he goes before moving at all is in my view, fraught with greater risks.[113]

The question remained of how to proceed. Wilson pointed out that since 'Europe' was a sensitive issue they should consider discussion of less contentious subjects to get the ball rolling.[114] Since de Gaulle had called a referendum on constitutional issues and made it an issue of confidence in his government, there was no point in trying to start talks until Stewart and Debré met at NATO Council in Washington after Easter: perhaps they could discuss Nigeria or the Middle East.[115] The proposal for talks was put to the French at low level, and Debré quickly agreed.[116] Although there were still some voices hostile to France (and thus to Soames' advice) within the FCO, Soames continued to advise that Stewart should 'try and bury the past as speedily as possible'.[117]

Stewart followed Soames' advice in his meeting with Debré. The French foreign minister expressed his sadness at the state of Anglo-French relations. He insisted that de Gaulle had intended a genuine opening with his proposals to Soames and would have been prepared to discuss them with Wilson. As for talks, for the present, the line was down. Not enough time had passed. However, Debré's reluctance seemed only to apply to discussion of Britain's role in Europe: he said that he would be happy to discuss issues like the Middle East and Nigeria after the forthcoming referendum. Stewart thought that Debré was suggesting that 'nothing was certain until the referendum and that the situation might well be different thereafter', and he clearly felt that the meeting had helped to ease the tension.[118] Wilson seemed to be relieved that relations were returning to a more normal footing, agreeing that they should wait until after the referendum and then take stock. In a cryptic note, Wilson indicated that he felt he had been 'taken for a ride' over the Soames Affair by elements within the FCO – presumably those elements most hostile to the French.[119] Yet, as was seen, Wilson was quite happy to go along with FCO advice during the first half of February, a decision he took in the face of conflicting advice from Soames and Palliser.

Relations with the Five

Throughout the chilly relations with France, other Europeans continued to offer support. Nenni made a powerful speech in the Italian Senate against the 'policy of vetoes', declining to accept that 'the refusal of a single government should hold up a movement which seeks first harmony and then unity'. He stressed that Italy would continue to pursue foreign policy co-operation in WEU as well as British entry into the EC. As Palliser commented, 'good rousing stuff!'[120] Others, like Dr Linthorst Homan, the chief representative of the Commission in the UK, and Dr Rainer Barzel, the leader of the Parliamentary CDU-CSU parties, made similarly positive statements.[121] The German foreign ministry even appeared to be considering a 'Northern European Community', including Britain, which might replace the EC if France persisted in opposing the latter's enlargement.[122] This initiative does not appear again in the official British record, but it indicates the extent of irritation with the French in parts of the German administration. Clearly Wilson had managed to convince some Europeans, at least, of the sincerity and determination underlying his application to the EC.

The Italian visit

Wilson had an opportunity to reinforce this impression and build an important alliance during the Italian state visit in April. Preparations for President Saragat's visit to the UK began in early March with plans for a joint declaration that would be a 'positive, outspoken and clear exposition of our ideas on the future of Europe.'[123] Wilson stressed that the centre of British policy was the application for membership, cemented in the political and economic strength of Europe and the defensive strength of the Atlantic Alliance. Saragat said it was in European interests to have Britain join: for Italy personally, British entry would help to defend the democratic tradition.[124] As well as these supportive words, however, Saragat also signed a joint declaration with Wilson. It said that the policy of the two countries was to enlarge the Communities and make its outward-looking traditions stronger, 'and to avoid enlargement becoming more difficult. At the same time they agree to consult and to intensify the exchange of all relevant information.' This agreement to consult and exchange information had most significance for Britain.[125] The commitment to avoid hindering enlargement meant in effect that Britain would have a voice, albeit indirect, in the internal discussion of the Community. While, as has been seen, the Italians and Dutch had previously said that they would prevent developments within the EC that would impede enlargement, and indeed, had taken action in this direction, the Anglo-Italian Declaration was the first instance of a formal written agreement to this effect.

The significance of the Declaration was quickly overshadowed, however. In one of his first meetings with Wilson, Saragat commented that 'de Gaulle was not immortal.'[126] His point was timelier than he possibly could have imagined: during his visit to London, de Gaulle lost his referendum and resigned as president.[127]

Conclusions

These few months in 1969 therefore saw a real advance in the success of British European policy. Added to their original refusal of the Harmel proposals the previous autumn, French actions in the 'Soames affair' and in WEU pushed the Germans towards overt support of Britain, in defiance of de Gaulle. The general had shown himself to be both intransigent and un-European. Wilson, in contrast, had not only continued to re-state his determination that Britain should enter the European Communities, but had committed the UK to extra-treaty co-operation and then demonstrated that commitment in a very practical way by revealing de Gaulle's proposals to Soames. He had shown, therefore, not only that he wanted Britain to be part of 'Europe', but that it should be the kind of Europe envisioned by the Five. It is, of course, impossible to say how long the newly-strong German position would have lasted had de Gaulle not resigned, but it should be remembered that German impatience with the French had been building up for almost a year, since the rejection of the first Brandt proposals the previous spring. The 'Soames affair' and French boycott of WEU brought Franco-German relations to breaking point.

There were in these months other indications of changes to come in the Community. Added to the inability of the French to prevent co-operation in WEU were more signs of a shift in the balance of power between France and Germany. Debré, interviewed on a French television show called 'Face to Face', agreed that it would be a good thing for Britain to be at France's side to help offset the power of Germany, whose recent growth and revival were leading to concern. The offer of bilateral talks would therefore be renewed at some point in the future.[128] Kissinger also disclosed that when Nixon was in Paris, the French talked a lot about the 'German problem', and he thought that de Gaulle was 'perhaps becoming obsessive about West Germany.'[129] French insecurity in the face of growing German strength will later be posited as one reason for the lifting of the veto.

There were also developments more worrying to Britain. Although the Dutch initially refused to agree to a Belgian proposal to press on with the internal development of the Community without reference to enlargement, the Five were prepared to discuss de Gaulle's suggestions, made to Kiesinger in mid-March, for the future development of the Community, and Thorn even suggested a meeting of the foreign ministers of the Six.[130] The maintenance of the British application had caused stagnation in the Community – it was a key aim of continuing to press for membership, although one that was not publicly expressed. The possibility of internal progress being resumed was therefore worrying: it raised the danger that British accession would become more difficult as the Six 'moved the goalposts'. Added to this unwelcome prospect were rumours on the continent that British European policy was about to change. [131] In the coming months, therefore, Wilson and his government would have to spend a good deal of time not only trying to prevent unwelcome developments, but also convincing their European colleagues that they really did want to join the Community. As Nenni said, de Gaulle's resignation had 'far-reaching consequences and the situation was now radically changed.'[132]

7

April – December 1969: after de Gaulle – the veto is lifted

De Gaulle's resignation entirely changed the enlargement question for Wilson's government, suddenly raising the possibility of the veto being lifted. The result for Britain was a shift in focus towards a sense of guarded anticipation; new frustration while waiting for a government to be formed in France; the awakening of 'anti-Europeans' in cabinet as the realisation dawned that Wilson's application might actually be successful; and jockeying for position and advantage in the final deal that would see the end of French efforts to keep Britain out of the European Communities.

It took a long time for the new French position to become clear. British hopes rose when Georges Pompidou, the Gaullist presidential candidate, made an electoral deal with the Independent Republicans, led by Valery Giscard d'Estaing. In exchange for the small party's support, Pompidou proposed, if elected, 'to pursue the construction of Europe, which it is desirable should be enlarged.'[1] Despite contradictory comments from hard-line Gaullists like Debré, Pompidou's initial comments proved sincere.[2] Meanwhile, the German response to the new circumstances was slightly unclear, with differing stances taken by Kiesinger, Brandt (who made a proposal for a summit meeting), Schmidt and Strauss.[3]

In these circumstances, the British decided to keep the pressure on. Chalfont sent out instructions stating that the British application remained in. He hoped the Six would consider it in their first meeting after a new French government was formed: if the French did not take the initiative, he hoped that the Five would suggest that negotiations be opened. The

British application should be the first business of any summit, and Britain should be able to participate in any talks on the future development of the Community. One point was made particularly clear: while the UK looked forward to the return of normal, friendly relations with France, there was 'no intention of dealing bilaterally with France on our approach to Europe, lest we be asked to pay a supplementary bilateral price first for the opening and then for the conclusion of negotiations with the Six.' Evidently the government still feared French underhandedness.[4] Meanwhile, all friendly member states supported the British application at a WEU meeting in June, and Stewart reported that they were 'extremely anxious to see our entry successful'.[5]

The Pompidou government and progress

The French position remained ambiguous even after Pompidou won on 15 June. Stewart did not expect changes in policy to be 'as rapid or as radical' as they might have been under the anglophile interim president, Alain Poher, but he did anticipate the eventual withdrawal of the veto on enlargement negotiations. Wilson agreed.[6] From Paris, Soames stressed that the new government would need time to think: Pompidou would have to take as long as possible to agree to negotiations, in order to pacify orthodox Gaullists. Even the tiny steps taken so far, such as Brandt's call for a summit, were interpreted by hard-line Gaullists as Britain trying to wear down 'French resistance before a new French government has even been formed', moving 'with indecent haste'.[7] Soames was pleased at the appointment of Maurice Schumann as foreign minister: he was 'a convinced European and a well known if not too well-known Anglophile.'[8] Soames felt that 'the composition of the government as Monsieur Pompidou had created it gave us as good an opportunity as we were likely to have' to re-establish good relations', but warned that HMG should be careful not to show 'excessive haste' or 'undue pressure.' He hoped that Wilson would continue to speak positively on the application. Wilson agreed, although he 'also had to keep in mind that there were those who were prepared to say that he was taking his fences too quickly.'[9]

The new French prime minister, Jacques Chaban-Delmas, made a statement of policy on 26 June, and while it appeared positive, it stressed the difficulties ahead of enlargement.

> The enlargement of the common market to new members, in the front rank of whom stands Britain, must be the subject of preliminary discussions and agreements with our Community partners. But it is essential that this accession, far from weakening the structure which has already been built, should strengthen

it....British accession must not lead to the dilution of the European concept: the enlargement of the dimensions of Europe must not compromise its vocation.[10]

Wilson felt that the statement was 'very cautious and even ambiguous....[It] could mean that the French wished to move but wished to cover this up by the use of old phrases.'[11] However, Soames noted that Chaban-Delmas had avoided reference to the classical Gaullist objections to British membership, and 'spoke as if the principle of entry were accepted.'[12] The well-connected governor general of the *Banque Nationale de Paris,* Jean Dromer, expected talks to begin before the end of the year and that, although these would be tough, they were to result in accession.[13] Clearly, the French would drive a hard bargain, but nevertheless, the locks on the door barring British accession were being drawn back.

Ministers in Britain and the Six therefore began to take tentative steps towards negotiations. Chalfont told the German ambassador that HMG stood by the application, was not interested in trade arrangements, and was confident that, by the time all EC rules applied to Britain, the country would be a 'strong and welcome' member of the Community. Blankenhorn welcomed Chalfont's words, saying they would 'strengthen the hand of those in Germany who were anxious to continue their support for our enlargement.'[14] Stewart asked Soames to tell Schumann that he hoped for better Anglo-French relations, explaining that he hoped to help the French to change their policy without too much loss of face. Once agreement had been reached to open negotiations, bilateral relations with France – with the Five kept informed, of course – might help.[15] French interest in bilateral talks with the British caused some suspicion, both in the UK and on the continent, but as the sincerity of the new French position became more evident, bilateral talks began to seem more attractive.[16]

All were aware, however, that only tentative steps could be taken, partly because of the autumn German elections, and partly because of the timetabled move from the 'transitional' to the 'definitive' period of the EC by the end of the year. Brandt said that his government would remain active in European policy during the election period, in order to facilitate for its successor the decisions that had to be made by the end of the year. Nevertheless, the prospect of elections could not but introduce an element of delay.[17] Progress was therefore slow, but the first inklings of the deal to be made at the end of the year emerged at a Franco-German meeting in July, when Brandt warned Schumann that failure to agree on enlargement might encourage failure to agree on an agricultural settlement

– 'though there would be no attempt to establish a formal link between the two issues.'[18]

Despite Schumann's comment to Brandt, in English, that '[w]e mean business', putting the elements together took six months.[19] From July, the idea of a straight exchange – the French vision for CAP in exchange for enlargement – was explicitly discussed at high level.[20] Pompidou insisted on the need to consolidate the Communities before enlargement, saying that France was 'not against going into all this: but we do not want negotiations to start without knowing first what the difficulties are, what prospects these hold out, and what might be the common attitude of the Six.' A summit could discuss these questions.[21] His inclusion of enlargement in the summit agenda gave the British hope, since it indicated a faster timetable than that implied by the prioritising of completion.[22] That hope was reinforced when Schumann said that completion and the consideration of enlargement by the Six could take place in parallel.[23]

Relations with the Five
The British continued to seek support from the Five. Harmel told Stewart that the Belgians wanted to go further than vague generalities by tying together negotiations for enlargement and for internal development. He warned that there was so much to discuss – financial regulations, commercial policy, development policy, CAP, monetary policy and technology – that fundamental decisions could not possibly be made before November. His plan was for the Six to draw up parallel programmes for completion and enlargement, to be finished by the end of the year. If France then refused to open negotiations, an 'untenable political situation' would result. He believed it was 'unthinkable' that France would not agree to open negotiations; still, 'it must be understood that as soon as there was a Government in Germany a time must be fixed for the opening of negotiations.' Davignon pointed out that France was still taking a fairly hard line. He and Harmel confirmed, however, that the Five would be firm. Stewart agreed that the situation was difficult: without knowing what the French were thinking, the Five did not know how much pressure they could apply, and in which forum to do so. Too much in the wrong place could be counter-productive. Harmel concluded, however, that those most able to influence French ministers should do so now, and 'tell them that people could wait no longer for negotiations for British entry' and that 'if no progress was made by September the French government would find themselves confronted with many difficulties.'[24] This situation would have been impossible without the Wilson government's careful diplomatic work over the previous months.

For the Commission, Rey believed that it was 'impossible' that once the negotiations started, a veto could be imposed. He expected a decision on negotiations by the end of the year. His optimism was reinforced by Stewart's promise that the British government was interested in political union, including building 'a political structure on the basis provided by the Rome Treaties.'[25] This kind of dialogue, of a reiteration of support for the British application in exchange for a reinforcement of the UK's European credentials, was seen often in the lead up to The Hague summit.[26]

The importance of keeping up pressure for entry was clear: the FCO received reports from Europe suggesting there was still some doubt about British readiness and ability to sustain membership, and perhaps also some hesitation about making progress with negotiations with the present government. Robinson concluded that 'we must continue to proclaim HMG's policy', suggesting Wilson's forthcoming speech at the Guildhall as the next opportunity.[27] Although given in a domestic context, the speech was therefore directed at continental ears. Wilson noted the frustrations and disappointments that the UK had suffered, and emphasised that his determination 'certainly will not weaken now.' He spoke also about political unity, and argued that the 'immediate task of this generation is to work, as we are pledged to work, for that degree of political unity which is within our immediate grasp.'[28]

As the summer wore on and British pressure for the opening of negotiations continued, encouraging noises emerged from France. The new finance minister, Giscard, declared that there were 'no insurmountable economic and financial obstacles to the enlargement of the Community.'[29] Schumann reciprocated Stewart's wish for better relations, and although he still stressed the need to settle the CAP before enlargement, he acknowledged that the Six could clearly not present a 'rigid front' on this issue to the four applicants.[30] That position was consolidated at a Council of Ministers meeting on 22 July, when the Six took the first formal steps towards new consideration of enlargement negotiations. Schumann proposed a summit in The Hague to consider completion, reinforcement and enlargement of the Community and the future role of Europe in the world. The 'single condition' for enlargement 'was that there should be no weakening of the Community', and he insisted that there should be 'prior agreement' on the three aims among the Six before enlargement. The Five welcomed Schumann's words, with Brandt and Zagari (a minister in the Italian foreign ministry) insisting that elections in Germany and Italy would not cause any delay. Summing up, Luns welcomed Schumann's 'eloquence and European sentiment', but also highlighted that the others had seen between the three aims 'a factual [link] of a political nature which led to parallelism.' The Six agreed to ask the Commission to update its 'Opinion' on enlargement, to instruct the permanent representatives to prepare a discussion on the three aims, and to hold a Council in September, at which political questions and the proposed summit could be examined.[31] Although the French had 'given little ground on matters of substance' and had won the argument of whether the summit should be of six (their preference) or seven (Brandt's and the British preference), they had nonetheless 'aroused expectations in their and other people's public opinion and among the governments of the Five which it will be difficult in the autumn to dash or to feed with no more than words, if French aims in the agricultural field are not to be jeopardised.' Further, the strong position of the Five would make it difficult for the French to try and sideline enlargement.[32]

Another step had therefore been taken towards agreement: the French minister of agriculture told Soames that 'the new French government had made it clear that the veto was lifted.'[33] A EURO paper concluded that all Six member states were now favourable to enlargement.[34] Moreover, the ability of the French government to reverse its position was undermined when, on 8 August, the franc was devalued without warning or consultation and measures were introduced to protect French agriculture. It was a severe setback for the CAP, while reinforcing both the ability of individual member states to protect their individual interests, and HMG's contention that it was not possible to quantify the cost of entry.[35] However, the French insisted that it was still their objective to get agreement among the Six on CAP before discussing enlargement, and Davignon warned that French officials would dig themselves in. The Belgians also believed that none of the Five would permit action that would drastically alienate the farming vote.[36] Nevertheless, Brandt argued that the forthcoming Franco-German meeting, the September Council of Ministers and the summit itself must decide the form for the opening of negotiations.[37] The rapid progress once de Gaulle had resigned reflected the unilateral nature of his anti-British position, and suggests that the rest of the French political establishment did not share his political arguments against British accession.

The Franco-German meeting and Council of Ministers
Kiesinger and Pompidou's meeting appeared to concentrate on the further development of the Communities. At lower levels, the French prioritised completion, and used 'very clear language' to make the point that agreement on agricultural finance by the end of the year was a condition both for negotiations for enlargement and for the existence of the Community itself.[38] Brandt was much firmer than Kiesinger, pressing Schumann for a date for the opening of negotiations – Schumann later

told Soames that he expected the Six to have reached agreement on a date by the time he visited London in January.[39]

From this meeting onwards, there was consensus among the Six that they should formally agree by the end of the year to open negotiations. Schumann told Soames in September that the French were 'determined not to appear to be dragging their feet'. He hoped to have something positive to tell Stewart in January, though he continued to stress the need for agreement on completion of the Communities first.[40] Ambassador de Courcel told Stewart that his government wished – as long as their partners would go as fast as France hoped – to be able to open negotiations as soon as the definitive phase of the Common Market had begun on 1 January 1970.[41] The French continued to deny any link between completion and enlargement of the Communities, but when asked by Stewart whether the French government was against British entry, reluctant but ready to accept it as inevitable, or positively in favour, Schumann chose the third option, emphasising again that careful preparation was necessary.[42] Brandt's and Luns' joint proposal to the French for a summit of the ten in February 1970, however, was rejected out of hand.[43] Instead the Six focused on arrangements for CAP.[44]

The Six formally agreed to hold a summit at the Council meeting in mid-September.[45] Schumann rejected setting a date for the opening of negotiations, and insisted again that there could be no link between completion and enlargement. On the other hand, there must clearly be links between strengthening and enlargement, which the Six would have to discuss for some months after the summit. The Commission would update its Opinion by the end of the month. Marjoribanks described the French position as one of 'utter complacency in allowing the preparatory stage for negotiations to drag on as long as possible.'[46] Fortunately for the British, Luns said that whatever the French said, 'there was a political link in the Dutch mind between enlargement and completion, and that the Dutch would not agree to completion as the French wanted without firm guarantees about enlargement.'[47] The Germans too were considering withholding ratification of the new agricultural arrangement in order to force the French to accept enlargement.[48] British efforts to win over the Five were paying off.

The Commission Opinion and the German elections

There were two significant events in October. First, the Commission published a revised 'Opinion' on enlargement, reiterating that negotiations should open as soon as possible. It went into some detail before stressing that reinforcement and enlargement of the Communities must be considered simultaneously.[49] Marjoribanks described the document as 'considerably more favourable to our application than its predecessor', and considered that it was in part a lecture directed at the Six about the problems that they had thus far failed to solve, and in part a road map for the future development of an enlarged Community.[50]

The second significant event in October was, of course, the German federal election. On 21 October Brandt became Chancellor after an alliance with the liberal FDP enabled his SDP to form a government without the CDU/CSU. The German ambassador in London told O'Neill, back in the FCO as deputy under-secretary, that the position in Bonn would now be easier from the British point of view.[51] In addition to the usual congratulations, Wilson sent a personal and confidential message to Brandt almost straight away, reminding him of the 'importance and urgency of the decisions in prospect in Europe', suggesting that all needed to show determination in the coming weeks, and asking Brandt to use his 'immeasurably stronger position...in Community affairs' to ensure that the summit resulted in a decision to open negotiations early in 1970.[52] Brandt said that this message strengthened 'once again my conviction that the German policy of seeking to open up and enlarge the European Community is necessary and right.'[53]

Brandt made a first statement to the Bundestag on 28 October, saying that

[t]he enlargement of the European Communities must come. The Community needs Great Britain as much as the other applicant countries. In the chorus of European voices the voice of Britain must not be missing, unless Europe wants to inflict harm on herself. We are gratified to note that the decisive forces in British policy continue to be convinced that Britain in turn needs Europe.[54]

Brandt's statement acknowledged the importance of Wilson's efforts to bring the UK closer to membership of the Communities, and Wilson was 'very much encouraged'.[55] Brandt's election as chancellor transformed Germany's earlier verbal support for British accession into action. He felt that Britain belonged in Europe: they had 'already demonstrated their membership in Europe's darkest hour'.[56] He believed that he could use the partnership with France as 'the key to European unification – more concretely, to the cardinal problem of how to bring the dispute over British entry to a favourable conclusion.[57] Perhaps most importantly, the *Ostpolitik* for which he is most often remembered was rooted in a foreign policy directed towards the west. First, only from secure foundations in the west could the FRG reach out to the east. Second, *Ostpolitik* deprived the French of their old diplomatic weapon of threatening to pursue closer relations with the Soviet Union or to recognise the GDR. Lahr, now the German ambassador in Rome, was outspoken in a talk with O'Neill about the difficulties caused to the UK by Kiesinger, saying that progress on enlargement had been impossible and that there had been 'floods of tears' in the chancellery when de Gaulle resigned. Brandt and his new cabinet would be much better from the British point of view.[58] Arguably, therefore, the election of Brandt was equally or even more important to the eventual success of the British application as was the resignation of de Gaulle.

Domestic difficulties

These months did not pass without ministerial debate. In April the FCO had been reviewing European policy: Robinson noted that the enormous paper that resulted was as valid in the new situation as it would have been had de Gaulle remained in office. Coming after the Soames affair, the paper detailed contingency planning for the consideration of alternative European policies, centred around the possibility of fundamental change occurring in the Communities. Interesting for its analysis of past British European policy since 'Plan G', the paper repeatedly came to the same conclusion: the Communities were *not* likely to disappear or radically change. While alternative organisations, such as an industrial free trade area with no agricultural content, might be more attractive to the UK, they were unlikely to attract the Six. The reality was that the Communities existed and British policy had to be forged in that environment. Therefore, the 'best, and probably the only, way to change the Communities into a system which suits us better will be to join them and change them from the inside.' The FCO's considered recommendation, therefore, was 'to maintain our application and our present policy unchanged.'[59] A slightly tongue-in-cheek annex to the paper addressed supposed 'francophobia' in the FCO, but concluded that it had 'generally been a case of reacting to moves by de Gaulle which were clearly contrary to British policy or interests... "Degaullophobia" [had] a respectable ancestry from Mr Churchill's wartime days'. The annex concluded that de Gaulle's resignation had 'drawn a line under the account': it would be 'particularly important for HMG to show by their actions that they are not motivated by any permanent hostility towards France.'[60] The paper remained confined to the FCO for fear that it would lead to accusations that the government was considering a change in policy, but, as Chalfont noted, 'we are ready with detailed arguments, if they are needed, to substantiate the view that there is no realistic and advantageous alternative for us to membership of the Communities.'[61]

Despite the early uncertainty about the new French position, the FCO quickly sought and received Wilson's authority to instruct officials to begin bringing the negotiating position up to date.[62] When Stewart reported to cabinet that 'within a reasonable time European affairs and the question of the entry of Britain and other candidates for membership of the European Economic Community would come to the fore again' there was no discussion: ministers simply took note.[63] Crosland suggested a new attempt to cost entry, but did so direct to the Cabinet Office rather than to his colleagues: Robinson noted that a small official group would prepare this work and that the FCO 'therefore need not fear the outcome.'[64] Ministers' acquiescence in Wilson's European policy thus continued.

Wilson himself remained proactive. In a speech at the twentieth anniversary celebrations of the Council of Europe, he said that

> [t]he policy of Her Majesty's Government remains firmly based on our application for full membership of the European Communities. Our determination to join the Communities did not weaken in the face of delay in opening negotiations on our application, negotiations which the European Commission recommended should start over eighteen months ago. And it certainly will not weaken now.

Going on to discuss the future role of a united Europe in the world, Wilson said that HMG would press on, 'in the conviction that [the Communities'] enlargement and development provide the obvious, the natural and the best way forward.' He concluded that '[w]e have been right to persist. When that persistence is rewarded by the enlargement of the Communities, as it will be, the road to a united Europe will again be open.'[65]

As the prospect of negotiations crept closer, the question of the cost of entry was raised increasingly often in the UK, and Wilson used all his powers as prime minister to control the answers. He initially rejected moves to establish the total cost due to the likelihood of press speculation and the difficulty of making valid assumptions about CAP when the Six had not yet agreed on a definitive system.[66] Stewart agreed that no detailed figure was necessary, and suggested that this decision should be made clear to other departments, in case there was 'private enterprise' going on. However, he insisted that official studies must continue so that the negotiating position could be prepared, and Wilson agreed, provided that the task be done by officials, not ministers.[67] Within Whitehall, FCO officials knew that the 'worries of the Treasury [and] the Board of Trade about our ability to shoulder the additional burden of joining the Common Market [would] have to be faced at some stage.'[68]

Cabinet

Likewise, cabinet discussed the cost of entry, concerned that France might try to extract their full demands in agriculture as the price for British entry. Wilson insisted that collective responsibility for the policy must be retained.[69] In mid-September, Crosland had written to him about divisions on European policy within the cabinet's 'management committee,' set up in May 1969 to take the place of the 'parliamentary committee', an informal 'inner' cabinet. Crosland classed himself with the anti-Europeans Castle and Peart in describing a dispute with Stewart, and effectively suggested a u-turn on European policy.[70] Castle's and Crossman's diaries reveal how Wilson dealt with such objections. When he stressed the damage that would be done abroad by the appearance of divided counsels, Crossman wrote that 'I suppose I felt that was right but I also couldn't help feeling that in this, as in so many other issues, Cabinet no longer minds. We are all too tired, too absorbed in our own interests to feel any great collective responsibility.'[71] He also seemed to feel that a French veto - 'another snub' - was still likely, but felt that in forcing Wilson to agree to future discussion, he had retained the possibility of a u-turn for the future.[72] Castle too saw hope in Wilson's promise of a review of the costs of entry, perhaps assuming that those costs would prove unpalatable.[73] Continuing apathy, the possibility of a renewed French veto, and the prospect of significant discussion in the future all dissuaded anti-accession ministers from forcing their objections on Wilson in the summer of '69. His skilful management of his cabinet colleagues and insistence that the application must be pursued were crucial in the furtherance of European policy in the run up to the summit.

At the beginning of August, therefore, Stewart sent guidance to several missions, stating that the government's policy was based on the application, with 'massive parliamentary approval' for full membership. The government's determination had not weakened, and it was prepared to go 'as fast as our European partners are prepared to go' in terms of the future development of the Communities. Meanwhile, it was not yet possible to provide a sensible estimate of the cost of entry: as soon as 'meaningful' information was available, it would be provided.[74] The government continued to respond to the need of the Five for reassurance that the UK was sincere: Chalfont argued that the government should publicise <u>every</u> ministerial Common Market speech in order to win the 'information battle'.[75]

Preparations for negotiations

As well as maintaining the momentum for negotiations, the British were also working on their own position. There was discussion of the form and content of negotiations both domestically and with the Six.[76] In May, Robinson began planning a special section in the FCO with responsibility for preparing material for negotiations.[77] EURO began to update George Brown's 'opening statement' of 4 July 1967, and work was done even on the personnel and accommodation aspects for negotiations as well as substantive points like the introduction of a value added tax.[78] After Pompidou was elected, a 'Common Market Publicity Working Party' (EURO PB) was set up in the FCO to organise the British information effort on the continent. It had a wide remit, from publication of ministerial speeches to bringing influential European editors to the UK.[79] More informally, a private group was set up to help with European contacts, including people like Dr Roy Pryce from the University of Sussex and Dr Raymond Carr from the University of Oxford.[80]

The CAP, which had emerged in 1967 as the most difficult negotiating problem, continued to draw the most attention, and officials considered whether or not the UK should try to influence the settlement. Schmidt said Germany would prefer Britain to participate in the final settlement, since their interests coincided.[81] Brandt advised that the British should concentrate on the Italians, who were most likely to be sympathetic to the French position.[82] Even the French conceded that a truly 'definitive' agreement might not be reached by the end of the year.[83] Robinson concluded that the UK would therefore probably be a full member in time for the next review. Nevertheless, studies on the cost of CAP should continue and when complete, should be used bilaterally to 'try discreetly' to further British objectives.[84] British officials continued to work on the cost of British entry – a cost that one Treasury official described as 'very worrying.'[85] At the Labour Party conference in September, Wilson promised that when the estimates were ready, they would be made available to Parliament, for public discussion and debate.[86]

Another important question was that of the political aspects of the treaties and the argument over federalism and supranationality. Marjoribanks warned that on the continent there was 'unmistakeably an inclination to assume that Britain is less than sincere in this matter.'[87] When Wilson made public comments about a directly elected European parliament and a federal European state, for example, they were noticed on the continent: a minister in the Dutch embassy questioned the FCO on their importance. When officials reassured him, he remarked that 'for domestic Parliamentarian reasons controversial points like this would inevitably from time to time be dealt with by somewhat different formulae' and that they would doubtless be 'minutely scrutinised' on the continent.[88] He was correct.[89]

British policy received a boost in July, however, with the presentation of the long-anticipated reports on British accession to Monnet's Action Committee. The Committee was 'confirmed in its conviction that the problems raised by Great Britain's entry into the Common Market can be solved' and called on the Six to open negotiations.[90] Stewart and the Conservative representatives Alec Douglas Home and Reginald Maudling had an opportunity to discuss the CAP with their Community counterparts in a friendly setting.[91] The support was significant: all the major political parties in Europe apart from the communists and Gaullists were represented, and Stewart considered that the membership of the three main British political parties had brought 'considerable advantage'.[92]

Management of cabinet divisions
In response to the continental worries as well as anti-European sentiment closer to home in *The Guardian* and from Enoch Powell, among others, Chalfont suggested that ministers needed to take the lead, with consistency and conviction, to 'demonstrate that our Europeanism is not an esoteric foreign office gimmick but a crucial factor in the survival of this country as a world power of any real influence, consequence and prosperity.' Otherwise 'domestic vacillation' could prevent success in the approach to Europe, 'unquestionably the most important foreign policy issue that faces us.' Stewart and Wilson agreed, and decided to press ministers to make speeches during the autumn.[93] More significantly, Wilson suggested that the reshuffle planned for October could be used 'to emphasise our commitment to Europe', and left the choice of FCO ministers 'entirely' up to Stewart.[94] Crosland's defection to the anti-Europeans may therefore help to explain his move from the Board of Trade to Local Government and Regional Planning. Other cabinet-level changes included the pro-European Roy Mason replacing Crosland at the Board of Trade, while George Thomson became chancellor of the Duchy of Lancaster and took over responsibility for European affairs. With the abolition of the Department of Economic Affairs, Peter Shore became minister without portfolio.[95] While these changes did not change the balance of pro-Europeans and anti-Europeans in the cabinet as a whole, it certainly did in the key ministries concerned with the approach to Europe. The level of trust and commonality of vision for European policy between Wilson and Stewart that they revealed was remarkable. Wilson's comment in his memoir that he moved Thomson to the Duchy in order to have the Common Market negotiator in the cabinet seems, therefore, to be rather an understatement.[96]

On 21 October the two asked junior ministers from all departments to speak in favour of the European policy, for 'it was the policy of the whole government.'[97] Later Wilson sent a similar message to all ministers, asking them

> in speeches, press interviews and other public appearances – to support the Government's European policy....If we are to carry through successful negotiations, on which everything will depend, it is important that the whole Government should present a determined and united front both to our future partners in Europe and to those who are trying to undermine the Government's policies at home.

There was, Wilson added, 'no need to be obsessed by safeguards and the negative aspects of our application, though the Government has these fully in mind.' Instead, there were 'plenty of positive points to put across about the opportunities that membership would offer for our influence abroad and economic well-being at home.'[98] Neither the reshuffle nor the imprecation to collective responsibility healed the divisions in the cabinet. Stewart reprimanded Callaghan at the end of October for comments about CAP and food prices in a parliamentary debate, saying he had given ammunition to opponents of the policy.[99] The request for speeches was repeated in cabinet in November, but Crossman replied, '[w]e will if you like but I shall take the proper posture the Prime Minister recommends, which is that we haven't changed our view that we should enter if the conditions are right because we are now strong enough to ensure that they are right.' It was not the most diplomatic position to take as negotiations drew closer. Wilson, Crossman wrote, 'looked a bit peeved and his face puckered', knowing that in this case Cabinet was 'registering a check on him and Michael Stewart, who are still hell bent on getting the negotiations going as fast as they possible can.'[100] The difficulty of maintaining ministerial discipline was evident.

In the atmosphere of growing expectation, collective responsibility seemed more necessary than ever, but Wilson guarded responsibility for decision-making in significant areas for himself, without consulting other ministers. The cabinet secretary wrote to Wilson towards the end of October, seeking ministerial authority for a host of official projects. Sir Burke Trend requested decisions on the form and content of the paper on the cost of joining the EC, promised at the Labour Party conference.[101] Wilson asked for a list of assumptions on which the figures would be calculated, and a range of estimates of the costs, which could perhaps be included in a series of white papers.[102] When he saw the resulting work at the end of the month, he commented, again apparently without consulting other ministers, '[t]his is very good. I'd like them to go ahead broadly on this basis.'[103] The postponement of the summit to December gave a little more leeway, and Wilson discussed the preparations with Stewart on 12 November, apparently for the first time.[104] The two agreed that the paper must be white, providing factual information on a given government policy, and not green, implying government proposals open to debate, and Sir William Nield, now permanent secretary to the Cabinet Office, agreed to hurry the work to be ready for publication in the new year.[105] Wilson agreed that the draft paper would go to ministers in January 1970.[106] The details of the cost of entry would be kept from cabinet for as long as possible, to prevent any attempts to re-open European policy.

With ministers lagging in pro-European speeches, the task was left to those at the top. Through the medium of the Queen's speech at the opening of parliament, it was announced that the government would 'maintain their application to become full members of the European Communities and desire an early commencement of negotiations. They will take a full part in promoting other measures contributing to European unity.'[107] Wilson himself made another speech in Guildhall, saying that he was facing a new move forward in relations with the EEC in the spirit of faith in British stability and native British common sense. He said that Britain's growing economic strength was recognised as a potential source of strength to Europe itself. While the UK was strong enough to survive outside Europe, this result would only emerge if 'through decisions not our own, we are denied entry', and it would be at a high price both for the UK and for Europe.[108] All by himself if necessary, Wilson was sending a clear message to the EC.

The superpowers, EFTA, the Commonwealth and WEU

As usual, the EC was not the only institution with which the British had to deal, although events in 1969 again demonstrated the priority placed on European relations. While ambassador John Freeman in Washington worried that British participation in the European gas centrifuge project would upset the Americans, for example, its importance in demonstrating Britain's European credentials and commitment to European technology overruled any such concerns.[109] Freeman was probably over-reacting: when Wilson briefly met Nixon during the latter's flying visit to RAF Mildenhall in August, the American president confessed that he 'had not been able to put his mind to these questions'. He welcomed Wilson's offer to talk at greater length.[110]

The British government continued to ask for discrete support for the application from the US, and despite their growing concerns about the effect of EC enlargement on American commercial interests, the Nixon administration obliged.[111] Stewart and secretary of state William Rogers agreed that 'it would be unwise to say it too loud', although in September Rogers revealed that since they no longer felt that the French were likely to object, they had been more active in their private support of the British application.[112] Still, the Americans waited for the summit results before Rogers gave a gentle public welcome to the signs of progress. He said that the administration saw the renewed impetus as 'a major step toward realisation of the full constructive potential of Europe. An enlarged European community would reflect more accurately than is now the case the reality of Europe's collective influence and potential – not only in an Atlantic context but in world affairs in general.'[113] He made similar comments bilaterally, telling Pompidou that the Nixon administration had assessed the difficulties and problems of EC enlargement for the US, and considered them entirely manageable. He said that the US government warmly welcomed the outcome of the summit.[114]

There were few concerns in EFTA as British entry began to seem more likely. A Swedish minister commented that the worst thing for the Swedish economy would be a long period of uncertainty before arrangements could be made for his country.[115] The Danes were concerned with their own application, hoping for separate but parallel negotiations with Britain, while the Irish were anxious that no tariff wall should be erected between Britain and Ireland.[116] The Austrians too hoped that they would not have to wait for British membership before their own relations with Europe could be resolved.[117] The president of Finland, Dr Urho Kekkonen, revealed that earlier British concerns about the development of Nordic Union had been misplaced: to his sorrow, the Norwegian and Danish governments 'had made it all too clear that their first priority was entry into the EEC and...they regarded Nordek as very much of a second best.'[118] There was therefore no pressure for EFTA to be considered as an alternative to the EC.

The Commonwealth, however, remained a time-consuming institution for Britain in 1969, with unrest in Anguilla, civil war in Nigeria and continuing difficulties in Rhodesia all taking cabinet time and British resources.[119] Yet most Commonwealth countries understood the new focus on Europe. When the governor-general of Australia called on Wilson in June, he commented on the strain caused to Anglo-Australian relations by the British decision to apply to the EC and withdraw from East of Suez. However, he 'thought that nevertheless Australia had been very understanding and, as a result, no Australian of consequence had tried to deter us from joining Europe if that is where we thought our interests lay.' Wilson acknowledged that Australia had legitimate interests in Britain's application, and promised to consult if there were any developments that would affect its interests.[120] The Canadians were more generous, telling Stewart in September that they 'fully understood and sympathised with our wish to seek entry' but 'hoped our entry might encourage liberal trade policies which would be more to Canada's liking than the present Community's.'[121] In return, when Canadian domestic politics forced prime minister Trudeau's government to take a harder line, the British offered to discuss Canadian 'special anxieties' whenever necessary.[122] When the deputy prime minister of New Zealand visited in mid-October, he and Wilson spent more time discussing the sincerity of the French change of position than New Zealand interests – which the British had long agreed to try and protect.[123] Smaller Commonwealth countries too, like Jamaica, were concerned for their 'vital interests'.[124] In general, however, as the summit drew closer, the Commonwealth only provided an obstacle to European policy insofar as its troubles provided a time-consuming diversion for Wilson and his ministers.

Political and technological collaboration

Co-operation in WEU continued in this period, although still without France. However, its importance had diminished: when progress was made on the British application, the question of political consultation would arise in the EC, at a level qualitatively higher than that possible in WEU.[125] The British felt that the work was useful since the time when it could be moved or merged into the EC was far off, and the Five agreed.[126] The forum was not only used for discussion of the British application: there continued to be substantive efforts to co-ordinate foreign policies. In June the six countries represented agreed to make individual but concerted representations to Greece, whose military government left it in danger of being expelled from the Council of Europe; Rhodesia was also discussed.[127] While rebuilding relations with France was important to Britain, luring them back to WEU was not a priority. As Stewart told Harmel, if the French attitude had changed sufficiently for them to contemplate British entry it would be hoped that they would also be prepared to co-operate in WEU.[128]

Technological collaboration also continued, although the effects of British economic retrenchment were still being felt in 1969, and ministers seriously considered cancelling Concorde.[129] The FCO, focused on rebuilding good relations with France, was appalled at the suggestion. The project was retained, although not without further deliberations over its usefulness.[130] At the end of October, the British were invited to participate in scientific and technological co-operation with the Communities: the invitation was accepted, with Wilson's qualification that the British job was 'to prove that real co-operation is impossible outside a united (and widened) community.'[131]

The nuclear question again...

More dramatically, Conservative leader Edward Heath openly discussed the idea of European nuclear collaboration, describing an Anglo-French nuclear deal as 'a key issue' in relation to British entry.[132] Stewart and Healey periodically discussed the nuclear option, concluding that a deal was possible, but that France, not Britain, should make any approach.[133] Wilson himself pointed out that the French nuclear deterrent was not committed to NATO, and when Heath apparently publicly suggested that the European partners should have a nuclear deterrent, he argued that such a move was forbidden by the nuclear non-proliferation treaty, describing it as 'the most dangerous and irresponsible' suggestion.[134] At the end of July Fred Mulley, then a minister of state in the FCO, took the opportunity of a question in the House of Commons to make the government's position clear. He said that 'it would be extremely unwise to link this with negotiations for entering into the Common Market. I have seen no disposition on the part of the Six to attempt to extract from us a deal of that kind, linking two things which are very different indeed.'[135]

The British embassy in Paris acknowledged that British aid to the *force de frappe* might help with the long-term French attitude to Britain, but pointed out the high cost of such a project, and revealed that the French had 'more than half a mind to go "direct to the fountain head" by trying (with whatever chance of success) for special defence relationship direct with the US.'[136] Stewart and Healey agreed again in October that the idea of Anglo-French nuclear co-operation was 'difficult and dangerous', with no reward for Britain unless France changed their attitude to NATO. The position of the new German government also needed to be taken into account.[137] Robinson's never-identified 'French friend' reported that the idea of an Anglo-French nuclear deal was possibly being revived in Paris, but nothing more was heard.[138] Heath's position might have been more dramatic than that of the Wilson government, but the simple fact was that the price the Six expected for British entry was clear, acceptance of the Treaties including the CAP, and there seemed to be no need to offer any other inducement at this time.

The Hague Summit

Throughout these diversions, the British continued to prepare for the summit. Two new bodies were created, a European Communities Information Unit, and a sub-committee of EURO to co-ordinate official information work within the UK.[139] Agriculture remained the main focus. Stewart decided, after consultation, not to try and influence CAP reform: among other dangers, he did not want to reveal the UK's detailed negotiating position on agriculture too soon.[140] In the meantime, the Germans – who shared the British desire for a revamp of the CAP – could be relied on to press for reform. Fortunately for this aim, the German perception of their power relative to France seemed to be changing. Frank, the state secretary in the foreign ministry, said that 'he could not see how the new Government could accept the position on which the French seemed determined to dig themselves in'. The British concluded that the CAP was an issue 'on which the Federal Government could not afford to give way to French wishes'.[141] Brandt told Jackling that he thought the complicated situation over agriculture could prove to have its advantages, and that he intended to make clear to the French in friendly but firm fashion that a beginning must now be made.[142] The British were in something of a Catch 22 situation: in order to demonstrate the sincerity of their conversion to Europe and pay the French price for British membership, they had to accept the principle of CAP: lobbying for change could be used by France as evidence that the UK was not truly 'European.' On the other hand, retention of CAP in its present form could make the cost of entry prohibitive for the UK. Indications that Germany might take a stand on agricultural policy were therefore welcome. In return, the improving British trade figures and balance of payments were welcomed in Bonn, according to Jackling, perceptibly changing the climate for the discussion of enlargement.[143]

A sense of urgency developed as the probability of a deal on enlargement increased. Soames said that 'there is now a tide in Europe, which, if we take it at its crest, will lead to our entry into the Community. If we miss this tide he [could] not himself see that we will ever again have a comparable opportunity.'[144] To some extent the French desire to complete the Communities' transitional period by the end of the year was therefore useful to the British: the faster the Community entered its definitive period, the sooner negotiations could open. Moreover, Pompidou continued to say that he looked forward to negotiations being opened and that 'he hoped that they would be brought to a successful conclusion.' In a meeting with Soames, Pompidou also raised the question of the British election timing – not, he hastened to add, because it would make any difference to him whether there was a Labour or a Conservative government in power, but because the Six should deal with a government that would have some time in power.[145] In response, Stewart emphasised 'HMG's determination to maintain their candidature for full membership of the Communities and seek negotiations as soon as possible. All three political parties support this. We are ready when the Six are.'[146]

Nonetheless, the after-effects of the 'Soames Affair' continued to be seen: the German government asked for an account of Soames' talk with Pompidou.[147] The residual distrust of France was significant, and the Five did not lift their pressure. At a lunch meeting of the foreign ministers of the Six, the Five 'emphasised clearly and unanimously to Schumann that the summit would be a political failure if a decision were not...taken on enlargement.'[148] The British continued to believe that the French would at least allow negotiations to open, although they were not yet convinced that Pompidou intended them to end in success.[149] Evidence of the firmer German position was reassuring, although the federal government still required constant reassurance from the British that the application was sincere.[150]

In this atmosphere of expectation the heads of state and government of the Six gathered at The Hague on 1-2 December.[151] President de Jong of the Netherlands opened by saying that the stagnation in the Communities would disappear when the member states reached agreement on the admission of new member states. If there were no difficulties on the principle of enlargement, then the Six could fix a time to begin. He was 'convinced that unless the European Communities are enlarged, and unless they are strengthened, they will mark time and even go into reverse.'[152] Pompidou initially made only a short reference to enlargement. He conceded that the candidatures of 'Great Britain and the three other candidates must be approached in a positive spirit but without losing from sight the interests of our Community and its members.' The Six should forge a community position, and negotiations should be conducted 'in the name of the Community and in the spirit of the Community.'[153]

Brandt followed, and spoke with authority. He pointed out the seriousness of the occasion, saying that if 'all were well in Europe, we would not have met today...the success or failure of this conference will rightly be read from whether we can steer the craft of the European Communities back into navigable waters.' He also noted that 'the German Parliament and public expect me not to return from this conference without concrete arrangements regarding the Community's enlargement.' The question could not be put off any longer: 'experience has shown us that postponing the question of enlargement threatens to paralyse the Community.' Brandt even drew attention to Germany's growing strength, saying that 'those who fear that the economic strength of the Federal

Republic of Germany could upset the balance within the Community ought to favour enlargement for this very reason.' He closed by saying that the choice was 'between a courageous step and a dangerous crisis....Europe needs our success.'[154] The Italians, Luxembourgers and Belgians added their support for the early opening of negotiations.[155]

When it came to the discussion on the first day, however, evidence of French hesitation emerged, and the British had to rely on the Five to fight their case. Pompidou said that he

> could feel no certainty that the applicant countries would be ready to accept the Community's ideas and it was therefore necessary to discuss the co-operation which ought to exist between the Six before discussing the extension of this co-operation to the candidates. "We must talk about what we are ourselves and what we want, before we ask others to join us."

He did concede, though, that conversations with the applicants could start in parallel with the development of the Community. The others agreed that completion was also a priority, and spent some time discussing issues like the financing of CAP and the election of the European parliament. As a result both the British and others expressed some disappointment at the outcome of the first day of the summit, Luns speaking for all when he described the results of the first meeting as 'not so very comforting.' After the dinner that evening, however, Scheel admitted feeling 'qualified optimism': Schumann had protested to him that the French position had changed. Not only had they said that they were in favour of enlargement in principle: they now wished the negotiations success.[156]

The optimism gained foundation during bilateral meetings on 2 December. Brandt laid great importance on these meetings, writing that 'President Pompidou and I finally succeeded in establishing the conditions under which Britain and other countries could enter the European Community.[157] In the plenary session, Pompidou interrupted twice to make clear his good intentions. First he described a plan for 'completion', and claimed that France was 'willing to go through these problems in a progressive spirit notably with regard to the candidates.'[158] Later he stressed again that he was in favour of enlargement and thought that the decisions necessary for reaching a common position could be taken '*dans les délais les plus utiles et plus rapide*' – although he insisted that there was no need to set a date for the opening of negotiations.[159] Schumann provided added reassurance when he said in a press conference that the preparatory work should not take longer than six months, rewriting history when he added that 'France had always wished for enlargement'. And in a separate press conference, Scheel said that he felt confident that there was no danger of failure in the preparations for negotiations.[160] The Summit Communiqué stated that the Heads of State and Government had agreed to the opening of negotiations, and 'that the essential preparatory work for establishing a basis of negotiation could be undertaken as soon as practically and conveniently possible. By common consent, the preparations would take place in a most positive spirit.'[161] The French veto had formally been lifted.

After The Hague

As he had promised before the summit, Brandt sent Frank to report to Wilson. He said it 'had not been easy to convince the French but now mutual confidence among the Six on the issue of enlargement was so involved that it would be exceedingly difficult for the French to go back on what had been agreed.'[162] Frank said the French had agreed that the preparations for negotiations must be completed by 1 July 1970, and stressed that 'this result had only been achieved after two private conversations between Chancellor Brandt and M. Pompidou.' The initial French attitude on a date for negotiations 'had been a disappointment and a rupture had been near', but Brandt had extracted Pompidou's 'word of honour' on the above agreement. Moreover, 'everyone knew' that ratification of the new CAP agreement could be held up if the French obstructed enlargement. Frank did not take all the credit for Brandt though: 'all the others had helped as well. A moment had been reached in the Community where the mutual trust between the members really meant something. It would be impossible to go back on this now without a deadly crisis.'[163]

The British were less effusive. Nield felt that the summit was a 'first small breach in the dyke of French obstructionism to both the development and the enlargement of the Community.' Nevertheless, it would be difficult for France to go back on its word. The government must now take great care on the substance and timing of the white paper, on any attempt to influence the Six's Community deliberations, and on continuing to strengthen the British economy. Wilson commented that Nield was '[v]ery realistic. Of all the commentaries I have seen this seems to be the best analysis.[164] Stewart took a more positive approach, describing the results of the summit as 'encouraging', meaning that 'the feeling for unity in Europe is moving strongly forward and that the Europeans fully understand that to get results, Britain has to be a part of this.'[165]

Cabinet and preparations for negotiations

Cabinet did not see the summit as a turning point. Thomson detailed the results, and his colleagues agreed that the results were 'as good as could be expected.' They were still concerned that France would impose an excessive price for lifting the veto, but agreed to discuss the matter further on receipt of the forthcoming white paper – Wilson again putting off discussion.[166] Shortly afterwards, Stewart told ministers that the Five were not prepared to brook delaying tactics from the French, and that they expected to deal with their internal affairs and then open negotiations with Britain within Six months. There was no recorded comment in reply to this news: anti-Europeans did not raise any objections.[167]

British preparations therefore continued in an atmosphere of heightened expectation. The FCO was considering its views on the Commission as negotiator, on transitional periods, and on replying to a German request to know the effect of levy and customs duty payments for Britain.[168] Efforts to display good European credentials continued, with Wilson even telling the French finance minister that the UK would go as far as European colleagues in monetary integration, 'not excluding a common currency', and Jenkins also holding detailed discussions on monetary co-operation with Giscard.[169] There were other substantive talks. During his visit to report on the summit, Frank also discussed agriculture, structural policy and political integration with the British.[170] Such talks were important, and not just in terms of pre-negotiations. When Soames met de Lipowski a few days after the summit the latter was not only celebrating the fact that it was 'all over bar the shouting.' He also said that 'the remaining doubt in Georges Pompidou's mind was the attitude and intention of HMG in regard to the whole European question and anything that could be said by HMG which would serve to set these fears at rest would be advantageous.' De Lipowski explicitly suggested that HMG should welcome the summit resolution to make progress on economic and monetary integration.[171] These comments were firm evidence, if any more were needed, that the UK needed not only to maintain pressure for the opening of negotiations, but also to show itself willing to discuss the future development of the Communities. The British also continued to fight suggestions that the British general election would affect the opening of negotiations, arguing that it was in the interests of the Six, if they wanted smooth negotiations with Britain, to start them with the present government and taken them as far as possible before the election. Either it would be the same government, and time would have been saved and the atmosphere improved by the Six showing their confidence in the present government; or there would be a new government, and the continuation of the bipartisan policy made more certain if negotiations were already in train.[172]

The white paper

Work on the white paper went on, and Wilson described the first drafts as 'a most impressive effort'.[173] Plans for its publication were put back to February, after officials expressed worries that Wilson's planned trip to the US and Canada would create an opportunity for anti Common Market briefing 'as soon as [he] had embarked on the plane.' Wilson himself, frightened of leaks, wanted even discussion of the paper before his trip to be restricted to 'a small high-powered group of ministers.'[174] Hints of the difficult economic picture given in the paper were revealed when Nield suggested that the closing paragraphs be reinforced with a fuller and firmer exposition of the political case for joining before the paper went before ministers.[175] Wilson agreed, and personally made several changes to the paper to make it more positive, including stressing the fact that the vote on the application in 1967 had been 'one of the largest majorities in a vote in the House of Commons in peacetime.'[176] Wilson was wary of relying on the political arguments: he did not want to lay the government open to the charge that they were 'seeking to disguise the economic effects by vague political arguments', so the paper should simply refer to his own parliamentary comments on the political arguments. Within the economic parts, attention should be drawn to the advantages to industry and technology. On some drafts of the paper, Wilson even checked the arithmetic in his trademark green ink.[177]

Community business

Meanwhile the Six moved towards an agreement on agricultural finance.[178] As it appeared that a definitive agreement could make it impossible for Britain to join unless substantially modified, an urgent debate ensued within the government over whether or not to try and intervene. When on balance the British decided that greater risk lay in not making known their preferences, they sent out telegrams to the capitals instructing ambassadors to make the position clear: if the UK contributed all its customs duties and levies to the agricultural fund, the amount would be far above the figure that would correspond to the British percentage of an enlarged Community's gross national product. The principle of equity must be included in the new arrangements.[179] In talks on 20-22 December, the French again agreed not to block the opening of negotiations in return for a commitment from the Five that they would agree to work out a new agreement on agricultural finance by 31 December. In fact, the Six did not manage to come to agreement – to extend the present system for one more year – until February 1970, thus relieving the urgency of the British representations.[180]

Conclusions

Ironically, the fourth Polaris submarine, 'Revenge', was commissioned at Birkenhead on 4 December, just two days after the lifting of the French veto at the summit. De Gaulle had used the British arrangement to buy Polaris nuclear weapons from the United States in December 1962 as a pretext for his veto of the first British application in 1963.[181] Yet there was no question of any re-imposition of the veto. The 'personality, position and performance of Willy Brandt', the weakened position of France itself after the downfall of de Gaulle and devaluation of the franc and consequent need for Community support in the agricultural, commercial and financial fields, and the threat of continued stagnation to the Community itself together dictated a deal on enlargement.[182] Brandt's independent foreign policy raised the spectre of a self-confident Germany, tipping the balance away from France within the Community. His opening statement at The Hague raised this very issue, and Debré later cited disquiet about German intentions as a reason for bringing Britain into the EC.[183] Equally, the Five now had something to offer France in reform of the CAP. This deal, which started to emerge six months before the summit, worked two ways. First, the Five let it be known that they would block a definitive arrangement for agriculture unless the French opened the door to enlargement. Second, the Five were willing to accept an arrangement that did not best fit their interests as the price of British entry. This deal meant, of course, that the British had to accept it too.

For Wilson, the decision that negotiations would be opened in mid-1970 marked a personal triumph. The British application had been pursued, doggedly, 'in the face of many frustrations and delays'.[184] Wilson's activity in controlling antagonistic ministers, in directing the preparation of Britain's negotiating position and in presenting the European policy at home and abroad was crucial both in building support and in minimising opposition. In 1970, as the potential costs of entry became clearer and the opening of negotiations drew closer, Wilson's continuing determination would remain vital.

8

January – June 1970: towards negotiations

From January 1970, however, British preparations for enlargement negotiations accelerated, and the nature of interaction with the Community states therefore changed to some extent, as each side worked to finalise its bargaining position. Opposition in cabinet to the European policy became more vocal as the likelihood of entry into the Communities increased, meaning that Wilson, Stewart and their officials had to work extra hard to convince their European allies of the sincerity of the government's application.

Britain's European credentials
Stewart stressed the need to maintain the pressure for accession. He wrote to Wilson in January that they 'must continue to press for substantive negotiations to take place in the summer of 1970. Otherwise we may find the timetable slipping until the end of the year.' As it was, Stewart did not expect negotiations, signature and ratification of the accession treaties to be complete until mid-1972 at the earliest, so it was vital to keep moving.[1] This need to maintain momentum was not only felt in Britain: friends across the continent advised the British to keep pressing their case.[2] Every opportunity was taken to advertise Britain's European nature.

Wilson set out his own views and hopes at a press conference at Chequers. He said that Britain would play a 'wholehearted part' in the future development of the Communities, mentioning technological co-operation, the development of European companies, and monetary co-operation. It would be important 'for us all to get closer and more and more into the habit of working together'; new institutions could be created as the need arose. He was not worried about a loss of sovereignty: 'human progress was based on the progressive derogation of sovereignty' and the 'important questions were to whom sovereignty should be ceded and for what purpose.' Britain had made 'calculated derogations of sovereignty' to NATO, EFTA and the United Nations because the advantages were greater than the disadvantages. Wilson acknowledged that popular feeling for European integration had slipped since 1967, but argued that it would 'develop positively' once membership was seen to be a possibility: 'the whole issue was much more exciting.' When asked for his personal reasons for accepting that Britain's future lay in Europe, Wilson mentioned not only the technological possibilities but said that 'on the political level he had become convinced that the world needed a more coherent voice from Europe.'[3] The fact that this press conference was non-attributable suggests that Wilson gave an honest account of his views. They were greeted with pleasure: the Italian newspapers, for example, stated that 'Britain has demonstrated her determination to press ahead with her candidature for the Common Market, that she is decided to accept the terms of the Treaties of Rome and that Europe herself has much to gain from British accession in the economic, technological and political fields.'[4] Wilson suggested that the press cuttings be sent to a British newspaper editor.[5] In a more orthodox way, he also continued to stress the British position in private meetings with European ministers.[6]

Stewart and Thomson provided backup. In a speech to the Franco-British Society, Stewart said that 'it must be accepted now by even the most sceptical, that Britain has made her determination, the strength of her desire to enter the Community, plain beyond doubt. We go forward resolutely'.[7] Thomson stressed the political aspects of the British application, which were 'overriding for Britain....there was a deep feeling in Britain that Europe must get together politically if it was to make its views felt.'[8] Together, Wilson, Stewart and Thomson presented a consistent and formidable front on European policy, and were successful in convincing their European counterparts of the sincerity of Britain's turn to Europe.

Preparations

Meanwhile, work on the British position was continuing. The negotiating team, although not announced until 11 April, was at least partially selected in January, with Thomson and O'Neill leading.[9] Thomson specified that team members should 'feel a strong sense of commitment to the success of the negotiations.'[10] The full team consisted of GR Bell (third secretary to the Treasury); GR Denman (on promotion to deputy secretary, Board of Trade); FM Kearns (deputy secretary, MAFF); WP Shovelton (under-secretary at the Ministry of Technology); John Robinson, IM Sinclair (legal adviser), and Marjoribanks and Christofas from the British representation to the EC.[11] Likewise, preparations were being made both on the timetable for negotiations and on the substantive British position.[12] An official sub-committee was set up to consider the financial and monetary aspects of the UK's application, and spent much of its time tracking developments within the Six as they pursued the summit's aim of monetary integration.[13] As with all work on European policy, Wilson kept up to date with progress in this committee, provided it with guidance and endeavoured to secure its conclusions within as small a circle as possible.[14] Likewise, he continued to follow the progress of EURO, asking for example in February if anything was being done for 'Britain's developing country friends similar to Yaoundé'.[15] A legal sub-committee was set up in March, to give legal assistance to the negotiating team and to prepare the legislation necessary for accession.[16] By March, Nield had provided Wilson with a long and detailed brief on negotiating strategy: the details of the brief are beyond the scope of this book, but Wilson's grasp of economic questions was again demonstrated when he minuted Nield to ask if on 'different target prices can it be shown that elasticity of consumption and production response are such as exactly to balance the saving by lower target [and] import prices?'[17] Relatively late on, in April, a ministerial sub-committee consisting of Thomson, Mason, Hughes (now minister of agriculture), John Diamond (chief secretary to the Treasury) and Harold Lever (paymaster general) was set up to supervise the negotiations and report to EURM – the latter, however, did not meet.[18] Full cabinet decisions, O'Neill said, would not be required until October at the earliest.[19] When Nield reported that draft negotiating briefs would be ready in mid-May, Wilson agreed that, for reasons of security and inter-departmental rivalry, ministers would not need to see them until detailed negotiations were underway in the autumn.[20]

The white paper and the costs of entry

This preparatory work continued almost in isolation from the domestic presentation of European policy. In January much time was taken up in drafting the white paper, of which there were still at this point two versions. Wilson's assertion in his memoir that it was 'drawn up by officials, economists and statisticians, and free from all ministerial interference' was clearly a misrepresentation, since his own close involvement continued.[21] Nield noted that the prime minister had kept 'in close touch' with the drafting process.[22] Moreover, Wilson continued to manage the progress of the paper extremely carefully. An 'inner group' of ministers was set up consisting of Stewart, Jenkins, Castle, Healey, Benn, Thomson, Mason, and Hughes. In a letter to their private secretaries, Richard Lloyd-Jones (private secretary to Nield) stressed the need for secrecy, and passed on Wilson's request that in view of 'the risk of premature disclosure of the government's intentions at this stage', knowledge of the composition of the group should be confined to the ministers themselves and the officials directly involved in briefing them. Copies of the white paper were attached 'for personal use only.'[23] It was also in the spring of 1970 that Wilson decided that appeals from cabinet committees to full cabinet would only be allowed after consultation with the chairman of the committee concerned: the committees received a 'devolution of authority' from full cabinet and so their decisions should stand as far as possible. For this reason, ministers should themselves attend committees of which they were members, rather than sending representatives.[24]

The secrecy was for a good reason: as Nield wrote to the permanent under secretaries, the preparation was 'as difficult as that of any White Paper I can recall.' First, the remit was not to produce a paper setting out why the UK should join if the terms were right, but a 'factual and objective assessment of the economic advantages and disadvantages, quantified so far as possible, whilst reaffirming the policy set out in 1967 of joining if acceptable terms can be negotiated.' Second, there were three readerships: the UK, European countries and third countries, 'all with differing and often opposing interests in the negotiations.' The conflict between forming a negotiating position and domestic presentation was clear, and Nield acknowledged that it would cause a 'major debate.'[25] Wilson insisted that the paper contain as much quantification as possible, so that it would be a full assessment of the economic effects of entry: however, the reason why only partial quantification (that is, of the costs but few of the benefits) was possible should also be given. At the same time, of course, since much of the quantification would be adverse, it would fortify the British negotiating position to have the potential costs of entry baldly spelled out. Finally, presenting the paper in such a way would allow the government, in the concluding paragraphs, to

lift the discussion to a higher plane than that of an argument about figures – namely that what is at stake here is the future welfare and security of Britain and Europe in the last three decades of the twentieth century – a judgement to be taken on the judgement of responsible citizens and not by slide rule or computer.[26]

Wilson was aware that 'everyone would see [the white paper] as reinforcing their own prejudices' but argued that the figures were less alarming than he had expected, partly because the figures were for 1977 (the end of the expected transition period) not 1972 (as expected when the application was made in May 1967).[27] Nield warned that the picture might prove 'too gloomy', and Wilson acknowledged that the paper should indicate that, 'of course, if negotiations did not produce acceptable conditions we should decline.'[28]

Wilson was not the only person to point out the costs of entry might prove to be too high for Britain: a Treasury official pointed out that this point 'should be stated clearly in the concluding paragraphs'.[29] Nield concluded that 'painful economic adjustments' could be avoided provided that national income grew by 3.4% each year, but Wilson believed that an acceptable bargain could – indeed, must – be found through negotiation.[30] Wilson's comments thus had a different nuance to those of some of his ministers who felt that unacceptable costs could be used as an excuse for rejecting accession.[31] Wilson's position was, perhaps ironically, best expressed by Brandt. In an address to the Foreign Press Association in London, Brandt said that negotiations

> will involve many difficult technical problems and will not be without complication.
>
> But as long as we remain convinced that the Community must be enlarged to enable Europe to hold its own in the political, economic and technical fields, and as long as the will for enlargement remains strong, those difficulties can be overcome. An enlargement of the Community is in line with our common interest in European consolidation and solidarity.[32]

The difficulty of reaching acceptable terms did not mean, therefore, that the attempt should be abandoned.

Eventually, other ministers had to see the white paper. Part of the reason for restricting it to economics had been to avoid 'too extensive a debate' on political issues in cabinet.[33] The tactic was successful: when the above-mentioned ministerial committee met, its discussion was confined to economic detail and the need to publish as much factual information as possible so that the press would not be tempted to make its own calculations. If it appeared that the government was trying to conceal its estimates, the committee agreed, 'this in itself would generate opposition to the Government's policy of opening negotiations'. Not only did Wilson again stress the need for confidentiality, the members of the sub-committee were not allowed to receive copies of the minutes.[34]

The white paper was by far the most contentious European issue dealt with in cabinet in 1970: some senior ministers described it as 'horrifying.'[35] Castle recorded her 'delight at the revelations of the document' – bizarrely, since she was part of the ministerial committee that had already seen and approved the paper – and the 'shocked reactions of some of the most devoted adherents of going in.'[36] Yet its contents and structure – apart from two concluding paragraphs on the political benefits of joining the Community – were generally approved. Ministers were discouraged (some rather encouraged) by the high cost of entry as set out in the paper, noting that it 'could well be the case that we should not be able in the end to afford the cost which was demanded.' After some discussion Wilson concluded that the paper was approved for publication on 10 February, subject to the amendments suggested. He again stressed the need for secrecy and asked that ministers not discuss the paper between its publication and the debate in parliament.[37] When the Paper returned to cabinet two days later, revisions had been made to only five paragraphs. It was agreed that Wilson would present it to Parliament by himself, without other ministerial speeches but taking account of the comments of ministers in drafting his statement. BBC coverage would be factual and educational and aim to avoid political controversy.[38] Significantly, most ministers had only a week, from receiving the draft white paper on 29 January, to approving its publication on 5 February, to consider a long and enormously detailed paper that had been several months in the preparation by officials, Wilson, Stewart and Thomson.[39]

In presenting the white paper to the House of Commons and the wider public, Wilson was able to set its economic tone in the political context of his European policy, a context that ministers had resisted being included in the paper itself. Wilson saw the press summary of the paper before any other minister, suggesting one amendment to make the economic consequences of entry seem less drastic.[40] The FCO had warned that omitting a re-statement of the basic position would be 'widely interpreted abroad as representing a retreat from our publicly declared policy' and Wilson did not disappoint.[41] In the Commons he insisted that the figures had been calculated in 'a completely objective and neutral way' and that the government's European policy was 'not in question.' Political as well as economic factors were involved. No decision on entry had to be taken yet: it would depend on the negotiations. He concluded that the

> Government will enter into negotiations resolutely, in good faith, mindful both of British interests and of the advantages of success in the negotiations to all the members of an enlarged Community. We have made clear that if the negotiations produce acceptable

conditions for British entry we believe that this will be advantageous for Britain, for Europe, and for Europe's voice in the world. Equally, we have made clear that if the conditions which emerge from the negotiations are in the Government's view not acceptable, we can rely on our own strength outside the Communities. But I repeat what I have said on a number of occasions in the House and outside that this outcome – a failure of the negotiations – would involve a cost for Britain, a cost for Europe, and a diminution of Europe's influence in world affairs.[42]

There was nevertheless some 'pretty wild political speculation' in the British press about the meaning of the paper, and Nield advised Wilson to follow a 'steadying operation' in the Commons debate on the subject.[43] The same emphasis was given in instructions to missions in the Six, which stated that 'Her Majesty's Ministers have since [May 1967] repeatedly stressed our determination to join the European Communities on terms fair for all.'[44]

The response of the Six suggested that Wilson had succeeded in finding the right balance among his different audiences: continental press coverage commented that the paper would give solace to 'anti-Europeans' in Britain but did not see it as an obstacle to the opening or success of negotiations.[45] Brandt at least felt that the British were seeking a fair bargain.[46] The Italians too, as debtors to the EEC themselves (because they imported so much food) felt the British position keenly and were convinced that there should be an equitable sharing of burdens.[47] The principle was one on which the Wilson government would insist until the end of its term.[48]

The white paper was not the only instance where different interpretations were made or given to different audiences. As during the previous year, Wilson and others made comments in the House of Commons that then had to be 're-phrased' for the continental ear. Fortunately, friends in Europe understood that there was anti-accession opinion in the House of Commons, but they welcomed the clarifications nonetheless. For example, when MP Neil Marten asked a question about majority voting and political unification in the Community and Thomson's answer could be taken to indicate that the British rejected the concept, a guidance telegram was sent to European missions explaining both that the UK accepted the current rules on majority voting and that the government looked forward to participating in discussions on political unification.[49]

Despite the remaining divisions in cabinet, ministers were genuinely shocked when Shore made a speech on 25 March, implying that the Government no longer wished or intended to make a real effort to join the Communities, without first consulting the Foreign Secretary or Chancellor of the Duchy of Lancaster. Crossman called it 'an act of total recklessness.'[50] Shore defended himself vigorously, but was reminded in discussion that all had agreed that whatever differences of opinion of emphasis there existed among individual ministers, the Government would speak with one voice in public in endorsement of the policy. It was essential, he was told, in what Castle described as 'the biggest trouncing in Cabinet I can remember for a long time', to avoid any appearance of disunity or allow the impression to be created that the Government was prepared to treat a major issue of national policy as the subject of mere party political controversy in the period before the general election. The Government's policy should therefore be reaffirmed in the terms already approved collectively by cabinet, and Shore should seek an early public opportunity to put his speech in better perspective, making it clear that it remained the Government's declared purpose to join the EC if acceptable terms could be obtained.[51]

Shore's March speech had repercussions on the continent: Soames wrote from Paris of the importance placed on the fact that all three main British political parties supported entry into the Community, and the danger of doing anything that might undermine it.[52] Herr Blankenhorn, the German ambassador in London, told Thomson that Shore's speech had caused 'considerable misgivings' in Europe.[53] Sir Anthony Part, permanent under-secretary to the Board of Trade, was asked about the speech during a visit to Bonn and responded by quoting Wilson's statement in the House of Commons on 26 March that Britain was 'extremely anxious to get into the Common Market if we can get the right terms and we will proceed to negotiate with full determination to that end.'[54] The European credentials that Wilson had taken such care to build had been undermined.

Shore's speech was particularly galling since, prompted by officials, Wilson had asked Stewart in January again to encourage his colleagues to make positive speeches on entry into Europe.[55] Castle pointed out that there was a difference between saying nothing and speaking in favour of the policy: the latter 'was really straining loyalty too much. I was prepared to keep my mouth shut, but not to speak if I could avoid it.'[56] Nevertheless, in May Shore followed instructions and made a more positive speech in Stepney. He still stressed the costs of entry, stating that, for 'its part the Government is determined to get on with negotiations with all speed in the conviction that we can secure fair terms for all. In short we are prepared to make sacrifices if, and only if, the total package is in the interests of Britain and of Europe.'[57] Perhaps as a consequence of Castle's comment, Wilson told cabinet ministers in April to clear the text of any speech about the forthcoming negotiations with the chancellor of the Duchy of Lancaster and the chairman of EURO.[58] The commitment to collective responsibility could only, it seemed, be trusted so far.

Relations with the Six

While ministers were thus engaged, the rebuilding of relations with France continued. There was still considerable uncertainty in the UK about the sincerity of the French about-turn. Once again there were suggestions of the possibility of an Anglo-French nuclear deal, but these were only ever vague hints, without substance, and Stewart and Healey concluded that the first move, if any happened, would have to come from France.[59] The French expressed more concrete concerns about the future of the sterling balances and their impact on future monetary co-operation in an enlarged Community, and the British remained suspicious that any such matters raised by the French would be used as excuses to keep the UK out, rather than genuine negotiating points.[60] Some officials stressed the need for the UK to accept all the Community's rules, implying that there was continuing concern that British entry might change the EC's nature: even Schumann asked whether 'the rules and principles of the EEC will remain sacrosanct' when Britain joined.[61] In February de Courcel appeared 'distrustful' of the British insistence on limiting negotiations to the essential questions, worried that once inside, the British would refuse to agree to particular regulations or directives already accepted by the Six.[62] Indeed, Palliser, now in the British embassy in Paris, worried that the scepticism of de Courcel's reports from London was reinforcing the lingering doubts in Paris.[63] The French minister of commerce, Jean Wahl, suggested that 'if only one could find a way around the mutual suspicions of the *Quai d'Orsay* and the Foreign and Commonwealth Office, the chances of a successful negotiation for entry into the Common Market would be greatly increased.'[64] Couve – more Gaullist than de Gaulle – discussed the subjects of negotiation and future developments with Stewart. He warned Stewart that the US had expressed concern at some Community developments, implying that he still felt the 'special relationship' could cause problems for Britain.[65] He was 'smilingly icy' at a meeting of the Foreign Affairs club, showing that he regarded an enlarged Community as 'an impossibly unmanageable affair.'[66] De Gaulle's former *chef de cabinet*, Etienne Burin des Roziers, now French ambassador in Rome, made a similar speech with the old Gaullist excuse: British entry would change the nature of the EC.[67]

However, there were also encouraging noises coming from the very top of the new French establishment: Schumann told Harmel that he regarded the decisions at The Hague as a European 'bible'.[68] In a speech in

Brussels, he said that 'in the long term there will be no Europe without England for the sufficient reason that without England thirty years ago there would without doubt be no Europe today.'[69] The US embassy in Paris passed on information that Pompidou had told the French cabinet that 'it was now in France's interests to have Britain in the Market.'[70] Likewise, ambassador de Courcel told Stewart that 'whereas his government had previously sought to delay enlargement of the EEC, they were now seeking to bring it about.'[71] Officials from the French ministry of agriculture even suggested that Britain come forward with ideas for structural reform of Community agriculture: normal contacts between the two countries were beginning again at every level.[72] By March, Gaullists previously opposed to Britain's entry were reported to be 'resigned' to that event.[73] Duhamel, French minister of agriculture and responsible for the sector likely to be the key issue in negotiations, was in favour of British entry on economic and political grounds and thought the British 'economic miracle' would enable her to pay the price.[74]

When Schumann visited London at the end of January, the new warmth of the relationship was evident. Schumann said that 'it was essential that if negotiations were begun they must be successful' and added that there was no reason why they should not start in the early summer.[75] He said that he was 'deeply encouraged' at the development of Anglo-French relations – although he noted as well the need to get on with building the Channel Tunnel.[76] Chaban-Delmas said publicly that he was 'favourable' towards British entry and that negotiations would be opened 'in the most constructive spirit.'[77] As always, Monnet was encouraging, telling Stewart in March that he was convinced that the problems of Britain's entry would be solved without much difficulty during the negotiations.[78] Pompidou too told a California audience that negotiations would open soon and that '*finalement nous aboutirons à un accord et à l'entrée de la Grande Bretagne dans le Marché Commun.*'[79] By April, Thomson was holding the same kind of pre-negotiation discussion with the French as with all other members of the Six, covering political co-operation as well as the form and content of enlargement negotiations.[80] When the French completed their own studies of the effects of British entry in early June, they let it be known that they were convinced that there were no problems which Britain could not solve or manage with the help and time of the kind that the Six had given each other over the years.[81]

The significance of Brandt's leadership of Germany continued to be recognised. Jackling commented that

Kiesinger had not been able to conceive of a Europe without Great Britain but equally he had not been able to conceive how to secure

British entry into the Community. Brandt was determined to see the Community enlarged not least because he was convinced that the best way to make real progress with the eastern policy was through enlargement of the Community.[82]

Having struggled against Kiesinger's more cautious attitude towards Britain during 1967-1969, Brandt in 1970 reassured Wilson that his 'assumption that negotiations for entry will begin in the middle of this year remains unchanged.'[83] As Stewart told Wilson, 'Anglo-German relations are excellent...For the first time in history we have a German Government about whose attitude towards Britain there are no lurking doubts and to whose Chancellor we can talk pretty well without inhibitions.'[84] Later, Brandt reported that the Six were making good progress on the work that needed to be done before negotiations could open, but that Britain need not worry that internal Community work was moving too fast: the Six had been discussing economic and monetary union but 'no one in Britain need fear that progress on this aspect would advance too far before negotiations'. The British and Germans agreed on all other aspects – the timing of the opening of negotiations, their focus, economic and political integration, and continued European co-operation within NATO. Wilson again stressed the British attitude: 'Britain would be entering these negotiations in the determination to succeed if that lay in our power'.[85] Brandt promised to keep the British government closely informed as discussions proceeded within the Community.[86] Brandt was not above delivering a little flattery to the British parliament, telling the House of Lords that when it soon had to take a decision on the 'weighty and far-reaching questions' involved in British entry, 'the experience and far-sightedness which distinguish this Parliament [would] come into their own.'[87]

Moving goalposts

Of course, the summit at The Hague concerned matters other than enlargement, and some Community business that had stagnated during the veto period accelerated from December. The use of WEU for the co-ordination of foreign policies remained a point of contention. The French maintained their boycott of WEU until June 1970, only returning on condition that there was no discussion of 'any technical or economic questions related to the enlargement of the ECs, nor any political questions directly linked therewith.'[88] In contrast, the Germans were determined to intensify the political consultations at ministerial meetings until 'something better' might be available.[89]

Little was done in the direction of the co-ordination of foreign policy or 'political unification', and in any case, the member states assured Britain that they would keep the Government informed of any decisions about the future form of political co-operation in Europe: there was no question of final decisions being taken in its absence.[90] As in 1961 and 1967, when the British had hoped to influence or even participate in the discussions on agricultural finance at the same time as negotiating for accession, in 1970 they hoped to take part in talks on political co-operation in parallel with enlargement negotiations.[91] The Germans warned that 'absolute priority' must be given to persuading France to contribute to the success of the economic negotiations, and if necessary, the political talks could be delayed, but the British continued to push for inclusion.[92] This was not just a public position: in a draft statement for a Labour Party discussion of policies to be followed in the next parliament, Stewart included that 'we shall wish to play a full part as soon as possible in the discussions with our European partners on European political unification.'[93] Eventually Schumann said clearly that there could be no question of setting up political co-operation among the ten before the end of negotiations for enlargement.[94] The French had acknowledged to Stewart that the Community would not get very far with its consideration before British entry, so the UK could take part in its eventual discussions later.[95] Nevertheless, the Dutch continued to block political consultation without British participation, determined that they should be involved from the start.[96] The extent to which the British were looking to the future was revealed in a meeting of heads of European missions in March: while some time was spent on the usual subjects of CAP and the cost of entry, more was devoted to discussion of political unification and even defence.[97]

More significant in terms of the opening of negotiations were economic developments that would affect the cost of entry for Britain. The French were not the only country to raise uncomfortable points about British entry. The Belgians suggested in February that Britain could not expect to have full membership rights in terms of voting during the transition period, although they backed down in response to the fierce British rebuttal.[98] All six member states were determined that 'completion' must be reached within the EEC before enlargement negotiations began.[99] But the desire to finalise internal business did not mean delay for enlargement: the Commission wanted to 'get down to business' before the summer holidays; even the French did not believe that anything done as part of the 'reinforcement' of the Community would be unacceptable to Britain or cause delays.[100] Interestingly, when Wilson heard that Jenkins had told French finance minister Giscard d'Estaing that Britain 'did not want to reserve the monetary field from the Community, and we were prepared to move far in this field', he commented '[y]es. Very interesting. Chancellor gave all the right answers.'[101] The Commission even suggested that economic and monetary union would facilitate British acceptance of the CAP without correctives, and that the Six should press on for that reason.[102] Other members of the Six were 'delighted' to hear Jenkins' views, passed on by Giscard, since they had supposed that monetary developments might be a real obstacle for Britain.[103]

Although agreement on agricultural finance was held up by differences over a common market for tobacco, a common wine policy – which Schumann described as 'a great bore' – the future budgetary powers of the Parliament and final details of the arrangements for future European Agricultural Fund expenditure, these issues were finally settled at Council meetings held in February.[104] The previous chapter demonstrated British efforts to ensure that the UK share of agricultural funding would be equitable, and there was a 'good deal' of support for this view amongst Europeans.[105] The same dichotomy that had been seen between enlargement and agricultural finance at The Hague was seen through 1970. Leverage over the French was retained in that the financial agreement had to be ratified by each member state: the Germans planned to take at least until the end of 1970 in order to force the French to negotiate seriously with Britain. But on the other hand the French suggested that negotiations with Britain 'could not finish...before ratification was complete nor indeed could they reach a very advanced stage.'[106] Schumann said that negotiations could reach their 'decisive stage' once ratification of the agricultural finance agreement was complete.[107] The British, Belgians and Dutch were extremely annoyed by what they saw as a new French delaying tactic, and the French re-phrased their comment. According to the Belgians, they 'were ready to open negotiations in the summer and to negotiate seriously, but they would watch the process of ratification slowly and implied that, 'if it seemed to be dragging, this would naturally affect their own zeal in the enlargement negotiations'.[108] Ultimately, it was Heath and not Wilson who had to deal with this problem: the Labour Government continued to insist that nothing should hold up the enlargement negotiations.

Agreements were also reached within the Six on a common commercial policy, the postponement for some members of the introduction of value added tax (VAT), a reduction in size of the Commission, and monetary co-operation, while negotiations for association with Greece, Turkey, Yugoslavia, Israel and Spain continued.[109] For Britain, these agreements represented moving goalposts, or a raising of the barrier to entry into the Communities. However, differences within the Six, particularly between

France and Germany, helped to ensure that the Community did not take 'reinforcement' so far that it would endanger Britain's entry.[110] And as soon as agreement had been reached on agricultural finance, the Six turned their attention to preparing their own joint negotiating position: the Dutch saw no reason why it should not be complete by the end of May or beginning of June.[111]

Throughout the last months of the Wilson government, the Six therefore discussed amongst themselves and with the British the form that negotiations should take. There were many possibilities: should the Commission negotiate on behalf of the Six, or the foreign ministers collectively, or a combination of both? Should they be held with the four applicants together or separately, and should all four enter at the same time? Should discussions focus, as the British hoped, on the 'big issues' with the detail left for after entry?[112] The British stood by George Brown's statement in WEU in July 1967, and resisted efforts to introduce new subjects, like monetary co-operation, into the primary negotiations.[113] Throughout, the British continued to insist on their determination. Stewart stressed that

> [w]e must be absolutely clear that our first priority was to get into the Community....we needed to concentrate single-mindedly on joining the Community. The primary reason why matters had reached their present conjuncture was that we had steadfastly persisted in this single aim; we had refused to be diverted by suggestions of a trade arrangement; we had refused to nibble at the suggestions President de Gaulle had put to Mr Soames.[114]

In pursuit of this aim, the British continued to demand that negotiations open before the summer holidays.[115] From mid-May they knew from Luns that the Six were planning a 'family portrait' meeting with all four applicants at the end of June, and the work of the committees was timetabled accordingly.[116]

The superpowers, EFTA and the Commonwealth

British relations with other countries therefore continued to evolve. An FCO planning committee paper in January explicitly recognised a shift from Churchill's 'three circles' policy of the equal importance in foreign policy of the USA, the English-speaking world (or Commonwealth) and Europe. It suggested that the lifting of the French veto would mean that the changing relationship with the United States would now have to be considered. It was not a straight choice between the US and Europe, because the influence of both Britain and the other European states would collectively increase as the Communities were enlarged and strengthened. The US had consistently supported this development, although the continuation of that support depended on political integration in Europe concomitant with economic integration. The paper concluded that the British,

> while taking care to avoid the implication that we are in any sense a representative of the United States, we shall have to try to ensure that European integration does not upset too many American interests at the same time, that Europe continues to develop as an outward-looking Community, and that in the defence field Western Europe maintains and if possible improves its contribution to the Alliance.[117]

This paper informed Anglo-American contacts over the remaining months of the Wilson government.

Freeman in Washington believed European political integration to be 'the most important single element' in the talks between Nixon and Wilson that month, and that Wilson and Stewart should concentrate on 'deploying the political case for our entry.'[118] He argued that Nixon 'needed to have ammunition with anti-European integration lobbies in the United States' and that impressing the president now with the 'rightness of the general strategy of our European policies' would help to discount in advance the strains that were bound to emerge in Anglo-American relations as the negotiations proceeded. Wilson pointed out that British participation in a more united Europe would help to reduce the responsibility which the US had to carry for Germany, although he acknowledged that the UK might have to 'disassociate' themselves somewhat from the US on issues like the gas centrifuge.[119] Freeman was correct about US worries: the embassy warned London of American concerns about Community price support for agriculture and the increasing number of preferential arrangements with third countries.[120] It should be noted that these concerns were not totally one-sided: officials from the US state department told the British that they assumed that if the negotiations failed, the UK 'would become a permanent liability to the US requiring continual bailing out.'[121] Economically, then, British entry was the lesser of two evils for the United States.

Wilson's speech to the state dinner in the White House therefore stated that it was as important for the US as for Britain 'that Europe should grow stronger and more united'.[122] He told Nixon that the political case for British entry was strong, and perhaps even being reinforced, at least in French eyes, by their growing fear of a revanchist Germany. He acknowledged that British entry into a Europe 'which at present looked only inwards' would have an adverse effect on short-term American economic interests. However, political benefits would come from what he called a 'Vietnamisation' (meaning 'Europeanisation') of Europe: a stronger, more cohesive Europe would be able to take some of the burden off the United States and make an increased contribution to NATO. Nixon responded with the standard American line: the US favoured British entry but would 'allow their policy to be inferred rather than declared.'[123] These lines were repeated at the special meeting of the National Security Council to which Wilson and Stewart were invited in imitation of Nixon's attendance of a British cabinet meeting in January 1969. Nixon said that he 'favoured a strong Europe – economic, political and, in the end, defence – including Britain. The hope was that such a Europe would, of its own free choice, follow a parallel course with the US.'[124] When Wilson later wrote to Nixon to inform him of his talks with Brandt, Nixon promised that he would 'convey to the Chancellor as I did to his predecessor, my strong conviction that British entry into the Common Market will be a major milestone in the building of our Western partnership.'[125] He also wrote to Rey on the twentieth anniversary of the Schuman Declaration that had led to the creation of the European Coal and Steel Community, 'to reaffirm the full support of the United States on the renewed effort of broadening and strengthening the European Community.'[126] In recognition of the American interest, arrangements were put in place, replicating those of 1961-3, to brief the Americans about once a week on the progress of the negotiations once they started.[127]

As they drew closer, Sir Duncan Wilson commented that there was in the Soviet Union 'an element of genuine concern at the likely shape of an integrated Western Europe', so the UK should take care to put their ideas frankly to the Soviets. Wilson (the prime minister) replied that one problem of dialogue with the Russians (sic) was knowing whether one's point had registered. For example, he had made the point to Kosygin that the British presence in Europe acted 'as a restraint on the Germans'. Sir Duncan concluded that once Britain was a member of the EC, 'the Soviet Union would be realistic about it and make the best of it.'[128]

EFTA was more acquiescent. The Irish were anxious that the negotiations should be successful, and that their entry should come as soon as possible after Britain's.[129] There were hints that the Swiss might abandon their neutrality and apply for some kind of economic association with the EEC.[130] For the Scandinavians, progress continued with Nordic Union: the Swedish prime minister Olaf Palme continued to state after The Hague that 'Nordek is no half-way house but a customs union standing on its own feet.' However, it was clearly secondary to entry into or association with the EEC, and did not cause Britain any problems – indeed, the Swedes hoped that the British would be successful.[131] Wilson and Palme knew each other personally, and when they met in April Wilson encouraged the Swede to consider applying for full membership.[132] As membership of the Communities became increasingly likely, EFTA consequently declined in importance for the British and the other members alike.

In contrast, as the negotiations drew closer, Commonwealth countries began to speak out for their interests. The Canadians were anxious that British entry should cause them as little difficulty as possible, and premier Trudeau's government felt that failing to insist on close consultation would result in domestic trouble. Wilson resisted adding to the already extensive bilateral machinery between the two countries.[133] New Zealand was more insistent, but again, the British managed to put off their requests for consultations until after the election.[134] EURO did consider consultations with other governments, and emphasised that it would be important not to exclude Arnold Smith, the secretary general of the Commonwealth, at least for presentational reasons.[135] Wilson intervened to note that if HMG allowed extra consultations with one government (apart from New Zealand, which had been mentioned in George Brown's opening statement on 4 July 1967) it would have to allow them with all.[136] He sent a message to Commonwealth and dependent territories' governments, reassuring them that Thomson, a former Commonwealth secretary, had first hand knowledge of the problems that British entry would cause them and that all Commonwealth governments would be informed 'fully and promptly' of discussions of interest to them, via their representatives in Brussels and London as the negotiations unfolded.[137] Wilson's message precipitated a flurry of replies, with New Zealand again pressing for consultations before the negotiations opened, but others pronouncing themselves satisfied with the suggested arrangements.[138] The New Zealanders were again put off until after the elections, to which all eyes now turned.[139]

The general election
Concerns were raised throughout the year that the British general election might upset the timing for the negotiations, and the government felt it necessary regularly to re-state that, since both main parties supported British entry into the Communities, the election need not cause any delay.[140] In May, Nield and Trend advised Wilson that if they were asked about the relative timing of the election and the 'family portrait' meeting, he should say that the government would be reconstituted well before 30

June and that he expected all necessary preparation to be completed in time. He did not expect a change of government, and questions about the Conservatives' position on timing should be directed to the leader of the opposition.[141] Wilson agreed that Stewart should make this position clear, and Stewart told Rey on 19 May – the day after the date for the general election was announced – that the government would be ready on 30 June. Indeed, it would be better for the negotiations that the government should have the election behind it rather than yet to come.[142] Schumann agreed: speaking in the French cabinet, he said that when the negotiations opened, the EEC could expect to be dealing with a British government of guaranteed stability and could therefore advance more rapidly to the nub of the problems at issue. The French would therefore be active in ensuring that the Council of Ministers would also be ready.[143] Thomson and Wilson therefore agreed that no new ministerial authority was needed before the election, but that cabinet should meet immediately afterwards to decide on an opening statement for 30 June. In the meantime officials would continue to work on a steering brief.[144]

On 11 June 1970, Harmel, in his capacity as president of the Council of Ministers, issued the official invitation:

J'ai l'honneur de porter à votre connaissance que lors de sa session tenue à Luxembourg le 8 juin 1970 le Conseil des Communautés Européennes a décidé... d'ouvrir négociations qui font l'objet de la demande d'adhésion que le Gouvernement de sa Majesté a adressée au Conseil de Communautés Européenes par ses lettres du 10 mai 1967.

En conséquence j'ai l'honneur d'inviter le Gouvernement de sa Majesté à une premiere réunion le 30 juin 1970 à Luxembourg pour l'ouverture des négociations.[145]

Although no formal reply was sent until after the election, the FCO News Department was briefed to say that 'we are pleased to receive and accept this invitation.'[146]

Conclusions

All the efforts of the previous two and a half years had paid off. By the day of the British general election, 18 June 1970, the date for the opening of negotiations was set, the British team had been selected and the preparation of the negotiating position was well underway. In agreeing to a date for the opening of negotiations, the French had demonstrated that their former veto had genuinely been lifted, and the Six had made considerable progress towards defining their own negotiating position and format. In twelve days' time, negotiations for Britain's entry into the European Communities would begin.

Conclusions

> Harold Wilson is almost certainly one of those few men but for whom Britain could not have entered the Community…[there is] little doubt that, had the election turned out differently, it would have been for Harold Wilson to have collected the prizes for European statesmanship that several foundations lavished on Edward Heath at the end of 1971. What is more, he would have amply deserved them – and, for his earlier historic role, deserves them anyway.[1]

Kitzinger is one of the few authors to acknowledge Wilson's role in winning British membership of the European Communities. The British application was maintained after General de Gaulle's veto in November 1967 at least in part because Wilson was a consistent and determined supporter of Britain's accession to the EC, rejecting 'alternatives' such as a North American free trade association or 'going it alone'. His participation was not only in the overall direction, management and implementation of European strategy. Wilson, 'the footnote fiend', also took an interest in minute tactics, from the wording of the Anglo-German Declaration of February 1969 to the mathematics of the 1970 white paper.[2] Palliser commented that Wilson 'was a European of the head and not of the heart', but that 'he had…become genuinely committed to getting us in' and that 'the head was very sound.'[3] Parr noted that, once the decision was taken in 1966, Wilson was 'absolutely determined that the bid should succeed.'[4] When Wilson lost the 1970 election, therefore, it was also a defeat of his aim of being at the head of the government that took the UK into the EC, thus claiming for himself a place in history. Nevertheless, the importance of his role prior to June 1970 cannot be over-stated.

The book also shows that the application was maintained through the deployment of a number of domestic and overseas strategies. Domestically important were Wilson's control over his colleagues, and the acquiescence of many in the pursuit of a policy with which they did not agree. Ministers in the key offices in the FO/FCO, including George Brown, Michael Stewart and Alun Chalfont were already or became whole-hearted 'pro-Europeans'. Wilson maintained this predominance by bringing pro-Europeans like George Thomson into cabinet and removing from relevant positions those like Peter Shore, who opposed the policy, and Anthony Crosland, who had a slightly different focus, as negotiations drew closer. In this way, Wilson ensured that his preferred policies were implemented. The most renowned 'pro-European', Roy Jenkins, was side-lined first by being based, during the whole of the veto period, in the 'euro-sceptic' Treasury, and second by the threat that he posed to Wilson as a potential rival for the leadership. Palliser comments, however, that Jenkins accepted being somewhat excluded from European policy-making in part because he recognised the strength of Wilson's determination to succeed in winning membership. Wilson

> certainly talked to Jenkins about Europe, and he knew Jenkins was extremely keen, and I think probably for that reason Jenkins himself didn't fight to be involved in all the European policy-making. Of course he went to meetings with European finance ministers....So he was involved *in Europe* but not so much in official European policy-making.[5]

With these ministers on side, Wilson's policy had a certain force in cabinet meetings that other ministers were not willing to oppose. When objections were voiced, Wilson and his foreign ministers either ignored them or deflected attention by means of semantic nuance or by promising a later review.

Control of cabinet was supplemented through the use of committees. Wilson's use of 'inner' and 'kitchen' cabinets is well known, and European policy was no exception. Once the initial authority for the continued pursuit of entry after the veto was obtained, European policy was kept away from full cabinet wherever possible. Brown, Stewart and other ministers colluded in the use of small ministerial committees for decision-making. This practice was about more than efficient decision-making: ministers like Crosland on occasion pressed for full cabinet discussion and were refused.[6] The use of committees was intended to keep European policy safe from the oversight of those, like Castle and Crossman, who would have preferred that the British application be withdrawn or at least left dormant. Therefore Philip Giddings' assertion that the use of committees was 'simply for convenience' rather than to override full Cabinet or to avoid confrontation is clearly incorrect, and Wilson's management of European policy fits more closely with Peter Hennessy's assertion that 'the most strategic decisions would often be removed from the purview of the full Cabinet.'[7] In the case of obtaining ministerial authority for a British initiative in 1968, it took three different committees

(EURM, the ministerial sub-committee on technology and MISC 224) before Wilson and Stewart managed to achieve their aim.

The relative lack of protest from euro-sceptic ministers was also significant. Wilson's cabinets were divided on the subject – indeed, had there been unity Wilson would have had no need for the committees mentioned above. Why, then, did ministers like Shore, Castle and Crossman not protest more forcefully? First, there was an element of collective responsibility: cabinet *had* agreed in 1967 to apply, unconditionally, for entry, and that decision had been reinforced by the largest peace-time majority then achieved in the House of Commons. Second, the decision had been taken by 'a defeated cabinet.'[8] By the time of de Gaulle's veto, devaluation had compounded the defeat initially inflicted by the various sterling crises and the failure of the national plan. Ministerial acquiescence thereafter suggests that they did not see any realistic alternative to the continued pursuit of membership. Third, some ministers at least believed that, given de Gaulle's opposition to British entry, Wilson's approach could never succeed. There was no need to take a stand when the general would do the euro-sceptics' job for them.[9] Finally, in a cabinet that saw battles over issues like the Rhodesian settlement, selling arms to South Africa and the reform of industrial relations, European policy was simply not important enough a subject over which to resign.[10] In combination, these factors created an opportunity space for Wilson, Brown and Stewart in which to pursue accession to the Communities.

Did the maintenance of the application have any importance for the future success of negotiations for British entry? When Sir Edward Heath was later asked to judge the importance of British diplomacy after the veto in winning over the Six to the British cause, he replied – perhaps naturally in a party politician – that it was of 'no importance.'[11] In contrast, Harmel wrote to Stewart on the opening day of accession negotiations: *'En cette journée ouverture négociations, veux vous addresser message personnel amitié et souvenir pour tout ce que vous avez accompli en préparation de ce jour.'*[12] Stewart replied to say that he 'believe[d] there is now real prospect that our work will bear fruit, even though I shall have to watch it from a distance.'[13] Clearly, Harmel and Stewart believed that they had achieved *something* over the previous thirty-one months. The British government had forged close relations with most members of the Six, based on regular and close bi- and multilateral consultation. With two countries, the FRG and Italy, this closeness was reinforced with joint declarations encapsulating commitments to work together for each other's interests and in the interest of a united Europe.

Partially as a result, the Wilson government won what have been described in this book as good 'European credentials'. They had succeeded in convincing Europeans that UK foreign policy was now focused on Europe, that the application was sincere and that the government was willing to accept the Rome Treaties without derogation. European trust in British intentions had to be regularly reinforced, and Wilson always complied, re-emphasising the authenticity of the application and his own determination whenever necessary. At the same time, maintaining the application in the veto situation won the UK a breathing space for economic recovery without losing European momentum. In this way the government was able to answer the criticisms made by de Gaulle in his November press conference that the UK was too economically weak and unstable to take on the burden of Community membership. The efforts to improve the economic situation were presented on the continent as part of Britain's preparation for entry into the Community, thus reinforcing the good credentials noted above.

Significantly, Wilson's government, with the help of friends like Italy and the Netherlands, succeeded in preventing the development of the Communities in ways that would have been undesirable to Britain or that would have made British entry more difficult. The years under consideration should have been busy ones for the Community as its transitional period ended and its 'definitive' period began. Instead, the British application was at the top of the agenda at most Council meetings, the Six were forced to spend time on consideration of 'interim arrangements' for Britain, and some members openly blocked particular developments in an explicit protest at the French veto. The resulting stagnation was blamed on France, not Britain, and when it came to the renegotiation of agricultural policy, it gave the Five a lever to use on France.

Not only was expected progress within the Community blocked. Wilson and the Five also built important foundations for the European Political Co-operation (in foreign policy) that began in 1974 in fulfilment of a Hague Summit aim. The Labour government succeeded in forging real and meaningful integration with the Five in this area by means of the Harmel proposals in WEU. Stewart and the Foreign Office had been integral in eliciting new proposals from the Five; Harmel had then closely consulted the British government as he drafted his proposals; and Stewart's diplomacy was crucial in bringing together Germany, Italy, Luxembourg and the Netherlands after the Rome WEU council in November 1968. Despite French protestations of illegality, the result was closer collaboration in the 'high politics' area of foreign policy than had ever occurred before, with Britain and the Five discussing subjects like the Middle East, Rhodesia and the military coup in Greece, and agreeing on a kind of common action (separate but concerted) in the case of the latter. This integration foreshadowed that later undertaken in the EC under the auspices of European Political Co-operation, in which Britain was involved from the start. Of course, it also again reinforced Britain's self-perception as a European state with common European interests.

Crucially, of course, the French veto was lifted under the Wilson government, not its successor. Six months before Heath took office, Pompidou agreed – was forced to agree – that negotiations would open by mid-1970. It cannot be assumed that Pompidou would have removed the French obstacle to negotiations without the pressure imposed by Britain and its European allies over the previous two years. Had Wilson withdrawn the British application in November 1967 the Community could have carried on with its own internal development, much as it had after the first French veto in January 1963. The resulting strengthening of the Community might even have meant that the Six could have entered into their 'definitive period' without the need for a summit at head of government level. Instead, the French were faced with a situation where they could not obtain their objectives in the Community without removing the veto on enlargement negotiations. While the increasingly predominant FRG cannot be overlooked as an explanation of the French decision to allow negotiations, this does not undermine the achievement of Wilson's government since that new German strength was directed at compelling France to lift the veto. As has been seen, Wilson's constant reiteration of his sincerity in making the application was an important part of convincing Brandt to fight the British cause.

Wilson's actions were also important as each side began to prepare for negotiations. He regularly stated that the UK could only join if the terms were right – and that, therefore, they *must* negotiate the right terms. This position was important in two ways. First, it allowed 'Euro-sceptics' in cabinet to believe that the 'wrong' terms might provide them with an escape route from membership, so that they allowed Wilson and Stewart to proceed with the application. Second, it reminded friends on the continent that Wilson had to account to cabinet, parliament and people, and that if the terms they offered were too unfavourable to British interests Wilson might feel compelled to decline, thus depriving them of the British membership that they felt was in the interests of Europe as a whole. Wilson won acknowledgement from members of the Community that the terms of entry must be fair and equitable for the UK: the French must not be allowed surreptitiously to re-impose the veto by insisting on terms that the UK could not accept. Wilson's insistence that the terms be fair, and the acknowledgement at least of the Five that this was a reasonable request, thus ensured that as the Six prepared for negotiation they had British interests, and not solely their own, in mind.

Finally, not only was the veto lifted and preparations begun, but the date for the opening of negotiations was set under Wilson's government for 30 June, twelve days after the forthcoming British general election. Continued British pressure after The Hague summit for talks to begin, and corresponding pressure from the Five on France, meant that the period of pre-negotiation was not allowed to drag on as a kind of veto in itself. The UK and the Five insisted that the Community quickly set its house in order and rapidly deal with the 'completion' part of the Hague triptych so that it could move on to enlargement as soon as possible. Conceivably, had Wilson and friends like Brandt relaxed their endeavours after the summit, France could have delayed 'completion' indefinitely, or insisted that the 'strengthening' of the Community be addressed before enlargement. It would not have been a new tactic: in 1968 Debré had insisted that the Community address all outstanding questions before even considering enlargement. Instead, the Six were forced to move swiftly through the issues remaining after the summit in order to open negotiations as soon as possible, and Wilson thus received a firm commitment, not just that negotiations would open, but *when* they would open.

The place of European policy in wider foreign policy
Wilson's focus on the EC was reinforced by changes in the wider British foreign policy, without the links between the two being explicitly acknowledged: indeed, Stewart referred to them as '[c]hicken + egg' (sic).[14] While the decision to withdraw from East of Suez was taken independently of the decision to apply for membership of the EC, it had consequences for European policy. At the most basic level, it made Britain seem more 'European', finally relinquishing the global role that was a hangover from Empire. On several occasions, Wilson stressed this development, telling the Royal Commonwealth Society, for example, that '[w]e are a European country. We have an inescapable duty to assist in the constructive process of unity in Europe. Europe is our natural base'.[15] As well as this apparent change in the character of Britain, the concentration of British defence in Western Europe created an opportunity for closer co-operation in defence policy, within NATO, that was suggested in the Benelux and Harmel proposals but ultimately taken by Healey with a degree of separation from 'mainstream' European policy.

This new focus had ramifications for Britain's other relationships, and most importantly, for relations with the United States. The latter developed in a somewhat peculiar manner, with the government both detaching itself from and relying for support on the American administration. Retaining influence with the US was still a key aim of British foreign policy, as it had been since the Second World War, but there was in these years a recognition that that influence could only be obtained through British membership of the EC. By distancing itself, the government could shrug off the taint of association with American policies like that on Vietnam; by increasing its influence, it could hope to have a greater say over such policies in the future. The important point is that the UK was willing to accept a changed relationship with the United States as part of the price of membership of the EC. Wilson's poor relations with Johnson and inability to act as a mediator between the US and the USSR may have been significant in his acceptance of this change. Ironically, Wilson continued to depend on the Johnson and Nixon administrations to support Britain's entry into Europe – support that could not be taken for granted as the EC continued to develop protectionist policies and American interests increasingly articulated their objections. Since both presidents maintained the long-lived American policy of supporting British entry, partly in the hope that the UK would be able to persuade the Community to re-orientate itself towards free trade, Wilson did not have to deal with the concerns expressed in particular by the departments of commerce and of agriculture. American insistence that a 'North American free trade association' was not on offer also helped Wilson to quash wishful thinking in that direction at home.

When it came to EFTA and the Commonwealth, transformations in those institutions radically decreased their influence over the UK. EFTA had been a disappointment from its inception: it was a reminder of Britain's botched attempt to de-rail the progress of the Six towards the Rome Treaties. In comparison with the EC, the EFTA countries had little to offer Britain economically, and nothing to offer politically. Moreover, Ireland, Denmark and Norway had made their own applications for membership, while others, like Austria, had applied for association. The Commonwealth saw a similar pattern of reorientation. While it began years before Britain's second application, the regionalisation of Commonwealth trade continued during the years 1967-1970, and several East African countries and Malta considered negotiating their own special agreements with the EC irrespective of the results of Wilson's application. In other words, just as the Commonwealth was becoming progressively less important to British trade, so too was the opposite true. With the exceptions of the Commonwealth Sugar Agreement and the New Zealand dairy industry, Britain made no promises to protect Commonwealth interests, arguing instead that they would be best served by a strong Britain working from within the Community. Strategic changes in Britain's wider foreign policy thus help to explain why the government pressed on with the application for membership of the Communities after the veto, while also playing a supporting role in the success of European policy.

Of course, the veto years form only part of the story of Harold Wilson's involvement in British European policy. As government and private papers are released, they may reveal the same determination on Wilson's part after 1970 as has been seen in this book.[16] His years in opposition and back in government, from 1970-74 and 1974-76 respectively, saw different and greater challenges of party politics than was the case in 1967-70. Nevertheless, future research on Wilson and European policy should be informed by the conclusions reached here.

Final remarks

It is clear that Heath would have faced a very different situation had Wilson withdrawn the application after de Gaulle's veto. Both Britain and the Communities would have been going their own way since 1967, undoubtedly making British entry more difficult by the time that Heath made his own application. Although Heath says that he would have applied immediately on taking office, he would have faced a Community focused on its own affairs, working according to its own timetable and certainly less careful of British interests than was in fact the case.[17] Certainly, negotiations would not have started in June 1970, but a minimum of six months later, to give each side time to prepare. Given the economic crises that rocked the world in the 1970s, even a six-month delay in the opening of negotiations could conceivably have de-railed a Heath application. Wilson thus played a vital role in bringing about Britain's integration into the EC. During the veto years and after The Hague summit, he was fiercely *interested* in European policy. As prime minister he had the power and resources to pursue his objectives, and as he told one journalist, 'what is power for except to carry out the ideals in which you believe?'[18]

NOTES

Introduction

1   Six European states – France, the Federal Republic of Germany, Italy, Belgium, the Netherlands and Luxembourg – were founding members of the European Communities (EC – including the European Coal and Steel Community (ECSC), the European Economic Community (EEC) and the European Atomic Energy Community (EURATOM)), sometimes colloquially known as the 'Common Market'.

2   Jeffrey Pickering, *Britain's Withdrawal from East of Suez: the Politics of Retrenchment*, Basingstoke: Macmillan, 1998.

3   Andrea Benvenuti, *The End of the Affair: Britain's Turn to Europe as a Problem in Anglo-Australian Relations (1961-72)*, unpublished DPhil thesis, University of Oxford, 2003.

4   Joseph Frankel, *British Foreign Policy 1945-1973*, London: Oxford University Press for the Royal Institute of International Affairs, 1975, p212; PMH Bell, *France and Britain 1940-1994: The Long Separation*, London and New York: Longman, 1997, pp210-217; Stephen George, *Britain and European Integration since 1945*, Oxford: Blackwell, 1991, p48; David Butler and Michael Pinto-Duschinsky, *The British General Election of 1970*, London: Macmillan, 1971, p45.

5   Uwe Kitzinger, *The Second Try: Labour and the EEC*, Oxford: Pergamon Press Ltd, 1968.

6   Oliver Daddow (ed), *Harold Wilson and European Integration: Britain's Second Application to join the EEC*, London: Frank Cass, 2003; 'Europe', in John Young, *The Labour governments 1964-1970, Volume 2 International Policy*, Manchester and New York: Manchester University Press, 2003; Helen Parr, *Britain's Policy Towards the European Community: Harold Wilson and Britain's world role, 1964-67*, Abingdon: Routledge, 2006.

7   See in particular Helen Parr, *Harold Wilson, Whitehall and British Policy towards the European Community, 1964-1967*, unpublished PhD thesis, Queen Mary College, University of London, 2002; 'Gone Native: The Foreign Office and Harold Wilson's Policy towards the EEC, 1964-67' in Daddow, *Harold Wilson*; and Parr, *Britain's Policy Towards the European Community*.

8   Daddow, *Harold Wilson*, p11.

9   Uwe Kitzinger, *Diplomacy and Persuasion*, London: Thames and Hudson, 1973, pp68-76.

10   Young, *The Labour governments*, p160.

11   David Gowland and Arthur Turner, (eds), *Britain and European Integration 1945-1998: A Documentary History*, London: Routledge, 2000, p128.

12   Young, *The Labour governments*, p160.

13   Sir Con O'Neill, *Britain's Entry into the European Community: Report on the Negotiations of 1970-1972*, London: Whitehall History Publishing in association with Frank Cass, 2000, p9.

14   Philip Ziegler, *Wilson: The Authorised Life of Lord Wilson of Rievaulx*, London: Weidenfeld and Nicholson, 1993, p336.

15   Paul Foot, *The Politics of Harold Wilson*, London: Penguin, 1968, p237.

16   Ben Pimlott, *Harold Wilson*, London: BCA, 1992, pp434-442.

17   Austen Morgan, *Harold Wilson*, London: Pluto Press, 1992, pp297, 396.

18   Kenneth Morgan, *Callaghan: a Life*, Oxford: Oxford University Press, 1997, p254.

19   Cecil King, *The Cecil King Diary 1965-70*, London: Jonathan Cape, 1972, 2 March 1968, p179.

20   Alun Chalfont, *The Shadow of My Hand*, London: Weidenfeld and Nicholson, 2000, p126; Michael Stewart, *Life and Labour*, London: Sidgwick and Jackson, 1980, p162.

21   Roy Jenkins, *A Life at the Centre*, London: MacMillan, 1991, p300.

22   Marcia Williams, *Inside No. 10*, London: Weidenfeld and Nicholson, 1972, pp126, 372.

23   George Brown, *In My Way*, London: Victor Gollancz, 1971, p219; Barbara Castle, *The Castle Diaries 1964-70*, London: Weidenfeld and Nicolson, 1984, 21 March 1967, p236.

24   Jean Monnet, *Memoirs*, London: Collins, 1978, p496.

25   Richard Crossman, *The Diaries of a Cabinet Minister, Volume 3, Secretary of State for Social Services, 1968-70*, London: Hamish Hamilton and Jonathan Cape, 1977, 10 August 1969, p612; Richard Marsh, *Off the Rails*, London: Weidenfeld and Nicholson, 1978, p96.

26   For the Labour Party and European policy, see Roger Broad, *Labour's European Dilemmas From Bevin to Blair*, Basingstoke: Palgrave, 2001; Alan Milward, *The Rise and Fall of a National Strategy, 1945-63*, London: Whitehall Publishing in Association with Frank Cass, 2002; Richard Heffernan, 'Beyond Euro-Scepticism? Labour and the European Union since 1945', in Brian Brivati and Richard Heffernan (eds), *The Labour Party: A Centenary History*, Basingstoke and London: Macmillan, 2000; and Kitzinger, *Diplomacy and Persuasion*, pp188-270.

27   Kitzinger, *Diplomacy and Persuasion*, pp188-250.

28   On the European Movement, see NA/PREM/13/2876; on the Action Committee, see letter, Wilson to Monnet, 3 October 1968; reply, 4 October 1968, NA/PREM/13/2632.

29   'The Wilson Tactic', *The Economist*, 14 February 1970, p9-10. See also anonymous survey: 'Public Opinion and the EEC', *Journal of Common Market Studies* Vol 6, No 3, 1967-8; Robert J Lieber, *British Politics and European Unity:*

Parties, Elites and Pressure Groups, Berkeley: University of California Press, 1970, especially pp258-260; and Kitzinger, *Diplomacy and Persuasion*, pp353-357.

Chapter One

1   Foreign Office files on British relations with the EC were labelled 'Approach to Europe'.

2   Wolfram Kaiser and Gillian Staerk, (eds), *British Foreign Policy, 1955-64: Contracting Options*, Basingstoke: Macmillan in association with the Institute of Contemporary British History, 2000, pxiii; Reginald Hibbert, 'Britain in search of a role, 1957-73: A Witness Account', in Brian Brivati and Harriet Jones, *From reconstruction to integration: Britain and Europe since 1945*, Leicester: Leicester University Press, 1993, p121.

3   Sean Greenwood, *Britain and the Cold War 1945-91*, Basingstoke: Macmillan, 2000, p168.

4   Kaiser and Staerk, *British Foreign Policy* (title).

5   James Ellison, 'Accepting the inevitable: Britain and European Integration' in Kaiser and Staerk, *British Foreign Policy*, p182.

6   Alan Sked and Christopher Cook, *Post-War Britain: A Political History 1945-1992* (4th ed) London: Penguin, 1993, p168.

7   N Piers Ludlow, *Dealing with Britain: the Six and the First UK Application to the EEC*, Cambridge: Cambridge University Press, 1997, p38.

8   John Young, *Britain and European Unity, 1945-1999*, Basingstoke: Macmillan, 2000, p72; Ludlow, *Dealing with Britain*, p41.

9   John Young, *Britain and European Unity*, p12.

10 Hugo Young, *This Blessed Plot: Britain and Europe from Churchill to Blair*, London: Macmillan, 1998, p137.

11 Anne Deighton, 'The Labour Party, Public Opinion and 'the Second Try' in 1967', in Daddow, *Harold Wilson*, p41.

12 Kitzinger, *The Second Try*, pp2-4.

13 Kenneth Morgan, *The People's Peace: British History 1945-1990*, Oxford: Oxford University Press, 1990, p236.

14 See Steven Fielding, *The Labour governments 1864-70, Volume 1 Labour and Cultural Change*, Manchester and New York: Manchester University Press, 2003.

15 Morgan, *The People's Peace*, pp315-316.

16 Daddow, *Harold Wilson*, p1.

17 Morgan, 'The Wilson Years, 1964-70', in Nick Tiratsoo (ed), *From Blitz to Blair: a New History of Britain since 1939*, London: Phoenix, 1998, pp132-133.

18 Morgan, *The People's Peace*, pp243-246; see also Jim Tomlinson, *The Labour governments 1964-70, Volume 3 Economic policy*, Manchester and New York: Manchester University Press, 2003.

19 Morgan, *The People's Peace*, p281.

20 Morgan, *The People's Peace*, p313.

21   David Butler, *British General Elections since 1945*, Oxford: Blackwell, 1995, pp25-27.

22   Morgan, *The People's Peace*, p251.

23   Morgan, *The People's Peace*, pp254, 274, 304.

24   Morgan, *The People's Peace*, pp254-255, 300-306.

25   FS Northedge, *Descent from Power: British Foreign Policy 1945-1973*, London: George Allen and Unwin Ltd, 1974, pp348-349.

26   Pickering, *Britain's Withdrawal*, pp137-138.

27   Pickering, *Britain's Withdrawal*, p140.

28   David Reynolds, *Britannia Overruled: British Policy and World Power in the 20th Century*, Harlow: Longman, 1991, pp227-229.

29   Harold Wilson, *The Labour Government 1964-1970: A Personal Record*, Weidenfeld and Nicholson and Michael Joseph, 1971, p297; Pickering, *Britain's Withdrawal*, pp157-158; Greenwood, *Britain and the Cold War*, p173.

30   Pickering, *Britain's Withdrawal*, pp158, 170-172.

31   On the Wilson-Johnson relationship, see especially Jonathan Colman, *A 'special relationship'? Harold Wilson, Lyndon B. Johnson and Anglo-American relations 'at the summit', 1964-1968*, Manchester and New York: Manchester University Press, 2004.

32   Brown, *In My Way*, p146.

33   Reynolds, *Britannia Overruled*, p227.

34   Greenwood, *Britain and the Cold War*, p168.

35   Greenwood, *Britain and the Cold War*, p174.

36   Pickering, *Britain's Withdrawal*, p148.

37   Reynolds, *Britannia Overruled*, pp227-228; Pickering, *Britain's Withdrawal*, pp148-149.

38   Robert Holland, *The Pursuit of Greatness: Britain and the World Role, 1900-1970*, London: Fontana Press, 1991, p327; Pickering, *Britain's Withdrawal*, p148.

39   Reynolds, *Britannia Overruled*, pp227-228.

40   Frankel, *British Foreign Policy*, p212; Reynolds, *Britannia Overruled*, p231.

41   Cited in Pickering, *Britain's Withdrawal*, p173.

42   Cited in Pickering, *Britain's Withdrawal*, p173.

43   Pickering, *Britain's Withdrawal*, pp156-157.

44   Reynolds, *Britannia Overruled*, p228.

45   20 March 1969, National Archives, Kew, London (henceforth NA) CAB/128/44/CC(69)13.

46   Richard Crossman, *The Diaries of a Cabinet Minister, Volume 1, Minister of Housing 1964-66*, London: Hamish Hamilton, 1975, 14 November 1965, pp377-378.

47   Reynolds, *Britannia Overruled*, p222.

48   Frankel, *British Foreign Policy*, p232.

49   See N Piers Ludlow, *The European Community and the Crises of the 1960s: Negotiating the Gaullist Challenge*, Abingdon: Routledge, 2006.

50   N Piers Ludlow, 'The Eclipse of the Extremes. Demythologising the Luxembourg Compromise', in Wilfred Loth (ed), *Crises and Compromises: the European Project 1963-1969*, Baden-Baden: Nomos Verlag, 2001, pp247-248.

51   Ludlow, *The European Community*, chapters 3-4.

52   Broad, *Labour's European Dilemmas*, pp58-62.

53   Pickering, *Britain's Withdrawal*, p156.

54   Frankel, *British Foreign Policy*, p227.

55   Cited in Foot, *The Politics of Harold Wilson*, p220.

56   Cited in Foot, *The Politics of Harold Wilson*, pp220-221.

57   Foot, *The Politics of Harold Wilson*, p224.

58   Cited in Foot, *The Politics of Harold Wilson*, p224.

59   Foot, *The Politics of Harold Wilson*, pp222-225.

60   'Prosperity with a Purpose', cited in FWS Craig, *British General Election Manifestos 1959-1987*, Dartmouth: Parliamentary Research Services, 1990, p56.

61   Holland, *The Pursuit of Greatness*, p321.

62   Parr, *Harold Wilson*, pp73-79.

63   Cynthia W Frey, 'Meaning Business: the British Application to join the Common Market, Nov 1966-Oct 1967', *Journal of Common Market Studies*, Vol 6, No 3, 1967-8.

64   Cited in Foot, *The Politics of Harold Wilson*, p226.

65   Foot, *The Politics of Harold Wilson*, p227.

66   Parr, *Harold Wilson*, pp66-80.

67   Foot, *The Politics of Harold Wilson*, pp228-230.

68   'Time for Decision', cited in Craig, *British General Election Manifestos*, p98.

69   Interview with the author, 12 July 2002.

70   Parr, *Harold Wilson*, pp105-106; Palliser, interview with the author, 12 July 2002.

71   Interview with the author, 12 July 2002.

72   Cited in Frey, 'Meaning Business', p198.

73   Parr, *Harold Wilson*, p43-44; Foot, *The Politics of Harold Wilson*, p231.

74   The papers of Sir Patrick Reilly held in the Bodleian Library, Oxford (henceforth Reilly papers), MS Eng c.6925, 'Britain and the EEC'.

75   Parr, *Harold Wilson*, pp89-90.

76   Parr, *Harold Wilson*, p2; Foot, *The Politics of Harold Wilson*, pp232-233.

77   Parr, *Harold Wilson*, pp168-170.

78   Peter Shore, *Leading the Left*, London: Weidenfeld and Nicholson, 1993, p96 and *Separate Ways: the Heart of Europe*, London: Duckworth, 2000, p41.

79   Interview with the author, 12 July 2002.

80   Brown, *In My Way*, p206.

81   Interview with the author, 12 July 2002.

82   Parr, *Harold Wilson*, p225.

83   Tony Benn, *Out of the Wilderness– Diaries 1963-67*, London: Hutchinson, 1987, 30 April 1967, p496; Parr, *Harold Wilson*, chapter five.

84   Telegram, Wilson to Brown, 20 April 1967, No 3790, NA/PREM/13/2108.
85   Lieber, *British Politics*, p254.
86   Castle, *The Castle Diaries*, 20 April 1967, p244.
87   Marsh, *Off the Rails*, p96.
88   King, *The Cecil King Diary*, p98.
89   King, *The Cecil King Diary*, pp111-114.
90   Interview with the author, 12 July 2002.
91   Crossman, *Diaries*, Volume II, 9 January 1967, p191.
92   King, *The Cecil King Diaries*, p123.
93   Wilson, *The Labour Government*, p341.
94   Parr, *Harold Wilson*, p287.
95   Memo, O'Neill to Hancock, 18 August 1967, NA/FCO/13/207.
96   Wilson, handwritten note on letter, Palliser to Day, 25 September 1967, NA/FCO/30/107.
97   Letter, Palliser to Day, 25 September 1967, NA/FCO/30/107.
98   Telegram, UKMis New York to FO, 24 September 1967, No 2420, NA/FCO/30/107.
99   Telegram, Bonn to FO, 3 October 1967, No 1325, NA/FCO/30/107.
100 Letter, Robinson to O'Neill, 27 July 1967, NA/FCO/30/107.
101 Letter, O'Neill to Statham, 28 July 1967, NA/FCO/30/107.
102 Draft Paper, 'Britain and the European Communities', 16 August 1967, NA/FCO/30/107.
103 EURO(67)117, 'Action to be taken in the light of an early French veto', 6 October 1967, NA/FCO/30/107.
104 Memo, Jackling to Brown's private secretary, 20 October 1967, NA/FCO/30/107.
105 Published 7 October 1967, *Keesing's Contemporary Archive* (henceforth *KCA*) 23169-23170 (1-8 February 1969).
106 KCA23170 (1-8 February 1969).
107 Treasury brief, 20 November 1967, NA/PREM/13/2058.
108 Letter, van den Boeynants to Wilson, 21 November 1967; see also letters, de Jong to Wilson, 23 November 1967; Werner to Wilson, 23 November 1967; unofficial translation of letter, Kiesinger to Wilson, 4 December 1967, all NA/PREM/13/2058.
109 Memo, Wilson to Brown, 24 November 1967, NA/PREM/13/2058.
110 Minute, Trend to Wilson, 20 November 1967, NA/PREM/13/2058.
111 Memo, Wilson to Brown, 24 November 1967, NA/PREM/13/2058.
112 KCA22373 (25 November - 2 December 1967).
113 KCA23170-23171 (1-8 February 1969). For a discussion of French policy-making, see Helen Parr, draft article, 'Success or Failure? French policy towards enlargement: Britain's Second Application in 1967', *Cold War History*, forthcoming.
114 Kitzinger, *The Second Try*, p14.

[115] De Gaulle had vetoed a British plan for a Free Trade Area in 1958 and the first application to the EC in 1963, Deighton, 'The Labour Party' in Daddow, *Harold Wilson*, p48.

[116] Lieber, *British Politics*, p272.

[117] Lieber, *British Politics*, p263.

[118] Frankel, *British Foreign Policy*, p242.

Chapter Two

[1] Paul-Henri Spaak on the first veto, *Combats inachevés*, Brussels: Vokaer, 1979, Vol 2, p406, cited in Jean Lacouture, *De Gaulle the Ruler: 1945-1970*, London: Harvill, 1991, p361.

[2] Reilly papers, MS Eng.c.6926; KCA22521 (10-17 February 1969).

[3] Minute, Palliser to Wilson, 27 November 1967, NA/PREM/13/2646.

[4] Telegram, Paris to FO, 27 November 1967, No 1191, NA/PREM/13/2646.

[5] Letter, Palliser to Maitland, 28 November 1967, NA/PREM/13/1464.

[6] KCA23172-23173 (1-8 February 1969); Wilson, *The Labour Government*, p469.

[7] *Hansard*, Vol 755, col 239, 28 November 1967.

[8] EUR(O)(67)202, NA/PREM/13/1488.

[9] Letter, Palliser to Maitland, 30 November 1967, NA/PREM/13/2454.

[10] Letter, Maitland to Dean, 6 December 1967, NA/FCO/30/225.

[11] Minute, Gore-Booth to Chalfont, 4 December 1967, NA/FCO/30/225.

[12] Telegram, FO to Bonn, 2 December 1967, No 3057, NA/FCO/30/192.

[13] Telegram, Brussels to FO, 12 December 1967, No 727, NA/FCO/30/225.

[14] Telegrams, Brussels to FO, 14 December 1967, No 747, NA/PREM/13/2402 and Washington to FO, 21 December 1967, No 4012, NA/FCO/30/225.

[15] See for example EUR(O)(67)117, 'Action to be taken in the light of an early French veto', 6 October 1967, NA/FCO/30/107.

[16] Telegram, Lisbon to FO, 19 December 1967, No 575, NA/FCO/30/89.

[17] Letter, FH Jackson to Statham, 27 November 1967, NA/FCO/30/89.

[18] Telegrams, Oslo to FO, 21 December 1967, Nos 404-5, NA/PREM/13/1488.

[19] Telegram, Copenhagen to FO, 22 December 1967, No 433, NA/PREM/13/1488.

[20] Brief for Wilson for meeting of Leaders of Socialist International at Chequers, 9 December 1967, NA/PREM/13/1591; letter, Palliser to Morphet, 11 December 1967, NA/FCO/9/21.

[21] Brief for Wilson for meeting of Leaders of Socialist International at Chequers, 9 December 1967, NA/PREM/13/1591.

[22] WEU was formed in 1955 on the basis of the 1948 Brussels Treaty, and consisted of the Six and Britain. Although its main provision was a mutual defence guarantee, it also served as a forum for discussion on a wide range of economic and political topics.

23 Commonwealth Liaison Committee: Minutes of a meeting held at Marlborough House at 3pm on Thursday, 14 December 1967, NA/FCO/30/243.

24 Young, *Britain and European Unity*, p72.

25 See for example Philip Alexander, 'From Imperial Power to Regional Powers: Commonwealth Crises and the Second Application', in Daddow, *Harold Wilson*, pp188-210.

26 Commonwealth Liaison Committee: Minutes of a meeting held at Marlborough House at 3pm on Thursday, 14 December 1967, NA/FCO/30/243.

27 'Record of Conversation between the Secretary of State and Mr Marshall, Deputy Prime Minister of New Zealand, on 29 November' 1967, NA/FO/800/969.

28 Transcript of meeting between the Prime Minister and Mr McEwen, Prime Minister of Australia, Melbourne, 23 December 1967, NA/PREM/13/1488.

29 Ludlow, *Dealing with Britain*.

30 KCA23173 (1-8 February 1969).

31 KCA23173 (1-8 February 1969).

32 Telegram, Bonn to FO, 29 November 1967, No 1622, NA/FCO/30/192. For a discussion of German policy on the British application, see Philipp Rock, *'With a little Help from my Friends': Die Rolle der Bundesrepublik Deutschland beim Beitritt Großbritanniens zu den Europäischen Gemeinschaften, 1967-1971*, Magister thesis, Humboldt University, 2005 (translated for the author by Ms Carmel Croukamp).

33 Telegram, FO to Brussels, 28 November 1967, No 2305, NA/FO/800/969. For the technology proposals see KCA23174 (1-8 February 1969).

34 Telegrams, The Hague to FO, 29 November 1967, Nos 499 and 500, NA/PREM/13/2637.

35 C(67)187, 'The Approach to Europe', Memorandum by the Secretary of State for Foreign Affairs, 28 November 1967, NA/CAB/129.

36 CC(67)69, 30 November 1967, NA/CAB/128/42.

37 Castle, *The Castle Diaries*, 30 November 1967, p332.

38 Shore, *Leading the Left*, p97.

39 Minute, Shore to Wilson, 28 November 1967, NA/PREM/13/2646.

40 Castle, *The Castle Diaries*, 30 April 1967, p250.

41 Background note, 'The Italian Attitude', in briefing for Wilson for the meeting of Leaders of Socialist International, 9 December 1967, NA/PREM/13/1591.

42 For example, telegrams, FO to Brussels, 2 December 1967, Nos 2364 and 2365; see also 'Record of Conversation between the Foreign Secretary and the Luxembourg Foreign Minister held at the Foreign Office on Friday 1 December at 3.30pm', both NA/FO/800/969; telegram, UKDel OECD to FCO, 30 November 1967, No 56, NA/PREM/13/2637.

43   Background note, 'The German Attitude', in briefing for Wilson for the meeting of Leaders of Socialist International, 9 December 1967, NA/PREM/13/1591.

44   Telegrams, FO to Brussels, 2 December 1967, No 2367, NA/FO/800/969; FO to Bonn, 1 December 1967, No 3050, NA/FCO/30/192.

45   Telegrams, FO to Brussels, 2 December 1967, No 2367; FO to Bonn, 8 December, No 3167 and 9 December 1967, No 3177, all NA/FO/800/969.

46   Letter, Palliser to Morphet, FO, 11 December 1967, NA/PREM/13/1591.

47   Wilson to Jean Rey, President of the European Commission, private meeting, at 10 Downing Street, 4 December 1967, NA/PREM/13/2104.

48   'Record of a Meeting between the Prime Minister and the President of the Commission of the European Communities at 10, Downing Street at 11.35am on Monday, December 4, 1967'; 'Record of a Meeting held at 10, Downing Street, SW1, on Monday, 4 December, 1967, at 12 noon'; 'Record of a Meeting between the Foreign Secretary and M. Jean Rey, President of the European Commission, at the Foreign Office on 4 December, 1967, at 5.00pm', all NA/PREM/13/2104.

49   NA/FCO/30/172-3.

50   Minute, James to Head of Chancellery, 6 December 1967, NA/FCO/30/173.

51   Letter, Campbell to Statham, 8 December; minute, Statham to Hancock, and appended comments, 13 December 1967, NA/FCO/30/173.

52   Lacouture, *De Gaulle*, p474. In an example of the frequent pettiness of relations, Wilson, trying to discredit the French, became intrigued for a few days with the question of the legality or otherwise of a French imposition of tariffs on imported Italian fridges. Letters, Palliser to Maitland, 28 November 1967 and 5 December 1967, and Maitland to Palliser, 6 December 1967, all NA/PREM/13/1464.

53   Telegram, UKDel Brussels to FO, 18 December 1967, No 413, NA/FCO/30/173.

54   Telegram, FO to Rome, 1 December 1967, No 3365, NA/FO/800/969.

55   'Record of Conversation between the Foreign Secretary and the Luxembourg Foreign Minister held at the Foreign Office on Friday 1 December at 3.30pm', NA/FO/800/969.

56   'Record of Conversation between the Foreign Secretary and the Netherlands Foreign Minister held at the Foreign Office on Tuesday, 5 December 1967 at 11.15am' and again at 3pm, NA/PREM/13/2637. Wilson had talks with Luns the same day: letter, Palliser to Maitland, 5 December 1967, NA/PREM/13/1464. For Foreign Office work see for example minute, Robinson to Hancock, 7 December 1967; Minute, Hancock to Jackling, 7 December 1967 and comments by Thompson, Barnes, Hildyard, Willan (8 December), Robinson and Hughes (11 December), all NA/FCO/30/108.

57   Telegram, FO to Bonn, 8 December 1967, No 3167, NA/FO/800/969.

58   Telegram, Bonn to FO, 3 December 1967, No 1653, NA/FCO/30/192.

59   Telegram, UKDel EEC to FO, 15 December 1967, No 411, NA/FCO/30/193.

60 Telegram, Bonn to FO, 15 December 1967, No 1742, NA/FCO/30/193.
61 KCA23174 (1-8 February 1969).
62 Minute, Chalfont to Brown, 12 December 1967, NA/FCO/30/108.
63 NA/FCO/30/192.
64 Telegram, Bonn to FO, 15 December 1967, No 1742, NA/FCO/30/193.
65 Telegrams, FO to Bonn, 15 December 1967, Nos 3245-6, NA/FCO/30/193.
66 Telegram, Bonn to FO, 12 December 1967, No 1716, NA/FCO/30/193.
67 Telegram, Bonn to FO, 14 December 1967, No 1736, NA/FCO/30/193.
68 Telegrams, Bonn to FO, 1 December 1967, Nos 1639–40; 2 December 1967, Nos 1651-2; 3 December 1967, Nos 1653-56; 4 December 1967, No 1959; 5 December 1967, No 1664; 6 December 1967, Nos 1671-2, all NA/FCO/30/192.
69 Telegram, Bonn to FO, 12 December 1967, No 1712, NA/FCO/30/193.
70 Telegram, Bonn to FO, 12 December 1967, No 1712, NA/FCO/30/193.
71 Minute, Robinson to Hancock, 14 December 1967, NA/FCO/30/116.
72 Minute, Robinson to Hancock and attached draft Dutch paper, 14 December 1967, NA/FCO/30/116.
73 Brown, handwritten note on minute, Robinson to Hancock, 14 December 1967; minute, Chalfont to Brown, 15 December 1967, NA/FCO/30/116.
74 EURO(67)134, 17 December 1967, NA/FCO/73/70.
75 Telegram, UKDel Brussels to FO, 19 December 1967, No 421, NA/PREM/13/1488.
76 KCA23174 (1-8 February 1969).
77 Telegrams, Brussels to FO, 20 December 1967, Nos 763 and 765, NA/PREM/13/1488.
78 Telegram, Hague to FO, 21 December 1967, No 573, NA/PREM/13/1488.
79 Record of meeting at Italian Ministry of Foreign Affairs, 29 December 1967, NA/PREM/13/1488.
80 'Record of a Meeting held at 10 Downing Street, SW1, at 12 noon on Monday, 11 March 1968', NA/PREM/13/2106.
81 Telegrams, Brussels to FO, 20 December 1967, Nos 763 and 765, NA/PREM/13/1488.
82 Minute, Brown to Wilson, Jenkins, Castle, Shore, Peart, Healey, Benn and Thomson, PM/67/120, 19 December 1967, NA/PREM/13/1488.
83 CC(67)73, 20 December 1967, NA/CAB/128/42.
84 Minute, Benn to Wilson etc, 20 December 1967, NA/PREM/13/1488.
85 CC(67)69, 30 November 1967 and CC(67)73, 20 December 1967, NA/CAB/128/42.
86 KCA23174 (1-8 February 1969).
87 Minute, Chalfont to O'Neill, 19 December 1967 and handwritten comment by O'Neill, 20 December 1967, NA/FCO/73/90.
88 Note on minute, Robinson to Morland, 19 December 1967, NA/FCO/30/173.

[89]   Telegram, FO to Rome, 20 December 1967, No 3628, NA/PREM/13/1488.

[90]   Telegram, FO to Rome, 20 December 1967, No 3629, NA/FCO/73/70.

[91]   Telegrams, FO to Hague, No 2331, and FO to Brussels, No 2610, both 20 December 1967, NA/FCO/30/122.

[92]   Telegram, Rome to FO, 22 December 1967, No 1262, NA/FCO/30/122.

[93]   Telegram, FO to Rome, 25 December 1967, No 3685, NA/FCO/30/122.

[94]   Telegrams, Rome to FO, 27 December 1967, No 1269, 29 December 1967, Nos 1272-1273, NA/FCO/30/122.

[95]   Telegrams, Hague to FO, 22 December 1967, Nos 574-575, NA/FCO/30/122.

[96]   Telegram, Hague to FO, 23 December 1967, No 577, NA/FCO/30/122.

[97]   Telegram, Hague to FO, 27 December 1967, No 578, NA/FCO/30/122.

[98]   Telegram, UKDel Brussels to FO, 21 December 1967, No 430, NA/FCO/30/122.

[99]   Telegram, Luxembourg to FO, 21 December 1967, No 239 and letter, Malcolm to O'Neill, 22 December 1967, NA/FCO/30/122. To clarify, a lower case 'four' is used to indicate the four applicant states to the EC. An upper case 'Four' is used to indicate the four member states of the EC that remained 'friendly' to the UK in the periods when Germany sided with France, hence 'the friendly Four'.

[100] Telegram, Brussels to FO, 21 December 1967, No 766, NA/FCO/30/122.

[101] Telegram, Brussels to FO, 22 December 1967, No 770, NA/FCO/30/122.

[102] Telegrams, FO to Netherlands, No 2382 and FO to Brussels, No 2675, 28 December 1967, NA/FCO/30/122.

[103] Telegram, Bonn to FO, 21 December 1967, No 1766, NA/PREM/13/1488.

[104] Telegram, Bonn to FO, 21 December 1967, No 1767, NA/FCO/73/70.

[105] Telegram, Bonn to FO, 22 December 1967, No 1775, NA/FCO/73/70.

[106] Telegrams, Bonn to FO, No 1773 and FO to Bonn, No 3338, 22 December 1967, NA/FCO/73/70.

[107] Telegram, Bonn to FO, 28 December 1967, No 1785, NA/PREM/13/1488.

[108] Telegrams, Rome to FO, 29 December 1967, Nos 1281-2, NA/FCO/30/122; 'Record of a Conversation between the Foreign Secretary and the Italian Foreign Minister before luncheon at the Palazzo Farnesina, Rome, on December 29, 1967', 'Record of a Conversation between the Foreign Secretary and the Italian Foreign Minister after lunch at the Palazzo Farnesina, Rome, on 29 December 1967, NA/FCO/70/73; 'Record of Meeting between the Foreign Secretary and the Italian Foreign Minister at the Italian Ministry of Foreign Affairs, 29 December 1967', NA/PREM/13/1488.

[109] Telegram, Rome to FO, 29 December 1967, No 1284 and telegram, Brussels to FO, 30 December 1967, No 781, NA/PREM/13/1488.

[110] Message, Brown to Brandt in telegram, Rome to FO, 29 December 1967, No 1283, NA/FCO/73/70.

[111] Letter, Roberts to O'Neill, 30 December 1967, NA/FCO/73/70.

[112] Kitzinger, *The Second Try*, pxi.

[113] For Franco-German relations during the first application, see Ludlow, *Dealing with Britain*.

Chapter Three

[1] Letter, Wilson to Kennet, 31 January 1968, NA/PREM/13/2239.

[2] Minute, Austee to Balogh to Wilson, 19 February 1968, NA/PREM/13/2107.

[3] 'UK Contribution to Discussion of the Agenda for a High Level Meeting between the Five and Britain', 1 January 1968, NA/FCO/73/111.

[4] Letter, Shuckburgh to O'Neill, 2 January 1968, NA/FCO/30/123; telegrams, Bonn to FO, 3 January 1968, No 13, and 4 January 1968, No 21, NA/PREM/13/2110; Brandt was not the only person upset by Brown: Reilly's early recall from Paris, to be replaced by Churchill's son-in-law Christopher Soames, was announced at the end of February and led to much bitterness on the part of the outgoing ambassador. Con O'Neill also resigned when he was not given the Bonn embassy on Sir Frank Roberts' retirement. See Reilly papers, MS Eng.c.6296.

[5] Note on Minute, Cambridge to Hancock, 5 January 1968, NA/FCO/30/123.

[6] JIC(68)(N)2, 11 January 1968 and Wilson's note thereon; minute, Day to Palliser, 22 January 1968, both NA/PREM/13/3216.

[7] 'Meeting at the House of the German Foreign Minister in Bonn at 12.45pm on 8 January' 1968, NA/PREM/13/2110.

[8] Telegram, Tokyo to FO, 9 January 1968, No 30, NA/FCO/30/123.

[9] Minute, Statham to Hancock, 15 January 1968, NA/FCO/30/123.

[10] Wilson's note on minute, Palliser to Wilson, 13 January 1968, NA/PREM/13/2110.

[11] Minute, Palliser to Wilson, 17 January 1968, NA/PREM/13/2110.

[12] Letter, O'Neill to Roberts, 4 January 1968, NA/FCO/73/70.

[13] Telegram, Bonn to FO, 7 February 1968, NA/FCO/62/84 and telegrams, Bonn to Foreign Office, 8 January 1968, Nos 40 and 41, NA/PREM/13/2110.

[14] Reilly papers, MS Eng.c.6296.

[15] Telegrams, Brussels to FO, 11 January 1968, No 20, NA/PREM/13/2110; 16 January 1968, No 33, NA/FCO/30/123; for the Benelux proposals and subsequent Harmel proposals, see also Vincent du Jardin, *Pierre Harmel*, Montigny-Le Bretonneux: Le Cri, 2004, pp474-513.

[16] Wilson's note on telegram, Bonn to FO, 11 January 1968, No 69, NA/PREM/13/2113.

[17] Telegram, Brussels to FO, 18 January 1968, No 46, NA/PREM/13/2110.

[18] Telegram, Hague to FO, 18 January 1968, No 60, NA/PREM/13/2110.

[19] Telegram, Brussels to FO, 18 January 1968, No 47, NA/PREM/13/2110.

[20] Telegram, Brussels to FO, 18 January 1968, No 48, NA/PREM/13/2110.

21 Telegrams, FO to UKDel Brussels, 26 January 1968, No 178, NA/FCO/30/125; UKDel Brussels to FO, 29 January 1968, No 34, NA/FCO/30/58 and 3 February 1968, No 39, NA/FCO/30/129.

22 Telegrams, Rome to FO, 25 January 1968, No 116, and 26 January, Nos 126-129; FO to Rome, 24 January 1968, No 390, and 29 January 1968, No 463, all NA/FCO/30/125.

23 Telegrams, Bonn to FO, 24 January 1968, No 146, NA/FCO/30/125; and 27 January 1968, No 174, NA/FCO/30/193.

24 Telegram, Paris to FO, 22 January 1968, No 88, NA/FCO/30/124.

25 Minute, Robinson to O'Neill, 22 January 1968, NA/FCO/30/173.

26 Telegrams, Luxembourg to FO, No 34 and Hague to FO, No 80, 23 January 1968, NA/FCO/30/124.

27 Minute, Nield to Wilson, undated but annotated by Palliser on 24 January 1968, NA/PREM/13/2110.

28 CC(68)10, 25 January 1968, NA/CAB/128/43.

29 Letters, Morphet to Palliser and Owen to Palliser, 19 January 1968, both NA/PREM/13/2110.

30 Telegrams, FO to Hague etc, Nos 292-3, and FO to Bonn, No 369, 25 January 1968, NA/FCO/30/125.

31 For example, telegrams, FO to Bonn, No 351, and FO to Rome, No 425, 25 January 1968, NA/FCO/30/125.

32 Letter, Reilly to Jackling, 12 January 1968, NA/FCO/30/193; telegrams, Bonn to FO, 17 January 1968, Nos 102 and 110, NA/FCO/30/184; No 112, NA/FCO/30/124; and Paris to FO, 18 January 1968, No 75, NA/PREM/13/2110.

33 Telegram, Paris to FO, 1 February 1968, No 110.

34 Letter, Roberts to Gore-Booth, 9 February 1968, NA/FCO/30/184.

35 Letter, Galsworthy to Statham, 31 January 1968, NA/FCO/30/173.

36 Letter, Statham to Hancock, 2 February 1968, NA/FCO/30/193.

37 Telegram, Bonn to FO, 6 February 1968, No 236, NA/PREM/13/2111.

38 For example, telegrams, FO to Bonn, 7 February 1968, No 529 and 9 February 1968, Nos 543-544, NA/FCO/30/173.

39 Telegrams, Bonn to FO, 9 February 1968, No 257 and 10 February 1968, No 260, NA/FCO/30/173.

40 Telegram, FO to Bonn, 7 February 1968, No 571, NA/FO/800/970.

41 Minute, O'Neill to Maitland, 7 February 1968 and letter, Maitland to Shuckburgh, 8 February 1968, both NA/FO/800/984.

42 Telegram, Bonn to FO, 9 February 1968, No 255, NA/FCO/30/184.

43 Telegram, Paris to FO, 15 February 1968, No 157, NA/FCO/30/173.

44 Telegram, Paris to FO, 15 February 1968, No 158, NA/FCO/30/184; minute, Robinson to Hancock, 15 February 1968, NA/FCO/30/125.

45 Telegram, Paris to FO, 18 February 1968, No 179, NA/FCO/30/184.

46 Unofficial FO translation, 16 February 1968, NA/PREM/13/2107.

47 Telegram, Paris to FO, 16 February 1968, No 165, NA/PREM/13/2107.

48   Telegram, Bonn to FO, 20 February 1968, No 306, NA/PREM/13/2107.

49   Telegram, FO to Bonn, 22 February 1968, No 704, NA/PREM/13/2111.

50   Telegram, Bonn to FO, 16 February 1968, No 287, NA/FCO/30/193.

51   Telegram, Paris to FO, 20 February 1968, No 198, NA/FCO/62/84.

52   Telegram, Paris to FO, 19 February 1968, No 183, NA/PREM/13/2107.

53   Telegram, Paris to FO, 22 February 1968, No 195, NA/FCO/62/84.

54   Telegram, Paris to FO, 22 February 1968, No 196, NA/PREM/13/2107.

55   Telegram, FO to Rome, 27 February 1968, No 801, NA/FCO/30/126.

56   For example, telegrams, Luxembourg to FO, 15 February 1968, No 9 Saving; Hague to FO, 17 February 1968, No 128, NA/FCO/30/184.

57   Telegram, UKDel Brussels to FO, 20 February 1968, No 60, NA/FCO/62/84.

58   Telegram, Paris to FO, 16 February 1968, No 167, NA/FCO/30/184.

59   Minutes, Palliser to Wilson, 16 and 17 February 1968, NA/PREM/13/2107.

60   Minute, Statham, 16 February 1968 and telegram, Paris to Foreign Office, 17 February 1968, No 177, both NA/PREM/13/2107.

61   Minute, Rhodes to Hancock, 19 February 1968, NA/FCO/30/184.

62   Telegrams, FO to Rome, 20 February 1968, No 698; FO to Brussels, 27 February 1968, No 518, NA/PREM/13/2111.

63   See for example telegram, Hague to FO, 17 February 1968, No 131, NA/PREM/13/2107; minute, Robinson to O'Neill, 23 February 1968, NA/FCO/30/184; telegrams, Luxembourg to FO, 22 February 1968, No 10 and Rome to FO, 20 February 1968, No 219, both NA/PREM/13/2107; telegrams, Rome to FO, 20 February 1968, Nos 220-221, NA/PREM/13/2107.

64   'Memorandum of the Italian Government relating to the forthcoming meeting of the EEC's Council of Ministers', 29 February 1968, NA/PREM/13/2111.

65   Wilson's note on minute, Meynell to Maitland, 12 January 1968, NA/PREM/13/2110.

66   CC(68)9, 18 January 1968, NA/CAB/128/43.

67   CC(68)15, 27 February 1968, NA/CAB/128/43, and C(68)42, 'Foreign Policy: Note by the Secretary of State for Foreign Affairs', NA/CAB/129.

68   CC(68)15, 27 February 1968, NA/CAB/128/43.

69   Castle, *The Castle Diaries*, 27 February 1968, pp382-383.

70   On the subject of boredom, see Castle, *The Castle Diaries*, 13 and 20 April 1967, pp242-243.

71   For response to devaluation, see NA/PREM/13/2058; KCA22489 (27 January – 3 February 1968).

72   NA/PREM/13, especially 13/2975.

73   For cuts in public expenditure, see KCA22489 (27 January – 3 February 1968).

[74] NA/CAB/128/43. See also EURO(68)6, 14 February 1968, NA/FCO/30/87; telegram, Bonn to FO, 3 January 1968, No 7, NA/PREM/13/2483.

[75] C(68)40, 'Technological Collaboration with Europe after the Veto: Note by the Minister of Technology', 23 February 1968, NA/CAB/129.

[76] CC(68)15, 27 February 1968, NA/CAB/128/43.

[77] Telegram, Washington to FO, 14 January 1968, No 185, NA/FO/800/955.

[78] Draft paper, 'British Foreign Policy for the Next Three Years', Planning Section, FO, 14 January 1968; Wilson's note on cover letter, Palliser to Wilson, 22 January 1968, both NA/PREM/13/2636; for similarities with the first application, see Ludlow, *Dealing with Britain*, pp32, 37.

[79] C(68)42, 'Foreign Policy: Note by the Secretary of State for Foreign Affairs', 23 Feb 1968, NA/CAB/129 and CC(68)15, NA/CAB/128/43.

[80] Chalfont, notes for Speech to Reading University, 30 March 1968, NA/FCO/73/86; Lord Max Beloff, *The United States and the Unity of Europe*, Washington: The Brookings Institution, 1963, p101.

[81] KCA22562 (2-9 March 1968).

[82] Telegram, Brown to Washington, 1 February 1968, No 1129, NA/PREM/13/2111.

[83] Telegram, FO to Paris, 12 January 1968, No 125, NA/FCO/30/123.

[84] There are many examples of this: see for example NA/PREM/13/3428, 3545-6.

[85] Telegram, Brown to Washington, 1 February 1968, No 1129, NA/PREM/13/2111.

[86] Letter, Dean to Hancock, 9 January 1968, NA/FCO/30/116.

[87] Telegram, Washington to FO, 29 January 1968, No 344, NA/PREM/13/2111.

[88] Telegram FO to Bonn, 12 January 1968, No 153, NA/FCO/30/123; telegram, Washington to FO, 17 January 1968, No 211, NA/FCO/30/225.

[89] Letter, Palliser to Morphet, 8 January 1968, NA/PREM/13/2110.

[90] Minute, O'Neill to Hancock, 10 January 1968, NA/FCO/30/225; telegram, Washington to FO, 19 February 1968, No 655, NA/FCO/30/184.

[91] For example, 'Record of a Conversation between the Prime Minister and Mr Kosygin at Dinner in the Hall of Receptions on the Lenin Hills on Monday, 22 January, 1968', NA/PREM/13/2402.

[92] Anglo-Soviet Communiqué, 24 January 1968, KCA22562 (2-9 March 1968).

[93] Minute, Greenhill to PUS, 29 January 1968, NA/PREM/13/2402.

[94] 'Summary Record of Discussion between Lord Chalfont and the Austrian Federal Chancellor in Vienna on 5 February [1968]', NA/FCO/73/79.

[95] Extract from conversation between the Prime Minister and Brezhnev, 23 January 1968, NA/PREM/13/2114.

[96] 'Record of a Conversation between the Prime Minister and Mr Kosygin at Dinner in the Hall of Receptions on the Lenin Hills on Monday, 22 January, 1968', NA/PREM/13/2402.

97   KCA22514 (3-10 February 1968).
98   Telegram, FO to Hague, 2 January 1968, No 16, NA/FCO/30/122.
99   EURO(68)1, 1 January 1968, NA/FCO/30/87.
100 Minute, Brown to Crosland, 3 January 1968; letter, Crosland to Brown, 5 January 1968; letter, Palliser to Morphet, 10 January 1968, NA/PREM/13/2110.
101 Letter, Brightly to Palliser, 3 January 1968; reply, 10 January 1968, NA/PREM/13/2454.
102 Draft paper, 'British Foreign Policy for the next three years', 14 January 1968, NA/PREM 13/2636.
103 KCA22798 (6-13 July 1968); KCA22566-8 (2-9 March 1968); KCA22683 (4-11 May 1968); KCA22730 (1-8 June 1968); KCA22874 (24-31 August 1968); KCA22765 (22-29 June 1968).
104 KCA22596 (16-23 March 1968).
105 Note, Campbell to Morrice, 14 February 1968, NA/FCO/62/68.
106 'Extract of Record of Conversation between the Prime Minister and the Prime Minister of Canada at the latter's residence in Ottawa on Saturday, February 10, 1968 at 10am', NA/PREM/13/2111. In his press conference of 28 November 1967, de Gaulle had called for a free Québec.

Chapter Four

1   For example, telegrams, Hague to FO, 1 March 1968, Nos 167-168; FO to Rome, 7 March 1968, No 905; Hague to FO, 5 March 1968, No 170, all NA/FCO/30/126.
2   Letter, Harmel to Brown, 1 March 1968; telegram FO to Brussels, 7 March 1968, No 590, both NA/PREM/13/2111; telegram, UKDel Brussels to FO, 7 March 1968, No 96, NA/FCO/62/84.
3   Telegram, FO to Rome, 6 March 1968, No 890, NA/PREM/13/2111.
4   See for example telegrams, Paris to FO, 2 March 1968, No 217, NA/FCO/30/173 and 7 March 1968, No 230, NA/FCO/30/174; Bonn to FO, 2 March 1968, No 381, NA/PREM/13/2111; minute, O'Neill to Hancock, 4 March 1968, NA/FCO/30/194.
5   Telegram, Paris to FO, 5 March 1968, No 226, NA/PREM/13/2111.
6   Letter, Marjoribanks to Statham, 4 March 1968, NA/FCO/30/126.
7   Letter, Roberts to Minister (Economic) etc, 7 March 1968, NA/FCO/30/194; note, Statham for the file, 4 March 1968, NA/FCO/30/117.
8   Telegram, Bonn to FO, 8 March 1968, No 419, NA/FCO/62/84.
9   Telegram, UKDel Brussels to FO, 8 March 1968, No 97, NA/PREM/13/2111.
10   Telegram, Bonn to FO, 9 March 1968, No 423, NA/PREM/13/2111.
11   Telegram, UKDel Brussels to FO, 10 March 1968, No 98, NA/PREM/13/2111.

[12] Telegram, Brussels to FO, 11 March 1968, No 175, NA/PREM/13/2111.

[13] Telegram, Bonn to FO, 11 March 1968, No 426, NA/FCO/30/126.

[14] Telegram, UKDel Brussels to FO, 10 March 1968, No 102, NA/FCO/30/126.

[15] Telegrams, UKDel Brussels to FO, 10 March 1968, No 99, NA/FCO/30/126 and No 100, NA/FCO/62/84; Brussels to FO, 11 March 1968, No 175, NA/PREM/13/2111; letter, Garran to O'Neill, 12 March 1968, NA/FCO/30/126.

[16] 'Record of a Meeting held at 10 Downing Street, SW1, at 12 noon on Monday, 11 March, 1968'; 'Record of a Meeting held at 10 Downing Street, SW1, at 11.15am on Tuesday 12 March' 1968, both NA/PREM/13/2111.

[17] Minute, Hancock to O'Neill, Morland and Private Secretary, 12 March 1968, and O'Neill's and Chalfont's notes thereon, all NA/FCO/30/126.

[18] Telegram, FO to Brussels, 16 March 1968, No 656, NA/PREM/13/2112.

[19] For details, see Pimlott, *Harold Wilson*, pp483-503.

[20] Minute and paper, Hancock to Morland etc, 18 March 1968, NA/FCO/30/117; letter, Roberts to Maitland, 19 March 1968, NA/FCO/30/194.

[21] 'George Brown', Reilly papers, MS Eng.c.6295.

[22] The papers of Lord Stewart of Fulham, held at Churchill College, Cambridge (henceforth 'Stewart papers' or 'Stewart diaries'), diaries, 23 April 1968, STWT/8/1/5; (however, no confirmation of this move has been found elsewhere).

[23] Castle, *The Castle Diaries*, 20 February 1968, p604.

[24] For example, telegrams, FO to Bonn, 21 March 1968, No 1015, NA/FCO/30/194, FO to Paris, 21 March 1968, No 1123, NA/FCO/30/174.

[25] Stewart diaries, 10 April 1968, STWT 8/1/5; minute, Maitland to Hancock, 19 March 1968, NA/FCO/30/117.

[26] Stewart diaries, 10 April 1968, STWT 8/1/5.

[27] Minute, O'Neill to Hancock, 21 March 1968, NA/FCO/30/117.

[28] Letter, Statham to Olver and other ambassadors in the Six and UKDel Brussels, 22 March 1968; telegrams, Rome to FO, 27 March 1968, No 337; Hague to FO, 30 March 1968, No 241; Luxembourg to FO, 27 March 1968, No 80; letters, Laskey to Statham and Wraight to Statham, 27 March 1968; telegrams, UKDel Brussels to FO, 28 March 1968, No 149; Paris to FO, 2 April 1968, No 304, all NA/FCO/30/117.

[29] Telegrams, UKDel Brussels to FO, 2 April 1968, Nos 157-159, NA/PREM/13/2112; Bonn to FO, 22 March 1968, No 483, NA/FCO/30/194.

[30] Telegram, UKDel Brussels to FO, 6 April 1968, No 172, NA/PREM/13/2112; letter, Marjoribanks to Hancock, 8 April 1968; telegram, Rome to FO, 10 April 1968, No 382, both NA/FCO/30/126.

31 Telegram, FO to Bonn, 25 April 1968, No 1335, NA/PREM/13/2112; Stewart diaries, 26 April 1968, STWT 8/1/5.

32 Telegram, Bonn to FO, 9 May 1968, No 732, NA/PREM/13/2112.

33 EUR(M)(68)2, 2 April 1968, 'European Space Activities', memo by SOSFA. Despite the numbering, Stewart's paper was written in response to EUR(M)(68)3 above.

34 EUR(M)(67)1, 24 May 1967, NA/FCO/30/114.

35 Minute, Palliser to Wilson, 6 April 1968, NA/PREM/13/2364.

36 'Record of Meeting between the Prime Minister and Sir Solly Zuckerman, Monday, 12.30pm, April 8th, 1968', NA/PREM/13/2364.

37 Minutes, Stewart to Wilson, 9 April 1968 (PM/68/37); Trend to Wilson, 10 April 1968, both NA/PREM/13/2364.

38 Minute, Stewart to Wilson, 9 April 1968 (PM/68/37); letter, Palliser to Maitland, 10 April 1968, NA/PREM/13/2364; C(68)26, 9 April 1968, NA/CAB/128/43.

39 Telegram FO and CO to certain missions, 11 April 1968, No 101 Guidance; 'Record of Conversation between the Foreign Secretary and the Netherlands Minister of Foreign Affairs at the Foreign Office on Tuesday, 16 April 1968, at 3pm', both NA/PREM/13/2364; 'Record of Conversation between the Foreign Secretary and Mr JMAH Luns at Lunch at 1, Carlton Gardens on Tuesday, 16 April 1968', NA/FCO/73/13; memo by C J Audland, 23 April 1968; telegram, Bonn to FO, 23 May 1968, No 810, both NA/PREM/13/2364; letter, Harmel (in Rome) to Stewart, 12 September 1968, NA/PREM/13/2113; letter, Harmel to Wilson, 26 September 1968, NA/PREM/13/2975.

40 Minute, Palliser to Maitland, 7 May 1968, NA/FCO/7/13; Stewart diaries, 7 May 1968, STWT 8/1/5.

41 Note for the Record, 'Meeting at No 10 Downing Street on European Technological Co-operation', 7 May 1968, NA/FCO/73/13.

42 EUR(M)(68)6, 'Europe', memorandum by the SOSFA, 17 May 1968.

43 Note, Stewart, undated (received in archives 16 May 1968); minute, Chalfont to Stewart, 8 May 1968, both NA/FCO/30/118; note by Wilson on minute, Palliser to Wilson, 10 May 1968, NA/PREM/13/2112; minute, Hancock to Morland and Private Secretary, 7 May 1968; minute, Robinson to Hancock and Private Secretary, 10 May 1968, both NA/FCO/30/118; Stewart diaries, 13 May 1968, STWT 8/1/5.

44 Minute, Hancock to Private Secretary, 18 May 1968, NA/FCO/30/118.

45 EUR(M)(68)2nd Meeting, 21 May 1968, NA/CAB/134/2805; EURM(68)7: 'Europe: Memorandum by the President of the Board of Trade', 20 May 1968, NA/FCO/62/69.

46 Minute, Palliser to Wilson, 24 May 1968, NA/PREM/13/2112.

47 Minute, Robinson to Hancock, 28 May 1968, NA/FCO/30/118.

48 Minute, Robinson to Hancock, 19 June 1968, NA/FCO/30/119.

49 Minute, Robinson to Hancock, 29 May 1969, NA/FCO/30/114; EUR(M)(69)2, 'Composition and terms of reference: note by the Secretary of

the Cabinet', 28 October 1969, NA/CAB/134/2806; NA/CAB/134/2824 passim for EURO papers.

50 CC(68)30, 30 May; CC(68)34, 4 July; CC(68)36, 18 July; CC(68)39, 24 September; CC(68)42, 17 October; CC(68)43, 24 October; CC(68)46, 12 November; CC(68)47, 22 November, all 1968 and NA/CAB/128/43.

51 Letter, Palliser to Maitland, 10 April 1968, NA/PREM/13/2364. The ministers were: Chalfont and Ministers of State at the Treasury, Board of Trade, Department of Science and Education, Ministry of Technology, and the Minister of Defence for Equipment, the Parliamentary Under-Secretary of the Department of Economic Affairs, and the Chief Scientific Adviser.

52 EUR(M)(T)1st Meeting, 10 May 1968, NA/CAB/134/2810.

53 EUR(M)(T)1st Meeting, 10 May 1968; EUR(M)(T)2nd Meeting, 17 June 1968; EUR(M)(T)3rd Meeting, 25 July 1968; EUR(M)(T)4th Meeting, 9 December 1968, all NA/CAB/134/2810.

54 For description of May events, see Lacouture, *De Gaulle*, pp527-558.

55 Telegram, Paris to Foreign Office, 23 May 1968, No 470, NA/PREM/13/2112.

56 Telegram, Brussels to FO, 24 May 1968, No 286, NA/FCO/30/127.

57 Minutes, Statham to Hancock, 14 May 1968, NA/FCO/30/174; Robinson to Hancock, 15 May 1968; letter, Mellon to Cambridge, 20 May 1968; telegrams, UKDel Brussels to FO, 17 May 1968, No 210, all NA/FCO/30/127, 24 May 1968, No 214; 30 May 1968, No 227, both NA/FCO/30/167; Hague to FO, 17 May 1968, No 339, NA/PREM/13/2112.

58 Minute, Robinson to Hancock, 28 May 1968, NA/FCO/30/195; letter, Marjoribanks to Hancock, 18 May 1968, NA/PREM/13/127.

59 'Record of a Conversation between the Foreign Secretary and the German Foreign Minister at Herr Brandt's residence in Bonn at 3pm on 24 May, 1968', NA/PREM/13/2112.

60 Telegram, FO to Bonn, 30 May 1968, No 1653, NA/FCO/73/13.

61 Letter, Edwards to Statham, 18 May 1968, NA/FCO/30/185.

62 Telegrams, UKDel Brussels to FO, 31 May 1968, Nos 233-234, NA/FCO/30/115.

63 Minute, Hancock to Tait, and Chalfont's note thereon, 6 June 1968; letter, Hancock to McIntosh, 10 June 1968, both NA/FCO/30/119.

64 Letter, Hancock to Reilly and other Community posts, 6 June 1968, NA/FCO/30/119.

65 Telegram, Paris to FO, 11 June 1968, No 580, NA/FCO/30/119; minute, Galsworthy to Robinson, 14 June 1968, NA/FCO/30/174; letter and enclosure, Overton to Robinson, 10 June 1968, NA/FCO/30/195; letters, Barclay to Hancock, 11 June 1968 and Jackling to Hancock, 15 June 1968; telegram, Hague to FO, 13 June 1968, No 384; letter, Olver to Morgan, 13 June 1968, and Malcolm to Hancock, 13 June 1968; telegram, Rome to FO, 14 June 1968, No 564; letter, Marjoribanks to Hancock, 13 June 1968, all NA/FCO/30/119; minute, Morland to Cambridge and Robinson, 19 June 1968, NA/FCO/30/167.

66   'Record of a Conversation between the Prime Minister and the President of the European Commission in the Prime Minister's Room in the House of Commons at 7.15pm on Tuesday, June 25, 1968', NA/PREM/13/2104.

67   Telegram, UKDel Brussels to FO, 1 July 1968, NA/PREM/13/2113.

68   Telegram, Bonn to FO, 6 July 1968, No 1027, NA/FCO/73/84.

69   'WEU: Minutes of the 348th Meeting of the Council, held at Ministerial level in Bonn on 8 and 9 July 1968', (CR(68)13, Part II), NA/FCO/73/25.

70   'Record of Conversation between the Foreign Secretary and the Foreign Ministers of Germany and Belgium at the German Foreign Minister's Residence at Venusberg, Bonn, on 9 July 1968, at 8.45am', NA/PREM/13/2113.

71   'Record of a Discussion between the Foreign Secretary and the Belgian Foreign Minister and their advisers at the Residence of the Belgian Ambassador at Bonn on Tuesday, 9 July at 1.15pm', NA/PREM/13/2113.

72   Letter, Jackson to Robinson, 23 July 1968, NA/FCO/30/127.

73   'Foreign Secretary and Lord Chalfont at the Unattributable Press Briefing for British Correspondents at HM Ambassador's Residence, Bonn, on 9 July 1968', NA/FCO/73/25.

74   Minute, Hancock to PUS, Tait and Maitland, 10 July 1968, NA/PREM/13/2113.

75   Telegrams, Paris to FO, 23 July 1968, No 756, NA/PREM/13/2113; 25 July, No 766, NA/FCO/30/174; see also Bonn to FO, 27 July 1968, No 1107, NA/PREM/13/185.

76   Letter, James to Robinson and Killick's note thereon, 9 August 1968, NA/FCO/30/127.

77   Letter, Ledwidge to Morgan, 24 July 1968, NA/FCO/30/119.

78   Telegram, Paris to FCO, 29 July 1968, No 772, NA/FCO/30/174.

79   Telegram, UKDel Brussels to FO, 30 July 1968, No 299, NA/FCO/30/127.

80   Telegram, UKDel Brussels to FO, 31 July 1968, No 301, NA/FCO/30/127.

81   Minute, Gore-Booth to Hancock, 10 July 1968, NA/FCO/30/119.

82   For example, 'Record of Conversation between the Foreign Secretary and M. Jean Monnet at lunch in Brown's Hotel on 21 February 1968', NA/PREM/13/2111; 'Record of Conversation between the Prime Minister and M. Jean Monnet at 10 Downing Street, at 3.00pm on Monday, July 15 1968, NA/PREM/13/2090.

83   Letter, Maitland to Palliser, 17 July 1968, NA/PREM/13/2632.

84   'Record of Conversation between the Prime Minister and M. Jean Monnet at 10 Downing Street, at 3.00pm on Monday, July 15 1968, NA/PREM/13/2090; letter, Stewart to Monnet, 22 July 1968; reply, 25 July 1968; letter, Palliser to Day, 25 September 1968; formal invitation, Monnet to Wilson, 28 September 1968, NA/PREM/13/2632.

85   'Record of Conversation between the Prime Minister and M. Jean Monnet at 10 Downing Street, at 3.00pm on Monday, July 15 1968, NA/PREM/13/2090.

86 NA/PREM/13/2632 and NA/PREM/13/2876.

87 CC(68)36, 18 July 1968, NA/CAB/128/43; for Peart comment, see Crossman, *Diaries*, Volume III, 18 September 1968, p192.

88 Letter, Hannay to Robinson, 12 July 1968, NA/FCO/30/127; 'Record of Conversation between the Secretary of State and the French Ambassador at the Foreign Office on Tuesday, 23 July 1968, at 4.30pm', NA/FCO/73/19.

89 'Record of a Meeting between Lord Chalfont and the Danish Ambassador, M. Erling Kristiansen, at the Foreign Office at 11am, on 11 July 1968', NA/FCO/73/79.

90 Minute, Hancock to Robinson, 17 July 1968; letter, Robinson to Olver, 22 July 1968, both NA/FCO/30/127.

91 Broad, *Labour's European Dilemmas*, p70.

92 Letter, Soames to Wilson, 30 April 1968, NA/PREM/13/2364.

93 Letter and enclosure, Soames to Maitland and Palliser, 24 July 1968, and Robinson's note thereon, NA/FCO/30/174; minute, Robinson to Hancock, 7 August 1968, NA/FCO/30/167.

94 Minute, Hancock to Cambridge, 14 August 1968, NA/FCO/30/174.

95 Text of Soames' speech, Hancock to Winchester, 15 August 1968, NA/FCO/30/174.

96 'Secretary of State's Discussion with Mr Soames, 15 September', NA/FCO/30/174.

97 Minute, Palliser to Wilson, 19 July 1968 and Wilson's note thereon, NA/PREM/13/2113.

98 Letter, Palliser to Maitland, 22 July 1968, NA/PREM/13/2113.

99 Letters, Marjoribanks to Hancock, 6 August 1968; Barclay to Hancock, 12 August 1968; Malcolm to Hancock, 20 August 1968; Jackling to Hancock, 27 August 1968, all NA/FCO/30/119.

100 Letter, Ford to Robinson, 8 August 1968, NA/PREM/13/2113.

101 Telegrams, Rome to FO, 11 August 1968, Nos 764-765 and 13 August 1968, No 766; FO to Rome, 12 August 1968, No 2129, all NA/PREM/13/2113.

102 Telegrams, FO to Rome, 15 August 1968, No 2134; Rome to FO, 16 August 1968, No 781, 26 August 1968, No 808, and 29 August 1968, No 825, all NA/PREM/13/2113.

103 Telegram, Paris to FO, 21 August 1968, No 835, and cover note, Hancock to Cambridge, both NA/FCO/30/174.

104 Telegram, Bonn to FO, 26 August 1968, No 1210, NA/FCO/41/284.

105 26 August 1968, KCA22995 (26 October – 2 November 1968).

106 Letter, Jackling to Stewart, 28 August 1968, NA/FCO/30/1195; see also letter, Maitland to Palliser, 29 August 1968, NA/PREM/13/2673.

107 Telegram, Paris to FO, 29 August 1968, No 860, NA/PREM/13/2113.

108 'Record of Conversation between the Foreign Secretary and the French Ambassador at the Foreign Office on Friday, 30 August, 1968 at 10am', NA/PREM/13/2113.

109 Telegrams, Paris to FO, 9 September 1968, No 883, NA/FCO/30/185; No 888, NA/PREM/13/2114 and 12 September 1968, No 907, NA/FCO/30/185; minute, Palliser to Wilson, 9 September 1968, NA/PREM/13/2646.

110 'Report: Sir Patrick Reilly's Farewell Interview with General de Gaulle', sent 12 September 1968, NA/PREM/13/2113.

111 Reilly papers, MS Eng.c.6925.

112 Telegram, UKMis Geneva to FO, 10 September 1968, No 105 Saving, NA/PREM/13/2113.

113 Telegram, Bonn to FO, 11 September 1968, No 1270, NA/FCO/30/185.

114 Telegram, Rome to FO, 9 September 1968, No 856, NA/PREM/13/2113.

115 Minute, Palliser to Wilson, 10 September 1968, NA/PREM/13/2113.

116 Letter, Wood to Cambridge, 20 March 1968, NA/FCO/30/225; telegram, Washington to FO, No 2885, 25 September 1968, NA/PREM/13/2113; see also letter, Buxton to Dean, 13 June 1968, NA/PREM/13/3016.

117 Telegram, Washington to FO, No 2793, 18 September 1968, NA/PREM/13/2443; letter, Palliser to Maitland, 25 September 1968, NA/PREM/13/2090; 'Record of Conversation between the Foreign Secretary and Mr George Ball, US Permanent Representative to the United Nations, at the Foreign Office, on Friday, 12 July, 1968 at 4pm', NA/FCO/73/19; minute, Robinson to Hancock, 19 September 1968, NA/FCO/30/185; letter, Washington Embassy to Foreign Office, 17 July 1968, NA/PREM/13/2113.

118 Telegram, UKMis Geneva to FO, 4 March 1968, No 80, NA/PREM/13/2111.

119 Telegrams, Copenhagen to FO, No 154 and UKMis Geneva to FO, No 161, 25 April 1968; letter, Holland to Palliser, 30 April 1968, all NA/PREM/13/2112.

120 Letter, Palliser to Holland, 30 April 1968, NA/PREM/13/2112.

121 Letter, Holland to Palliser, 3 May 1968, NA/PREM/13/2112.

122 Telegram, FO to Geneva, 10 May 1968, No 425 Saving, NA/PREM/13/2112.

123 Telegram, FO to Geneva, 10 May 1968, No 425 Saving, NA/PREM/13/2112.

124 For example, 'Record of Conversation between the Foreign Secretary and the Danish Ambassador at the Foreign Office on Wednesday, 31 July, 1968 at 3.30pm', NA/FCO/73/19; conversation between Wilson and Erlander, reported in letter, Palliser to Day, 30 September 1968, NA/PREM/13/2413.

125 Letter, Wright to Hancock, 11 July 1968, NA/FCO/30/119.

126 NA/PREM/13/2096 *passim*.

127 Conversation with Wilson recorded in letter, Palliser to Maitland, 17 May 1968, NA/PREM/13/2112.

128 Letter, Snelling to O'Neill, 8 March 1968, NA/FCO/30/194.

129 Minute, Smith to Shannon, 12 March 1968, NA/FCO/62/68.

[130] Letter, Palliser to Maitland, 12 September 1968, NA/PREM/13/2113.

[131] Minute, Robinson to Hancock, 17 September 1968, NA/PREM/13/2113.

[132] Letter, Harmel to Stewart, 12 September 1968, NA/PREM/13/2113.

[133] Telegram, Hague to FO, 15 September 1968, No 502, NA/PREM/13/2113.

[134] Telegram, Paris to FO, 13 September 1968, No 912, NA/PREM/13/2113.

[135] Palliser's note on telegram, Rome to FO, 13 September 1968, No 865, NA/PREM/13/2113.

[136] Telegrams, FO to Hague, No 1686 and FO to Rome, No 2222, both 16 September 1968, NA/PREM/13/2113.

[137] Telegrams, Hague to FO, 17 September 1968, Nos 510-512, NA/FCO/30/127.

[138] Telegram, FO to Hague, 17 September 1968, No 1689, NA/FCO/30/127.

[139] Telegrams, Paris to FO, 17 September 1968, Nos 919-920l; minute, Palliser to Maitland, 18 September 1968; see also telegram, UKDel Brussels to FO, 21 September 1968, No 329; FO to Paris, 26 September 1968, No 2490, all NA/PREM/13/2113.

[140] Telegrams, FO to Brussels, 18 September 1968, No 1319; Brussels to FO, 20 September 1968, No 465, both NA/PREM/13/2113.

[141] Minute, Hancock to Robinson, 19 September 1968, NA/FCO/30/195; telegrams, Hague to FO, 20 September 1968, Nos 521-522, 527-528 and 530; see also FO to Bonn, 24 September 1968, Nos 1711-1712; letter, Overton to (unclear), cc Robinson, 24 September 1968, all NA/FCO/30/127.

[142] Telegrams, Rome to FO, 21 September 1968, No 885; Hague to FO, Nos 536-537; Luxembourg to FO, No 152; Paris to FO, No 958, all 25 September 1968; minute, Hancock to Robinson, 26 September 1968, all NA/FCO/30/127.

[143] Telegram, UKDel Brussels to FO, 27 September 1968, No 337, NA/FCO/30/127.

[144] Letter, Palliser to Maitland, 23 September 1968, NA/PREM/13/2113; telegrams, Hague to FO, No 535; Paris to FO, No 955, all 24 September 1968, NA/FCO/30/127.

[145] Telegram, Bonn to FO, 26 September 1968, No 1329, NA/PREM/13/2113.

[146] Letter, Wilson to Kiesinger, 26 September 1968, PMPM Serial No T198/68.

[147] Minute, Jackling to Hood, 28 September 1968, NA/PREM/13/2113.

[148] Since Article XXIV of the GATT stated that groups of countries could only reduce the tariffs amongst themselves as a step towards forming a customs union, insisting that an 'arrangement' be compatible with GATT was a way of linking it with eventual British membership of the Communities.

[149] Telegram, UKDel Brussels to FO, 27 September 1968, No 338, NA/PREM/13/2113; minute, Marjoribanks to Mellon etc, 28 September 1968, NA/FCO/30/127.

[150] Telegram, UKDel Brussels to FO, 27 September 1968, No 339, NA/PREM/13/2113.

[151] Letter, Mellon to Morland, 30 September 1968, NA/FCO/30/127.

152 Minute, Robinson to Hancock, 27 September 1968, NA/PREM/13/2113.

153 Wilson's note on minute, Jackling to Hood, 28 September 1968; telegrams, Bonn to FO, 29 September 1968, Nos 1340, 1343 and 1344 and Wilson's note thereon; Paris to FO, 30 September 1968, No 974 and Wilson's note thereon; Paris to FO, 3 October 1968, No 989, all NA/PREM/13/2113.

154 Minute, Robinson to Hancock, 20 September 1968, NA/PREM/13/2113; see also minute, Hancock to private secretary, 20 September 1968, NA/FCO/30/120.

155 Minute, Robinson to Hancock etc and Chalfont's and Maitland's notes thereon, 26 September 1968, NA/FCO/30/120.

156 For example, letters, Jackson to Robinson, 11 and 16 September 1968, NA/FCO/30/167; minute, Robinson to Hancock, 19 September 1968, NA/FCO/30/185.

Chapter Five

1   Crossman, *Diaries*, Volume III, 16 October 1968, p225.

2   Letter, Wilson to Monnet, 3 October 1968; reply, 4 October 1968, NA/PREM/13/2632.

3   Letters, Palliser to Maitland, 23 October 1968; Monnet to Palliser, 6 November 1968; Rumor to Wilson, 22 November 1968, all NA/PREM/13/2632.

4   Minute, Robinson to Hancock, 28 November 1968, NA/PREM/13/2632.

5   'Record of Conversation between the Foreign and Commonwealth Secretary and M. Monnet at the Foreign and Commonwealth Office, at 4pm on Tuesday, 28 January, 1969'; 'Record of a Conversation between the Prime Minister and Monsieur Jean Monnet at 10 Downing Street at 6.45pm on Wednesday, January 29, 1969', NA/PREM/13/2632.

6   Telegram, FO to Brussels, 1 October 1968, No 1341 and Palliser's note thereon, NA/PREM/13/2113; minutes, Robinson to Hancock and Barrington; Hancock to Lord Hood, both 1 October 1968, NA/FCO/30/393.

7   Telegram, FO to Brussels, 2 October 1968, No 1345, NA/PREM/13/2113

8   '*Allocution prononcée par M. Pierre Harmel, Ministre des Affaires Étrangères, devant l'Organisation des Journalistes Européenes, à Val Duchesse, le 3 Octobre 1968*', advance copy, NA/PREM/13/2113.

9   Telegram, Bonn to FO, 4 October 1968, No 1368, NA/FCO/30/433.

10 Letter, Mellon to Morland, 4 October 1968, NA/FCO/30/393.

11 Minute, Palliser to Wilson, 4 October 1968, NA/PREM/13/2113.

12 Minutes, Palliser to Day, both 7 October 1968, NA/PREM/13/2113 and NA/PREM/13/2627.

13 Letter, Morphet to Palliser, 11 October 1968, NA/PREM/13/2627.

14 Minute, Hancock to private secretary, 4 October 1968; note by Maitland, 6 October 1968; minute, Hancock to Robinson, 7 October 1968, all NA/FCO/30/531; minutes, Palliser to Day and Palliser to Gruffydd Jones,

both 7 October 1968, NA/PREM/13/2627; Philip Giddings, 'Prime Minister and Cabinet' in Donald Shell and Richard Hodder-Williams, *Churchill to Major, the British Prime Ministership since 1945*, London: Hurst and Company, 1995, pp41-44.

15   Minute, Day to Hancock and Robinson, 4 October 1968, NA/FCO/30/395.

16   Telegram, FO to Paris, 3 October 1968, No 2516 and Palliser's note thereon, NA/PREM/13/2113.

17   Telegram, Paris to FO, 8 October 1968, No 1001; letter, Galsworthy to Robinson, 9 October 1968, both NA/FCO/30/445.

18   Telegram, Stewart (in New York) to FO, 13 October 1968, No 2491, Prime Minister's Personal Message (PMPM) Serial No T218/68, NA/PREM/13/2627.

19   Telegram, Stewart (in New York) to FO, 13 October 1968, No 2492, PMPM Serial No T219/68, NA/PREM/13/2627.

20   Telegram, Stewart (in New York) to FO, 13 October 1968, No 2490, PMPM Serial No T217/68, NA/PREM/13/2627.

21   Brief, 'MISC 224 – European Policy', RRD McIntosh, 15 October 1968, NA/PREM/13/2627. See also telegram, Bonn to FO, 15 October 1968, No 1424, NA/FCO/30/433.

22   Minute, Palliser to Wilson, 15 October 1968, NA/PREM/13/2627.

23   Minute, Robinson to Hancock, 15 October 1968, NA/FCO/30/533.

24   MISC 224(68)1st Meeting, 16 October 1968, NA/CAB/130/398.

25   Minute, Robinson to Hancock, 17 September 1968, NA/PREM/13/2112; Crossman, *Diaries*, Volume III, 16 October 1968, p225 and 17 October 1968, p226; CC(68)42, 17 October 1968, NA/CAB/128/43.

26   Castle, *The Castle Diaries*, 5 November 1968, pp544-545.

27   'Record of Conversation with the Minister of State and the Joint Secretary of State, Federal German Ministry of Economics, held at the Foreign Office on Monday, 14 October, at 5.15pm', NA/FCO/30/433.

28   Lord Chalfont's speech to WEU Assembly, Paris, 15 October 1968, NA/FCO/30/531.

29   Telegram, Bonn to FO, 16 October 1968, No 1436, NA/PREM/13/2627.

30   Telegram, Bonn to FCO, 18 October 1968, No 1449, NA/PREM/13/2627. The Foreign Office and Commonwealth Relations Office merged in October to form the Foreign and Commonwealth Office, FCO.

31   Telegram, FO to Bonn, 16 October 1968, No 2245 and Palliser's note thereon, NA/PREM/13/2627; see also letter, Jackling to Hood, 16 October 1968, NA/FCO/30/433.

32   Telegram, FO to Bonn, 16 October 1968, No 2246, NA/PREM/13/2627.

33   Telegram, Bonn to FCO, 18 October 1968, No 1449, NA/PREM/13/2627; see also telegram, Lisbon to FCO, 18 October 1968, No 497, NA/FCO/30/433.

34   Telegram, Paris to FO, 15 October 1968, No 1022, NA/PREM/13/2627.

35   Minute, Chalfont to Stewart, 16 October 1968, NA/PREM/13/2627.

36 Telegram, FCO to Paris, 17 October 1968, No 2546, NA/PREM/13/2627.

37 Telegrams, Paris to FCO, 17 October 1968, Nos 1030 and 1033, NA/FCO/30/445.

38 Telegram, Bonn to FCO, 19 October 1968, No 1462, NA/FCO/30/433.

39 Telegram, Paris to FCO, 21 October 1968, No 1047, NA/PREM/13/2627.

40 Telegram, Hague to FCO, 17 October 1968, No 587, NA/FCO/30/433.

41 Telegram, Bonn to FCO, 17 October 1968, No 1445, NA/PREM/13/2627.

42 Telegram, FCO to Bonn, 17 October 1968, No 935, NA/FCO/30/433.

43 'Record of a Conversation between Lord Chalfont and State Secretary Jahn at the German Embassy at Rome at 11pm on 20 October 1968', NA/FCO/30/533.

44 Telegram, Bonn to FCO, 18 October 1968, No 1456, NA/FCO/30/433.

45 Letter, Robinson to Barclay, 23 October 1968, NA/FCO/30/533.

46 Telegram, Stewart (in Rome) to FCO, 22 October 1968, No 1005, NA/PREM/13/2627.

47 Telegram, Stewart (in Rome) to FCO, 22 October 1968, No 1006, NA/PREM/13/2627.

48 Telegram, FCO to Rome, 24 October 1968, No 714 Saving, NA/FCO/30/531.

49 Telegram, Stewart (in Rome) to FCO, 22 October 1968, No 1007, NA/PREM/13/2627.

50 Accounts in *Figaro* and *Le Monde*, cited in telegram, Paris to FCO, 22 October 1968, No 1052, NA/PREM/13/2627.

51 CC(68)43, 24 October 1968, NA/CAB/128/43.

52 Telegram, FCO to Bonn, 24 October 1968, No 2266, NA/PREM/13/2627.

53 Telegram, FCO to Bonn, 24 October 1968, No 2271, NA/FCO/30/534.

54 Telegram, FCO to certain missions, 24 October 1968, No 259, NA/FCO/30/533.

55 Letter and enclosed speech, Galsworthy to Robinson, 25 October 1968, NA/FCO/30/455.

56 Telegram, Paris to FCO, 31 October 1968, No 1083, NA/PREM/13/2628.

57 Letter, Marjoribanks to Robinson, 28 October 1968, NA/FCO/30/401; telegram, FCO to Rome, 29 October 1968, No 2373, NA/FCO/30/276; letter, Guidotti to Stewart, 29 October 1968, NA/FCO/30/433.

58 'Summary of Conversations between Lord Chalfont and the Luxembourg Ambassador M. Andre Clasen and the Belgian Ambassador, Baron Jean van den Bosch, on Friday, 25 October, 1968, at the Reception for the Austrian National Day at 18, Belgrave Square, SW1', NA/PREM/13/2627.

59 Telegram, Rome to FCO, 27 October 1968, No 1022, NA/FCO/30/533.

60 Telegram, Brussels to FCO, 30 October 1968, No 527, NA/FCO/30/533.

61 Telegram, Stewart to Brussels, 31 October 1968, No 1384, NA/PREM/13/2627.

62 Minute, Hood to Hancock, 28 October 1968, NA/FCO/30/533.

[63] Initial translation of message, Brandt to Stewart, 5 November 1968, NA/FCO/30/534.

[64] Undated 'French proposals' to Council of Ministers, 4-5 November 1968, NA/FCO/30/372; minute, Robinson to private secretary, 4 November 1968, NA/FCO/30/395.

[65] Telegram, FCO to certain missions, 7 November 1968, No 270 Guidance, NA/FCO/30/395.

[66] See for example letter, Jackling to Hancock, 4 November 1968, and Killick's notes thereon, NA/FCO/30/433.

[67] 'Note for the Record: Europe: Secretary of State's Office Meeting', Maitland, 5 November 1968, NA/FCO/30/395.

[68] Telegram, FCO to Bonn, 6 November 1968, No 2312, NA/FCO/30/534.

[69] Telegram, Bonn to FCO, 7 November 1968, No 1537, NA/FCO/30/534.

[70] Telegram, Hague to FCO, 9 November 1968, No 665, NA/FCO/30/534.

[71] Telegram, Hague to FCO, 7 November 1968, No 662, NA/FCO/30/534.

[72] Telegrams, Hague to FCO, No 669; FCO to Paris, No 2597, both 9 November 1968, NA/FCO/30/534.

[73] Telegrams, Paris to FCO, No 1123 and Brussels to FCO, No 539, both 12 November 1968, NA/FCO/30/534.

[74] Minute, Trend to Wilson, 11 November 1968, NA/PREM/13/2627.

[75] C(68)123, 'NATO and our Policy towards Europe: Memorandum by the Secretary of State for Foreign and Commonwealth Affairs', 8 November 1968, NA/CAB/129/139.

[76] CC(68)46, 12 November 1968, NA/CAB/128/43.

[77] NA/CAB/128/43; Castle, The Castle Diaries, 15 January 1969, p590 (first mention by name).

[78] Letter, Kiesinger to Wilson, 12 November 1968, PMPM Serial No T262/68, NA/PREM/13/2114.

[79] Minute, Gore-Booth to Stewart, 14 November 1968, NA/FCO/30/433. Ludlow argues that French threats to leave the Communities in the 1960s were not credible, since French interests were too bound up in the organisation: Ludlow, 'The indirect route to the Elysée: de Gaulle's European policy from a Quai, Matignon and Brussels perspective', paper presented to the Maison Française, University of Oxford, 14 January 2002. In this case however, German perceptions of de Gaulle's intentions were more important.

[80] Telegram, Paris to FCO, 13 November 1968, No 1134, NA/FCO/30/534.

[81] Telegram, Stewart (in Brussels) to FCO, 14 November 1968, Nos 544, NA/PREM/13/2627.

[82] Telegrams, Stewart (in Brussels) to FCO, 14 November 1968, Nos 545 and 546, NA/PREM/13/2627.

[83] Italian aide memoire, Ricciulli to Hancock on 19 November 1968, NA/FCO/30/534.

[84] Minute, Robinson to Hancock, 19 November 1968, NA/FCO/30/534.

85   Telegram, UKDel Brussels to FCO, 21 November 1968, No 380, NA/PREM/13/2627.

86   Telegrams, FCO to Bonn, 5 December 1968, No 2388, NA/FCO/30/535; Rome to FCO, 26 November 1968, No 1105, NA/FCO/30/534.

87   Letter, Hancock to Ledwidge, 29 November 1968, NA/FCO/30/534.

88   Letter, Barclay to Hood, 3 December 1968, NA/FCO/30/535.

89   1 July 1968, KCA22975 (19-26 October 1968).

90   Crossman, *Diaries*, Volume III, 26 November 1968, p273.

91   KCA23089-23093 (21-31 December 1968).

92   Letter, Garran to Hancock, 28 November 1968, NA/FCO/30/535; 'Extract from Chancellor's Speech at Assembly of Council of Europe, Strasbourg, Wednesday 29 January', 1969, NA/PREM/13/2627.

93   Telegram, UKDel Brussels to FCO, 10 December 1968, No 397, NA/PREM/13/2627.

94   Telegram, Rome to FCO, 11 December 1968, No 1145, NA/FCO/30/535.

95   'Record of Meeting between Lord Chalfont and Herr Birrenbach at the Foreign and Commonwealth Office on Wednesday, 11 December, 1968', NA/PREM/13/2627.

96   Minute, Robinson to Hancock, 17 December 1968; see also minute, Robinson to Hancock, 11 December 1968, both NA/FCO/30/535.

97   Telegram, FCO to Rome, 17 December 1968, No 2469, NA/FCO/30/535.

98   Telegrams, Bonn to FCO, 12 December 1968, Nos 1725-1726, NA/FCO/30/535.

99   Letters, Ledwidge to Morgan and Ledwidge to Palliser, both 18 December 1968, NA/PREM/13/2627.

100 See for example minute, Tait to Robinson, 18 December 1968; telegram, Luxembourg to FCO, 19 December 1969, No 197, both NA/FCO/30/535.

101 Telegrams, Rome to FCO, 19 December 1968, No 1172; FCO to Rome, 20 December 1968, No 2480; see also telegram, Brussels to FCO, 20 December 1968, No 593, all NA/FCO/30/535.

102 Draft of Italian paper, Robinson to Palliser, 23 December 1968, NA/PREM/13/2627.

103 Telegram, FO to Paris, 3 October 1968, No 2515, NA/PREM/13/2364.

104 KCA23075 (7-14 December 1968).

105 'Record of Conversation between the Foreign and Commonwealth Secretary and Signor Medici, Italian Minister of Foreign Affairs at the British Ambassador's Residence, The Hague, during lunch on Saturday 9 November', 1968, NA/PREM/13/2627.

106 Minutes, Zuckerman to Wilson, 4 and 14 October 1968, NA/PREM/13/2975.

107 Wilson's notes on minutes on the IIST by the secretaries of the EURM(T) and Benn, both 5 December 1968; Palliser to Wilson, 11 December 1968; telegram, FCO to UKDel OECD, 11 December 1968, No 180, all NA/PREM/13/2975.

108 MISC 224(68)2nd Meeting, 11 November 1968, NA/CAB/130/398. The ministers were: Wilson, Stewart, Shackleton, Morris, Peart, Benn, Diamond, Roberts and Williams, together with Zuckerman.

109 Wilson's note on telegram, Paris to FCO, 26 November 1968; minute, Palliser to Day, 2 December 1968, both NA/PREM/13/2627.

110 Letter, Barrington to Palliser and Palliser's and Wilson's notes thereon, 9 December 1968, NA/PREM/13/2627.

111 Minute, Wilson to Stewart, 17 December 1968, Prime Minister's Personal Minute No M74/68, NA/PREM/13/2627.

112 'Meeting on European Policy in Lord Chalfont's Office on 19 December', NA/FCO/73/90; minutes, Chalfont to Stewart, 19 December 1968 and Stewart's note thereon, NA/FCO/30/395; Stewart to Wilson, 20 December 1968, PM/68/110, NA/PREM/13/2627.

113 Minute, Palliser to Wilson, 23 December 1968 and Wilson's note thereon, NA/PREM/13/2627.

114 For French hints, see letter, Marjoribanks to Robinson, 28 October 1968, NA/FCO/30/401; minute, Hannay to HE, 29 November 1968, NA/FCO/30/445; telegram, Paris to FCO, 4 December 1968, No 91 Saving, NA/PREM/13/2627.

115 There is no mention of such discussions in the FCO files pertaining to the EC and US together: FCO files on relations with the US in a non-EC context were not examined.

116 Draft paper, Hancock to Soames, 7 January 1969, NA/PREM/13/2627.

117 Minute, Palliser to Wilson, 17 January 1969 and Wilson's comments thereon, NA/PREM/13/2627.

118 Minute, Palliser to Maitland, 24 January 1969, NA/PREM/13/2627.

119 14 January 1969, KCA23130 (11-18 January 1969).

120 'Governor Scranton's call on the Secretary of State, 4 October 1968, Record of Meeting'; minute, Palliser to Maitland, 5 October 1968, both NA/PREM/13/2443; 'Report: President Elect: Richard Milhous Nixon, Attitudes to Europe', US Information Service, 7 November 1968, NA/PREM/13/2627; 'Record of a Conversation between the Prime Minister and Senator Javits at No 10 Downing Street at 2.30pm on Monday November 18, 1968', NA/PREM/13/3020.

121 Minute, Palliser to Wilson, 2 December 1968, NA/PREM/13/2444; letter and notes, Bendall to Palliser, 23 December 1968, NA/PREM/13/3097; minute and enclosed notes, Palliser to Wilson, 23 December 1968 and Wilson's note thereon, NA/PREM/13/3097.

122 Memorandum by FCO officials, 17 December 1968, sent by Trend to Wilson, 23 December 1968, NA/PREM/13/2114.

123 Summary of Moscow Dispatch of 2 January 1969: Soviet Union's 'Annual Review', 1968, Sir D Wilson; letter, Giffard to Hayman, 13 January 1968, both NA/PREM/13/2959.

124 Minutes, Crosland to Stewart and reply, both 18 October 1968; Crosland to Stewart, 12 November 1968, and reply, 14 November 1968; telegrams,

Vienna to FCO, 21 November 1968, No 478 and 22 November 1968 No 482; minute, Crosland to Stewart, 25 November 1968, and reply, 11 December 1968; Crosland to Stewart, 18 December 1968, all NA/PREM/13/2627.

125 Telegrams, Stockholm to FCO, 25 October 1968, No 65; FCO to Stockholm, 2 November 1968, No 997, PMPM Serial No T236/68, NA/PREM/13/2627.

126 Letter, Robinson to East, 29 November 1968, NA/FCO/30/534; telegrams, UKMis Geneva to FCO, 5 December 1968, Nos 570-571, NA/FCO/30/372; minute, Robinson to Hancock, 16 January 1969, NA/FCO/30/536; see also 'Denmark: Annual Review for. 1968', Wright, 22 January 1969, NA/PREM/13/2572; letter, Scott Fox to Morgan, 29 January 1969, NA/FCO/30/372.

127 'Record of Conversation between the Foreign and Commonwealth Secretary and the Jamaican High Commissioner at the Foreign and Commonwealth Office on 18 October, 1968 at 12.25pm', NA/FCO/73/19.

128 C(69)9, Stewart, 'World Situation and Trends', 7 January 1969, NA/CAB/129/140.

129 CPM(69)9th Meeting, 13 January 1969; CPM(69)11th Meeting, 14 January 1969; communiqué, all NA/PREM/13/2539.

130 Minute and enclosed speaking note, Brind to Brighty, 20 January 1969, NA/FCO/30/395.

131 KCA22988 (9-16 October 1968).

132 Telegrams, Brussels to FCO, 17 January 1969, Nos 15 and 17; Rome to FCO, 19 January 1969, No 55; Luxembourg to FCO, 20 January 1969, No 18; letter, Robinson to Drinkall, 20 January 1969; telegram, FCO to Rome, 21 January 1969, No 38; minute, Robinson to Hancock, 21 January 1969; telegram, Hague to FCO, 22 January 1969, No 43; minute, Robinson to Hancock, 22 January 1969, all NA/FCO/30/536; telegram, FCO to Brussels, 23 January 1969, No 20, NA/FCO/73/32; telegrams, Luxembourg to FCO, 23 January 1969, No 20; FCO to Luxembourg, 23 January 1969, No 5; minute, Barrington to Hancock, 23 January 1969; telegrams, FCO to Rome, 24 January 1969, No 45; Rome to FCO, 24 January 1969, No 80; Luxembourg to FCO, 25 January 1969, No 22; FCO to Rome, 28 January 1969, No 50; Luxembourg to FCO, 30 January 1969, No 29; Brussels to FCO, 31 January 1969, No 30, all NA/FCO/30/536.

133 31 October 1968, KCA23006 (2-9 November 1968).

134 Speech at the Lord Mayor's Banquet, Guildhall, London, on Monday 11 November 1968, MS WILSON 1149.

135 Stewart diaries, 1 January 1968, STWT 8/1/6.

Chapter Six

1   Minute, Palliser to Wilson, 5 February 1969, NA/PREM/13/2628. This chapter has appeared in a slightly altered form as 'British personal diplomacy and public policy: the Soames Affair', *JEIH*, Vol 10, No 2, 2004, pp59-76.

2   Minute, Palliser to Wilson, 1 February 1969, NA/PREM/13/2628. For British co-operation with Action Committee see for example 'Draft Record of Conversation between the Foreign and Commonwealth Secretary, the Minister of Agriculture, and M. Pisani in Room 21C at the House of Commons at 5pm on Wednesday, 26 February' 1969, NA/FCO/73/32. For Italian paper and Anglo-German Declaration see telegrams, Bonn to FCO, 28 January 1969, Nos 80-81 and 29 January 1969, No 83, letter, Maitland to Palliser, 30 January 1969, all NA/PREM/13/2672; Wilson's note on minute, Palliser to Wilson, 1 February 1969; minutes, Palliser to Maitland, 3 February 1969, and Maitland to Palliser, 5 February 1969, all NA/PREM/13/2628.

3   Telegram, Paris to FCO, 4 February 1969, No 121, NA/PREM/13/2628.

4   Telegram, Paris to FCO, 5 February 1969, No 123, NA/PREM/13/2628.

5   Telegram, Paris to FCO, 5 February 1969, No 124, NA/PREM/13/2628.

6   Telegram, Paris to FCO, 5 February 1969, No 125, NA/PREM/13/2628.

7   Minute, Palliser to Wilson and Wilson's note thereon, 5 February 1969, NA/PREM/13/2628.

8   Telegrams, Stewart (in Luxembourg) to Paris via FCO, 6 February 1969, No 1 and 7 February 1969, No 2; Paris to Stewart (in Luxembourg) via FCO, 6 February 1969, No 131, all NA/PREM/13/2628.

9   Telegram, Stewart (in Luxembourg) to FCO, 6 February 1969, No 35, NA/PREM/13/2628.

10 Telegram, Stewart (in Luxembourg) to Wilson, 6 February 1969, No 37 (PMPM Serial No T16/69), NA/PREM/13/2628.

11 Minute, Morgan to Hood, 7 February 1969, NA/FCO/30/416.

12 Minute, Andrews to Barrington, 7 February 1969, NA/PREM/13/2628.

13 'Record of Conversation between Lord Chalfont and M. de Lipowski, French Minister of State for Foreign Affairs, at Luxembourg on 6 February 1969', NA/FCO/30/414.

14 Telegram, Rome to FCO, 7 February 1969, No 132, NA/PREM/13/2628.

15 Telegram, Luxembourg to FCO, 4 February 1969, No 33, NA/FCO/30/537.

16 Telegrams, Paris to FCO, No 122; Rome to FCO, No 123, both 4 February 1969, NA/FCO/30/357.

17 'Record of a Meeting between the Foreign and Commonwealth Secretary and the Luxembourg Foreign Minister at the Luxembourg Ministry of Foreign Affairs at 7pm on Wednesday, 5 February 1969', NA/PREM/13/2628; 'Note of a Meeting between the Foreign and Commonwealth Secretary and the Netherlands Foreign Minister at the Kirchberg at 9.15am on 6 February, 1969', 'Note of a Meeting between the Foreign and Commonwealth Secretary and the Italian Foreign Minister at the Kirchberg at 9.45am on 6 February 1969'; 'Record of a Meeting between the Foreign and Commonwealth

Secretary and the Federal German Minister of Foreign Affairs at Buehlerhoehe at 4pm on Wednesday, 5 February', all NA/FCO/73/24.

18 Telegram, Luxembourg to FCO, 7 February 1969, No 41, NA/PREM/13/2628.

19 Telegram, Stewart (in Luxembourg) to FCO, 7 February 1969, No 42, NA/PREM/13/2628.

20 Telegram, Stewart (in Luxembourg) to FCO, 7 February 1969, No 43, NA/FCO/30/537.

21 Telegram, Paris to FCO, 7 February 1969, No 136, NA/FCO/30/537.

22 CC(69)8, 11 February 1969, NA/CAB/128/44.

23 'Note of a Meeting between the Foreign and Commonwealth Secretary and the Italian Foreign Minister at the Kirchberg at 11.30am on 7 February 1969', NA/PREM/13/2628.

24 Minute, Stewart to Wilson and Wilson's notes thereon, 7 February 1969, PM/69/13, NA/PREM/13/2673.

25 Reilly papers, MS Eng.c.6925; telegram, Paris to FCO, 8 February 1969, No 138, NA/PREM/13/2628.

26 Minute, Palliser to Wilson; telegram, Rome to FCO, No 133, both 9 February 1969, NA/PREM/13/2628.

27 Telegram, Rome to FCO, 9 February 1969, No 133 and Wilson's note thereon, NA/PREM/13/2628; see also letter, Garran to Hood, 11 February 1969, NA/FCO/30/414.

28 Report and attached paper, Hancock to Maitland, 10 February 1969, NA/PREM/13/2628.

29 Telegram, Paris to FCO, 10 February 1969, No 143, NA/PREM/13/2628.

30 Minutes, Palliser to Wilson, 10 February 1969 and Wilson's note thereon; 11 February 1969, both NA/PREM/13/2628.

31 Minute, Maitland to Palliser, 11 February 1969, NA/PREM/13/2628.

32 Speaking Note, 'Prime Minister's visit to Bonn, February 1969: General de Gaulle's Approach to HM Ambassador, Paris: Talking Points', Maitland to Palliser, 11 February 1969, NA/PREM/13/2628.

33 Telegram, FCO to Paris, 11 February 1969, No 77, NA/PREM/13/2628.

34 Telegram, FCO to Wilson (in Bonn), 11 February 1969, No 118, NA/PREM/13/2628.

35 Telegrams, FCO to Brussels etc, 11 February 1969, Nos 32-33, NA/FCO/30/414.

36 Telegram, Wilson (in Bonn) to FCO, 12 February 1969, No 145, PMPM Serial No T19/69.

37 Wilson, *The Labour Government*, pp610-611; Ziegler, *Wilson*, p337; others, like Kitzinger, reproduce Wilson's account: Kitzinger, *Diplomacy and Persuasion*, pp46-57.

38 'Record of a Meeting between the Prime Minister and the Federal German Chancellor at the Federal Chancellery, Bonn, at 4pm on Wednesday, February 12, 1969', NA/PREM/13/2628.

39 'Record of a meeting between the Prime Minister and the Federal German Chancellor at the Federal Chancellery, Bonn, at 5.15pm on Wednesday, February 12, 1969', NA/PREM/13/2628.

40 Draft telegram, Greenhill (in Bonn) to FCO, 12 February 1969, No 159, NA/PREM/13/2628.

41 Telegrams, FCO to Brussels etc, 12 February 1969, No 35, NA/FCO/30/414; FCO to UKDel Brussels, 13 February 1969, No 14, NA/FCO/73/32.

42 Telegram, Rome to FCO, 12 February 1969, No 153, NA/FCO/30/414.

43 Telegrams, Brussels to FCO, No 48; Luxembourg to FCO, No 49; Hague to FCO, No 80, all 13 February 1969; Rome to FCO, 15 February 1969, No 167, NA/FCO/30/414; minute, Robinson to Hancock, 17 February 1969, NA/FCO/30/415.

44 Telegrams, Washington to FCO, 12 February 1969, No 422; Rome to FCO, 13 February 1969, No 158, both NA/PREM/13/2628.

45 Telegram, FCO to Bonn, 12 February 1969, No 136, NA/FCO/30/414; minute, Killick to Morland and Robinson, 12 February 1969, NA/FCO/30/417.

46 Telegrams, UKDel Geneva to FCO, 24 February 1969, No 108, NA/FCO/30/415; 27 February 1969, No 127, NA/PREM/13/2628; 13 February 1969, No 20 Saving, NA/FCO/30/537.

47 'Extract from Record of Conversation between the Prime Minister and Herr Willy Brandt, Federal German Foreign Minister in Bonn, on Thursday February 13, 1969', NA/PREM/13/2628.

48 'Record of a Conversation between the Prime Minister and Herr Strauss, Federal German Finance Minister, after dinner at the British Embassy in Bonn on Thursday, February 13, 1969', NA/PREM/13/2628.

49 'Joint Declaration by the British Prime Minister and the Chancellor of the Federal Republic', Bonn, 13 February 1969, NA/FCO/30/418.

50 Minute, Palliser to Barrington and Wilson's note thereon, 10 March 1969, NA/PREM/13/2629.

51 Telegram, FCO to Washington, 18 February 1969, No 378, NA/PREM/13/3217.

52 Telegrams, FCO to Paris, 12 February 1969, No 81, NA/FCO/30/414 and No 82, NA/PREM/13/2628.

53 Telegram, Paris to FCO, 12 February 1969, No 154, NA/PREM/13/2628.

54 Telegram, Paris to FCO, 14 February 1969, No 158, NA/FCO/30/414.

55 Telegram, FCO to Oslo etc, 14 February 1969, No 30, NA/FCO/30/414.

56 KCA23265-6 (29 March – 5 April 1969).

57 Letter, French Ambassador to WEU to Secretary-General of WEU, 16 February 1969; see also telegram, Paris to FCO, 19 February 1969, No 175, both NA/PREM/13/2628; KCA23265-6 (29 March – 5 April 1969).

58 KCA23266 (29 March – 5 April 1969); letters, Palliser to Maitland and Maitland to Palliser; report of German Press Conference; telegram, Bonn to

FCO, No 203, all 19 February 1969; telegram, Bonn to FCO, 19 February 1969, No 203, all NA/PREM/13/2628.

59 OPD(69)6, 'General de Gaulle's Approach to HM Ambassador, Paris: Memorandum by the Secretary of State for Foreign and Commonwealth Affairs', 12 February 1969, NA/CAB/148/91.

60 Telegrams, Paris to FCO, 17 February 1969, No 167, and reply, 17 February 1969, No 88; Paris to FCO, 18 February 1969, Nos 169-170; Brussels to FCO, 18 February 1969, No 52, all NA/FCO/30/414; 'Record of Conversation between the Foreign and Commonwealth Secretary and the Belgian Ambassador at 12 Noon on 19 February', NA/FCO/73/32.

61 NA/CAB/128/44/CC(69)9, 20 February 1969.

62 Castle, Castle, The Castle Diaries, 20 February 1969, p604.

63 Crossman, Diaries, Volume III, 20 February 1969, p374.

64 Telegrams, Ottawa to FCO, No 178; UKDel Brussels to FCO, No 26; Paris to FCO, Nos 179 and 182; Rome to FCO, No 179; Luxembourg to FCO, No 60; Bonn to FCO, No 206; Hague to FCO, No 96; Brussels to FCO, Nos 62 and 64; FCO to Brussels etc, No 45, all 20 February 1969, NA/FCO/30/414.

65 Telegrams, Paris to FCO, Nos 184 and 187; Brussels to FCO, No 69, all 21 February 1969, NA/FCO/30/415.

66 Telegrams, Paris to FCO, 21 February 1969, Nos 188-189; see also telegram, Luxembourg to FCO, 22 February 1969, No 69, all NA/PREM/13/2628.

67 Telegrams, FCO to Rome, No 111; reply, No 183, both 21 February 1969, NA/FCO/30/415.

68 Telegram, FCO to Oslo etc, 21 February 1969, No 36, NA/FCO/30/415; Robin Haydon's unattributable briefing, 21 February 1969, NA/PREM/13/2628.

69 Castle, The Castle Diaries, 22 February 1969, p605.

70 Telegram, Paris to FCO, 22 February 1969, No 191, NA/PREM/13/2628.

71 Telegram, Paris to FCO, 22 February 1969, No 192, NA/PREM/13/2628.

72 Telegram, Paris to FCO, 22 February 1969, No 194, NA/PREM/13/2628.

73 Telegrams, Paris to FCO, 24 February 1969, Nos 195-196 and 199, NA/FCO/30/415; No 201, NA/PREM/13/2628.

74 Telegram, FCO to Paris, 24 February 1969, No 104, NA/PREM/13/2628.

75 Telegram, FCO to Paris, 24 February 1969, No 111, NA/FCO/30/416.

76 Minute, Chalfont to Stewart, 24 February 1969, NA/FCO/30/416.

77 Telegram, Paris to FCO, 25 February 1969, No 205, NA/FCO/30/416.

78 Telegram, Paris to FCO, 25 February 1969, No 209, NA/FCO/30/416.

79 Telegrams, FCO to Paris, 27 February 1969, No 114; Paris to FCO, 28 February 1969, Nos 217-218 and 1 March 1969, Nos 223-224, all NA/PREM/13/2628.

80 CC(69)10, 27 February 1969, NA/CAB/128/44.

81 Castle, The Castle Diaries, 23 February 1969, p605.

82 Messagero, 22 February 1969, reported in telegram, Rome to FCO, 25 February 1969, No 1 Saving. For other press reports, see for example, telegrams,

Brussels to FCO, No 75; Bonn to FCO, No 216; Hague to FCO, No 111; Rome to FCO, No 186, all 22 February 1969, NA/FCO/30/415.

[83] Telegram, FCO to Bonn, 21 February 1969, No 169, PMPM Serial No T22/69, NA/PREM/13/2628.

[84] Telegram Bonn to FCO, 21 February 1969, No 215, NA/PREM/13/2628.

[85] KCA23266-7 (29 March – 5 April 1969).

[86] KCA23266 (29 March – 5 April 1969): intriguingly, the French delegation split over the resolution: the six Gaullist deputies voted against, the four non-Communist left-wing deputies voted for and three others abstained.

[87] Letter, Marjoribanks to Robinson, 5 March 1969, NA/FCO/30/538; KCA23266 (29 March – 5 April 1969).

[88] On this question, see du Jardin, *Pierre Harmel*, pp513-516, and Ludlow, *The European Community*, p172.

[89] See for example telegram, Washington to FCO, 7 February 1969, No 377; 'Agenda for the Meeting between the Prime Minister and the President: Note by Mr Tomkins', 6 February 1969; telegram, Washington to FCO, 15 February 1969, No 468, all NA/PREM/13/3007.

[90] Paper, 'Foreign Affairs in the Next Two Years', JA Thomson to Trend, 3 February 1969; covering minute, Trend to Palliser, 7 February 1969, both NA/PREM/13/2636.

[91] Telegram, FCO to Washington, 5 February 1969, No 267, NA/PREM/13/3007; see also 'Record of a Meeting with Mr Stans, the United States Secretary of Commerce, at No 10 Downing Street on Friday, April 25, 1969', NA/PREM/13/3028.

[92] 'Record of a Meeting held at 10 Downing Street, SW1, on Tuesday 25th February, 1969 at 10am', NA/PREM/13/3008.

[93] Telegram, Washington to FCO, 5 March 1969, No 39 Saving, NA/PREM/13/3008.

[94] Letter, Freeman to Greenhill, 15 March 1969, NA/FCO/30/445.

[95] Letter, Freeman to Stewart, 18 March 1969, NA/FCO/73/40.

[96] See for example letter and enclosures, Freeman to Greenhill, 2 April 1969, NA/FCO/30/445.

[97] Conversation with Pierre Messmer, defence minister to de Gaulle and later Prime Minister of France, *Maison Française*, University of Oxford, 15 February 2002.

[98] 28 February 1969, KCA23242-3 (15-22 March 1968); dinner at the Waldorf-Astoria, 2 March 1969, KCA23920 (11-18 March 1969).

[99] 'Record of Conversation between the Foreign and Commonwealth Secretary and the German Foreign Minister held at Lancaster House on Tuesday, 11 March 1969 at 12 noon'; 'Record of Conversation between the Foreign and Commonwealth Secretary and Mr Joseph Luns held at the Foreign and Commonwealth Office on Tuesday, 11 March, 1969 at 4pm', both NA/FCO/73/33.

[100] Telegram, Paris to FCO, 14 March 1969, No 278, NA/PREM/13/2629.

[101] Telegram, Paris to FCO, 14 March 1969, No 279, NA/PREM/13/2629.

[102]   Telegram, Paris to FCO, 14 March 1969, No 280, NA/PREM/13/2629.

[103]   Telegram, Bonn to FCO, 20 March 1969, No 366; see also telegram, Bonn to FCO, 23 March 1969, No 373, both NA/FCO/30/445.

[104]   Telegram, Paris to FCO, 14 March 1969, No 281, NA/PREM/13/2629.

[105]   Telegram, Rome to FCO, 22 March 1969, No 270, NA/FCO/30/538.

[106]   Telegram, Bonn to FCO, 20 March 1969, No 368, NA/FCO/30/433.

[107]   Message, Brandt to Stewart, 18 March 1969, enclosed in letter, Blankenhorn to Stewart, 27 March 1969, NA/FCO/30/433.

[108]   Telegram, FCO to Bonn, 28 March 1969, No 281, NA/FCO/30/433.

[109]   Telegrams, Bonn to FCO, 2 April 1969, No 401, NA/FCO/30/433; FCO to Bonn, 15 April 1969, No 307, NA/FCO/30/445.

[110]   Letter, Soames to Wilson, 11 March 1969, NA/FCO/30/417.

[111]   Letter and enclosed record of conversation, Campbell to Morgan, 24 March 1969, NA/FCO/30/418.

[112]   Telegram, FCO to Paris, 14 March 1969, No 143; minutes, Palliser to Maitland, 18 March 1969; Hancock to Hood etc, 19 March 1969; Tait to Stewart, 19 March 1969; Maitland to Tait etc, 20 March 1969; telegram, FCO to Paris, 21 March 1969, No 150; letter, Soames to Stewart, 21 March 1969; telegram, Paris to FCO, 24 March 1969, No 312; brief, Robinson to Hancock etc, 25 March 1969, all NA/FCO/30/418.

[113]   Telegram, Paris to FCO, 24 March 1969, No 313, NA/FCO/30/418.

[114]   'Record of a Meeting between the Prime Minister, the Foreign and Commonwealth Secretary and HM Ambassador in Paris at No 10 Downing Street at 9.50am on Wednesday, March 26, 1969', NA/PREM/13/2629.

[115]   'Record of an Office Meeting on Europe held in the Foreign and Commonwealth Secretary's Office on Wednesday, 26 March at 10.30am', NA/PREM/13/2629; telegram, FCO to Paris, 27 March 1969, No 163, NA/FCO/30/419/1. For details of the referendum, see Lacouture, *De Gaulle*, pp572-576.

[116]   Telegrams, Paris to FCO, 28 March 1969, No 330 and 1 April 1969, No 337, NA/FCO/30/419/1.

[117]   See for example minutes, Killick to Hancock, 1 April 1969, NA/FCO/30/445; Hancock to Greenhill, 2 April 1969, NA/PREM/13/2629; note, Brind to Killick and private secretary, 3 April 1969; letter, Soames to Stewart, 2 April 1969, both NA/FCO/30/445.

[118]   Telegrams, Stewart (in Washington) to FCO, 12 April 1969, Nos 1158-1159, NA/PREM/13/2629.

[119]   Note, Youde to Wilson and Wilson's note thereon, 14 April 1969, NA/PREM/13/2629.

[120]   Telegram, Rome to FCO, 26 February 1969, No 194 and Palliser's note thereon, NA/PREM/13/2628.

[121]   'Some reflections' delivered at the luncheon of the European Luncheon Club, London, 5 March 1969, by Dr J. Linthorst Homan, Chief Representative in the UK of the Commission of the EC, NA/FCO/30/261; 'Record of a

Conversation between the Foreign and Commonwealth Secretary and the leader of the CDU/CSU Parliamentary Party at the Foreign and Commonwealth Office on Wednesday, 16 April 1969 at 11.15am', NA/PREM/13/2629; letter, Barzel to Wilson, 25 April 1969, NA/PREM/13/2668.

122 Letter and enclosed minute, Overton to Robinson, 19 February 1969, NA/FCO/30/433.

123 'Record of Conversation between the Foreign and Commonwealth Secretary and Signor Zagari held at the Foreign and Commonwealth Office on Wednesday, 6 March 1969, at 6pm' NA/FCO/73/33.

124 Extract from 'Record of Meeting between the Prime Minister and Signor Saragat on 24 April 1969', NA/PREM/13/2629.

125 Anglo-Italian Declaration, 28 April 1969, KCA23400 (7-14 June 1969); 'Record of a Conversation between the Foreign and Commonwealth Secretary and the Italian Foreign Minister held at the Foreign and Commonwealth Office on Thursday, 24 April, 1969 at 3.45pm', NA/FCO/73/33.

126 'Record of a Meeting held at the Italian Embassy, 14, Three Kings Yard, Davies Street, W1, on Thursday 24 April 1969 at 7pm', NA/PREM/13/2738.

127 For details of the resignation, see Lacouture, De Gaulle, pp572-576.

128 Telegram, Bonn to FCO, 7 March 1969, No 620, NA/FCO/30/417.

129 Letter, Freeman to Greenhill, 15 March 1969, NA/FCO/30/445.

130 Letter, Marjoribanks to Robinson, 5 March 1969, NA/FCO/30/538; letter, Edwards to Killick, 28 March 1969; telegrams, Hague to FCO, 30 March 1969, No 181; UKDel Brussels to FCO, 3 April 1969, No 59, all NA/FCO/30/419/1; note, Killick to Hancock and EID, 31 March 1969, NA/FCO/30/433.

131 Minute, Robinson to Killick, 23 April 1969, NA/FCO/30/397.

132 'Record of a Meeting held at 10 Downing Street, SW1, on Monday 28 April 1969 at 12 noon', NA/PREM/13/2629.

Chapter Seven

1 Telegrams, Paris to FCO, 30 April 1969, No 423 and 2 May 1969, No 26 Saving, NA/PREM/13/2655.

2 Telegram, Luxembourg to FCO, 20 May 1969, No 109, NA/FCO/30/540; see also Serge Berstein and Jean-Pierre Rioux, The Pompidou Years, 1969-1974, Cambridge: Cambridge University Press, 2000, pp25-27.

3 For Kiesinger, see telegrams, Bonn to FCO, 7 May 1969, No 539; Bonn to FCO, 2 June 1969, No 673 and 4 June 1969, No 680, all NA/FCO/30/434; for Brandt, see telegram, Bonn to FCO, 14 May 1969, No 586, NA/PREM/13/2629; letter, Overton to Robinson, 28 May 1969, NA/FCO/30/434; for Schmidt, see minute, Youde to Graham, 29 May 1969; letter, Youde to Barrington, 26 May 1969; letter, Schmidt to Wilson and Wilson's note thereon, 9 June 1969, all NA/PREM/13/2629; for Strauss, see

'Record of Conversation between the Chancellor of the Exchequer and Herr Strauss, Federal German Minister of Finance, on 19 May, 1969', and 'Record of a Conversation, May 19, 1969' including Strauss and Wilson, both NA/PREM/13/2633.

4   Telegrams, Bonn to FCO, No 645; UKDel Brussels to FCO, No 92-94; Paris to FCO, No 487-8, all 29 May 1969; Brussels to FCO, 30 May 1969, No 205; Rome to FCO, 31 May 1969, No 542, all NA/FCO/30/397.

5   Press conference, Northolt Airport, 6 June 1969, NA/FCO/73/23.

6   Minute, Stewart to Wilson and Wilson's note thereon, 13 June 1969, (PM/169/39), NA/PREM/13/2645.

7   Telegram, Paris to FCO, 18 June 1969, No 546, NA/PREM/13/2655.

8   Telegram, Paris to FCO, 23 June 1969, No 560, NA/PREM/13/2655.

9   'Record of a Meeting between the Prime Minister, the Foreign and Commonwealth Secretary and Mr Soames at 2.45pm on Wednesday, June 25, 1969 at No 10 Downing Street', NA/PREM/13/2629; telegram, Paris to FCO, 23 June 1969, No 561, NA/PREM/13/2655.

10   Telegram, Paris to FCO, 26 June 1969, No 573, NA/FCO/30/445.

11   'Record of Conversation between the Prime Minister and Dr Waldheim, the Austrian Foreign Minister, at 10 Downing Street on Friday, June 27, 1969', NA/PREM/13/2629.

12   Telegram, Paris to FCO, 27 June 1969, No 581, NA/FCO/30/445.

13   Minute and enclosed American telegram, 27 June 1969, NA/FCO/30/445.

14   'Record of Conversation between Lord Chalfont and the German Ambassador, Herr Blankenhorn, at the Foreign and Commonwealth Office on Friday, 27 June 1969 at 3pm', NA/FCO/30/434.

15   Telegrams, FCO to Paris, 30 June 1969, Nos 321-322, NA/FCO/30/445.

16   Letters, Rooke to Killick, 3 July 1969; Beith to Robinson, 2 July 1969, both NA/FCO/30/446/1.

17   Telegrams, Bonn to FCO, 2 July 1969, No 816 and 3 July 1969, No 820, both NA/FCO/30/434.

18   Telegrams, Paris to FCO, 4 July 1969, No 610, NA/FCO/30/446/1; Bonn to FCO, 5 July 1969, No 835, NA/PREM/13/2629.

19   Telegram, Paris to FCO, 7 July 1969, No 616, NA/FCO/30/446/1.

20   For example, letter and enclosure, Overton to Robinson, 9 July 1969, NA/FCO/30/434; telegram, Paris to FCO, 15 July 1969, No 647, NA/PREM/13/2637; letter, Jackling to Brimelow, 16 July 1969, NA/FCO/30/434.

21   Telegram, Paris to FCO, 10 July 1969, No 632, NA/FCO/30/446/1.

22   Telegram, Paris to FCO, 11 July 1969, No 638, NA/FCO/30/446/1.

23   Telegram, Paris to FCO, 12 July 1969, No 646, NA/PREM/13/2629.

24   'Record of Conversation between the Foreign and Commonwealth Secretary and the Belgian Minister of Foreign Affairs in the Belgian Ministry of Foreign Affairs at Brussels on Monday 14 July at 5.30pm', NA/PREM/13/2629.

25 'Record of discussion at dinner between the Foreign and Commonwealth Secretary and the President of the European Commission at the Residence of the British Ambassador to the European Communities in Brussels on Monday, 14 July at 8.15pm', NA/PREM/13/2629.

26 For example, conversation between Wilson, Stewart and Luns, recorded in letter, Youde to Graham, 21 July 1969, NA/PREM/13/2629.

27 Minute, Robinson to Brimelow, 18 July 1969, NA/FCO/30/446/1.

28 Wilson papers, speech by the Prime Minister at the European Dinner at Guildhall on Tuesday, 29 July 1969, MS WILSON 1251; see also Wilson, *The Labour Government*, pp686-688.

29 Telegram, UKDel Brussels to FCO, 18 July 1969, No 129, NA/FCO/30/446/1.

30 'Record of Conversation between the Secretary of State and the French Ambassador at the F.C.O. on Tuesday, 22 July 1969 at 4.45pm', NA/PREM/13/2629.

31 Telegrams, UKDel Brussels to FCO, 22 July 1969, No 137-8, NA/PREM/13/2629.

32 Telegram, UKDel Brussels to FCO, 23 July 1969, No 141, NA/PREM/13/2629.

33 Telegram, Paris to FCO, 25 July 1969, No 682, NA/FCO/30/446/1.

34 Minute, Robinson to Thomson, 7 August 1969, NA/FCO/30/390/1.

35 Minute, Robinson to private secretary, 29 August 1969, NA/FCO/30/401; the franc was devalued from $1 = FF4.94 to $1 = FF5.55 on 10 August, despite promises to maintain parity on 26 June: KCA23521 (23 – 30 August 1969). The deutschmark was re-valued in October: KCA23681 (22 – 29 November 1969).

36 Minute, Greenhill to private secretary, 4 September 1969; letter, Beith to Palliser, 18 September 1969, both NA/FCO/30/447.

37 Telegram, FCO to Bonn, 10 September 1969, No 650, NA/PREM/13/2629.

38 Telegrams, Bonn to FCO, 9 September 1969, Nos 1103-1104, NA/FCO/30/446/1; FCO to Bonn, 11 September 1969, No 656, NA/FCO/30/435.

39 Telegrams, Bonn to FCO, 9 September 1969, No 1106, NA/FCO/30/435 and Paris to FCO, 11 September 1969, No 809, NA/PREM/13/2629.

40 Telegrams, Paris to FCO, 11 September 1969, No 809; UKMiss New York (Stewart) to FCO (Wilson), 20 September 1969, No 1926, PMPM Serial No T147/69, both NA/PREM/13/2629.

41 'Record of Conversation between the Foreign and Commonwealth Secretary and the French Ambassador at the Foreign and Commonwealth Office on Friday, 12 September at 10am', NA/FCO/73/35.

42 Letter, Palliser to O'Neill, 12 September 1969, NA/FCO/30/446/1; telegram, Stewart (in New York) to Wilson, 20 September 1969, No 1926, PMPM Serial No T147/69, NA/PREM/13/2629.

43 Telegrams, FCO to Hague, 13 September 1969, No 243, NA/FCO/30/435; Paris to FCO, 14 September 1969, No 828, NA/FCO/30/446/1.

44 For example, letter, Palliser to Robinson, 15 September 1969, NA/FCO/30/446/1.
45 Telegram, Paris to FCO, 22 September 1969, No 861, NA/FCO/30/446/1.
46 Letter, Marjoribanks to Robinson, 17 September 1969, NA/FCO/30/446/1.
47 'Record of a conversation of a meeting [sic] between the Foreign and Commonwealth Secretary and the Dutch and West German Foreign Ministers over lunch at the Waldorf at 1.15pm on Monday 22 September' 1969, NA/FCO/30/436.
48 Minute, O'Neill to Robinson, 22 September 1969, NA/FCO/30/436.
49 Telegrams, UKDel Brussels to FCO, 2 October 1969, Nos 186, 188-195 and 197, NA/PREM/13/2630.
50 Telegram, UKDel Brussels to FCO, 2 October 1969, No 198, NA/PREM/13/2630.
51 Minute, O'Neill to private secretary, 21 October 1969, NA/FCO/30/436.
52 Telegrams, FCO to Bonn, 24 October 1969, Nos 756-7, NA/FCO/30/436.
53 Letter and enclosed message, Blankenhorn to Wilson, 27 October 1969, PMPM Serial No 173/69, NA/FCO/30/436.
54 28 October 1969, published by the Press and Information Office of the Federal Government, NA/PREM/13/2664.
55 Telegram, FCO to Bonn, 30 October 1969, No 769, NA/FCO/30/436.
56 Brandt, *People and Politics*, p160.
57 Brandt, *People and Politics*, p157.
58 Minute, O'Neill to Robinson, 27 October 1969, NA/FCO/30/436. On *Ostpolitik*, see Brandt, *People and Politics*.
59 Draft paper, 'European Policy', Robinson to Tait, 28 April 1969, NA/FCO/30/421.
60 Annex, 'Allegations of Francophobia in the Foreign Office', Robinson to Tait, 28 April 1969, NA/FCO/30/421.
61 Minute, Chalfont to Tait, 30 April 1969, NA/FCO/30/421.
62 Telegram, FCO to certain missions, 5 May 1969, No 100 Guidance, NA/FCO/30/445; letter, Barrington to Youde, 30 April 1969, reply, 1 May 1969, both NA/PREM/13/2629.
63 CC(69)20, 1 May 1969, NA/CAB/128/44.
64 Minute, Robinson to Brind etc, 2 May 1969, NA/FCO/30/445.
65 Wilson papers, speech, XXth Anniversary Celebrations of the Council of Europe, Banqueting House, London, 5 May 1969, MS WILSON 1154.
66 Letter, Youde to Graham, 14 July 1969, NA/PREM/13/2480.
67 Letter, Graham to Youde; minute, Youde to Wilson and Wilson's note thereon, both 18 July 1969, NA/PREM/13/2629.
68 Comment, Brimelow, 20 July 1969, on minute, Robinson to Brimelow, 18 July 1969, NA/FCO/30/446/1.
69 CC(69)33, 16 July 1969; CC(69)35, 22 July 1969; CC(69)45, 25 September 1969, NA/CAB/128/44.

[70] Minute, Crosland to Wilson, 15 September 1969, NA/PREM/13/2629. The management committee records contain no reference to this discussion, which Crosland said occurred at Chequers, but it was not uncommon for no records to be kept: NA/CAB/134/3118 and 3119.

[71] Crossman, *Diaries*, Volume III, 22 July 1969, p586.

[72] Crossman, *Diaries*, Volume III, 24 September 1969, p653.

[73] Castle, *The Castle Diaries*, 25 September 1969, p711.

[74] Telegram, FCO to certain missions, 1 August 1969, No 164 Guidance, NA/PREM/13/2629.

[75] For example, letter and enclosed paper, Overton to Robinson, 28 August 1969; Telegram, FCO to Bonn, 29 August 1969, No 630, both NA/FCO/30/435; 'Record of Conversation between the Foreign and Commonwealth Secretary and the Italian Ambassador held at the Foreign and Commonwealth Office on Wednesday, 3rd September, 1969, at 11.30am', NA/FCO/73/35; Chalfont's note, 29 August 1969, on minute, Robinson to Killick, NA/FCO/30/446/1.

[76] For example, telegrams, Bonn to FCO, 14 May 1969, No 583, NA/FCO/30/434; Rome to FCO, 7 August 1969, No 768, NA/FCO/30/435; letter, Overton to Robinson, 15 July 1969; reply, 21 July 1969, NA/FCO/30/434; letter, Hannay to Robinson, 21 October 1969; reply, 12 November 1969; 'Conversation between Dr Harkort and Sir Con O'Neill', 14 November 1969, all NA/FCO/30/437; 'Record of conversation with Dr Per Fischer on 27 June', Robin O'Neill to Morland, 1 July 1969, NA/FCO/30/434; letter, Galsworthy to Marjoribanks, 24 July 1969, NA/FCO/30/446/1.

[77] Minute, Curson to Peck, 29 May 1969, NA/FCO/26/176.

[78] Minute, Robinson to Killick and Brimelow, 30 May 1969, NA/FCO/30/397; minute, Hartles to Youde, 30 October 1969, NA/PREM/13/2630.

[79] EURO PB/1, 18 June 1969, NA/FCO/26/386.

[80] Minute, Chalfont to Stewart, NA/FCO/30/176.

[81] Minute, Youde to Graham, 29 May 1969, NA/PREM/13/2629.

[82] 'Record of a Meeting between the Foreign and Commonwealth Secretary and Herr Willie [sic] Brandt during Dinner on board the M.V. 'Pieter Caland' in Rotterdam Harbour on the Evening of Thursday, 5 June', 1969, NA/FCO/73/23.

[83] Telegram, Paris to FCO, 16 July 1969, No 654, NA/FCO/30/446/1.

[84] Minute, Robinson to Youde, 25 June 1969, NA/PREM/13/2629.

[85] Minute, Graham to Halls, 31 July 1969, NA/PREM/13/2629.

[86] Wilson papers, speech to conference, 30 September 1969, MS WILSON 1252.

[87] Letter, Marjoribanks to Robinson, 30 May 1969, NA/FCO/30/425.

[88] Letter, Morphet to Youde, 5 June 1969, minute, Killick to Brimelow, 5 June 1969, both NA/PREM/13/2629.

[89] For example, minute, McCluney to Stewart, 24 July 1969, NA/FCO/73/27; minute, Overton to minister (economic), 4 August 1969, NA/FCO/30/435; letter, Faber to Robinson, 29 October 1969, NA/FCO/30/425.

[90] Letter, Monnet to Wilson, 22 July 1969, NA/PREM/13/2632.

[91] Minute by Barrington, attached to letter, Graham to Youde, 23 July 1969, NA/PREM/13/2632.

[92] Letter, Graham to Youde, 23 July 1969, NA/PREM/13/2632.

[93] Draft minute, Chalfont to Stewart, 7 September 1969, NA/FCO/73/90; minute, Stewart to Wilson, 10 September 1969, NA/PREM/13/2629.

[94] Draft minute, Wilson to Stewart, 13 September 1969, NA/PREM/13/2629.

[95] For full details of the reshuffle, see KCA23605 (11 – 18 October 1969).

[96] Wilson, *The Labour Government*, p713.

[97] Minute, Haines to Youde, 21 October 1969, NA/PREM/13/2630.

[98] Prime Minister's Personal Minute No M/62/69 to all Ministers and Junior Ministers, 30 October 1969, NA/PREM/13/3197.

[99] Minute, Stewart to Callaghan, 30 October 1969, NA/FCO/30/399.

[100] CC(69)53, 6 November 1969, NA/CAB/128/44; Crossman, *Diaries*, Volume III, 6 November 1969, p719.

[101] Minute, Trend to Wilson, 22 October 1969, enclosing minutes, Nield to Trend and Thornton to Nield, 20 October 1969, all NA/PREM/13/2630.

[102] Minute, Youde to Nield, 24 October 1969, NA/PREM/13/2630.

[103] Minute, Youde to Nield, 3 November 1969, NA/PREM/13/2630.

[104] Minute and paper, Nield to Youde and Wilson, and Wilson's comments thereon, 7 November 1969; note for the record, Youde, 12 November 1969, NA/PREM/13/2631.

[105] Minute, Nield to Youde and Wilson's note thereon, 14 November 1969, NA/PREM/13/2631.

[106] Minute, Nield to Youde and Wilson's note thereon, 1 December 1970, NA/PREM/13/2631.

[107] 29 October 1969, KCA23647 (1-8 November 1969).

[108] Wilson papers, speech at the Lord Mayor's Banquet, Guildhall, London, 10 November 1969, MS WILSON 1253.

[109] Telegrams, Washington to FCO, 4 May 1969, No 1367, and 10 May 1969, No 1430; minute, Zuckerman to Wilson, 2 June 1969, all NA/PREM/13/2556.

[110] 'The Prime Minister's account of his conversation with President Nixon at Mildenhall on Sunday, August, 3, 1969', NA/PREM/13/3009. The arrangements for Nixon's visit were overseen by Squadron Leader David Pine, the author's grandfather.

[111] Telegram, Washington to FCO, 16 September 1969, No 2511, NA/PREM/13/2629; minute, Youde to McCluney, 22 September 1969, NA/PREM/13/2625.

[112] Minute, Graham to WED, 26 May 1969, NA/FCO/30/430; 'Extract from record of Conversations between the Foreign and Commonwealth Secretary and the United States Secretary of State at the United States Mission to the

United Nations in New York at 11.30am on Tuesday, 23 September 1969',
NA/FCO/30/431.

113   Speech, Rogers to the 25ᵗʰ anniversary dinner of the Belgo-American
Association, Brussels, 6 December 1969, United States Information Service,
NA/FCO/30/431.

114   Letter, Palliser to O'Neill, 19 December 1969, NA/FCO/30/448.

115   'Record of Conversation between the Secretary of State for Foreign and
Commonwealth Affairs and the Swedish Minister for Industry at the Foreign
and Commonwealth Office at 9.45am on Wednesday, 19 June', 1969,
NA/FCO/73/34.

116   Draft unnumbered telegram, FCO to Copenhagen, 25 June 1969,
NA/FCO/73/74; 'Record of a meeting between the Foreign and
Commonwealth Secretary and the Foreign Minister of the Republic of Ireland
at the Residence of the British Ambassador in Brussels on Monday, 14 July at
6.45pm', NA/FCO/73/22; 'Record of Meeting between Lord Chalfont and
Mr Hilmar Baunsgaard, Prime Minister of Denmark, on Monday, the 8ᵗʰ
September, 1969 at 3pm at Christiansborg Castle', NA/FCO/73/74.

117   'Record of a Meeting between the Prime Minister and Dr Waldheim, the
Austrian Foreign Minister at 10 Downing Street on Friday, June 27, 1969',
NA/PREM/13/2500.

118   'Record of a Meeting held at 10 Downing Street, SW1 on Thursday, 17 July
1969 at 4.45pm', NA/PREM/13/3203.

119   See for example CC(69)23, 15 May 1969; CC(69)30, 26 June 1969; CC(69)22,
8 May 1969, all NA/CAB/128/44.

120   Letter, Youde to Brighty, 5 June 1969, NA/PREM/13/2496. See also
Benvenuti, *The End of the Affair.*

121   Telegram, Ottawa to FCO, 15 September 1969, No 924, PMPM Serial No
T143/69, NA/PREM/13/3203.

122   Telegrams, Ottawa to FCO, 18 December 1969, No 1221; reply, 23
December 1969, No 737, NA/PREM/13/3545.

123   'Record of a Conversation between the Prime Minister and the Deputy Prime
Minister of New Zealand at No 10 Downing Street at 12 noon on Friday,
October 17, 1969', NA/PREM/13/2815.

124   For example, 'Record of Conversation between the Prime Minister and Prime
Minister Shearer of Jamaica, 10 Downing Street, Thursday September 18,
1969, at 12 noon', NA/PREM/13/2629.

125   'Extract from Record of Anglo-German Talks – Bonn – 12 May 1969',
NA/FCO/30/434.

126   Telegrams, FCO to Luxembourg, 21 May 1969, No 43; The Hague to FCO, 6
June 1969, No 325, NA/FCO/30/540.

127   CC(69)26, 9 June 1969, NA/CAB/128/44.

128   Minute, Barrington to Robinson, 9 June 1969, NA/FCO/397.

129   CC(69)24, 22 May 1969, NA/CAB/128/44.

130   Minute, Killick to Brimelow, 29 May 1969, NA/FCO/30/445; C(69)163,
'Concorde: Memorandum by the Minister of Technology', and C(69)164,

'Concorde: Memorandum by the President of the Board of Trade', both 4 December 1969, NA/CAB/129/146.

[131] Minute, Cottrell to Wilson, 31 October 1969, 'Proposals by the European Communities for Scientific and Technological Co-operation between European Countries'; letter, Youde to Barrington, 7 November 1969, both NA/PREM/13/3511.

[132] For example, minute, Morland to Brind and Robinson, 14 July 1969, NA/FCO/30/398.

[133] 'Record of a Meeting between the Foreign and Commonwealth Secretary and the Defence Secretary on Tuesday, 7 October'; 'Record of a Meeting between the Foreign and Commonwealth Secretary and the Defence Secretary, with officials present, on 14 October 1969', both NA/FCO/73/27.

[134] Wilson papers, speech to the Yorkshire Women's Federation, Barnsley, 7 June 1969, MS WILSON 1154.

[135] Speech, Mulley in Commons adjournment debate, 25 July 1969, NA/PREM/13/2483.

[136] Letter and enclosed paper, Marshall to Robinson, 29 August 1969, NA/FCO/30/446/1.

[137] 'Record of a Meeting between the Foreign and Commonwealth Secretary and the Defence Secretary on Tuesday, 7 October', 1969; 'Record of a Meeting between the Foreign and Commonwealth Secretary and the Defence Secretary, with officials present, on 14 October 1969', both NA/FCO/73/27.

[138] Letter, Mellon to Robinson, 17 December 1969, NA/FCO/30/448.

[139] EURO PB, 3rd meeting, 7 October 1969; 4th meeting, 23 October 1969, both NA/FCO/26/386.

[140] Telegrams, Bonn to FCO, 2 October 1969, No 1227; Paris to FCO, No 888 and Brussels to FCO, No 311, both 3 October 1969; Rome to FCO, 6 October 1969, No 918; FCO to Paris, 16 October 1969, No 477, NA/PREM/13/2630.

[141] Letters, Overton to Robinson, 3 October 1969; Brooks Richards to Robinson, 8 October 1969, both NA/FCO/30/436.

[142] Telegram, Bonn to FCO, 30 October 1969, No 1358, NA/PREM/13/2630.

[143] Telegram, Bonn to FCO, 16 October 1969, No 1290, NA/FCO/30/436.

[144] Minute, Youde to Wilson and Wilson's note thereon, 7 October 1969, NA/PREM/13/2630.

[145] Telegram, Paris to FCO, 10 October 1969, No 914, NA/PREM/13/2630.

[146] Telegrams, FCO to Paris, 18 November 1969, Nos 555-556, NA/PREM/13/2631.

[147] Telegram, FCO to Bonn, 16 October 1969, No 719, NA/FCO/30/447.

[148] Telegram, Brussels to FCO, 21 October 1969, No 341, NA/PREM/13/2630.

[149] For example, minute, Robinson to O'Neill, 6 November 1969, NA/FCO/30/448.

[150] For example, letter and enclosed 'Extract from a statement to the Bundestag by the Federal Foreign Minister on 29 October 1969', Robin O'Neill to

Morland, 7 November 1969; letter, Overton to Robinson, 10 November 1969, both NA/FCO/30/437.

151 For a full account of the summit, see *Journal of European Integration History*, Volume 9, No 2, 2003.

152 Telegram, Hague to FCO, 1 December 1969, No 607, NA/PREM/13/2631; KCA24167-8 (5 – 12 September 1970).

153 Telegram, Hague to FCO, 1 December 1969, No 604, NA/PREM/13/2631.

154 'Introductory Statement by the Chancellor of the Federal German Republic at the EEC Summit Conference in The Hague on 1 December 1969', NA/PREM/13/2631.

155 Telegrams, Hague to FCO, 1 December 1969, No 607-608, NA/PREM/13/2631.

156 Telegrams, Hague to FCO, 1 December 1969, Nos 609-610; 2 December 1969, No 614, all NA/PREM/13/2631.

157 Brandt, *People and Politics*, p237.

158 Telegram, The Hague to FCO, 2 December 1969, No 616, NA/PREM/13/2631.

159 Telegrams, The Hague to FCO, 2 December 1969, Nos 619-620, NA/PREM/13/2631.

160 Telegram, The Hague to FCO, 2 December 1969, No 621, NA/PREM/13/2631.

161 KCA24168-9 (5 – 12 September 1970).

162 'Record of Conversation between the Prime Minister and Dr Frank of the German Foreign Office at 10 Downing Street at 12.30pm on December 3, 1969', NA/PREM/13/2671.

163 'Record of a Conversation between the Foreign and Commonwealth Secretary and the Deputy Under-Secretary for European Affairs of the Foreign Ministry of the Federal Republic of Germany at No 1 Carlton Gardens at 9.15am on Wednesday, 3 December', 1969, NA/FCO/30/437.

164 Minute, 'The Results of the Summit Meeting of the Six', Nield, 3 December 1969, NA/PREM/13/2631.

165 'Summary of the Secretary of State's Remarks of the Summit at the Airport', 3 December 1969, NA/PREM/13/2631.

166 CC(69)58, 4 December 1969, NA/CAB/128/44.

167 CC(69)60, 11 December 1969, NA/CAB/128/44.

168 Letter, O'Neill to Nield, 1 December 1969; letter, Robinson to Brooks Richards, 4 December 1969, both NA/FCO/30/437.

169 'Record of Conversation between the Prime Minister and the French Minister of Finance at No 10 Downing Street at 6pm on December 4', 1969, NA/PREM/13/3207; telegram, FCO to Paris, 5 December 1969, No 591, NA/FCO/30/769.

170 'Record of Conversation between the Prime Minister and Dr Frank of the German Foreign Office at 10 Downing Street at 12.30pm on December 3, 1969', NA/PREM/13/2671; see also 'Record of a Conversation between the

Chancellor of the Duchy of Lancaster and the French Foreign Minister at the Quai d'Orsay on Thursday, 11 December at 6.30pm', NA/FCO/30/448.

171 'Record of Conversation with M. Jean de Lipowski', Soames, 5 December 1969, NA/FCO/30/448; see also CC(69)61, 18 December 1969, NA/CAB/128/44.

172 Letter, Palliser to Robinson, 8 December 1969, and reply, 11 December 1969, both NA/FCO/30/448.

173 Draft white paper, Nield to Youde and Wilson's note thereon, 5 December 1969, NA/PREM/13/2631.

174 Minutes, Halls to Wilson, 10 December 1969; Nield to Halls and Wilson's note thereon, 12 December 1969, both NA/PREM/13/2631.

175 Covering letter to first full draft white paper, Nield to Youde, 15 December 1969, NA/PREM/13/3198.

176 Minute, Nield to Youde and Wilson's comments thereon, 19 December 1969, NA/PREM/13/3198.

177 Minute, Youde to Nield, 22 December 1969, NA/PREM/13/3198.

178 Telegram, UKDel Brussels to FCO, 10 December 1969, No 297, NA/PREM/13/2631.

179 Minutes, Nield to Youde, Youde to Wilson, O'Neill to Barrington, Williamson to Graham and Everett to Barrington, all 12 December 1969 and telegram, FCO to European Missions, 13 December 1969, No 617, NA/PREM/13/2631.

180 KCA24169-24170 (5 – 12 September 1970).

181 Ludlow, *Dealing with Britain*, pp198-199.

182 Minute, 'The Results of the Summit Meeting of the Six', Nield, 3 December 1969, NA/PREM/13/2631.

183 Michel Debré, *Trois Républiques pour une France: Gouverner Autrement*, (Mémoires), Paris: Albin Michel, 1993.

184 Paper, Graham to Andrews, 18 December 1969, NA/FCO/73/42.

Chapter Eight

1 Minute, Stewart to Wilson, 8 January 1970, PM/70/2, NA/PREM/13/3199.

2 See for example note for the record, John Anson, 8 January 1970, NA/FCO/30/769.

3 'Draft record of a non-attributable Press Conference given on 11 January, 1970 at Chequers by the Prime Minister, the Secretary of State and the Chancellor of the Duchy of Lancaster to a group of European journalists invited by the International Publishing Corporation', NA/PREM/13/3199.

4 Telegram, Rome to FCO, 14 January 1970, No 41, NA/PREM/13/3199.

5 Letter, Barrington to Everett and Wilson's comment thereon, 21 January 1970, NA/PREM/13/3199.

6 For example, 'Note of the Prime Minister's meeting with M. Gaston Thorn, Foreign Minister of Luxembourg, at 3pm on Monday, April 27th', 1970,

NA/PREM/13/3306; 'Record of the Prime Minister's meeting with Signor Emilio Colombo, Italian Minister of the Treasury, at 11am on Monday, May 18 at No 10 Downing Street', NA/PREM/13/3281.

[7] Stewart, speech to mark the 25th anniversary of the Franco-British Society at the Dorchester Hotel, London, 22 January 1970, NA/FCO/30/731.

[8] 'Record of conversation between the Chancellor of the Duchy of Lancaster and Hr. Scheel at the German Foreign Ministry in Bonn at 10.15am on 14 April, 1970', NA/FCO/30/764.

[9] NA/FCO/30/703.

[10] Minute, Thomson to Wilson, 13 January 1970, NA/PREM/13/3199.

[11] Announcement of team, 11 April 1970, NA/PREM/13/3201.

[12] NA/FCO/30/732 and 30/734 respectively.

[13] NA/FCO/59/565 *passim*.

[14] Minutes, Nield to Halls, 12 February 1970, and Trend to Wilson, 17 February 1970, and Wilson's comments on both, NA/PREM/13/3200.

[15] Minute, Nield to Moon, 18 February 1970 and Wilson's note thereon, 18 February 1970, NA/PREM/13/3200.

[16] NA/FCO/30/725 *passim*.

[17] Minute, Nield to Moon, 19 March 1970, and Wilson's note thereon, NA/PREM/13/3201.

[18] EURM(N)(70)1, 16 April 1970, composition and terms of reference, NA/CAB/134/2809.

[19] Minute, O'Neill to private secretary, 16 June 1970, NA/FCO/30/735.

[20] Minute, Nield to Moon, 24 April 1970, and Wilson's note thereon, NA/PREM/13/3201.

[21] Wilson, *The Labour Government*, p706.

[22] Minute, Nield to Moon, 16 January 1970, NA/PREM/13/3199.

[23] Letter, Lloyd-Jones to private secretaries, 7 January 1970, NA/PREM/13/3199.

[24] Prime Minister's Personal Minute No M23/70 to all cabinet ministers, ministers in charge of departments, law officers and the chief whip, 17 March 1970, NA/FCO/73/49.

[25] Letter, Nield to PUSs, 8 January 1970, NA/PREM/13/3199.

[26] Minute, Nield to Moon, and Wilson's comments thereon, 9 January 1970, NA/PREM/13/3199.

[27] Letter, Everett to Williams, 14 January 1970, NA/PREM/13/3199.

[28] Minute, Nield to Halls, and Wilson's comments thereon, 14 January 1970, NA/PREM/13/3199.

[29] Minute, Graham to Halls, 15 January 1970, NA/PREM/13/3199.

[30] Minute, Nield to Moon, 16 January 1970, NA/PREM/13/3199.

[31] See for example Crossman, *Diaries*, Volume III, 20 April 1970, pp893-894.

[32] 'Address of the Chancellor of the Federal Republic of Germany to the Foreign Press Association, London, 3 March 1970', NA/PREM/13/3222.

[33] Letter, Everett to Williams, 14 January 1970, NA/PREM/13/3199.

[34]   'Minutes of a Meeting held at 10 Downing Street SW1, on Monday 19th January 1970 at 4.30pm', NA/PREM/13/3199.

[35]   Wilfred Sendall, 'Price of Europe brings big shock', *Daily Express*, 4 February 1970, clipping in NA/PREM/13/3200.

[36]   Castle, *The Castle Diaries*, 3 February 1970, p759.

[37]   CC(70)5, 3 February 1970, NA/CAB/128/45.

[38]   CC(70)6, 5 February 1970, NA/CAB/128/45; C(70)19, 'United Kingdom Application for Membership of the EEC: Draft White Paper: Note by the Secretary of the Cabinet', 4 February 1970, NA/CAB/129.

[39]   NA/CAB/129/C(70)17, 'United Kingdom Application for Membership of the EEC: Draft White Paper: Note by the Secretary of the Cabinet', 29 January 1970.

[40]   Minute, Nield to Moon, 6 February 1970 and Wilson's comment thereon, NA/PREM/13/3200.

[41]   Minute, Nield to Halls, 4 February 1970, NA/PREM/13/3200.

[42]   Statement, Wilson in Commons, 10 February 1970, NA/PREM/13/3200; see also Wilson, *The Labour Government*, pp762-763.

[43]   Minute, Nield to Moon, 17 February 1970, NA/PREM/13/3200.

[44]   Telegram, FCO to certain missions, 9 February 1970, Guidance No 27, NA/PREM/13/3200.

[45]   Telegrams, Bonn to FCO, No 136; The Hague to FCO, No 46; Paris to FCO, No 151, all 11 February 1970; Paris to FCO, No 154; Luxembourg to FCO, No 27, both 12 February 1970, NA/PREM/13/3200.

[46]   Telegram, Bonn to FCO, 21 February 1970, No 194, NA/PREM/13/3222.

[47]   'Record of Conversation between the Foreign and Commonwealth Secretary and the Italian Minister of the Treasury, in the Foreign and Commonwealth Office at 7.30pm on 18 May 1970', NA/FCO/73/54.

[48]   For example, 'Record of a Conversation between the Chancellor of the Duchy of Lancaster and State Secretary Harkort held at the Federal Foreign Ministry, Bonn, at 11.15am on 14 April, 1970', NA/FCO/30/764.

[49]   Telegram, FCO to Certain Missions, 4 March 1970, Guidance No 42, NA/PREM/13/3201.

[50]   Crossman, *Diaries*, 26 March 1970, p875.

[51]   NA/CAB/128/45/CC(70)14, 26 March 1970; Castle, *The Castle Diaries*, 26 March 1970, p782.

[52]   Letter, Soames to Stewart, 1 April 1970, NA/PREM/13/3201.

[53]   Minute, Tickell to Robinson, 9 April 1970, NA/FCO/30/764.

[54]   'Visit to Bonn and Dusseldorf 31 March-2 April 1980, Note by the Permanent Secretary to the Board of Trade', NA/FCO/30/764.

[55]   Letter and drafts, Williams to Everett, 28 January 1970; minute, Everett to Wilson and Wilson's note thereon, 29 January 1970, both NA/PREM/13/3199.

[56]   Castle, *The Castle Diaries*, 26 March 1970, p783.

[57]   Speech, 6 May 1970, NA/PREM/13/3201.

58 Minute, Moon to Wilson, 13 April 1970, NA/PREM/13/3197; CC(70)17, 16 April 1970, NA/CAB/128/45.

59 See for example letters, Galsworthy to Robinson, and Mellon to Robinson, both 2 January 1970, NA/FCO/30/769; 'Record of Conversation between the Foreign and Commonwealth Secretary and the Defence Secretary at the Foreign and Commonwealth Office on Monday, 9 February, 1970', NA/FCO/73/53.

60 Minute, Robinson to O'Neill, 5 January 1970, NA/FCO/30/769.

61 Minute, Morland to Fielding, 29 January 1970; letter, Galsworthy to Adams, 10 March 1970, both NA/FCO/30/769.

62 Minute, Thomson to O'Neill, 11 February 1970, NA/PREM/13/3200.

63 Letter, Palliser to Greenhill, 6 March 1970, NA/FCO/30/769.

64 Minute, Lloyd-Hughes to Wilson, 25 March 1970, NA/PREM/13/3194.

65 'Record of a Meeting between the Foreign and Commonwealth Secretary and M. Maurice Couve de Murville at the Foreign and Commonwealth Office on Tuesday, 14 April at 12 noon', 1970, NA/FCO/73/54.

66 Minute, Figgures to Bell, 14 April 1970, NA/FCO/30/769.

67 Record, Selby to Robinson, 16 April 1970, NA/FCO/ 30/770.

68 Minute, Brimelow to O'Neill, 20 January 1970, NA/FCO/30/769.

69 Letter, Soames to Stewart, 21 January 1970, NA/PREM/13/3208.

70 Letter, Marshall to Robinson, 9 January 1970, NA/FCO/30/769.

71 Telegram, FCO to Paris, 13 January 1970, No 27, NA/FCO/73/53.

72 Minute, Galsworthy to minister, 16 January 1970, NA/FCO/30/769.

73 For example, on Boegner, letter, Marjoribanks to O'Neill, undated but received 6 March 1970; on Brunet, minute, O'Neill to Robinson, 17 March 1970, both NA/FCO/30/769.

74 Minute, Galsworthy to Adams, 18 March 1970, NA/FCO/30/769.

75 'Extract from Record of Prime Minister's discussion with M. Schumann, 23 January 1970', NA/PREM/13/3199.

76 'Record of Conversation between the Foreign and Commonwealth Secretary and the French Foreign Minister at the Foreign Office on Friday, 23 January at 11.30am', NA/FCO/73/53.

77 Telegram, Paris to FCO, 29 January 1970, No 110, NA/FCO/30/769.

78 Minute, Barrington to Robinson, 16 March 1970, NA/FCO/73/53.

79 Letter and enclosure, Rose to Robinson, 18 March 1970, NA/FCO/30/769.

80 'Visit of the Chancellor of the Duchy of Lancaster to Paris: Records of conversations at the Quai d'Orsay, 3-5.45pm, Friday, 17 April 1970, NA/FCO/30/770.

81 Minute, Tickell to Statham, 8 June 1970, NA/FCO/30/770.

82 Meeting of Heads of Mission from Certain European Posts, 9-10 March, 1970, NA/PREM/13/3201.

83 Message, Brandt to Wilson, 14 April 1970, PMPM Serial No T68/70, NA/PREM/13/3219.

84   Minute, Stewart to Wilson, 26 February 1970, PM/70/35, NA/PREM/13/3222.

85   'Record of a Meeting held at 10 Downing Street on Monday, 2nd March 1970 at 4pm', NA/PREM/13/3222.

86   Letter, O'Neill to Robinson, 4 March 1970, NA/FCO/30/764.

87   Brandt's reply to Lord Chancellor's speech of welcome, 3 March 1970, NA/PREM/13/3222.

88   KCA24081 (20 – 27 June 1970).

89   Telegram, Bonn to FCO, 20 January 1970, No 62, NA/FCO/30/763.

90   Minute, Everett to Wilson, 9 January 1970, NA/PREM/13/3199; CC(70)1, Tuesday 13 January 1970, NA/CAB/128/45.

91   For 1961, see Ludlow, Dealing with Britain, pp99-104; for 1967, see John Young, Britain and European Unity, p93.

92   For example, minute, Thomson to O'Neill, 5 March 1970; 'Record of Conversation between the Chancellor of the Duchy of Lancaster and Frau Focke in the Federal Chancellor's Office in Bonn at 9.30am on 14 April 1970, both NA/FCO/30/764.

93   Letter and enclosed draft, Stewart to Shore, 13 May 1970, Stewart papers, STWT 9/7/28.

94   Telegram, Paris to FCO, 28 April 1970, No 425, NA/FCO/30/770.

95   Telegram, FCO to Paris, 13 January 1970, No 27, NA/FCO/30/53.

96   'Record of Conversation between the Foreign and Commonwealth Secretary and the Netherlands Secretary of State for Foreign Affairs, in the Foreign Office, on Friday 1 May at 12.30pm'; see also 'Record of a Conversation between the Luxembourg Foreign Minister and the Foreign and Commonwealth Secretary at the Foreign and Commonwealth Office on Tuesday, 28 April at 11.30am', both NA/FCO/73/54.

97   Meeting of Heads of Mission from Certain European Posts, 9-10 March, 1970, NA/PREM/13/3201.

98   Letter, Galsworthy to Robinson, 2 February 1970, NA/FCO/30/769.

99   See for example 'Record of a Conversation between Sir Con O'Neill and State Secretary Harkort at the Federal Ministry of Foreign Affairs, Bonn at 11am on 3 February 1970', NA/FCO/30/763.

100   Telegram, UKDel Brussels to FCO, 6 March 1970, No 72, NA/PREM/13/3201; letter, Marjoribanks to O'Neill, undated but received 6 March 1970, NA/FCO/30/769.

101   'Note of a Meeting held in the Ministry of the Economy and Finance, 93 rue de Rivoli, Paris, Ter, at 11.30am and 4.30pm, Friday 27th February, 1970'; letter, Figgures to O'Neill, 2 March 1970 and Wilson's comment thereon, both NA/PREM/13/3201.

102   Telegram, UKDel Brussels to FCO, 6 March 1970, No 24 Saving, NA/PREM/13/3201.

103   Telegram, Luxembourg to FCO, 9 March 1970, No 49, NA/FCO/30/769.

[104] KCA24169 (5-12 September 1970); telegram, Paris to FCO, 25 March 1970, NA/FCO/30/769.

[105] CC(70)1, Tuesday 13 January 1970, NA/CAB/128/45.

[106] Minute, Robinson to O'Neill, 12 January 1970, NA/FCO/30/763; telegram, Paris to FCO, 12 February 1970, No 158, NA/FCO/30/769.

[107] Telegram, Paris to FCO, 20 February 1970, No 183, NA/FCO/30/769.

[108] Minutes, O'Neill to private secretary, 20 February 1970 and Robinson to O'Neill, 27 February 1970; telegrams, Brussels to FO, 23 February 1970, No 83; Hague to FCO, No 67 and Paris to FCO, No 211, both 26 February 1970, all NA/FCO/30/769.

[109] KCA24170-2 (5-12 September 1970).

[110] Letter, Overton to Statham, 10 June 1970, NA/FCO/30/764.

[111] For example, letter, Christofas to Robinson, 9 March 1970, NA/FCO/30/764.

[112] For example, minute, Brimelow to O'Neill, 20 January 1970, NA/FCO/30/769; 'Record of a Conversation between the Permanent Secretary of the Board of Trade and State Secretary Harkort, held at the Federal Ministry of Foreign Affairs, Bonn, at 4pm on 1 April 1970', NA/FCO/30/764; 'Record of a Conversation between Sir Con O'Neill and State Secretary Harkort at the Federal Ministry of Foreign Affairs, Bonn at 11am on 3 February 1970', NA/FCO/30/763; minute, Gildea to Mrs Healey [sic] 6 April 1970, NA/FCO/30/764.

[113] Letter and enclosure, Overton to Robinson, 21 January 1970 and reply, 23 January 1970, NA/FCO/30/763.

[114] Meeting of Heads of Mission from Certain European Posts, 9-10 March, 1970, NA/PREM/13/3201.

[115] Telegram, FCO to Bonn etc, 20 April 1970, No 261, NA/FCO/30/769.

[116] Minute, Nield to Isserlis, 12 May 1970, NA/PREM/13/3201.

[117] 'Implications for Anglo-United States Relations of Britain's European Policies', 1 January 1970, NA/PREM/13/3198.

[118] 'Prime Minister's visit to the United States, January 26-28, 1970: Record of Discussion at 10 Downing Street at 1530 hours on Monday, January 12, 1970'; telegram, Washington to FCO, 15 January 1968, No 113, NA/PREM/13/3545.

[119] 'Record of a Conversation between the Prime Minister and HM Ambassador, Washington, at No 10 Downing Street on January 16, 1970, at 11.30am', NA/PREM/13/3545.

[120] Minute, Wood to Rose, 21 January 1970; minute, Hannay to Christofas, 24 March 1970, both NA/FCO/30/760.

[121] Minute, Robinson to O'Neill, 27 May 1970, NA/FCO/30/760.

[122] Draft speech, 22 January 1970, NA/PREM/13/3428.

[123] 'Extract from Note of Meeting held in the White House, Washington, on Tuesday 27 January, 1970, at 11.00am', NA/PREM/13/2199; see also Wilson, The Labour Government, p753.

[124]   Record of special NSC meeting, 29 January 1970, NA/PREM/13/3546.

[125]   Telegram, FCO to Washington, 5 March 1970, No 544, PMPM Serial No T40/70; letter, Nixon to Wilson, 11 March 1970, PMPM Serial No T47/70, both NA/PREM/13/3222.

[126]   Letter and enclosed letter, Cleveland to O'Neill, 14 May 1970, NA/FCO/30/760.

[127]   Minute, Brind to Tickell, 12 May 1970, NA/PREM/13/760.

[128]   Meeting of East European and Soviet Department, 16 January 1969, NA/PREM/13/3203.

[129]   'Record of Conversation between the Foreign and Commonwealth Secretary and the Irish Ambassador in the Foreign and Commonwealth Office on Friday, 6 February at 11.30am', NA/FCO/73/53.

[130]   Minutes, Nield to Moon, 4 March 1970 and 17 March 1970, NA/PREM/13/3201.

[131]   Letter, Ross to Stewart, 9 March 1970; telegram, Stockholm to FCO, 20 March 1970, No 99; 'Record of a Conversation between the Foreign and Commonwealth Secretary and the Swedish Ambassador at the Foreign and Commonwealth Office on 24 March, 1970, at 4.30pm', all NA/PREM/13/3509.

[132]   Wilson's note on minute, Trend to Wilson, 13 February 1970; 'Note by Prime Minister of conversation at private dinner with Mr Olaf Palme, Prime Minister of Sweden, on April 6', both NA/PREM/13/3509.

[133]   'Record of Meeting held at 10am on Monday, 26 January, 1970, at the Parliament Buildings (Cabinet Room), Ottawa', NA/PREM/13/3428.

[134]   Telegrams, Wellington to FCO, 20 March 1970, Nos 154-155; letter, Barrington to Moon, 9 April 1970; telegram, FCO to Wellington, 19 May 1970, No 189, all NA/PREM/13/3369.

[135]   EURO(70)4, 'Negotiations with the European Communities, Consultation with other Governments: Note by the FCO', 12 February 1970, NA/CAB/134/2826; minute, Moon to Wilson, 13 February 1970, NA/PREM/13/3200.

[136]   Wilson's note on minute, Croft to Thomson, 16 April 1970, NA/PREM/13/3202.

[137]   Telegram, FCO to ACCRA, 7 May 1970, No 345, NA/PREM/13/3202.

[138]   Letter, Blundell to Wilson, 14 May 1970, PMPM No T95A/70; message, Pant to Wilson, 19 May 1970, PMPM No T99/70; telegram, Kampala to FCO, 25 May 1970, No 578, PMPM No T101/70; undated letter, prime minister of Swaziland to Wilson; telegrams, Kingston to FCO, 29 May 1970, No 181; Gaborone to FCO, 16 June 1970, No 976, PMPM No T112/70, all NA/PREM/13/3202; Benvenuti, *The End of the Affair*, pp245-246.

[139]   Telegram, FCO to Wellington, 19 May 1970, No 189, NA/PREM/13/3202.

[140]   See for example, minute, W Adams to Robinson, 13 January 1970, NA/FCO/30/769; minute, Gildea to Mrs Healey [sic], 6 April 1970, NA/FCO/30/764.

141 Minute, Nield to Trend, 15 May 1970, and Trend's note thereon, NA/PREM/13/3201.

142 Letter, Moon to Tickell, 19 May 1970; 'Record of a Conversation between the Foreign and Commonwealth Secretary and the President of the European Commission at the Foreign and Commonwealth Office at 3.45pm, on Tuesday, 19 May 1970', both NA/PREM/13/3201.

143 Telegram, Paris to FCO, 20 May 1970, No 491, NA/FCO/30/770.

144 Minute, Thomson to Wilson, 21 May 1970, PM/GT/70/67, and Wilson's note thereon, NA/PREM/13/3201.

145 Telegram, UKDel Brussels to FCO, 10 June 1970, No 217, NA/PREM/13/3201.

146 Letter, Graham to Moon, 11 June 1970, NA/PREM/13/3201.

Conclusions

1 Kitzinger, *Diplomacy and Persuasion*, p276.

2 Minute, Palliser to Barrington, 4 February 1969, NA/PREM/13/2673; 'Conclusions of a Meeting between the Prime Minister and the Foreign and Commonwealth Secretary at 10 Downing Street at 11.40am on Monday, February 10, 1969', NA/PREM/13/2674; drafts of White Paper, and Wilson's comments, NA/PREM/13/3198 and 13/3199; Gerard Noel, 'Harold Wilson', in van Thal, Herbert (ed), *The Prime Ministers: Volume Two From Lord John Russell to Edward Heath*, Chatham: George Allen and Unwin Ltd, 1975, p386.

3 Interview with the author, 12 July 2002.

4 Parr, *Britain's Policy Towards the European Community*, p194.

5 Interview with the author, 12 July 2002.

6 For example, note on letter, Crosland to Stewart, 6 May 1968; letter, Palliser to Maitland, 7 May 1968, NA/PREM/13/2111.

7 Philip Giddings, 'Prime Minister and Cabinet' in Donald Shell and Richard Hodder-Williams, *Churchill to Major: the British Prime Ministership since 1945*, London: Hurst and Company, 1995, pp41-44; Peter Hennessy, *The Prime Minister: The Office and its Holders since 1945*, London: Penguin, 2000, pp312, 288.

8 Benn, *Out of the Wilderness*, 30 April 1967, p496.

9 Marsh, *Off the Rails*, p96.

10 Compare Castle's threat to resign over the 'Fearless' negotiations, Castle, *The Castle Diaries*, 13 November 1968, p548.

11 Correspondence with the author, 10 March 2003.

12 Stewart papers, letter, Belgian ambassador to Stewart, 30 June 1970, STWT 9/7/47.

13 Stewart papers, letter, Stewart to Harmel via Belgian ambassador, 2 July 1970, STWT 9/7/47.

14 Stewart papers, handwritten note on undated draft document, possible for a parliamentary Labour Party meeting in 1970, STWT 7/1/9.

15 Wilson papers, 23 May 1968, MS WILSON 1149.

16 See for example, Bernard Donoughue, *Downing Street Diary: with Harold Wilson in No. 10*, London: Random House, 2005, chapters 9-13 and 15, especially pp251 and 402; John W Young, 'Europe', in Anthony Seldon and Kevin Hickson (eds), *New Labour, Old Labour: The Wilson and Callaghan Governments, 1974-79*, London: Routledge, 2004, pp139-153; David Allen, 'James Callaghan, 1974-76' in Kevin Theakston (ed), *British Foreign Secretaries since 1974*, London and New York: Routledge, 2004, pp47-65.

17 Correspondence with the author, 10 March 2003.

18 Wilson papers, interview with Leslie Smith, recorded at No 10 on Thursday, Feb 20, for Radio, 9 March 69, MS WILSON 1249.

Bibliography

Interviews and correspondence
Conversation with M. Pierre Messmer at *Maison Francaise*, University of Oxford, 15 February 2002
Interview with Sir Michael Palliser at his home in London, 12 July 2002
Correspondence with Sir Edward Heath, 10 March 2003

Primary Documents
The Papers of Lord Wilson of Rievaulx, held in the Bodleian Library, Oxford
The Papers of Lord George-Brown, held in the Bodleian Library, Oxford
The Papers of Sir Patrick Reilly, held in the Bodleian Library, Oxford
The Papers of Lord Stewart of Fulham, held at Churchill College, Cambridge
Government archives held at the Public Record Office, Kew, London:
      CAB128
      CAB129
      PREM 13
      FO and FCO
House of Commons Parliamentary Debates (cited as Hansard)
Bennett and Hamilton (eds), *Documents on British Policy Overseas*, Series III, Volume I, HMSO, 1997
Labour Party Archives, held on microfiche in the Bodleian Library, Oxford

Newspapers and Magazines
The Economist
Keesing's Contemporary Archive
The New Statesman

Autobiographies, Biographies, Diaries and Memoirs

Acheson, Dean, *Present at the Creation: my years in the State Department*, London: Hamish Hamilton, 1970

Baker, Kenneth, *The Prime Ministers: an Irreverent Political History in Cartoons*, London: Thames and Hudson, 1995, section on Wilson

Barber, Anthony, *Taking the Tide: A Memoir*, Norwich: Michael Russell, 1996

Benn, Tony, *Out of the Wilderness – Diaries 1963-67*, London: Hutchinson, 1987

Benn, Tony, *Office Without Power – Diaries 1968-72*, London: Hutchinson, 1988

Brandt, Willy, *A Peace Policy for Europe*, London: Weidenfeld and Nicholson, 1969, tr. Joel Carmichael

Brandt, Willy, *People and Politics: the Years 1960-1975*, London: Collins, 1978

Brown, George, *In My Way*, London: Victor Gollancz, 1971

Cairncross, Alec, *The Wilson Years: A Treasury Diary 1964-1969*, London: Historians' Press, 1997

Callaghan, James, *Time and Chance*, London: Collins, 1987

Castle, Barbara, *The Castle Diaries 1964-70*, London: Weidenfeld and Nicolson, 1984

Chalfont, Alun, *The Shadow of My Hand*, London: Weidenfeld and Nicholson, 2000

Cole, John, *As it seemed to me: Political Memoirs*, London: Weidenfeld and Nicholson, 1995

Crossman, Richard, *The Diaries of a Cabinet Minister, Volume 1, Minister of Housing 1964-6*, London: Hamish Hamilton, 1975

Crossman, Richard, *The Diaries of a Cabinet Minister, Volume 2, Lord President of the Council and Leader of the House of Commons, 1966-68*, London: Hamish Hamilton, 1976

Crossman, Richard, *The Diaries of a Cabinet Minister, Volume 3, Secretary of State for Social Services, 1968-70*, London: Hamish Hamilton and Jonathan Cape, 1977

Debré, Michel, *Trois Républiques pour une France: Gouverner Autrement*, (Mémoires), Paris: Albin Michel, 1993

Donoughue, Bernard, *The Heat of the Kitchen*, London: Politico's, 2004

Donoughue, Bernard, *Downing Street Diary: with Harold Wilson in No. 10*, London : Random House, 2005

Foot, Paul, *The Politics of Harold Wilson*, London: Penguin, 1968

Galbraith, John Kenneth, *Ambassador's Journal: A Personal Account of the Kennedy Years*, London: Hamish Hamilton, 1969

Gladwyn, *The Memoirs of Lord Gladwyn*, London: Weidenfeld and Nicholson, 1972

Gordon Walker, Patrick, *Political Diaries 1932-1971*, London: the Historians' Press, 1991

Greenhill, Denis, *More By Accident*, York: Wilton 65, 1992

Haines, Joe, *The Politics of Power*, London: Jonathan Cape, 1977

Healey, Denis, *The Time of my Life*, Harmondsworth: Penguin, 1989

Healey, Denis, *When Shrimps Learn to Whistle: Signposts for the Nineties*, London: Michael Joseph, 1990

Heath, Edward, *The Course of my Life*, London: Hodder and Stoughton, 1998

Hellicar, Eileen, *Prime Ministers of Britain*, Newton Abbot and London: David and Charles, 1978, chapter on Wilson

Isaacson, Walter, *Kissinger: A Biography*, London: Faber and Faber, 1992

Jenkins, Roy, *A Life at the Centre*, London: Macmillan, 1991

du Jardin, Vincent, *Pierre Harmel*, Montigny-Le Bretonneux: Le Cri, 2004

Kay, Ernest, *Pragmatic Premier: An Intimate Portrait of Harold Wilson*, London: Leslie Frewin, 1967

Kellner, Peter and Hitchens, Christopher, *Callaghan: The Road to No. 10*, London: Cassell, 1976

King, Cecil, *The Cecil King Diary 1965-70*, London: Jonathan Cape, 1972

Kissinger, Henry, *Years of Renewal*, London: Weidenfeld and Nicholson, 1999

Kissinger, Henry, *Years of Upheaval*, London: Weidenfeld and Nicholson and Michael Joseph, 1982

Kissinger, Henry, *The White House Years*, London: Weidenfeld and Nicolson and Michael Joseph, 1979

Lacouture, Jean, *De Gaulle the Ruler: 1945-1970*, London: Harvill, 1991, (tr. Alan Sheridan)

Marjolin, Robert, *Architect of European Unity: Memoirs 1911-1986*, London: Weidenfeld and Nicholson, 1989 (tr. William Hall)

Marsh, Richard, *Off the Rails*, London: Weidenfeld and Nicholson, 1978

Marshall, Barbara, *Willy Brandt*, London: Cardinal, 1990

Marshall, Barbara, *Willy Brandt: A Political Biography*, Basingstoke: Macmillan, 1997

Monnet, Jean, *Memoirs*, London: Collins, 1978 (tr. Richard Mayne)

Morgan, Austen, *Harold Wilson*, London: Pluto, 1992

Morgan, Kenneth, *Callaghan: a Life*, Oxford: Oxford University Press, 1997

Nixon, Richard, *President Nixon's Foreign Policy Report 1972*, United States Information Service, 1972

Nixon, Richard, *The Memoirs of Richard Nixon*, New York: Grosset and Dunlap, 1978

Noel, Gerard, 'Harold Wilson', in van Thal, Herbert (ed), *The Prime Ministers: Volume Two From Lord John Russell to Edward Heath*, Chatham: George Allen and Unwin Ltd, 1975

Paterson, Peter, *Tired and Emotional: the Life of Lord George-Brown*, London: Chatto and Windus, 1993

Pimlott, Ben, *Harold Wilson*, London: BCA, 1992

Prittie, Terence, *Willy Brandt: portrait of a statesman*, London: Weidenfeld and Nicolson, 1974

Roberts, Frank, *Dealing with Dictators: the Destruction and Revival of Europe 1930-1970*, London, Weidenfeld and Nicholson, 1991

Rogers, Bill, *Fourth Among Equals*, London: Politico's, 2000

Schlesinger, Arthur, *A Thousand Days. John F. Kennedy in the White House*, London: Deutsch, 1965

Schroeder, Gerhardt, *Decision for Europe*, London: Thames and Hudson, 1964

Shore, Peter, *Separate Ways: the Heart of Europe*, London: Duckworth, 2000

Shore, Peter, *Leading the Left*, London: Weidenfeld and Nicholson, 1993

Shore, Peter, 'The Case Against Entry: the United Kingdom and the European Communities, the Answer to the White Paper', *New Statesman*, 1971 (pamphlet edition)

Short, Edward, *Whip to Wilson*, London and Sydney: Macdonald, 1989

Smith, Dudley, *Harold Wilson: A Critical Biography*, London: Robert Hale Limited, 1964

Stewart, Michael, *Life and Labour*, London: Sidgwick and Jackson, 1980

Thomson, George Malcolm, *The Prime Ministers: from Robert Walpole to Margaret Thatcher*, London: Secker and Warburg, 1980

Thorpe, D R, *Alec Douglas-Home*, London: Sinclair Stevenson, 1997

Unger, Irwin and Unger, Debi, *LBJ: A Life*, New York: John Wiley and Sons, 1999

Weidenfeld, George, *Remembering My Good Friends: An Autobiography*, Glasgow: Harper Collins, 1995

Williams, Charles, *The Last Great Frenchman: A Life of General de Gaulle*, London: Abacus, 1995

Williams, Marcia, *Inside No. 10*, London: Weidenfeld and Nicholson, 1972

Wilson, Harold, *Memoirs, 1916-1964: the Making of a Prime Minister*, London, Weidenfeld and Nicolas and Michael Joseph, 1986

Wilson, Harold, *The Labour Government 1964-1970: A Personal Record*, London: Weidenfeld and Nicholson and Michael Joseph, 1971

Wilson, Harold, *The Wit of Harold Wilson*, London: Frewin, 1967

Zeigler, Philip, *Wilson: The Authorised Life of Lord Wilson of Rivaulx*, London: Weidenfeld and Nicholson, 1993

Zuckerman, Solly, *Monkeys, Men and Missiles: An Autobiography 1946-88*, London: Collins, 1988

Unpublished material
Audland, Christopher, remarks on 'The Heath Negotiations' at *Chatham House Conference on Previous Enlargement Negotiations*, 1993
Benvenuti, Andrea, *The End of the Affair: Britain's Turn to Europe as a Problem in Anglo-Australian Relations (1961-72)*, DPhil thesis, University of Oxford, 2003
Boehm, Lasse, *Our Man in Paris? The Paris Embassy and the Second British Application to Join the EEC, 1966-67*, MPhil thesis, 2003
Daddow, Oliver, *Rhetoric and Reality: The Historiography of British European Policy, 1945-73*, PhD thesis, University of Nottingham, 2000
Gaitanis, Vasiliki Vicky, *A British invention condemned to Anglo-French diplomacy: collaboration in defence industries in the 1960s and the case of the Anglo-French Variable Geometry plane*, MPhil thesis, University of Oxford, 2000
Kajiwara, Toru, *Britain's Second Application for Membership of the European Economic Community (EEC) in 1966-67: Essence of Decision's 3-model analysis in a British Context*, MPhil thesis, University of Oxford, 2002
Parr, Helen, *Harold Wilson, Whitehall and British Policy towards the European Community, 1964-1967*, PhD thesis, Queen Mary, University of London, 2002
Rock, Philipp, *'With a little Help from my Friends': Die Rolle der Bundesrepublik Deutschland beim Beitritt Großbritanniens zu den Europäischen Gemeinschaften, 1967-1971*, Magister thesis, Humboldt University, 2005

Secondary Literature
Allen, David, Rummel, Rheinhardt and Wessels, Wolfgang, *European Political Co-operation: towards a foreign policy for Western Europe*, London: Butterworth Scientific, 1982
Baker, Amy, *Prime Ministers and the Rule Book*, London: Politico's, 2000
Baker, David and Seawright, David (eds), *Britain for and against Europe: British Politics and the Question of European Integration*, Oxford: Clarendon Press, 1998
Ball, Stuart and Seldon, Antony (eds), *The Heath Government 1970-74*, London: Longman, 1996
Bange, Oliver, *The EEC Crisis of 1963: Kennedy, Macmillan, de Gaulle and Adenauer in Conflict*, Basingstoke: Macmillan in association with the Institute of Contemporary British History, 2000 (Contemporary History in Context Series, general editor Peter Catterall)
Barber, James, *The Prime Minister since 1945*, Oxford: Blackwell, 1991

Barclay, G St. J., *Commonwealth or Europe*, Queensland: University of Queensland Press, 1970

Barker, Elizabeth, *Britain in a Divided Europe*, London: Weidenfeld and Nicholson, 1971

Barnett, Correlli, *The Lost Victory: British Dreams, British Realities 1945-50*, London: Macmillan, 1995

Bartlett, Christopher, 'The Special Relationship' A Political History of Anglo-American Relations since 1945*, Harlow: Longman, 1992

Bell, P M H, *France and Britain 1940-1994: The Long Separation*, London and New York: Longman, 1997

Beloff, Lord Max, *The United States and the Unity of Europe*, Washington: The Brookings Institution, 1963

Beloff, Lord Max, *Britain and the European Union: Dialogue of the Deaf*, London: Macmillan, 1996

Beloff, Nora, *The General Says No: Britain's Exclusion from Europe*, Harmondsworth: Penguin, 1963

Berstein, Serge and Rioux, Jean-Pierre, *The Pompidou Years, 1969-1974*, Cambridge: Cambridge University Press, 2000

Birke, Adolfe, Brechtken, Magnus and Searle, Alaric (eds), *An Anglo-German Dialogue: the Munich lectures on the history of international relations*, Munich: K G Saur, 2000

Black, Jeremy, *Convergence or Divergence? Britain and the Continent*, Basingstoke: Macmillan, 1994

Bond, Martyn, Smith, Julie and Wallace, William (eds), *Eminent Europeans: Personalities who shaped contemporary Europe*, London: The Greycoat Press, 1996

Braunthal, Gerard, *The German Social Democrats Since 1969: A Power in Power and Opposition*, Boulder: Westview Press, 1994

Brivati, Brian and Jones, Harriet, *From reconstruction to integration: Britain and Europe since 1945*, Leicester: Leicester University Press, 1993

Brivati, Brian and Heffernan, Richard (eds), *The Labour Party: A Centenary History*, Basingstoke and London: Macmillan, 2000

Broad, Roger, *Labour's European Dilemmas From Bevin to Blair*, Basingstoke: Palgrave, 2001

Broad, Roger and Preston, Virginia (eds), *Moored to the Continent? Britain and European Integration*, London: Institute of Historical Research, 2001

Bulpitt, Jim, 'The European Question: Rules, National Modernisation and the ambiguities of *Primat der Innenpolitik*', in David Marquand and Anthony Seldon, (eds), *The Ideas that Shaped Post-War Britain*, London: Fontana Press, 1996

Burr, William (ed), *The Kissinger Transcripts. The top secret talks with Beijing and Moscow*, New York: The New Press, 1999

Butler, David, *British General Elections since 1945*, Oxford: Blackwell, 1995

Butler, David and Pinto-Duschinsky, Michael, *The British General Election of 1970*, London: Macmillan, 1971

Camps, Miriam, *European Unification in the Sixties: From the Veto to the Crisis*, London: Oxford University Press, 1967

Chase, James and Ravenna, Earl C. (eds), *Atlantis Lost: U.S.-European Relations after the Cold War*, New York: New York University Press, 1976

Childs, David, *Britain since 1945: A Political History*, London: Routledge, 1997

Colman, Jonathan, *A 'special relationship'? Harold Wilson, Lyndon B. Johnson and Anglo-American relations 'at the summit', 1964-1968*, Manchester and New York: Manchester University Press, 2004

Cook, Chris and Stevenson, John, *The Longman Companion to Britain since 1945*, London and New York: Longman, 1996

Craig, FWS, *British General Election Manifestos 1959-1987*, Dartmouth: Parliamentary Research Services, 1990

Daddow, Oliver (ed), *Harold Wilson and European Integration: Britain's Second Application to join the EEC*, London: Frank Cass, 2003

Darwin, John, *The End of the British Empire: The Historical Debate*, Oxford: Blackwell, 1991

Davidson, Ian, *Britain and the Making of Europe*, London: Macdonald, 1971

Deighton, Anne, 'The Past in the Present: British Imperial memories and the European question', in Jan-Werner Müller (ed), *Memory and Power in Post-War Europe*, Cambridge: Cambridge University Press, 2002

Deighton, Anne, 'The Second British Application for Membership of the EEC' in Loth, Wilfred, (ed) *Crises and Compromises: the European Project 1963-1969*, Baden-Baden and Brussels: Nomos Verlagsgesellscaft, 2001

Deighton, Anne and Milward, Alan (eds), *Widening, Deepening and Acceleration: The European Economic Community 1957-1963*, Baden-Baden: Nomos Verlag, 1999

Deighton, Anne, 'British-West German Relations, 1945-1972', in Klaus Larres (ed), *Uneasy Allies: British-German Relations and European Integration since 1945*, Oxford: Oxford University Press, 2000

Dell, Edmund, *The Schuman Plan and the British Abdication of Leadership in Europe*, Oxford: Oxford University Press, 1995

Dickie, John, *'Special' No More: Anglo-American Relations, Rhetoric and Reality*, London: Weidenfeld and Nicholson, 1994

Dyson, Kenneth, *European Détente: Case-studies of the politics of East-West Relations*, London: Pinter, 1986

Edmonds, Robin, *Setting the Mould: The United States and Britain 1945-1950*, Oxford: Clarendon Press, 1986

Ehrmann, Henry W., Schain, Martin A., *Politics in France*, New York: Harper Collins, 1992

Emery, Fred, *Watergate: The Corruption and Fall of Richard Nixon*, London: Pimlico, 1995

Fabian Society, *Europe: what next?*, Fabian Tract 389, 1969

Fielding, Steven, *The Labour Governments 1964-70, Volume 1 Labour and Cultural Change*, Manchester and New York: Manchester University Press, 2003

Fitzmaurice, John, *The Politics of Belgium: Crisis and Compromise in a Plural Society*, London: C Hurst and Company, 1983

Frankel, Joseph, *British Foreign Policy 1945-1973*, London: Oxford University Press for the Royal Institute of International Affairs, 1975

Garton Ash, Timothy, *In Europe's Name: Germany and the Divided Continent*, London: Vintage, 1994

George, Stephen, *An Awkward Partner*, Oxford: Oxford University Press, 1994

George, Stephen, *Britain and European Integration since 1945*, Oxford: Blackwell, 1991

Gladwyn, *De Gaulle's Europe or Why the General Says No*, London: Secker and Warburg, 1969

Gladwyn, Lord, *The European Idea*, London: Weidenfeld and Nicolson, 1966

Godt, Paul, *Policy-Making in France: From de Gaulle to Mitterrand*, London and New York: Pinter Publishers, 1989

Gordon-Walker, Patrick, *The Cabinet*, London and Glasgow: Fontana and Collins, 1972

Gowland, David and Turner, Arthur (eds), *Britain and European Integration 1945-1998: A Documentary History*, London: Routledge, 2000

Greenwood, Sean, *Britain and the Cold War 1945-91*, Basingstoke: Macmillan, 2000

Greenwood, Sean, *Britain and European Integration since the Second World War*, Manchester and New York: Manchester University Press, 1996

Grosser, Alfred, *The Western Alliance: European-American Relations since 1945*, London and Basingstoke: Macmillan, 1980

Haase, Christian (ed), *Debating Foreign Affairs*, Berlin: Philo Verlagsgesellschaft, 2003

Hamilton, Keith, *The Last Cold Warriors: Britain, Détente and the CSCE, 1972-1975*, St Anthony's College, University of Oxford European Interdependence Research Unit Discussion Paper 991, July 1999

Hayward, Jack, *Governing France: the One and Indivisible Republic*, London: Weidenfeld and Nicholson, 1987

Hennessy, Peter, *The Prime Minister: The Office and its Holders since 1945*, London: Penguin, 2000

Hennessy, Peter, *Whitehall*, London: Fontana, 1990

Holland, Robert, *The Pursuit of Greatness: Britain and the World Role, 1900-1970*, London: Fontana Press, 1991

Ifestos, Panayiotis, *European Political Cooperation: Towards a Framework of Supranational Diplomacy?*, Aldershot: Avebury, 1987

James, Simon and Preston, Virginia (eds), *British Politics since 1945: the dynamics of historical change*, Basingstoke: Palgrave, 2001

Jowell, Roger and Hoinville, Gerald, *Britain into Europe: Public Opinion and the EEC 1961-75*, London: Croom Helm, 1976

Kaiser, Karl and Schwarz, Hans-Peter (eds), *America and Western Europe*, Lexington: Lexington Books, 1977

Kaiser, Wolfram, *Using Europe, Abusing the Europeans: Britain and European Integration 1945-63*, Basingstoke: Macmillan, 1996

Kaiser, Wolfram and Staerk, Gillian (eds), *British Foreign Policy, 1955-64: Contracting Options*, Basingstoke: Macmillan in association with the Institute of Contemporary British History, 2000 (Contemporary History in Context Series, general editor Peter Catterall)

Kissinger, Henry, *American Foreign Policy*, New York: W. W. Norton and Company, 1977

Kissinger, Henry, *Diplomacy*, New York: Simon and Schuster, 1994

Kissinger, Henry, *Nuclear Weapons and Foreign Policy*, London: Oxford University Press, 1957

Kissinger, Henry, *The Necessity for Choice*, London: Chatto and Windus, 1961

Kissinger, Henry, *The Troubled Partnership: A Reappraisal of the Atlantic Alliance*, Westport: Greenwood, 1982

Kitzinger, Uwe, *Diplomacy and Persuasion*, London: Thames and Hudson, 1973

Kitzinger, Uwe, *The Second Try: Labour and the EEC*, Oxford: Pergamon Press Ltd, 1968

Lamb, Richard, *The Failure of the Eden Government*, London: Sidgwick and Jackson, 1987

Lieber, Robert J, *British Politics and European Unity: Parties, Elites, and Pressure Groups*, Berkeley: University of California Press, 1970

Lloyd, T O, *Empire, Welfare State, Europe: English History 1906-1992*, (4th Edition), Oxford: Oxford University Press, 1993

Lord, Christopher, *British Entry to the European Community under the Heath Government of 1970-4*, Aldershot: Dartmouth, 1993

Loth, Wilfred (ed), *Crises and Compromises: the European Project 1963-1969*, Baden-Baden: Nomos Verlag, 2001

Ludlow, N Piers, *The European Community and the Crises of the 1960s: Negotiating the Gaullist Challenge*, Abingdon: Routledge, 2006

Ludlow, N Piers, 'Constancy and Flirtation: Germany, Britain and the EEC, 1956-72' in Noakes, Jeremy, Wende, Peter and Wright, Jonathan, *Britain and Germany in Europe 1949-1990*, Oxford: Oxford University Press, 2002

Ludlow, N Piers, *Dealing with Britain: the Six and the First UK Application to the EEC*, Cambridge: Cambridge University Press, 1997

Maclean, Donald, *British Foreign Policy Since Suez, 1956-1968*, London: Hodder and Stoughton, 1970

Maitland, Donald, *The Running Tide: A View of International and other Public Affairs over Four Decades*, Bath: University of Bath Press, 2000

McCarthy, Patrick (ed), *France-Germany in the Twenty-First Century*, New York: Palgrave, 2001

McKie, David and Cook, Chris (eds), *The Decade of Disillusion: British Politics in the Sixties*, London: Macmillan, 1972

Middlemas, Keith, *Power, Competition and the State Volume 2: Threats to the Postwar Settlement, Britain, 1961-74*, Basingstoke: Macmillan, 1990

Milward, Alan, *The Rise and Fall of a National Strategy, 1945-63*, London: Whitehall Publishing in Association with Frank Cass, 2002

Morgan, Kenneth, *The People's Peace: British History 1945-1990*, Oxford: Oxford University Press, 1990

Morgan, Kenneth, *Labour in Power 1945-51*, Oxford: Oxford University Press, 1984

Morgan, Roger, *The United States and West Germany, 1945-73, A Study in Alliance Politics*, London : Published for the Royal Institute of International Affairs and the Harvard Center for International Affairs by Oxford University Press, 1974

Northedge, FS, *Descent from Power: British Foreign Policy 1945-1973*, London: George Allen and Unwin, 1974

Nuttall, Simon, *European Political Co-operation*, Oxford: Clarendon, 1992

O'Neill, Sir Con, *Britain's Entry into the European Community: Report on the Negotiations of 1970-1972*, London: Whitehall History Publishing in association with Frank Cass, 2000

Padgett, Stephen (ed), *Adenauer to Kohl: The Development of the German Chancellorship*, London: Hurst and Company, 1994

Palliser, Michael, *Britain and British Diplomacy in a World of Change*, annual memorial lecture, 11th December 1975, to the David Davis Memorial Institute of International Studies

Parr, Helen, *Britain's Policy Towards the European Community: Harold Wilson and Britain's world role, 1964-67*, Abingdon: Routledge, 2006

Pickering, Jeffrey, *Britain's Withdrawal from East of Suez: the Politics of Retrenchment*, Basingstoke: Macmillan, 1998

Reynolds, David, *Britannia Overruled: British Policy and World Power in the 20ᵗʰ Century*, Harlow: Longman, 1991

Robins, LJ, *The Reluctant Party: Labour and the EEC, 1961-1975*, Ormskirk: GW&A Hesketh, 1979

Robbins, Keith, *The Eclipse of a Great Power: Modern Britain 1870-1992*, London: Longman, 1994

Sanders, David, *Losing an Empire, Finding a Role: British Foreign Policy since 1945*, Basingstoke: Macmillan, 1990

Seldon, Anthony and Hickson, Kevin (eds), *New Labour, Old Labour: The Wilson and Callaghan Governments, 1974-79*, London: Routledge, 2004

Shell, Donald and Hodder-Williams, Richard, *Churchill to Major, the British Prime Minister-ship since 1945*, London: Hurst and Company, 1995

Shore, Peter, *Separate Ways: the Heart of Europe*, London: Duckworth, 2000

Simonian, Haig, *The Privileged Partnership: Franco-German relations in the European Community 1969-1984*, Oxford: Clarendon Press, 1985

Silberschmidt, Max, *The United States and Europe: rivals and partners*, London: Thames and Hudson, 1972

Sked, Alan and Cook, Chris, *Post-War Britain: A Political History 1945-1992*, 4th edition, London: Penguin, 1993

Spotts, Frederic and Wieser, Theodor, *Italy, A Difficult Democracy: A Survey of Politics*, Cambridge, Cambridge University Press, 1986

Taylor, Philip, *When Europe Speaks with One Voice*, London: Aldwych Press, 1979

van Thal, Herbert, *The Prime Ministers*, London: Allen and Unwin, 1974-5

Theakston, Kevin (ed), *British Foreign Secretaries since 1974*, London and New York: Routledge, 2004

Tint, Herbert, *French Foreign Policy since the Second World War*, London: Weidenfeld and Nicholson, 1972

Tiratsoo, Nick (ed), *From Blitz to Blair: A New History of Britain since 1939*, London: Phoenix, 1998

Tomlinson, Jim, *The Labour governments 1964-70, Volume 3 Economic policy*, Manchester and New York: Manchester University Press, 2003

Uri, Pierre (ed), *From Commonwealth to Common Market*, Middlesex: Penguin, 1968

Vital, David, *The Making of British Foreign Policy*, London: Allen and Unwin, 1968

Wallace, William, *Britain's Bilateral Links within Western Europe*, Chatham House Papers 23, London: Routledge and Kegan Paul Ltd, 1984

Wallace, William and Paterson, W, (eds), *Foreign Policy-making in Western Europe: a comparative approach*, Farnborough: Saxon House, 1978

Wallace, William, *The Foreign Policy Process in Britain*, London: RIIA, 1977

Wallace, William, *Foreign Policy and the Political Process*, London, Macmillan, 1971

White, Brian, *Britain, Détente and Changing East-West Relations*, London: Routledge, 1992

Wilson, Harold, *The Governance of Britain: a unique insight into how Britain is run from the top*, London: Sphere Books, 1977

Wilson, Harold, *A Prime Minister on Prime Ministers*, London: Weidenfeld and Nicholas and Michael Joseph, 1977

Wurm, Clemens (ed), *Western Europe and Germany: the beginnings of European Integration, 1945-1960*, Oxford: Berg Publishers, 1995

Young, Hugo, *This Blessed Plot: Britain and Europe from Churchill to Blair*, London: Macmillan, 1998

Young, John, *The Labour governments 1964-70, Volume 2 International Policy*, Manchester and New York: Manchester University Press, 2003

Young, John, *Britain and European Unity, 1945-1999*, Basingstoke: Macmillan, 2000

Young, John, *The Heath Government and British Entry into the European Community*, Leicester: University of Leicester Discussion Papers on Britain and Europe No BE95/1, 1995

Articles

Journal of Common Market Studies (JCMS)
Journal of European Integration History (JEIH)

Special edition on the Summit of the Hague, *JEIH*, Vol 9, No 2, 2003

Allott, Philip, 'Britain and Europe: a Political Analysis', *JCMS*, Vol 13, 1975

Anonymous Survey: 'Public Opinion and the EEC', *JCMS*, Vol 6, No 3, 1967-8

Brittan, Samuel, 'Some Common Market Heresies', *JCMS*, Vol 8, No 4 1969-70

Byrd, Peter, 'The Labour Party and the European Community, 1970-1975', *JCMS*, Vol 13, 1975

Fitzgerald, Maurice, 'Ireland's Relations with the EEC: From the Treaties of Rome to Membership', *JEIH*, Vol 7, No 1, 2001

Frey, Cynthia W, 'Meaning Business: the British Application to join the Common Market, Nov 1966-Oct 1967', *JCMS*, Vol 6, No 3, 1967-8

Frøland, Hans-Otto, 'Choosing the Periphery: The Political Economy of Norway's European Integration Policy, 1948-73', *JEIH*, Vol 7, No 1, 2001

Hack, WGCM, 'The Economic Effects of Britain's entry into the Common Market', *JCMS*, Vol 11, No 2, 1972-3

Henig, Stanley, 'Britain and Europe – the Middle Way', *JCMS*, Vol 6, No 2, 1967-8

Kitzinger, Uwe, 'Britain's Crisis of Identity', *JCMS*, Vol 6, No 4, 1967-8

Lieber, Robert, 'European Elite Attitudes Revisited: The Future of the European Community and European-American Relations', *British Journal of Political Science*, 1975

Miller, Linda B, 'Europe's Futures – Change and Continuity?' in *JCMS*, Vol 9, 1970-71

Niblock, Michael, University of Bristol, Review of Pickles, William, *Britain and Europe: How Much has Changed?*, Blackwell, 1967, *JCMS*, Vol 6, No 1, 1967-8

Paavonen, Tapani, 'From Isolation to the Core: Finland's Position towards European Integration, 1960-95', *JEIH*, Vol 7, No 1, 2001

Parr, Helen, draft article, 'Success or Failure? French policy towards enlargement: Britain's Second Application in 1967', *Cold War History*, forthcoming

Pickles, William, Review of David Butler and Uwe Kitzinger, *The 1975 Referendum*, London: Macmillan, 1976, in *JCMS*, Vol 5, No 4, 1976-7

Pine, Melissa, 'British Private Diplomacy and Public Policy: the Soames Affair', *JEIH*, Vol 10, No 2, 2004

Preston, Christopher, 'Obstacles to EU Enlargement: The Classical Community Method and the Prospects for a Wider Europe', *JCMS*, Vol 33, No 3, 1995

Rifflet, Raymond, 'After the Hague', *JCMS*, Vol 8, No 4, 1969-70

Ruano, Lorena, 'Elites, public opinion and pressure groups: the British position in agriculture during the negotiations for accession to the EC, 1961-1975', *JEIH*, Vol 5, No1, 1995

Steininger, 'The Americans are in a Hopeless Position': Great Britain and the War in Vietnam, 1964-65', *Diplomacy and Statecraft*, Vol 8, No 3, 1997

Wallace, William, 'British External Relations and the European Community: the Changing Context of Foreign Policy-Making', *JCMS*, Vol 12, No 1, 1973-4

Wilkins, Andreas, 'Westpolitik, Ostpolitik and the Project of the Economic and Monetary Union. Germany's European Policy in the Brandt era (1969-1974)', *JEIH*, Vol 5, No 1, 1995

Wulf, Wilhelm E A, Review of John Costello and Terry Hughes, *The Battle for Concorde*, Salisbury: Compton Press Ltd, 1971, *JCMS*, Vol 10, 1971-2

Wyn Rees, G, 'British Strategic Thinking and Europe, 1964-1970', *JEIH*, Vol 5, No1, 1995

Young, John, 'Britain and 'LBJ's War', 1964-68', *Cold War History*, Vol 2, No 3, April 2002

Dramatis personae

United Kingdom

Adams, W James	First Secretary, Paris, 1965-69
Andrews, Derek	Private Secretary to Wilson, 1966-70
Anson, John	Financial Counsellor, Paris, 1968-70
Audland, Christopher	Head of Science and Technology Department, FCO 1968-70
	Counsellor and Head of Chancellery, Bonn from 1970
Austee, Miss M J	FCO (unspecified position and dates)
Balogh, Thomas	Economic Adviser to the cabinet, 1964-67
	Consultant to Wilson 1968
Barclay, Roderick	HM Ambassador to Belgium, 1963-69
Barnes, James	Under-Secretary, Board of Trade, 1966-70
Barrington, Nicholas	Assistant Private Secretary to Secretary of State for Foreign Affairs, from 1968
Beith, John	HM Ambassador to Belgium from 1969
Bell, George	Third Secretary to the Treasury from 1966
	Member of Negotiating team from 1970
Bendall, David	Counsellor, Washington, 1965-69
	Assistant Under-Secretary of State in FCO superintending SED, WED and WOD, from 1969
Benn, Tony	Minister of Technology 1966-1970
Bessell, Peter	Labour MP for Bodmin, 1964-70
Bridges, Thomas	Counsellor and Head of Chancery in Moscow from 1969

Brighty, David	Foreign Office 1967-69 (unspecified position)
Brimelow, Thomas	HM Ambassador to Poland, 1966-1969
	Deputy Under Secretary in FCO for EESD, Disarmament Department and SED, from 1969
Brind, Henry	Diplomatic Service from 1960 (unspecified position)
Brooks Richards, F	British embassy, Bonn (unspecified position and dates)
Brown, George	Deputy Prime Minister 1964-1968; Foreign Secretary 1966-March 1968
Buxton, Paul	Counsellor, Washington from 1967
Callaghan, James	Chancellor of the Exchequer 1964-1967
	Secretary of State for Home Affairs November 1967-70
Cambridge, Sydney	Foreign Office, 1966-70 (unspecified position)
Campbell, Alan	Counsellor, Paris from 1967
Carr, Raymond	St Anthony's College, Oxford; adviser to the government
Castle, Barbara	Minister for Transport, 1965-68
	First Secretary of State, 1968-70
	Secretary of State for Employment and Productivity 1968-70
Chalfont, Lord Alun	Minister of State in FO and FCO 1964-70
Christofas, Kenneth	Minister, UK Delegation to the EC from 1969
Churchill, Winston	Conservative Prime Minister 1951-55
Crosland, Anthony	President of the Board of Trade 1967-69
	Minister for Local Government and Regional Planning 1969-70
Crossman, Richard	Lord President of the Council 1966-68
	Secretary of State for Social Services 1968-70
Cudlipp, Hugh	Chairman, Daily Mirror Newspapers Ltd, 1963-68

	Chairman, International Publishing Corporation Ltd, 1968-73
Curson, Bernard	Information Policy Department, FCO, 1968-70
Day, Derek	Assistant Private Secretary to the Secretary of State for Foreign Affairs, 1967-68
Denman, Roy	Deputy Secretary, Board of Trade, 1967-70
	Member of Negotiating Team from 1970
Dean, Patrick	HM Ambassador to the USA, 1965-69
Diamond, John	Chief Secretary to the Treasury, 1964-70
Douglas-Home, Alec	Conservative Prime Minister, 1963-64
Drinkall, John	British embassy, Brussels, 1967-70
	Head of West European Department, FCO, from 1970
East, Kenneth	Counsellor and Head of Chancery, Oslo embassy, 1965-70
Eden, Anthony	Conservative Prime Minister, 1955-57
Edwards, David	British embassy, Bonn (unspecified position and dates)
Everett, Christopher	Private Secretary to Ambassador then First Secretary, Chancellery, Washington, 1963-67
	Planning Staff, FCO, 1967-70
Faber, Richard	Counsellor, The Hague from 1969
Fielding, Leslie	British embassy, Paris, 1966-70 (unspecified position)
	Deputy Head of Planning Staff, FCO from 1970
Figgures, Frank	Third Secretary to the Treasury, 1965-68
	Second Secretary to the Treasury, from 1968
Ford, John	Counsellor, Rome, 1966-70
	Assistant Under-Secretary supervising European Integration

	Department and European Communities Information Unit from 1970
Freeman, John	HM Ambassador to the USA from 1969
de Freitas, Geoffrey	Labour MP for Kettering, 1964-79
	President, Assembly of Council of Europe, 1966-69
	Labour Committee for Europe, 1965-72
Gaitskell, Hugh	Leader of the Labour Party 1955-63
Galsworthy, John	Counsellor and then Minister (European Economic Affairs), Paris from 1967
Garran, Peter	HM Ambassador to the Netherlands, 1964-69
Giffard, (Charles) Sydney,	Head of Eastern European and Soviet Department, FCO from 1968
Gildea, JRD	Board of Trade (unspecified position and dates)
Gore-Booth, Paul	Permanent Under-Secretary of State, FCO 1965-69
Graham, Andrew	Assistant Economic Adviser to the Cabinet, 1966-68
	Economic Adviser to the Prime Minister, 1968-69
Graham, John	Principle Private Secretary to the Foreign and Commonwealth Secretary from 1969
Greenhill, Denis	Deputy Under-Secretary of State, FCO, 1966-69
	Deputy Under-Secretary of State and Head of the Diplomatic Service, FCO from 196
Greenwood, Anthony	Minister of Housing, 1966-69
Gruffydd-Jones, Daniel	Private Secretary to Secretary of Cabinet, 1967-69
	Assistant Secretary, 1969
Haines, Joe	Chief Press secretary to the Prime Minister, 1969-70
Halls, AN (Michael)	Principal Private Secretary to the Prime Minister 1966-70

Hancock, Patrick	Assistant Under-Secretary of State, FO, 1965-68
	Deputy Under-Secretary of State, FCO, 1968-69
	HM Ambassador to Italy from 1969
Hannay, David	Second and then First Secretary, British Delegation to the EC, 1965-70
	Member of British Negotiating Team from 1970
Harrison, Geoffrey	HM Ambassador to the USSR, 1965-68
Haydon, Robin	Head of News Department, FO, from 1967
Hayman, Peter,	Assistant Under-Secretary of State, FO, 1966-69
	Deputy Under-Secretary of State, FCO from 1969
Healey, Denis	Secretary of State for Defence 1964-1970
Heath, Edward	Leader of the Opposition, 1965-70
Hilary, David	Cabinet Office, 1967-69 (unspecified position)
Hildyard, David	Head of Economic Relations Department, FO, 1965-68
	Minister and Alternate UK Representative to the UN from 1968
Holland, David	Chief Economic Adviser, FCO from 1967
Hood, Viscount Samuel	Deputy Under-Secretary of State, FCO, 1962-69
Hooper, Sir Robin	Deputy Secretary, Cabinet Office from 1968
Hughes, Cledwyn	Minister for Agriculture, Fisheries and Food, 1968-70
Hughes, Albert	Consul-General, Washington, 1964-68
	Head of Finance Department, FCO, from 1968
Isserlis, Alexander	Under-Secretary, Cabinet Office, 1969

	Under-Secretary, Ministry of Housing and Local Government, 1969-70
	Principal Private Secretary to the Prime Minister from 1970
Jackling, Roger	Deputy Under-Secretary of State, FO, 1967-68
	HM Ambassador to the FRG from 1968
Jackson, Frederick	Counsellor and Deputy Head, UK Delegation to the EC, 1967-69
James, CM (Kenneth)	Paris embassy, 1965-69 (promoted to counsellor 1968)
Jenkins, Roy	Chancellor of the Exchequer, 1967-70
Kaufman, Gerald	Parliamentary Press Liaison Officer, 1965-70
Kearns, Fred	Under-Secretary for External Relations, MAFF, 1964-68
	Meat and Livestock Group, MAFF, 1968-69
	Deputy Secretary, MAFF from 1969
	Member of Negotiating Team from 1970
Kennet, Lord Wayland	Parliamentary Secretary and Minister of Housing and Local Government (Lords), 1966-70
Killick, John	Counsellor and Head of Chancery, Washington, 1963-68
	Assistant Under Secretary, FCO from 1968
King, Cecil	Chairman, International Publishing Corp, 1963-68
Laskey, David	Minister, Bonn, 1967-68
Ledwidge, Bernard	Minister, Paris, 1965-69
Lever, Harold	Paymaster-General, 1969-70
Lloyd-Hughes, Trevor	Press Secretary to the Prime Minister, 1964-69
	Chief Information Adviser to the Government, 1969-70
Lloyd-Jones, Richard	Private Secretary to Secretary of the Cabinet, 1969-70

Macmillan, Harold	Conservative Prime Minister 1957-63
Maitland, Donald	Principal Private Secretary to Foreign and Commonwealth Secretary, 1967-69
	Chief Press Secretary, 10 Downing Street, from 1970
Malcolm, Dugald	HM Ambassador to Luxembourg, 1966-70
Marjoribanks, James	HM Ambassador and Head of British Delegation to the EC from 1965
Marsh, Richard	Minister for Power 1966-68
	Minister for Transport 1968-69
Marten, Neil	Conservative MP for Banbury from 1959
Marshall, Peter	Counsellor, UK Mission Geneva, 1966-69
	Counsellor and Head of Chancery, Paris from 1969
Mason, Roy	Minister of State at the Board of Trade, 1964-67
	Postmaster General and Minister of Power, 1968-69
	President of the Board of Trade from 1969
Maudling, Reginald	Conservative MP for Barnet from 1950
McCluney, Ian	FCO, 1969-70 (unspecified position)
McIntosh, Ronald	Deputy Secretary, Cabinet Office, 1968-70
Mellon, James	Head of Chancery at British Delegation to the EC from 1967
Moon, Peter	Private Secretary to the Prime Minister from 1970
Morgan, John	Minister, Moscow, 1965-67
	FO, 1968
	Counsellor and Head of Far Eastern Department, FCO, from 1970
Morland, Martin	Private Secretary to Lord Chalfont, 1967-68
	European Integration Department, FCO from 1968

Morphet, David	Assistant Private Secretary to Foreign Secretary, 1966-68
Morrice, Philip	CO and FCO 1967-69 (unspecified position)
Mulley, Fred	Minister of State, FCO, 1967-69 Minister of Transport from 1969
Nield, William	Deputy Under-Secretary, Cabinet Office, 1966-68 Permanent Under-Secretary of State, Department of Economic Affairs (DEA), 1968-69 Permanent Secretary, Cabinet Office from 1969
Olver, Stephen	Counsellor, The Hague, 1967-69
O'Neill, Con	Deputy Under-Secretary of State, FO, 1965-68 Deputy Under-Secretary of State, FCO from 1969
O'Neill, Robin	British embassy, Bonn from 1968 (unspecified position)
Overton, Hugh	British embassy, Bonn (unspecified position and dates)
Owen, Glendwr	Under-Secretary, Treasury from 1959
Palliser, A Michael	Private Secretary to the Prime Minister, 1966-1969 Minister, Paris from 1969
Part, Anthony	Permanent Under-Secretary, Board of Trade, 1968-70
Peart, Fred	Minister of Agriculture, 1964-68 Lord Privy Seal, 1968 Lord President of the Council, 1968-70
Peck, Edward	Deputy Under-Secretary of State, FCO, 1968-70
Powell, Enoch	Conservative MP for Wolverhampton from 1950
Pryce, Roy	University of Sussex; adviser to the government
Reilly, Patrick	HM Ambassador to France, 1965-68
Roberts, Frank	HM Ambassador to the FRG, 1963-68
Robinson, John	Counsellor, FO, 1967

	Head of European Integration Department, 1968-70
	Member of negotiating team from 1970
Rooke, James	Minister (Commercial), Canberra, 1966-68
	Minister (Economic), Paris from 1968
Rose, Clive	Counsellor, Washington from 1969
Ross, William	Secretary of State for Scotland, 1974-70
Scott Fox, David	HM Ambassador to Finland, 1966-69
Selby, Ralph	Chargé d'Affaires, Paris (unspecified dates)
Shackleton, Lord Edward	Minister without Portfolio, 1967-68
	Lord Privy Seal, 1968
	Paymaster-General, 1968
	Lord Privy Seal, 1968-70
Shannon, Godfrey	Assistant Under-Secretary of State, Commonwealth Office, 1956-68
Shore, Peter	Secretary of State for Economic Affairs 1967-69
	Minister without Portfolio 1969-70
Shovelton, Walter	Under-Secretary, Ministry of Technology, 1966-70
	Member of Negotiating Team from 1970
Shuckburgh, Evelyn	HM Ambassador to Italy, 1966-69
Sinclair, Ian	Legal Adviser to Negotiating Team from 1970
Smith, George	First Secretary, Commonwealth Office, 1966-68
Snelling, Arthur	Deputy Under-Secretary of State, Commonwealth Office and FCO, 1961-69
Soames, Christopher	HM Ambassador to France from 1968
Statham, Norman	Head of European Integration Department, FCO 1965-68 and from 1970

Stewart, Michael	Secretary of State for Economic Affairs 1966-67
	First Secretary of State 1966-68
	Secretary of State for Foreign Affairs/Foreign and Commonwealth Affairs, 1968-70
Tait, Michael	Private Secretary to Lord Chalfont, 1968
Thomson, George	Secretary of State for the Commonwealth 1967-68
	Minister without Portfolio October 1968-69
	Chancellor of the Duchy of Lancaster, 1969-70
Thomson, John	Head of Planning Staff, FO, 1967
	Cabinet Office, 1968
	Chief of Assessments Staff, Cabinet Office from 1968
Thornton, Peter	Assistant Under-Secretary of State, DEA, 1964-67
	Deputy Under Secretary, Cabinet Office and President of working group on Europe from 1970
Tickell, Crispin	Paris embassy, 1964-70 (position unspecified)
Tomkins, Edward	Chargé d'Affairs, Washington, 1967-69
	HM Ambassador in The Hague from 1970
Trend, Sir Burke	Secretary of the Cabinet from 1963
Willan, Edward	Head of Scientific Relations Department, FO, 1966-68
Williams, Marcia	Private and Political Secretary to Harold Wilson from 1956
Williams, Nigel	Private Secretary to Minister of State, FO, 1968
	Private Secretary to Chancellor of Duchy of Lancaster, 1969
Williamson, David	Principal Private Secretary to successive Ministers of Agriculture from 1967

Wilson, Duncan	HM Ambassador to Yugoslavia, 1964-68
	HM Ambassador to the USSR from 1968
Wilson, Harold	Prime Minister 1964-1970
Winchester, Ian	FO and FCO, 1967-70 (unspecified position)
Wood, Andrew	Second then First Secretary, Washington, 1967-70
Wraight, John	Minister and Consul-General, Milan from 1968
Wright, Oliver	HM Ambassador to Denmark, 1966-69
	Deputy Under-Secretary of State, FCO, 1969-70
Youde, Edward	Private Secretary to Harold Wilson, 1969-70
Zuckerman, Solly	Chief Scientific Adviser to the Government, 1964-70

France

Alphand, Hervé	Secretary General of the *Quai d'Orsay* from 1965
Angles	First Counsellor, London (unspecified dates)
de Beaumarchais, Jacques	Director of Political Affairs, *Quai* from 1965
Boegner, Jean-Marc	Permanent Representative to the EC, 1961-72
Brunet, Jean-Pierre	Director of Economic Affairs, *Quai* (unspecified dates)
Burin des Roziers, Etienne	de Gaulle's *chef de cabinet,* 1962-67
	Ambassador in Rome, 1969
Chaban-Delmas, Jacques	Prime Minister from 1969
de Courcel, Geoffroy	Ambassador to the UK from 1962
Couve de Murville, Maurice	Foreign Minister 1958-68
	Finance Minister 1968
	Prime Minister 1968-69
Debré, Michel	Minister of Finance, Economics and Social Affairs, 1966-68
	Foreign Minister, 1968-69

Dromer, Jean	Governor General of *Banque Nationale de Paris*
Duhamel, Jacques	Minister of Agriculture from 1969
Faure, Edgar	Minister of Education, 1968
	Minister of Social Affairs, 1969
de Gaulle, Charles	President , 1958-69
Giscard d'Estaing, Valèry	Finance Minister from 1969
Lipowski, Jean de	Minister of State, MFA from 1968
Messmer, Pierre	Minister for Armaments, 1960-69
Monnet, Jean	'Father of European integration'; founder of Action Committee for a United States of Europe
Pisani, Edgar	Minister of Agriculture, 1961-62 and 1962-66
	Minister for Equipment and Housing, 1967
	Deputy for Maine-and-Loire, 1967
Poher, Alain	Interim President, 1969
Pompidou, Georges	Prime Minister 1962-68
	President from 1969
Schumann, Maurice	Foreign Minister from 1969
Tricot, Bernard	Secretary-General at the *Elysée*
Wahl, Jean	Minister of Commerce from 1969

Germany

Barzel, Rainer	Leader of CDU-CSU in the *Bundestag* from 1964
Birrenbach, Kurt	CDU politician from 1957
Blankenhorn, Herbert	Ambassador to the UK from 1965
Brandt, Willy	Vice-Chancellor and Foreign Minister 1966-69
	Chancellor from 1969
Breer, Franz	First Counsellor at German embassy in London (unspecified dates)
von Dohnanyi, Klaus	German Permanent Representative to the EC (unspecified dates)
Duckwitz, Georg	State secretary in the MFA
Fischer, Per	MFA (unspecified position and dates)
Focke, Frau	Chancellor's Office (unspecified position and dates)
Frank, Paul	State Secretary in the MFA

Harkort, Gunther	State Secretary in the MFA
Jahn	State Secretary in the MFA
Kiesinger, Kurt-Georg	Chancellor 1966-69
Lahr, Rolf	State Secretary in the MFA
	Ambassador in Rome from 1969
Lübke, Heinrich	Federal President, 1959-69
Naupert	German embassy, London
Scheel, Walter	Foreign Minister from 1969
Schmidt, Helmut	SPD Parliamentary leader, 1967-69
	Deputy chairman of SPD from 1968
	Defence Minister from 1969
Strauss, Franz	Minister of Finance 1966-69

Italy

Colombo, Emilio	Minister of the Treasury, 1963-70
	Prime Minister from 1970
Fanfani, Amintore	Foreign Minister, 1966-68
	President of the Senate from 1968
Guidotti	Ambassador to the UK
Manzini	Ambassador to the UK, 1969
Medici, Giuseppe	Foreign Minister, 1968
Nenni, Pietro	Foreign Minister, 1968-69
Ricciulli	London embassy
Rumor, Mariano	General Secretary of Christian Democrats, 1964-69
	Prime Minister, 1969-70
Saragat, Giuseppe	President 1964-71
Zagari	Minister of State, MFA

Belgium

van den Boeynants, Paul	Prime Minister, 1966-68
van den Bosch, Jean	Ambassador to the UK
Davignon, Etienne	*Chef de cabinet* to Harmel, 1963-69
	Political Director, MFA, from 1969
Eyskens, Gaston	Prime Minister from 1968
Harmel, Pierre	Foreign Minister from 1966
Spaak, Paul-Henri	'Founding father' of European integration

Netherlands

de Jong, Petrus (Piet)	Prime Minister from 1967
de Koster, Henri (Hans)	Foreign Minister

Luns, Joseph   Foreign Minister, 1956-71

Luxembourg
Clasen, André   Ambassador to the UK
Grégoire, Pierre   Minister of Foreign Affairs, 1967-69
Thorn, Gaston   Foreign Minister from 1969
Werner, Pierre   Prime Minister, 1959-74

European Commission
Homan, Linthorst   Chief Representative of the EC in
                                the UK
Marjolin, Robert   Vice-President, 1958-67
Rey, Jean   President 1967-70

EFTA
Andersen, Nyboe   Danish Minister of the Economy and
                                European Market Relations
Baunsgaard, Hilmar   Prime Minister of Denmark from
                                1968
Erlander, Tage   Prime Minister of Sweden, 1957-69
Kekkonen, Urho   President of Finland, 1956-82
Klaus, Josef   Austrian Federal Chancellor, 1964-70
Kreisky, Bruno   Leader of Austrian Socialist Party
                                from 1966
                                Austrian Chancellor from 1970
Kristiansen, Erling   Danish ambassador to the UK
Lange, Gunnar   Swedish Trade Minister, 1955-70
Palme, Olaf   Swedish Prime Minister from 1970
Waldheim, Kurt   Austrian Foreign Minister, 1968-70

Commonwealth
Blundell, Denis   High Commissioner for New
                                Zealand to the UK from 1968
Gorton, John   Prime Minister of Australia 1968-71
Holt, Harold   Prime Minister of Australia, 1966-68
Holyoake, Keith   Prime Minister of New Zealand
                                1960-72
Marshall, Jack,   Deputy Prime Minister of New
                                Zealand 1960-1972
McEwen, John   Prime Minister of Australia 1967-68
Pant, Apasaheb   Indian High Commissioner to the
                                UK since 1969

Pearson, Leslie	Prime Minister of Canada, 1963-69
Ramgoolan, Seewoosagur	President of Mauritius from 1968
Shearer, Hugh	Prime Minister of Jamaica from 1967
Smith, Arnold	Secretary-General of the Commonwealth from 1965
Trudeau, Pierre	Prime Minister of Canada from 1969

USA

Acheson, Dean	Secretary of State 1949-53
Ball, George	Permanent Representative to the UN from 1968
Cleveland, James	Representative to NATO from 1965
Fowler, Henry	Secretary of the Treasury, 1965-68
Katzenbach, Nicholas	Under Secretary of State, 1967-69
Kennedy, John	President, 1960-1963
Kissinger, Henry	Assistant to the President for National Security Affairs from 1969
Javits, Jacob	Senator from 1957 and author of the 'Javits Plan' for NAFTA
Johnson, Lyndon	President, 1963-69
Nixon, Richard	President from 1969
Rogers, William	Secretary of State from 1969
Roosevelt, Franklin	President, 1923-45
Rusk, Dean	Secretary of State, 1961-1969
Scranton, William	Governor of Pennsylvania, 1963-67 Emissary of president-elect Nixon, 1968
Stans, Maurice	Secretary of Commerce from 1969

USSR

Brezhnev, Leonid	Secretary General of the CPSU from 1964
Kosygin, Alexsie	Chairman of Council of Minister (Prime Minister) from 1964

INDEX